How To Get Y
Back

Step By Step Formula On How To Get Your Ex Back And Keep Him/her For Good

PS: I Owe You!

Thank you for stopping by.

My name is Antony and I am passionate about teaching people literally everything I know about different aspects of life. I am an author and a ghostwriter. I run a small ghostwriting company with slightly over 100 writers. My wife (Faith) and I manage the business along with several other members of the team (editors).

Nice to meet you!

I started publishing (at Fantonpublishers.com) because I'd love to impart the knowledge I gather every single day in my line of work (reading and editing over 10 ghostwritten books every single day). My ghostwriting company deals with literally every topic under the sun, which puts me at a very unique position to learn more in a month than I learnt in my 4 years as a Bachelor of Commerce, Accounting, student. I am constantly answering questions from my friends, relatives and even strangers on various topics that I come across every day at work.

After several years of helping people to achieve different goals (e.g. weight loss, making money online, human resources, management, investing, stress reduction, depression, budgeting, saving etc.) offline thanks to my 'street' as well as 'class' knowledge on different topics, I realized I could be of better help to the world by publishing what I learn. My books are a reflection of what I have been gathering over the years. That's why they are not just focused on one niche but every niche possible out there.

If you would love to be part of my lovely audience who want to change multiple aspects of their life, subscribe to our newsletter or follow us on social media to receive notifications whenever we publish new books. You can also send me an email; I would love to hear from you!

PS: Valuable content is my bread and butter. And since I have lots of it to go around, I can share it freely (not everything is about money - **changing lives comes first!**)

I promise; I am busy just as you are and won't spam (I hate spam too)!

Antony,

Website: http://www.fantonpublishers.com/

Email: Support@fantonpublishers.com

Twitter: https://twitter.com/FantonPublisher

Facebook Page:
https://www.facebook.com/Fantonpublisher/

Private Facebook Group For Readers:
https://www.facebook.com/groups/FantonPublishers/

Pinterest: https://www.pinterest.com/fantonpublisher/

Some of the best things in life are free, right?

As a sign of good faith, I will start by giving out content that will help you to implement not only everything I teach in this book but in every other book I write. The content is about life transformation, presented in bit size pieces for easy implementation. I believe that without such a checklist, you are likely to have a hard time implementing anything in this book and any other thing you set out to do religiously and sticking to it for the long haul. It doesn't matter whether your goals relate to weight loss, relationships, personal finance, investing, personal development, improving communication in your family, your overall health, finances, improving your sex life, resolving issues in your relationship, fighting **PMS** successfully, investing, running a successful business, traveling etc. With a checklist like the one I will show you, you can bet that anything you do will seem a lot easier to implement until the end. This checklist will help you to start well and not lose steam along the way, until the very end. Therefore, even if you don't continue reading this book, at least read the one thing that will help you in every other aspect of your life.

Send me a message on support@fantonpublishers.com and I will send you my 5 Pillar Life Transformation Checklist.

Your life will never be the same again (if you implement what's in this book), I promise.

Introduction

I want to thank you and congratulate you for downloading the book, *"How To Get Your Ex Back: Step By Step Formula On How To Get Your Ex Back And Keep Him/her For Good"*.

This book has actionable steps and strategies on how get your ex back.

Most of the times, when we break up with someone who we were in a relationship with, we are told to move on and forget him or her. But what if we do not want to forget them? What if you really know that you can make things right? What if he or she is the one?

Love hopes in all things and never gives up. So if there is someone you love and you two broke it off, it's time to get back what's yours. You already know that they will be truly happy with you by their side. But they do not know that yet so you need to take the initiative and help them open their eyes. Help them see why the two of you are meant to be.

Well, I do not mean that you should go back to them crawling on all fours. You need to get your act together, dust yourself off then try again. Yes, you need to wash yourself clean and ensure that you are sparkling. Surely, you can make a few changes here and there for the sake of both your happiness. Isn't it all worth it for true love?

That is what this book is all about; it is all about dusting yourself, trying and then succeeding in getting back the one person that you truly love. Now breath in and then breath out because we are about to do some serious business.

In this book, we will learn:

- **What to do immediately after a break up**

- **The no-contact rule and how you can apply it**

- **Why taking some time off is the best thing you can do for yourself and the relationship**

- **What you should be doing during the time off**

- **How to analyze your relationship during the time off**

- **Important considerations you should take before going back**

- **Getting back together; what you need to know**

- **Increasing your odds of staying together for the long haul**

- **And much, much more!**

Thanks again for downloading this book. I hope you enjoy it!

Table of Contents

If you really want to have your ex back and have him/her stay, it is important that you follow a systematic process. That's why you don't start establishing contact immediately after a breakup. I know it sounds counterintuitive but trust me; not following the system will reduce your chances of getting together. That's why we will start from the beginning after the breakup so that you set yourself up for success i.e. getting him/her back effortlessly. Follow this step by step process and you will have him/her to yourself.

Step 1: Take Time Off

You just broke up and your heart is killing you. All you can think about is your lover and how you cannot live without them. You just want to go back there and let them see that it was just a simple misunderstanding. You are even willing to apologize for their mistakes just so that you can get back together. Take my word for it. Stay away.

Am I being real? Oh yes I am. Acting all desperate is not the way; you need to give your ex some space to breathe and don't be up on their face. At the moment, the reason for your break up is still fresh so they do not want to see you and you going to them all the time just pisses them off. You may even end up causing them to have an angry outburst, which will only hurt you and make matters worse, so stay away.

When I say stay away, I mean the following:

1. Do not call just to say hi or pretend that it was an "accident"

2. Do not send instant messages or stalk them in social media

3. No texting

4. No funny statuses online

5. No "bumping" into them because 'you were in the neighborhood'

6. No hanging out with common friends

Simply stay away and keep it that way. The both of you need space. It might just turn out that your relationship was great; all you needed was a bit of space from each other. In relationships that the both of you are in it for the long term, one of you may feel like they are suffocating or begin panicking when things start to get serious. This does not mean that they don't love you; it simply means that they are afraid of screwing things up. It is totally normal. You may not realize it just yet but you were also in need of space – this will become clear to you during your time apart and you will thank God for it. Trust me, space will do the both of you some good.

This is known as no contact rule so observe it religiously if you really want to get your ex back.

I Love My Ex, Why Should I Take Time Out?

Yes, I know how you really feel but it's not only your feelings that we are dealing with here; we are also looking at your ex. You need to pause for a while and weigh all things.

You may think that going back to them is the best thing to do but it is not. You are not sober because your heart has just been wounded so why are you going back to the gun yet you need a bandage on the wound?

Let us attend to the wound first, shall we? This is why.

1. Your head is full of clutter and you are wondering why your ex is leaving you. Your mind is tortured by self-destructive thoughts such as is it because I have gained a few pounds? Is it because I'm not good at cooking? Is it because the stunning new neighbor? Is it because I am boring? There is no way you can come up with anything constructive at such a state. You need to take a break from your ex and any other thing that is likely to contribute to your stress so that you can think clearly.

2. Going back immediately means that you do not want to know the mistakes you made that could have contributed to the situation. Relationships are quite funny; your partner can break up with you even if they are the ones at fault. For example, you can catch your partner in a lie and instead of them explaining him/herself, they end up getting mad at you and breaking up with you. If you don't take some time apart, you will not understand why your ex lied and why he or she got mad when you confronted them. Your ex might have lied not to worry you or was trying to surprise you and your confrontation and accusations over his or her good gesture pissed them. With the hostile feelings still fresh, your ex cannot explain himself or herself and you will break up for good.

3. Nobody eats the same type of food all the time. Give your ex the room to miss you. Seeing you all the time makes them resent you. I mean, has a person ever done something that annoyed you so much that when you run into him or her the next day you feel seething rage and resentment? This is because whatever the person did to you is still fresh in your mind and is all you can think of when you see them. This is exactly what your ex feels when they see you after the big argument that led to your break up. Wounds take time to heal so give your ex the time to cool off and to miss you.

Those three reasons should get you thinking if you are serious about winning somebody back.

Yes, now I know you are asking me what you are supposed to do during this period of silence. Well, let us find out.

Step 2: What Do I Do During Time Off?

During the time off is when you are prone to messing everything up. This is because as much as it is time off for you and your ex, you should be busy working on yourself. It is fine for you to grieve the loss of the relationship but if you want to ignite the sparkle of that love again, then you need to get up and start working on your road to recovery.

Let us look at some of the things that you could do during this period.

1. Changing your appearance

The old you is gone. Behold, you are now a new creature! Do something about your look. Trust me, you will feel good about yourself plus it will boost your self-esteem and if your ex sees you, they too will be amazed. As an added bonus, it also takes your mind off the loss of your relationship. Don't just change your appearance to please your ex, do it because you want to and because it makes you happy.

If you have long hair, you can get a nice short haircut. Go see the dentist and get your teeth whitened for that wonderful smile. (For ladies, you can go to the salon and get a makeover).

You can also go to the gym and lose some pounds while toning your muscles – this doesn't mean that you are fat. Exercise does wonders for your skin and helps in elevating your moods. Then lastly, you can change your wardrobe. Go for clothes that project confidence and make you feel smart.

This is not the time to be spending nights in bars drinking until dawn or eating lots of ice cream and crying yourself to sleep. This is the time to rebrand yourself, not waste away. After all, how will getting drunk and binging on ice cream help your situation? It only makes you feel good for a while but does not help in any way to get your ex back. So get back on your feet and "re-model" yourself.

2. Change your mentality

Your attitude determines your altitude so you should do something about your attitude towards your ex and life in general. Embrace gratitude in everything. Be grateful for the good times and the bad times you had with your ex. Be grateful for the experience of true love and everything you learn during your time apart.

Be happy and confident about yourself. Remember that only you alone can put a smile or a frown on your face. You are solely responsible for your happiness. You cannot say that you are sad because of your ex or that you are drinking because of your ex. You make the choice to be sad and to drink; it is totally up to you. So instead of drowning in self-pity, choose happiness. Go around and have some fun. Go for trips, go to the beach, visit your parents, hang out with your friends, treat yourself with some fine dining and anything else that will make you feel happy. Find ways to fill your heart with joy and contentment.

1. Keep a journal

Record your day-to-day experiences. What you are going through is a process but you won't know it until it is completed. Write what you learnt or what you found challenging. For instance, you can write about how you feel when your ex behaves in a certain way or the sort of mistakes you think you made during your time together or what you loved about your ex and such things; things that will make your relationship better when the both of you decide to give it another shot. Keep this journal well because when you get back with your ex, you will read it together; each of you will get the chance to analyze their feelings and come up with ways to right the wrongs as a couple.

A journal also helps you to release all the emotions that you have inside. Break ups are not easy at all and they bring with them a lot of feelings and emotions, which you should not ignore. It has never been healthy to bottle up your emotions because the more you suppress them, the more they eat at you. Use your journal to let it all out because once you let go, you feel more free and happier.

2. Meditate

During this period when you feel alone, it is time to go on a spiritual path. Meditation is the perfect exercise for you since it is best known for keeping things such as stress levels, anxiety and depression at bay. Taking on this practice on a serious note is sure to make your break up easier to handle and make you the perfect partner anyone could ever ask for.

And why is that?

Well, meditation makes you calmer and more sensible, improves your self-awareness, helps you acquire inner peace, inspires forgiveness, helps in getting rid of negative feeling and many other delightful things.

Meditate on everything-Meditate on how to:

- Handle the break up in a healthy way

- How to give your ex some space

- How to let go of all the negative emotions

- How to get back with your ex

- How to avoid arguments with your ex in the future when you get back together

- How to control your emotions

- And how to improve your relationship

You will be able to know yourself better in terms of weaknesses and strengths. Most importantly, you will be able to accept yourself and love yourself just as you are. This is what will generate confidence since there are no doubts holding you back. You are in the know.

3. Learn something new

Do you know how to cook or bake? Can you paint or play an instrument? Look; the last time you were with your ex, there are certain things you couldn't do.

Why not learn new things? Why not learn a new language such as Spanish or French?

If you don't know how to swim then this is the perfect time for you to learn. We all have that one thing that we have always wanted to know how to do. Don't just see this break up as a dark time; it can also be an opportunity to learn something new and explore the world.

This is not only about killing time but also reinventing yourself and increasing your skills. It also makes you feel good about yourself – knowledge is power.

4. Make new friends

You do not want to be too nostalgic about your ex so why not make new friends and have a good time with them? Besides, obsessing over something or in this case someone has never been healthy. In most cases, it drives you to make crazy decisions and you end up freaking out your ex, which ruins any chance of the two of you getting back together.

Now we don't want that, do we? Making new friends is a healthy way of taking your mind off your ex and you can learn quite a lot about yourself in your newly found friendships. Other than that, you get to hang out with new people and share experiences - a good way to help in mending your heart.

After going through the steps of time off, you are now sober enough to analyze the relationship that you had with your ex.

Step 3: Analyzing Your Relationship

You now know who you are and probably have met new people who have even shown interest in you so why do you still want to go back to your ex?

You really have to be honest with yourself and have a damn good reason why you want to go back.

I know some of the answers for wanting to go back could be:

- You still love them

- You cannot live without them

- You were meant to be together

- You are miserable without them

- They complete you

Now these are still the same reasons you had at the beginning. I need you to go deeper into yourself and really find out the reason why you want your ex back.

Be true to yourself - no judgment. If you want to get back with your ex because of the fear of spending the rest of your life alone, own it. If it is because your ex made you feel special, don't deny it; if it is because of the cooking, accept it. Just ensure that you are being honest with yourself.

This is where you have to consider certain factors before you say you want to go back to your ex.

The Considerations You Must Weigh Before Going Back

There are many questions that you had in your mind when you broke up with your ex but now the next hardest thing to ask yourself is if you should give the relationship another shot. Are you ready to risk it all even if you are going to end up with a broken heart again?

Are you prepared to go back to whatever it is you called a relationship? Are you ready to be a team with your ex once again? Are you willing to accept your ex and his/her flaws?

Is this the best thing for the both of you? Well, if your answer is yes then, there are several factors that you must weigh.

1. Why did you break up?

There are different causes of break ups. It could be abuse, an affair, or non-compatibility, whereby you feel things are not just working out for the two of you and you are not good together.

So think back to the kind of relationship you had before the break up. If the reason behind your break up was abuse, come up with possible answers for the abuse. Was it when you did not agree with them or maybe after having too much to drink or a stressful day at work?

If the break up was because of an affair, when did it start? What pushed them to have the affair? How frequent was their meeting?

If it was non-compatibility, which areas are you not compatible? When did you notice that you were not compatible or when did it start bothering you – because you surely would have noticed this before you got into the relationship with them in the first place; I mean, that is what dating is for, to know whether you are compatible with someone or not. After knowing why you broke up, you need to ask yourself if you are able to live with the issue because it will certainly pop up one of these days.

The both of you need to compromise in order to come up with a solution to your issues. For the abuse, your ex should hit the brakes on getting drunk and find better ways to handle stress e.g. meditation and as for you, if it is something you can agree with them on, disagree with them in a calm and polite way so as not to trigger them.

If it was the affair, what was it that you did not give your ex enough of that he/she felt they could only get it from another man/woman? Find this out and see whether you can give your ex more of it. If it is the non-compatibility, since your ex is the only one who has the ability to change him/herself, you can talk to them about trying (not now but when you establish contact, which I will show you when) and on your part, you have to decide whether you can stay with them despite it.

2. Why do you want to go back?

Ask yourself what is your motivation for going back. Is it for the kids or are your friends and family pressuring you to do so? Is it that you find so hard to start again with another person or is it that the financial burden is too much for you?

Don't just do it because everyone says it is the best thing to do because you are the one to be miserable if you are not on board with the idea – and you will probably break up again if it is not your choice.

Do it because you want to and because you really feel that it is the best thing for the both of you. You really need a good reason to actually say that you are going back. What is the point of going back if you know you are not going to be happy or if you know that your ex is not the "one"? Remember that you are in charge of your life and what you feel; therefore, going back to your ex should be entirely your choice.

3. Look at the entire relationship

Do not just focus on the break up. Try to analyze everything including what happened months before you went your separate ways. Were things so bad that you two broke up over a silly issue simply so that you can have an excuse to leave? Did the two of you confront and admit the issue because they are going to come back.

If you did not confront and admit the issue, what do you think it was? Sometimes the issue can be neither of you. Maybe during the past couple of months, you were facing a financial crisis and the pressure was getting to you guys so you began arguing to vent out which escalated and got out of hand leading to the break up.

If the both of you want to get back together, you need to know that financial issues are a part of life and it is better to go through it together rather than alone. Problems rise but they also end so be patient with each other.

At other times, the issue can be spending too much time with each other. As stated earlier, you cannot eat the same type of food everyday. Your ex may have been struggling with getting a job and you decided to be sweet enough to get them a job at your office. Having your lover as a colleague at work is likely to create space issues. If you wake up at the same time, go to work together, eat lunch together, go home together and eat dinner together each day with your partner, it tends to be annoying, infuriating and boring. You will not even have anything to discuss at dinner such as "how was your day" since you were in the same place.

The break up could just be about wanting space to breathe. If the issues with your ex began showing just a few months earlier, then it is nothing that cannot be fixed.

4. Is the issue chronic?

Did you break up because of something that kept occurring all the time and you got tired handling the same thing always? Some things are psychological and are ingrained in us since childhood.

So the question is; are you willing to go through this chronic issue with your ex and help them deal with it?

If you truly love your ex and they love you back, why not take the time to help them in overcoming their chronic issues? They might be willing to change and only require a slight push from you (well, only do this when you establish contact and when you are together- I will explain this later). If the issue is not chronic, then it is much easier to help them handle it better but you need to be really patient with them.

5. Are you ready to truly forgive?

Take time to think of what your ex did to you and how the relationship was when you were together. Is it something that you can look past or is it something that will always linger whenever you are around them? You are going back but you must be able to forgive all the mistakes. You are not to be bringing up the issue since you know it is your ex's Achilles heel.

If you do decide to forgive, you also decide to let go of the issue. It should never come up when a new argument arises. We are all human and we are all prone to mistakes so you also have your own. Just imagine what it would feel like if someone forgave you then kept throwing your mistake at your face every time you disagree. Annoying, isn't it? You need to let it be and move on to other important matters. There is no use re-uniting with your ex if you truly cannot forgive because it won't be long till you break up again and maybe this time for good.

6. Do not dive in; try being friends first-approach with caution!

When something breaks, e.g. a glass, you don't just repair it; you start from scratch to re-make it. The same applies to your relationship; don't just pick up where you left off. You need to do this because it is the only way you can be close to your ex and observe if they have actually changed. It is also a great way to know whether you want to spend the rest of your life with them or not, to see whether you can really forgive them and overlook their issues whether chronic or not. Do this without your hormones being in charge because even if you have great sex, it does not mean that you are back together. It means that you will not have time to talk through your issues with your ex and come up with solutions in order to ensure that you don't repeat the same mistakes. Remember that you have already been down this road before so why not be cautious this time? Why not take things slowly and reap the benefits later on when your relationship works? Trust me, your patience truly will pay off.

7. Go with the actions

It is easy to be carried away with words but do not be fooled; actions show the true intentions of the heart. Don't get weak in the knees even if they tell you everything you have been yearning to hear from them. Be strong.

Don't risk making your life miserable over a couple of sweet words. Words are just that, words. Demand action. As the saying goes, "actions speak louder than words."

I'm not saying that you should not listen- just check to see whether they back their words up with actions. If they promise not to drink any alcohol and they still hang around friends who drink, then you should smell a rat.

Don't be too anxious to get back to them that you end up missing the signs that the both of you are not yet ready.

If you are seriously thinking about going back to your ex, then you should give a serious thought to it. So now that you know what to weigh, how do you go to them?

Step 4: Go With This In Mind

Your attitude to the break up is positive. You have spent time alone rediscovering yourself and becoming a better person. Now you want to present this new person to an ex who only knows the former you.

So how do you go about it? Here are some things to remember and do:

1. Know that loving someone is a decision

Ask anyone in a long-term relationship how many times they wanted to walk out and they will tell you many. However, they decided to look for reasons to stay instead of leaving. The more you focus on building a relationship and being committed to it, there will be very few instances that you will be looking at the exit because you made up your mind and decided to love.

Love is about being patient, trusting, faithful, united, caring, happy and such things. If you decide to love someone, you don't go criticizing them for their mistakes or listening to hearsays about them or picking silly fights with them - and you certainly don't run away when things get tough.

If you love your ex, accept them the way they are, listen to them instead of listening to gossip and avoid fighting with them as much as possible; and when things get tough, stick together and try to come up with a solution as a team.

2. Forgiveness is not weakness

As I had stated before, if you want to go back, you should be ready to forgive and move on. Guess what? Forgiveness is not weakness. Everybody makes mistakes but only the brave forgive and decide to face the future.

So, are you brave enough to forgive your ex and accept them back into your life? You never know; maybe it was a one-time mistake that they wish had never happened which is bothering them as much as it is bothering you.

Wouldn't you want them to forgive you if you were in their shoes?

3. You are not the only one who has changed

Do not go back thinking that you are the only one who got themselves cleaned up. Go there with a leveled head. This is because you will also have to learn how to accept those changes.

Don't go thinking that you are better than them or they are better than you. Remember that you are going there to fix things not make them worse. Couples learn a lot during their time apart. What you learned and the things you decided to change is probably the same awakenings that your ex got. If your ex also has the intention of getting back together with you, he/she has also taken up measures to ensure that your relationship will work out when you try again. Change is hard to implement but not impossible.

Most people simply like hopping back into an old relationship but that is not how to go about it. Simply go about it with the right attitude and everything will work out; not like magic but as a timely process.

Step 5: It Is Now Time To Be Friends

You do not hop; step and jump back to your ex; you friend your way to them. I am not just talking about being friendly; I mean being a true friend and doing all that pertains to friendship.

So tell your hormones to relax and use the following stops to friend a way into your ex's heart.

1. Be kind to them

It may sound simple but it is quite a hard thing to do. Being kind means going out of your own way and being sensitive to your ex's needs. Be concerned about them and help them in solving their personal problems.

This may be quite hard because you have your own problems and you need to look past how they hurt you during the break up. You need to do this even if you do not make their world go round. Getting back together with you may not be their intention but showing kindness can change this.

2. Do not harbor resentment

When you harbor resentment, it is a sign that you did not forgive. During a breakup, there are no winners; you both lost a relationship. You need to put aside the issues that can make you get angry at what your ex did.

Sure, you got hurt during the break up but so was your ex. If you want to get back together, it means forgiving them for the mistake and forgetting about it and forgetting about it means letting go of the resentment you felt towards them.

Just ask yourself this simple question, "what good will resenting your ex for their mistake do?" let me answer you, NONE! All it does is destroy you. It already happened and there is nothing you can do about it.

So why not forgive and forget and save your heart from hurting more?

3. It takes time

The friendship thing won't blossom instantly but it requires time and patience. Also, do not crowd each other's space. Give your ex enough space. It is hard, I know when you know you no longer own someone's heart but still miracles happen through time and space.

If you are truly willing to re-build your relationship, you need to be really patient. Even normal friendships take time to get there. Your ex needs to trust you once again and embrace the idea of having you back in their life again. Don't force it on them; it has to be their choice. Give them time to miss you and want you back.

4. Kill the green eyed monster

This is not the time to try to make your ex jealous. You might even kill the little spark that they had burning for you. So long as you were once in love, you seeing someone else will make the ex to feel somehow bad. So do not try to show them how happy you really are without them because I would ask why then do you want them back?

Moreover, it is likely to backfire on you because showing your ex that you are moving on might also push them to move on from you. If you really love your ex, why hurt them by making them feel that you are better off without them?

If you want your ex back, don't use dangerous shortcuts to get there; do it the right way.

5. Spend time with them but not all your time

It is vital that you make your ex feel like they were missed but this does not meant that you spend all your time together. You will find yourselves in awkward situations and before you know it, you will be back at one that is in your old relationship with the old issues coming up.

When you have free time set aside time for your ex and time for yourself too. Whenever you meet, ensure you both enjoy yourselves and avoid talks that may lead to something negative then end your meet on a high note such as a joke or a fun memory.

This will make your ex miss having you around more often. Thereafter, during your "me-time", note how you think the meet with your ex was, how you felt and how you think your ex felt.

If the friendship graduates into a relationship then, you should ensure that it comes with a set of rules.

6. No sex with the ex

You are building a relationship here so the two of you having sex is a big relapse. This where you need your brain to take control of your heart and not the other way around. You are a new person and you have to maintain that status because a backslide will only bring in blurred lines.

Let it not be seen that you were using friendship to get into their pants.

Sex is not the most important part of a relationship, love is. If you jump right into the sex, you will not get the time to fix the issues you had with your ex before the break up so your relationship will solely be based on sex, not love.

If you are really serious about getting back with your ex, start by fixing the issues you had in your previous relationship. There will be plenty of time for sex later on when you are back together for the right reasons.

7. No touching

If you want tip number six to be successful then you better employ tip number seven. No touching. You can hug but kissing or holding hands and other things of the sort are a no go zone.

It all begins with an innocent kiss and before you know it, you fail at tip number six. So, instead of putting yourself through the struggle of dealing with temptation, no touching should be your motivation. It might be hard to keep your hands to yourself after having your ex all to yourself for all that time you were together but it will all be worth it when you have them back in your arms for good.

8. Offer your support

If it is their birthday, wish them the best and even surprise them with a gift. If things are not going on well for them back at work, encourage them. Let them know that you are there for them not only during the good times but the hard times as well.

You know what they value and truth is, if there was anyone they would want closer, it would be a friend. So as you build a new friendship with your ex, ensure that you are genuine so that they may feel as if they can count on you when things get tough.

Your support might be all they needed to regain their trust in you.

9. Say that you are sorry

Remember that you have decided to forgive but your ex does not know this. You also need to admit your faults. Let them know that you are sorry for the times you acted stupidly yet you knew better.

Don't be one of those people who cannot apologize first. Take the high road. Be the bigger person. Apologizing when you are wrong is not only good for your ex, it is also good for you because as you hope to be forgiven for your mistakes, it also helps you to forgive the mistakes that were made to you.

Show them that you are serious enough about them to admit the mistakes you made during your relationship and the part you played in the break up. Admission and confession are very powerful when it comes to reconciliation; it brings the parties involved closer.

10.   Always have a joke about something in the past

Laughter has always been the best medicine. You can always remember the good old times by recalling the funniest and the silliest things the two of you did.

Laugh about the time you had a dance off and neither of you knew how to dance, or how you both tricked a friend into eating hot pepper or how your ex slipped and fell on their bum but didn't get hurt.

Such jokes serve as proof to your ex that you still value what the two of you shared. They also bring the two of you closer by showing how happy you were when you were together. A little reminder of the good times will do the both of you some good as it also restores some lost feelings

Next, we will discuss how to tell when the newfound friendship is blossoming into something.

Step 6: How Do I Know That The Friendship Is Turning Into Something?

I am sure you are asking yourself if you did all you had to do for nothing. But remember that time is of great essence. Now I want to share the signs that will give you the green light that your ex is responding positively to you and that their heart is creating room to accommodate you once again.

I need you to know that just because your ex will show the signs, it does not mean that you stop doing what you were doing and now tell them you are in it too.

See the signs then discern them; I will show you how to seal the deal.

1. They make time to see you. Your ex will start having lots of free time. They will ask you what is your plan for the day and if you don't have nothing planned for later on, the two of you might just be having lunch or dinner together every other day. With the bitter feelings out of the way and with the great friendship that you have going on, your ex will want to spend more time with you. It is just like falling in love all over again. They have seen how much you have changed and have also changed in the process. You have totally gained their trust and interest. Since you always have a good time whenever you meet but you also give them space, they decide to make a bold move of asking you out.

2. They will call you often. Yes, your phone won't stop ringing or even getting instant messages. You have

become their favorite person. Do not be surprised that you will be talking on the phone just as you used to while dating. Remember the flare you guys had when you began dating? Well, its back! Whenever you guys are not together, you will still be talking as if you are - voice calls, video calls and instant messages. Your time together with your ex has proved to be really fun for them (and for you too) that they really can't get enough of you. You will truly enjoy this because you know that your plan is working – your hard work is finally starting to pay off.

3. Their friends will be the FBI. Yes, because they are too shy to ask you some questions, they will have their friends do that for them. Questions like "what do you think of so and so nowadays..." will be common. Somebody wants to know if you are still available or have closed shop. However, you have to be careful about how you answer these questions. Don't appear too happy as if it is all you have been waiting to hear then again don't act as if it is something that had never crossed your mind. Give answers such as "I think so and so is quite fun to have around..." with a calm expression on your face.

4. They also try to improve on themselves. You came back with a new haircut and they can see that you actually made some changes to your wardrobe plus you can now speak French. They will make an effort to complement the improvements that you have made. Very soon, they will also try to do something to look better in your eyes – maybe a new hair cut or a change in behavior. They may feel a little guilty to bring the same old things back to the

relationship whereas you have made some quite big changes to both your physical appearance and emotional stability. So you may notice a few romantic gestures here and there, some extra politeness, improved gentleness and such. At this time, it is your ex's intention to get back with you so they are making an effort to win you back.

5. They will become self-conscious, they will get nervous while speaking to you and when you look at them, they might blush or look away. By now, your ex has noticed that things are going quite well with the both of you and they don't want to screw it over. They now think that it is their idea for you guys to get back together and that's why they are self-conscious. They are trying to get you to fall back in love with them. In short, it will be like the early days when you first dated. Don't give them a hard time. They probably feel a lot of pressure trying to keep up with how improved you have become. Acknowledge each of their efforts and try to make them comfortable around you.

6. They will flirt with you. From the fullness of the heart, the mouth speaks but not only the mouth but also the body. Your ex will flirt with you and give suggestive talks. Their body language will also speak large volumes that they want you back. For instance, women will touch their hair all the time when they are with a guy they like while men love to play with things when they are with a lady who drives them crazy. For instance, if they have a glass, they will just rotate in their hand or be hitting it with something. Pupils will dilate and they will sit while facing

your direction. They want to make it clear that they are not in this for just the friendship, that they really want you back. I know that as this happens your heart is jumping with joy and all you want to do is to declare that you also want them but don't; hold your horses. It is not yet time. You have already come too far to mess it all up now. When you feel yourself about to give in to your body's demands, just breathe. Remember what you are going to gain in the end, it is truly worth the wait.

7. They talk to you about the future. Someone who wants to spend a lifetime with you does not only concentrate on going to the movies. If they are with you for the long ride, most of their statements will begin with the phrase "we will". They will talk about mortgages, children, cities and everything else that the two of you could have in the future including a wedding. Talking about the future is definitely a good sign because it means that you are definitely getting back together. Don't agree with them just yet but listen to whatever they have in stored and see whether it is in line with your own future plan. If there is something that you don't agree with them about it, then you can make some sort of suggestion about making a change.

8. Bursts of anger. Yes, I know this one here sounds crazy but it is the gospel truth. When your ex gets angry because you were talking to someone else or someone else was flirting with you, then you've got yourself a winner because that is the true sign of "I want you back for me". Take it from me; its sweet jealousy. Why the jealousy?

Technically, you are not together; you are just friends. So according to your ex, there is the possibility of someone else snatching you from them. This is quite infuriating as they are doing their very best to get you back. You may be tempted to enjoy this, but don't. Don't allow someone to flirt with you on your ex's face. It wouldn't be fun for you either if the tables were reversed.

9. Funny Facebook updates. They do not tell it to your face but everyone on social media knows that their heart is bleeding for someone. Nowadays, people use social media to express their feelings and your ex is no exception. Your ex is in-love once again and they want everyone to know about it. You are always on their mind every moment of every day and all they can think about is getting you back. And if we are being honest, it is also like this for you. Don't worry, it won't be long now.

10. Avoiding potential dates. Your ex is being approached by other people for dates but they are not interested. This is because all that they want and whom they want it with is you. You may notice that when your ex gets a call from the opposite sex wanting to hang out with them, they turn them down. They may even end up being rude in order to ensure that it does not happen again. You know, once you are in love with someone, other people flirting with you even pisses you off. Now you don't need to worry about other people snatching what is yours. You now know that your ex loves you and is serious about building a new relationship with you. You are both on the same page now but it doesn't mean it's time; it means you are in the right

path. Just a little more time till you get your so-deserved reward.

11. Getting touchy. Your ex is suddenly holding your hands or looking straight into you with deep set eyes. The gazes are smooth and the touches are soft. My friend; you are on the right track. Your ex can no longer keep their hands to their self and when they look at you, it is with deep admiration. They even end up getting lost in your eyes just as you get lost in theirs. Some say that rekindled love is usually as strong as, if not stronger, than the first love. I'll let you be the judge of that.

The above are just some of the many signs that your ex wants you back. You know them better and might just include some of the things they used to do while the two of you were together.

Let's move to the next step.

Step 7: You Have Scored A Goal

Now clap for yourself and even congratulate yourself or you can just turn up the volume and dance to your favorite song because you actually did it. You actually got your ex looking in your direction and now they want you back. Not for the sex but to try once again being in a relationship.

After the celebration, I need you to get your head together. I need you to know that as much as you won them back, the ex knows that they are taking a risk. That is why I need you to change how you love them.

I mean that you should not love them like you used to; rather, you should improve on the loving.

1. Be sensitive to their feelings while communicating with them. Just because they have got you back in their heart doesn't mean that they will not be using their head. This is not the time to speak to them just the way you want because you already know that they want you back. Give them more reason to want you back in their lives. When you are talking to them, ensure that what you say does not hurt them in any way or make them feel insufficient. If you are giving things another shot, then certain changes are due. If you feel as if you don't agree with what they are saying, be calm about it and approach them with humility. For example, "in addition to what you have said, we can also try…" When you approach with negativity e.g. "you are wrong" or "it cannot work" you are bound to have an argument; plus, it's a big step backwards.

43

2. Take initiatives. Do not be the kind of person who waits for their lover to do something. Do it and ask questions later in a gentle manner. One person cannot build a relationship; it requires the both of you. Don't say that your lover is best at deciding what is best for the both of you. You are also part of that relationship. Just come up with something that the both of you can do to improve the quality of your relationship; it's not rocket science.

3. Take baby steps. Love is not a horse race. Take it one day at a time. The both of you have admitted that you love one another and now it is time to be patient with each other. You don't need to rush back to where you were before the break up. This is a new relationship so allow nature take its course. If you are in a hurry, you miss out on all the wonderful things happening in the present and it also means that you wanted your ex back for the wrong reasons. You have all the time in the world so enjoy each and every moment with your lover.

4. Little things count. Use words like I'm sorry, thank you and please. These words mean a lot. "Please" denotes that you do not take the person's efforts for granted. I'm sorry shows that you are not the type that is always on the defensive. Thank you shows that you are grateful for whatever it is that has been done for you. Being polite does not cost you anything; it in fact cultivates your relationships. Using the above words will make your lover feel respected, loved, appreciated and important and it may inspire them to do the same for you.

5. Correct with love. If now they do something that does not please you, do not just shout it out. Go to the person quietly and tell them; "darling, you know I love you but I didn't like ABC". Watch your tone and body language when doing this; correcting someone with love brings out the best in them. As stated earlier, everyone makes mistakes but how you handle their mistake determines whether or not they will repeat it. When you are rude about it, your lover may intentionally make another mistake just to piss you off and make you feel bad as you did to them. But did you really work that hard to get back your ex just so you can criticize them whenever they make a mistake? Before you do anything, just think for a moment how you would feel if it was someone else doing it to you. Don't do it if it would make you feel bad.

6. Surprise them. They thought they knew you better but now do things that will make them widen their eyes and wonder where they have been all this time. Make them see that indeed by making up, the future holds the best things in store for them. Don't allow your relationship to go stale. Surprise your lover every once in a while – keep things interesting. Make your lover feel that they made the perfect choice in choosing to be with you. Make them feel special because they truly are since you went to all that trouble for them.

7. Continue improving yourself. Remember you won their heart but now you need to maintain it that way. This simply means that you need to improve on yourself every single day. Buy books with tips about life and

relationships and read them, watch programs on TV that can teach you to be a better lover, do some online research on how you can improve the quality of your relationship and such things. Be their dream come true. Just because your plan of getting your ex back worked doesn't mean that you stop making effort – you still need to maintain the relationship. Keep improving yourself, not just for your lover but also for you.

8. Be the whole package. Be a lover and a friend. This is the best combination so far. Take them out on romantic dates but also stay at home with them when they have a cold and make them some chicken soup. Listen keenly when they talk and try your best to always be there for them. When they have something bothering them, help them to come up with possible solutions. If they get laid off work, don't think about the reduction in your finances, support them. Encourage them by telling them that there are many other job opportunities for them; you can even help them in their job hunt by checking the newspapers and advertisements online. Let them know that you are there for them through the thick and thin.

There is nothing as beautiful as growing in love. Ensure that you and the one you love grow together. Let them know what you are doing and they will appreciate that you are making an effort to make the relationship work. When you have a thought about something you can both do together as a couple in order to better your relationship, share it with them and listen to their views about it. If there is need to make a big decision, ensure you consult with them to know whether it is okay with them or not.

Conclusion

We've come to the end of the book. Thank you for reading until the end.

I hope this book was able to help you to understand how to get your ex back.

Love is a beautiful thing but it is also a complicated issue. Understand that there is a time for everything underneath the sun. Most of all, there is a time for crying and a time for laughing, a time for sowing and a time for harvesting.

Sowing is not a pleasant experience and that is what happens when after a break up; you take the time to give your ex space and develop yourself. Do not be afraid or worry that they will get someone else. People who were in a serious relationship never get into one immediately. This is because what they had was so good and they cannot believe that it is now gone.

But there is hope; after sowing comes the harvest and I believe that you can get back the one you love. You only need to work on a few things and everything will be alright. Just ensure that this second time around, that you give them your all and show them all your cards.

Expose all the skeletons in your closet so that they can be in love with the real you. If you give your everything then you have nothing else to lose. Most of all, I need you to keep the hope alive. You need this to keep your love strong and remember that loving someone is a decision so stick to it.

Now you have all that you need to face what is ahead of you. Go get them.

No more ex, it is just you and the one you love presently.

The next step is to start implementing what you have learnt in restoring your relationship.

Do You Like My Book & Approach To Publishing?

If you like my writing and style and would love the ease of learning literally everything you can get your hands on from Fantonpublishers.com, I'd really need you to do me either of the following favors.

6 Things

I'll be honest; publishing books on what I learn in my line of work gives me satisfaction. But the biggest satisfaction that I can get as an author is knowing that I am influencing people's lives positively through the content I publish. Greater joy even comes from knowing that customers appreciate the great content that they have read in every book through giving feedback, subscribing to my newsletter, sending emails to tell me how transformative the content they read is, following me on social media and buying several of my books. That's why I am always seeking to engage my readers at a personal level to know them and for them to know me, not just as an author but as a person because we all want to belong. That's why I strive to use different channels to engage my readers so that I can ultimately build a cordial relationship with them for our mutual success i.e. I succeed as an author while at the same time my readers learn stuff that takes days and sometimes weeks to write, edit, format and publish in a matter of hours.

To build this relationship, I'd really appreciate if you could do any or all the following:

1: First, I'd Love It If You Leave a Review of This Book on Amazon.

Let me be honest; reviews play a monumental role in determining whether customers purchase different products online. From the thousands of other books that are on Amazon about the topic, you chose to read this one. I am grateful for that. I may not know why you read my book, especially until the end considering the fact that most readers don't read until the end. Perhaps you purchased this book after reading some of the reviews and were glued with reading the book because it was educative and engaging. Even if you didn't read it because of the positive reviews, perhaps you can make the next customer's purchasing decision a lot easier by posting a review of this book on Amazon!

I'd love it if you did that, as this would help me spread word out about my books and publishing business. The more the readers, the bigger a community we build and we all benefit! If you could leave your honest review of this book on Amazon, I'd be forever grateful (well, I am already grateful to you for purchasing the book and reading it until the end- I don't' take that for granted!). Please Leave a Review of This Book on Amazon.

2: Check Out My Other Books

As I stated earlier, my biggest joy in all this is building an audience that loves my approach to publishing and the amazing content I publish. I know every author has his/her style. Mine is publishing what I learn to readers out there so that they can learn what is trending, what other readers are also searching for in the nonfiction world and much more. As such, if you read the other books I have published, you will undoubtedly know a lot more than the average person on a diverse range of issues. And as you well know, knowledge is power- and the biggest investment that you can ever have on your life!

3: Let's Get In Touch

Let's get closer than just leaving reviews and buying my other books. Reach out to me through email, like or follow me on social media and let's interact. You will perhaps get to know stuff about me that will change your life in a way. As we interact, we will also influence each other in a way. I' definitely would love to learn something from you as we get to know each other.

Antony

Website: http://www.fantonpublishers.com/

Email: Support@fantonpublishers.com

Twitter: https://twitter.com/FantonPublisher

Facebook Page:
https://www.facebook.com/Fantonpublisher/

Private Facebook Group For Readers:
https://www.facebook.com/groups/FantonPublishers/

Pinterest: https://www.pinterest.com/fantonpublisher/

4: Grab Some Freebies On Your Way Out; Giving Is Receiving, Right?

I mentioned this at the start of the book. If you didn't download it then, now is the time to get it now.

5: Suggest Topics That You'd Love Me To Cover To Increase Your Knowledge Bank. As I

stated, I love feedback; any type of feedback- positive or negative. As such, make sure to reach out. I am looking forward to seeing your suggestions and insights on the topic. You could even suggest improvements to this book. Simply send me a message on Support@fantonpublishers.com. As a publisher, I strive to publish content that my readers are actively looking for. Therefore, your input is highly important.

6: Subscribe To My Newsletter To Know When I Publish New Books.

I already mentioned this earlier; I love to connect with my readers. This is just another avenue for me to connect to you. As such, if you would love to know whenever I publish new books and blog posts, subscribe to my newsletter. You will be the first to know whenever I have fresh content!

My Other Books

Weight Loss Books

You can search for the titles on Amazon.

Binge Eating: Binge Eating Disorder Cure: Easy To Follow Tips For Eating Only What Your Body Needs

Lose Weight: Lose Weight Fast Naturally: How to Lose Weight Fast Without Having To Become a Gym Rat or Dieting Like a Maniac

Lose Weight: Lose Weight Permanently: Effective Strategies on How to Lose Weight Easily and Permanently

Hair & Beauty Books

Hair Loss: How to Stop Hair Loss: Actionable Steps to Stop Hair Loss (Hair Loss Cure, Hair Care, Natural Hair Loss Cures)

Relationships Books

Wedding: Budget Wedding: Wedding Planning On The Cheap (Master How To Plan A Dream Wedding On Budget)

How To Get Your Ex Back: Step By Step Formula On How To Get Your Ex Back And Keep Him/her For Good

SEX POSITIONS: Sex: Unleash The Tiger In You Using These 90-Day Sex Positions With Pictures

Money Problems: How To Solve Relationship Money Problems: Save Your Marriage By Learning How To Fix All Your Money Problems And Save Your Relationship

Body Language: Master Body Language: A Practical Guide to Understanding Nonverbal Communication and Improving Your Relationships

Travel Books

Kenya: Travel Guide: The Traveler's Guide to Make The Most Out of Your Trip to Kenya (Kenya Tourists Guide)

Personal Finance & Investing Books

Real Estate: Rental Property Investment Guide: How To Buy & Manage Rental Property For Profits

MONEY: Make Money Online: 150+ Real Ways to Make Real Money Online (Plus 50 Bonus Tips to Guarantee Your Success)

Money: How To Make Money Online: Make Money Online In 101 Ways

Health & Fitness Books

PMS CURE: Easy To Follow Home Remedies For PMS & PMDD

Testosterone: How to Boost Your Testosterone Levels in 15 Different Ways Naturally

World Issues Books

ISIS/ISIL: The Rise and Rise of the Islamic State: A Comprehensive Guide on ISIS & ISIL

See You On The Other Side!

See, I publish books on just about any topic imaginable!

If you have any suggestions on topics you would want me to cover, feel free to get in touch:

Website: http://www.fantonpublishers.com/

Email: Support@fantonpublishers.com

Twitter: https://twitter.com/FantonPublisher

Facebook Page:
https://www.facebook.com/Fantonpublisher/

Private Facebook Group For Readers:
https://www.facebook.com/groups/FantonPublishers/

Pinterest: https://www.pinterest.com/fantonpublisher/

PS: You can subscribe to my mailing list to know when I publish new books:

Hey! This is not the entire list! You can check an updated list of all my books on:

My Author Central: amazon.com/author/fantonpublishers

My Website: http://www.fantonpublishers.com

Stay With Me On My Journey To Making Passive Income Online

I have to admit; my writing business makes several six figures a year in profits (after paying ourselves salaries). Until recently, I didn't realize just how hard we worked to build this business to what it has become so far.

However, while it is profitable and I want to do it in the long term, I understand its limitations. I know I cannot have an endless number of writers at a time especially if we are to continue delivering high quality products to our customers and readers consistently.

That's why I have recently started getting more serious with self-publishing to help me build a passive income business i.e. income that is not pegged on the number of writers and hours that we put to develop our products.

Thanks to my vast experience and dedication to get things done, I am committed to building a six figure passive income publishing business.

To make sure you are part of this journey, I am inviting you to subscribe to our newsletter to know my progress as far as passive income generation is concerned. That's not all; if making passive income, just like me, is something you'd love to venture into, you can follow my 'tell it all' blog, which I explain everything I have done to promote every book and how the results are turning out with figures and images.

My goal is to make sure that while I add value to my audience through the different topics that I publish about to solve various problems for instance, I also add massive value to readers in ways that go beyond just one book. Subscribe to our newsletter to know when I publish new books, how I did market research, how I make money with the books and much, much more.

You can even ask questions on anything you want me to answer regarding publishing and everything else related to the topics of discussion.

Antony

Website: http://www.fantonpublishers.com/

Email: Support@fantonpublishers.com

Twitter: https://twitter.com/FantonPublisher

Facebook Page: https://www.facebook.com/Fantonpublisher/

Private Facebook Group For Readers: https://www.facebook.com/groups/FantonPublishers/

Pinterest: https://www.pinterest.com/fantonpublisher/

I look forward to hearing from you!

PSS: Let Me Also Help You Save Some Money!

If you are a heavy reader, have you considered subscribing to Kindle Unlimited? You can read this and millions of other books for just $9.99 a month)! You can check it out by searching for Kindle Unlimited on Amazon.com!

Printed in Great Britain
by Amazon

18515721R00038

THE GROUNDWORK

OF THE

CHRISTIAN VIRTUES.

THE GROUNDWORK

OF THE

CHRISTIAN VIRTUES.

A Course of Lectures

BY

ARCHBISHOP ULLATHORNE.

"The soul advances in light as she advances in humility, and the
knowledge of humility is the knowledge of God and of self."
SIMEON JUNIOR THEOLOGUS.

FOURTH EDITION.

LONDON: BURNS & OATES, LIMITED.
NEW YORK: CATHOLIC PUBLICATION SOCIETY CO.
1890.

Dedication.

To the Reverend Mothers and the Sisters of the English Dominican Congregation of St. Catherine of Sienna.

DEAR SISTERS IN CHRIST,—

You will give a hospitable welcome to this book. It is yours by right of origin, yours by right of possession, and yours by right of your prayers for its success. It took its beginning from instructions directed to the formation of your first members, and the light of its principles is already implanted in your minds and hearts.

The holy Bishop St. Aldhelm, who was the first Englishman, as he tells us, who ever cultivated literature, dedicated his chief work to a conventual circle of "Christ's most holy Virgins"; and he assigns these reasons for thus addressing them : their purity of life, their loyalty to their vows, their concord in religious discipline, and their sagacious pursuit of the sweet wisdom hived in the holy Scriptures. He tells them that he never received their letters without lifting his hands to Heaven in gratitude; and that, touched with their devout urbanity, he gave thanks to the King of Heaven, who had given him to behold on earth such daughters of grace and handmaids of Christ. He says that, under the motherly guidance of Hedelitha, those Virgins of Christ were well instructed in holy doctrines, and well trained in the exercises of the soul to run their course with energy and skill. For Hedelitha I may substitute the names of Margaret and Imelda, the first venerable Mothers of your religious life, now happily with God.

To the motives assigned to his spiritual daughters by St. Aldhelm twelve hundred years ago, for dedicating his book to them, I may add one more. Having watched over your Congregation from its cradle, having co-operated with its holy Foundress in its formation and expansion, I have desired, among the responsibilities of the episcopal office, to complete this book, and to place it in your hands as some token of my paternal affection, as some memorial of my solicitude for your solid instruction, which your filial gratitude may pass on to the generations that come after you.

Next to the God of all condescension, who is the lover of humble souls, to whom but to you should I dedicate this book? So long as your motto expresses your life, so long as you seek God ALONE, and find in Him the supreme object of your desires; so long as you are earnest as well in the second object of your life, to draw to God the poor, the ignorant, and the suffering, whom Christ has redeemed; so long will the charity and sweet peace of God be with you, and the fragrance of your cheerful virtues will attract other souls to follow your example. This, my dear Sisters, is the earnest prayer of your devoted Father in Christ,

✠ W. B. ULLATHORNE.

BIRMINGHAM, *April* 10, 1882.

CONTENTS.

———

CONTENTS.

LECTURE I.

THE DIVINE LAW OF PROBATION.

"The Lord your God trieth you, that it may appear whether you love Him with all your heart, and with all your soul, or not."—DEUTERONOMY xiii. 3.

THE noblest building demands the costliest foundation to secure its firmness and solidity. The magnificent structure of the Christian virtues, by which the soul ascends to God, can only rest firmly and rise securely upon the receptive virtue of humility,—a virtue most costly to our corrupted nature, yet of wonderful strength when brought to its perfection. This virtue has its ground in the nature of things, its reason in the unchangeable order of justice, and the whole knowledge of God and of one's self for the compass of its motive. And whilst as a virtuous force of the will it keeps the soul in her just and true position, it opens her powers to every good and perfect gift that descends from the Father of lights.

In our former course of lectures we considered the endowments of man in their relations with his final end, and took a general survey of the broad and deep foundations of this virtue, and we thus prepared the way for a more precise and exact consideration of its nature, its origin, its force and efficacy; and upon this we have now to enter. We shall have further to consider the relations which humility bears to the other Christian virtues, its qualities as their essential groundwork, and as the preparation, sustaining power, and protection of them all. For the foundation of the Christian virtues is itself a strong and a most comprehensive virtue, and a virtue without which there is no Christian virtue. As the moral groundwork of God's building in the soul, this virtue has rightly obtained the name of humility. For as the

1*

word *humus*, from which it is derived, signifies the lowly ground that is opened by the labours of man to the fertilizing influence, of the heavens, *humilitas*, or humility, is the lowly condition of the soul, opened by the self-cleansing and self-subduing labours of the spiritual man to the benign influences of God.

God alone is independent; every creature is dependent on God. But as man is made for God, he has a vast capacity, and wants in full proportion to his capacity for God, and is therefore immeasurably more dependent on his Creator than the irrational creatures, whose wants are limited to this world. To be deeply conscious of this dependence is to have the soul filled with the most important moral truth with which we are concerned; and to enter with good-will into this truth is to place ourselves on the secure foundation of all justice. This dependence has its foundation in the divine pre-eminence and absolute sovereignty of God, and in His bountiful goodness, and in the need we have of receiving His divine help and bounty, that we may be united with Him, both as our first cause and as our final end: as our first cause, that we may receive His continual influence; and as our final end, that by His graces and blessings, as we are made to His images we may come to our Divine Original. So dependent is the ray of light upon the sun, that when separated it expires in darkness; and so dependent is our soul upon the divine beneficence, that when we are no longer subject to His gracious influence we decline into a moral death. As humility springs in the order of justice from the truth of our dependence on God, it is the virtue proper to the intellectual and moral creature, and the foundation of all those virtues whereby man is perfected unto God.

But as the pillar that led Israel from Egypt to the Land of Promise was both light and cloud, so this virtue of humility is light to the children of belief, whilst to the children of this world it takes the appearance of an obscure and unintelligible cloud. It enlightens the humble; it perplexes the proud. For the world without humility is the world without the sense of God, and consequently without the sense of dependence on God. But when for long ages pride had usurped the place of humility in human hearts, then came humility from Heaven in the person of God and the nature of man, that through its divine power and influence the souls of men might return to God.

But before entering into these great subjects we shall have to consider the divine law of probation, which has its reason in the law of subjection, and which establishes the connecting link between the subjects of our present and of our past course of lectures. Lest, however, what we have already said on the great qualities of humility should seem overcharged, especially to those who have hitherto seen but its cloudy side, and who can see nothing in it but an amiable weakness or a shameful degradation, we shall at once point out two facts that place the victorious force of this virtue on invincible foundations. The first is this, that by the divine exercise of humility the fallen race of man was redeemed from evil and brought back to God. The second is this, that by the exercise of this virtue the Christian soul is transplanted from dependence on her own native resources to dependence on the inexhaustible resources of God, and from reliance on her own feeble self-support to reliance on the strong support of God. A virtue that carries the soul over from her own foundation to place her on a divine foundation must be strong; and this virtue is humility.

God is the fountain of law. He gives to us the light of law, that by its guidance we may rule our wills in conformity with His divine will, which expresses both the eternal order of things and the order of progress in the creature from what is good to what is better. From this order all justice proceeds, and through justice all good is obtained. There are two orders of dependence in the creation: there is a necessitated order in the materia creation, which is without understanding or will; and there is a voluntary order of dependence in the spiritual creation, which determines its own free conduct by law and virtue, or by neglecting them becomes a failure.

In the material universe the order of dependence is fixed and determined by the will of God, the first Mover of all things, unless for great spiritual purposes He changes that order, and brings it under the higher motive of a higher law, that it may serve to the saving and sanctification of souls. Even in that fixed order and dependence of the material world, on which we habitually rely, what is inferior in it is perfected by what is superior. But in the spiritual world of created intelligences, where wills are free, the just and due order of dependence on God, whose needy clients we are, is one thing as it exists in the law of justice, and another as it exists in fact—that is to say, as it exists in the actual conformity of our will to the will of God as expressed in the law of justice. For the law of justice may be in our mind and conscience whilst our will is far from it. Thus whilst the material creation is necessarily dependent on God, our spiritual soul must be willingly subject to God, that we may be in just order and right dependence on God, to receive His sovereign bounty: a truth which redounds to our honour and dignity as free and intelligent spirits made to the image of God.

There is one truth more of vast importance in this relation. To every soul a certain portion of the elements of this material world is attached in the wonderful organization of the human body; and notwithstanding the general laws which regulate material things, the free soul exercises its free-will upon the body and upon the things dependent on the body that are external to it, and either subjects them to order or throws them by evil conduct or neglect into disorder. Now if the will of man can thus change the material order of things in so far as they are dependent on him, yet without seeming to interfere with the fixed and constant order of any part of the material creation, how much more can God for His high spiritual purposes do the same! For matter is made to be the servant of spirit.

The light of justice is therefore planted in our mind and the sense of God in our heart, and the choice is left to our will whether we will conform ourselves by the exercise of virtue to the just and due order of our dependence on God or not. But this moral conformity of our disposition and will to our real position before God, and the subordination of our will to the known will of God, is expressed by the subjection of our mind and will to the mind and will of God; and in virtue of this subjection, which is the becoming predisposition on our part, we are able to receive from God the gifts that bring us to perfection. Subjection is therefore to our free natures what dependence is to the irrational creature, and by this willing subjection we not only consult our greater good, which comes to us from the divine superiority, but we give that reverence and honour to God which is due to Him. Yet this reverence and honour, as St. Thomas observes, is not given to God as though a benefit to Him, to whose glory no creature can add anything, but it returns to our benefit, because our perfection consists in subjecting ourselves to God, even as everything is perfected by subjection to its superior.

So the body is perfected through subjection to the soul, the atmosphere through subjection to the sun, and the soul is united to God through subjection to Him, and by reason of that subjection she receives from Him whatever is needful for her perfection.*

The soul in her substance and powers is the free creation of God, who in creating willed that she should exist for ever. As the Book of Wisdom says: "God created man indestructible, and to the image of his own likeness he made. Him ".† Man has no power, therefore, over his own spiritual existence. Independently, moreover, of her own will, the soul receives whatever is necessary for her natural functions, such as the gift of reason and the natural sense of good and evil. But as she is destined for a good unspeakably higher than her nature, as God Himself is the Supreme Object of the soul, she cannot receive what is necessary for her union with God and her perfection without the free subjection of her will and the voluntary dependence of her hope on God. First, because divine gifts in the moral order must have a willing subject. Secondly, because their greatness and goodness must be gratefully recognized. Thirdly, because the lowly receiver of gifts so high must humbly understand and feel that they are not her own, but come from the bounty of God. Fourthly, because the soul must willingly open herself in response to the divine gifts to make them fruitful. Fifthly, because the will must enter into the intention of her Divine Benefactor.

Yet, so far is this willing subjection from debasing the soul, that it brings her to the majesty and submits her to the loving condescension of God, which brings honour to her nature and dignity to her character. Nor is the freedom of our nature lessened by subjection to the Divine Nature ; on the contrary, it is wonderfully increased ; we are set free in mind by the possession of greater truth, and free in heart by the possession of greater good. Our subjection to God is not a subjection by descending, but by ascending ; is not a deference to things lower than ourselves, but a movement towards what is incomparably higher than we are. In this subjection the soul deserts her self-love, and the base things to which self-love holds her captive and enchained, and moves towards God in the act of subjecting herself to Him, who is the perfect freedom and the source of all

* S. Thomas, *Sum.* ii. 2, q. 81, a. 7.   † *Wisdom* ii. 23.

freedom.   Is the spirit free that cleaves to her own nature, or the spirit that seeks the Divine Nature?   Is the mind most at liberty in her own light, or the mind that comes into the sphere of the divine and supernal light?   Is the soul enlarged through immersion in the body, or through union with the spiritual things of God?   The pride of independence is isolation, and isolation is poverty—poverty of mind, poverty of heart, and poverty of spirit. But he who is the subject of greater light than his own, and the servant of greater powers than his nature can supply, has reached to sources of freedom beyond the limits of his nature.   It is not the man, then, who isolates himself in the pride of self-sufficiency, but the man who unites himself by subjection to what is higher in power, better in wisdom, and greater in good—the man who looks hopefully to the Divine Fountain of light and grace, who is free with that freedom with which God sets us free.   Freedom is not of the night ; darkness is its adversary: freedom is of the day, and God is the sun of our freedom.

To put the law of dependence in a simple point of view, whatever is created is feeble and requires to be fed.   The heavens feed the earth, the earth the plants, the plants the animals, and all feed the body of man.   But whatever lives by food depends on the provider of that food : to rebel against that food or against its provider is to starve.   And spiritual creatures are also in a state of weakness and want of their proper food, all the greater because their capacity is too immense for anything but God to satisfy.   They, too, must be fed, and, since they are spirits, with spiritual food ; or they can neither grow, nor strengthen, nor advance to those better things, the appetite for which is deep within them, and for which they were really made.   The food of the mind is truth, and the food of the will is force and good. Hence the Divine Master of souls has said : " Not in bread alone doth man live, but in every word that proceedeth from the mouth of God ".*

Spiritual natures are on the summits of creation ; there is nothing but God above them.   Bearing the image of God in their nature and the consciousness of God in that image, they are His immediate subjects, and He their Father and Feeder. For the Lord God is the Pastor of souls, feeding them as a shepherd his sheep ; and when He appoints other shepherds, they feed

* S. Matthew iv. 4.

not from their own substance, but from His eternal stores. But unless the spiritual children be subject to the Father, how can they be fed? A stomach that loathes its food makes a weak and sickly body; and a soul that revolts against its nourishment cannot have spiritual strength. God is the first Giver and the first Mover; the will is the receiver and the second mover, meeting the gift, making it her own, and making it fruitful. But if the receiver responds not to the Divine Giver, if the gift be left unregarded, the mind is not enlightened, the heart is not nourished, the soul is in a worse plight through her neglect than before the gift was offered. There may be an idle, sentimental, passive submission to the gift, but this will do nothing for the soul's good. There must be an active subjection and an earnest correspondence to God and His grace, to meet and mingle with the good movements of God, to enrich and fertilize our powers with His gifts.

Government is as necessary to the soul as food, and spirits on their venturous way from ignorance to truth, from nothingness to God, require the Divine Wisdom to lead them, the Divine Lord to govern them. But there can be no government without subjection. You may choose a wise and beneficent master, who is interested in your well-being and advancement, or you may choose a tyrannical master, who thinks but of his own interests at the cost of yours; but a master you must have. If you choose the first, you choose freedom; if you choose the second, you bid farewell to liberty. There is no master so large-minded, so generous, or who is so well acquainted with you and your requirements, as God; no father so loving and bountiful; no friend so free from all jealousy; none who so completely loves you for your greater good. Whilst there is no tyrant so narrow-minded, so proud-hearted, so exacting, so suspicious, so utterly bent on keeping you to your own littleness, as the one we all know so well, of whose tyranny we have had such bitter experience, and who goes by the name of Myself. This name has such an unpleasant sound to all ears but our own, that even whilst cherishing what it signifies, we find it prudent to keep it as much away from other ears as we can. Yet God or yourself you must choose for your master.

The whole design of God's beneficent government of souls is to draw them out of themselves and to bring them to His truth and good. This is the true object of the divine law of probation, to draw us out of ourselves by means of those virtues which probation is intended to develop and promote. Unless you understand this grand truth, you will have but a faint notion of the good which God contemplates in providing temptation and probation for His spiritual creatures. As there are few truths more obscure to the general mind, or that more nearly concern our spiritual welfare, let us examine the principle of this divine law more closely.

The soul begins her everlasting existence in a feeble and contracted condition as well as the mortal body. Her first life is one of sense and instinct. What she first obtains is the consciousness of self, and of her own personal and separate existence; then a little experience adds to this keen self-consciousness the sense of limitation. Owing to the double sensation produced by what acts within us and what reacts upon us from external causes, these lines of limitation are at first obscure and indefinite; experience has yet to teach the difference between these two causes of sensation; both, however, have the same effect of increasing the sensibility of self-consciousness. But this inclines our nature to independence.

Consider the motive power within this young spirit. First, it is an instinct rather than a will, until reason dawns in the intelligence, and then it becomes a will. The infant seems at first to be almost a part of the mother, and finds its good and protection in her. When taken from her, the child suffers; when brought to her, it rejoices and clings to her for all good. But in passing from infancy to the dawning of reason there comes a change. Thinking has begun, self-consciousness has grown, the sense of independent life becomes definite, the will begins to assert itself, and to feel its own importance. The mother says: *You must.* The child replies: *I won't.* This little fit of self-assertion is the beginning of pride. Fear must come to check this first step to independence. The child receives reproof and some new command as a loving discipline to enforce subjection and obedience. This first trial of the young spirit is probation, helping the little soul to leave its selfishness and to submit to its mother's law. The obedience that follows is the beginning of self-knowledge and self-mastery.

This will serve to explain how the newly-created intelligence, whether angel or human soul, is engaged with the sense of her own existence and of her own limitations, and is thus inclined by nature to self-love, before that intelligence is drawn by grace to a greater Being than her own. The sense of personality comes first, because it is the foundation of responsibility. We therefore find ourselves before we completely find God, although the testimony of God is within us. Even the angels were not created in union with God or with virtue; they had first to receive the grace of God, and then acquire the virtues in a state of probation.

If we look for analogies between the visible and the invisible world, we shall find them in abundance, because both are created by one Spiritual Power and are formed from spiritual types. There are two great principles of movement in the visible world and two great principles of movement in the spiritual world, which, with great differences, have still a striking resemblance. To the fundamental principles of movement in the material universe we give the names of attraction and gravitation, names that cover our ignorance of their nature. By a mysterious influence beyond our perception, each mass of matter is attracted to its own centre, whereby it coheres together; whilst by another mysterious influence a body of less quantity is attracted to a body of greater quantity in proportion to its mass, density, and distance. In other words, what is less is attracted to what is greater, according to its greatness and proximity of influence. This is a shadow of the order that reigns in the spiritual world, where justice prevails; for whilst the movement of the material universe is necessitated, the movement of the spiritual world is free, and springs from will and choice. But the order of good in the spiritual world demands that whatever spirit has less of being, life, and good should overcome the tendency to self and the disposition to abide in self, and should tend to what has the greatest being, life, and good, that the less may partake of the greater. And as the movement of spiritual natures is by thought, desire, and love, and the attraction which influences these movements to the better things is the presence, light, and grace of God, they ought to tend, by the inclination of faith, desire, and love, to the Supreme Being, who is the Truth, the Life, and the Love, that they may become partakers of God.

This ever-moving earth is not only attracted to its own centre, as all that constitutes man is held together by the central force of the soul, but it is held on its rapid course by the attraction of the sun; and as it turns towards that mighty luminary it receives his image, and partakes his light, warmth, and fertilizing power. Yet his rays are intercepted by the vapours which the earth produces, and by the turbulence arising from their conflicts. And so by His creative influence does God hold the ever-active soul, in which He has placed His image, in her dependence. But when she turns her face with desire to Him who attracts her, He sends forth the celestial influence of His light, grace, and charity upon her, attracting her to move towards Him by faith, hope, and love, and she becomes a partaker of His goodness. But as the soul is not necessitated like the earth, but free to make her choice, if she prefers her own central attraction, and the drawing to herself of the small things around her, instead of the divine attraction, and her own uneasy love instead of the divine love, that soul is left in her own littleness, is clouded and darkened by her own vapours, and troubled in herself. For she is doing violence to the deepest appetite of her nature, and is oppressed far more than she can understand with the weight of that attraction to the greater good, whose object she is constantly misunderstanding, or which her pride is constantly resisting; and that spirit becomes more and more oppressed, and more and more impoverished.

Who can express the magnificence of the light of faith as compared with the light of reason? One who has had the gift of faith from infancy, and has no experience of a condition of soul without that supernatural light, can never realize the immensity of the sphere of faith as compared with the sphere of natural reason, or the difference of character that belongs to the one light as compared with the other. In the things of God and the soul reason but gropes among the shadows reflected here below; whilst faith, with its light direct from God, opens out the infinite and eternal prospect of divine truth, which, though obscurely seen, is yet surely seen by the humble mind, giving a breadth and firmness to that mind that nothing can explain but the action of God in the soul. For the truth of God, received by faith and embraced by charity, gives a largeness to the soul beyond every limit of nature, exalts the will above all that is merely human, and the joy of believing brings the heart nigh to God. The Divine Master of truth, knowing all her ways, has said, "You shall know the truth, and the truth shall make you free ".*

* *S. John* viii. 32.

In words that still vibrate with his awe and gratitude, St. Augustine records the first visit of that light of faith which drew him out of himself to the Eternal Truth. " Admonished," he says, " to return to myself, through Thy divine guidance I entered my interior. I was able to do this because Thou, O God, wast my helper. I entered, and with the eye of my soul I saw the unchangeable light. It was above the eye of my soul, above my mind. It was not this common light that shines to all mortals alike; nor a light of the same kind, embracing all things equally with its brightness. It was not this, but another light, exceedingly differing from all this. Nor was it upon my mind as oil is upon water, but was far above me, because It made me, and I was far beneath, because made by It. Whosoever knoweth the truth knoweth that light, and whosoever knoweth that light knoweth Eternity. Charity knoweth it. O Eternal Truth, true Charity, and dear Eternity, Thou art my God! To Thee I sigh both day and night. When first I knew Thee, Thou didst lift me up, that I might see it was not myself I beheld, but the truth. And thou didst beat down my sight with Thy vehement irradiation into me, and I trembled with dread and with love, finding myself far from Thee in a region of unlikeness. It was as though I heard Thy voice on high saying to me: ' I am the food of the strong; grow up and thou shalt partake of Me. Thou shalt not change Me into thee, but thou shalt be changed into Me.' And I knew that Thou dost correct man for iniquity, and dost make his soul to waste away like the spider. And I looked on the things beneath Thee, and saw that they neither are nor are not, because they are not as Thou art; for that alone hath true being that abideth unchangeable. My good, therefore, is to adhere to God; for unless I abide in Him I cannot abide in myself; but He, whilst abiding in Himself, reneweth all things. And Thou art the Lord my God, because Thou hast no need of my goods." *

If the gift of faith is so wonderful, how much more wonderful is the gift of charity! It is the flame of love descending from God into the humble soul, penetrating to the centre of her spirit, embracing the will, embraced by the will, carrying us gratefully out of the contracted limits of our self-love towards the Divine Author of all life and happiness. This love is the living bond

* S. August., *Confessiones*, lib. vii., c. 10, 11.

between God and the soul: on the one side, an extension of God's eternal love to us; on the other, a return of love to our Divine Benefactor, the free restoration to Him of the life He has given to us, the full homage of all we are and have received.

If we look to the earth for a symbol of the way in which spiritual natures are developed, we shall find it in the flowers. Those beautifiers of the earth that gladden all eyes are the fructifying organs of the vegetable world, yet they are beautiful and pure, a reminiscence of the world yet undefiled by sin. Fit offerings, therefore, are they to the heavenly purity, although, like all earthly things, they quickly fade. In their first life the flowers are closed upon themselves; but the sun shines upon the lily and it opens to the descending light, expands its sensitive petals to the glowing warmth, and its pure cup is filled with light, beauty, and sweetness; yet it gracefully bows its head in confession of its native weakness and dependence. In many flowers, when darkness comes or the tempest rages, like the faithful soul under trial, the beautiful creature folds itself in patience, awaiting the return of light to expand itself anew in joy.

There is an intimate and essential connection between the law of subjection and the law of probation; for probation is the test of subjection. To prove is to examine, to apply a test, to find out by experiment. Man is often an unconscious imitator of God. If he makes a thing for some great purpose on which much depends, he puts it to a severe test to try its firmness before it is adopted. If any one is intended for a great office, honour, or duty, he is proved and tried by a suitable discipline before he is advanced. The angelic spirit and the immortal soul are destined for the highest honour and the noblest end, but this demands great purity and constancy; and as they are not only free but weak by nature, they must be proved and tried whether they will hold to the strength of God or abide in their own weakness. As their advancement to their glorious end depends on their constancy to the ever-increasing gifts of God, on their sincerity in acknowledging them and their fidelity in responding to them, their virtue requires to be openly proved and strengthened by trial before they receive the great things of eternity.

In the Sacred Scriptures God is sometimes said to prove, and sometimes to tempt, but this is always by a revelation, a command, or an affliction. When the law was revealed from Sinai, Moses said to the people: "Fear not; for God hath come to prove you, and that the dread of Him might be upon you, and you shall not sin ".* The great revelation came with fear, that the souls of the people might be humbled for its reception. When the commandments of God were repeated with solemn circumstances, and the people bound themselves to obey them before entering the Promised Land, Moses said to them again: "Thou shalt remember the ways through which the Lord thy God hath brought thee forty years through the desert, to afflict and prove thee, that the things that were in thy heart might be made known, whether thou wouldst keep His commandments or not ".+ Here the trial of affliction is to reveal the disposition of the heart. Again the great Lawgiver says: "The Lord your God trieth you, that it may appear whether you love Him with all your heart, and with all your soul, or not ".‡ Here probation is shown to be the test of faithful love. Then the Prophet alleges another motive why they have been proved and tried: "After He had afflicted and proved thee, at the last He had mercy on thee; lest thou should say in thy heart: My own might, and the strength of my own hand, have achieved all these things for me. But remember the Lord thy God, that He hath given thee strength, that He might fulfil His covenant."§ The motive here assigned is, that through trial the gifts of God may be known to be His, and not the power of the creature.

The whole reason of divine probation is summed up in these grave sentences. But where the Scripture speaks of God as tempting, what is really meant is proving, as St. Thomas observes after St. Augustine. Where it is said, for example, that "God tempted Abraham," it was not an evil temptation to sin, but a proving of his virtue and fidelity by a most difficult command. Abraham was destined for great things, to be the friend of God, the prophet as well as ancestor of Christ, and the father of the faithful. He receives the command to sacrifice his son, a figure to all times of the sacrifice of the Son of God: he obeys, and a substitute is provided. He gives the required proof of his firm faith and obedience, and through His angel the Almighty said to him: "Because thou hast done this thing, and hast not spared

* *Exodus* xx. 20.   + *Deuteronomy* viii. 2.
‡ *Ibid.*, xiii. 3.   § *Ibid.*, viii. 16-18.

thy only-begotten son for My sake, I will help thee, and I will multiply thy seed as the stars of Heaven, and as the sand that is by the sea-shore: thy seed shall possess the gates of their enemies. And in thy seed shall all the nations of the earth be blessed, because thou hast obeyed My voice."* This exceptional example proves that when God himself tries the good, He tries them with good, and not with evil; for the trial was a divine command that God alone could give, because it arose to principles far higher than those of the law delivered to men. It arose by reflection to those principles which our Blessed Lord proclaimed when He said: "God so loved the world as to give His only-begotten Son ".† And Isaac became a figure of Christ.

The temptings of God are not seductions to evil; these belong to Satan and his followers. They are searchings of the spirit, that she may know herself, become more humble, understand her grace, find out what help she needs from God, and draw nearer to Him for strength and protection. For, as St. Augustine says: "No one knows what powers of love are in him, or are not in him, until through a divine experiment they are made known to him ".‡ If the spirit fails in the trial, it is expedient that her hidden infirmity be brought to light for the divine justification.

St. James gives us this solemn warning: "Let no man, when he is tempted, say that he is tempted by God. For God is not a tempter of evils, and He tempteth no man." The Apostle then points out where the temptation comes from: "But every man is tempted by his own concupiscence, being drawn away and allured. Then when concupiscence hath conceived, it bringeth forth sin." § The external tempter is powerless without the inward inclination to evil; but when the inward weakness yields to evil allurements, the sin is conceived, and death is its fruit. But God does not allure to sin; He proves the spirit by some new truth that asks for faith, or by some new command that calls for obedience; and the humility of obedience brings great good and enlargement to the soul. Hence St. Augustine observes, that "when God ceases to prove, He ceases to teach ".

From what has been said we may gather five reasons why

---

* *Genesis* xxii. 1, 16-18.   † *S. John* iii. 16.
‡ S. August., *Quæst in Genesim*, lib. iv., q. 59.   § *S. James* i. 13-15.

every rational creature who has received the grace of God should be submitted to probation.

1. The first reason is, that the spirit may be drawn out of herself, and be attracted to the sphere of eternal light and good, and so be enlarged in spirit and life for the reception of greater and diviner gifts. This is accomplished through some great and unexpected call upon faith and obedience. Thus in the innocent morning of their creation, after magnifying them with holy gifts, God suddenly proved the angels. He gave them a new and wonderful revelation prophetic of the mystery of the Incarnation, and commanded their adoration of the Eternal Word, their own Illuminator, in a nature made lower than their own: "When He bringeth in the First-Begotten into the world He saith, And let all the angels of God adore Him". * They were tried by good in a difficult mystery, and by their subjection and obedience they had to prove their faith and constancy. Those who stood their probation were confirmed in sanctity and passed to their reward in the Beatific Vision; but those who yielded to pride and resisted, proved their utter unfitness for union with God. As they would not accept the truth from God, they could not accept the God of truth; as they would not subject themselves to God in one command, they could not adhere to God for eternity.

2. The second reason for probation is, that the outward call upon the inward powers may act as a kind of awakening shock upon the sleeping energies, calling upon them to meet the new demand upon the spirit's faith and obedience. It is a call to active leaving of one's narrow self to adhere to God despite of difficulty. For it is one thing to receive light, another to enter into that light; one thing to obtain grace, another to act with that grace. But when an exterior revelation is added to the inward light, or an exterior command to the inward grace, or an exterior affliction to the inward gift of patience, that exterior call acts as an outward impulse to summon and help the will to exercise her inward gifts, and to use the powers divinely given to her. As the preacher gives us an outward stimulation to use our inward grace, so in the moment of probation God 'gives us an outward call to use our inward grace, and give proof of our fidelity. This trial is the culminating moment that determines the will to its root, deciding the habit and condition of the soul,

* *Hebrews* i. 6.

like a profession after a novitiate. It is said of the interests of this present life, that everybody has one opportunity, which followed up leads on to fortune. However this may be, the hour of probation is such an opportunity for the gaining of eternal life.

3. The third reason is, that through probation every spirit may obtain the knowledge of herself, what her weakness is, what her limitations, and what the strength received from God. "We must consider," says St. Aelred, "how every creature is changeable. If rational creatures were not changeable as well as others, they would not need their Creator's help, as they could neither advance to what is better nor fall to what is worse. But as they are changeful, they require to know this, and to learn by experience what is written : 'My good is to adhere to God'; that every mouth may be stopped, and every creature may be subject to God. But for angel and man to discover their mutability they required to be tempted, and through temptation to be proved, and through probation to be confirmed, that the victorious may receive glory, and they who sin through evident perversity may give proof of the justice that befalls them. For it concerns that beatitude and glory which the beneficent Creator bestows on His rational creatures that their merits be known to flow from the grace of their Creator, and that their happiness is His gift as well as their reward." *

There is another important view of the self-revelation brought out by trial. As the child who obtains the grace of baptism before the age of reason might never know the divine gifts received without the instruction of the Church, the newly created angel or man, who received the gifts of grace immediately upon creation, might confound those gifts with the natural powers, were they not taught by the probation of some difficult revelation and command that their nature is weak, and needs the special help and grace of God to believe and to obey.

4. The fourth reason for probation is to form, develop, and invigorate the virtues by which the soul is perfected for God. The first probation is the trial of faith, because, as St. Thomas observes, faith is the first virtue that submits the mind to God. The second is the trial of obedience, because thereby the will is made subject to the will of God. Through humility, temperance, and patience, the virtues whereby we renounce ourselves and

---

* S. Aelred, *Serm.* 17 *in Cap.* xiii. *Isaiæ.*

overcome our weakness, our subjection to God is made thorough, free, and constant. But the final end of all probation is to test our trust and try our confidence in God. This is summed up in the universal virtue of obedience, which embraces all the virtues. For to believe the eternal mysteries because God has revealed them is the obedience of faith; to abstain from all things that God has forbidden is the obedience of justice; and to love all that God commands us to love is the obedience of charity.

To be passively subject to God is to be only like the things that perish; to be actively subject to His sovereign will is alone worthy of a free and intelligent creature. When God, therefore, gave to the newly-created man the precious endowment of grace and the dignity of original justice, He would not give him entrance into Heaven until he had proved himself worthy by the active exercise of obedience. This was so necessary, and so befitting the Divine Providence, that although God knew that he would transgress the precept and fall into evil, He nevertheless imposed the command upon him to abstain from the tree of knowledge, and left him to his liberty, yet not without giving him ample grace to enable him to obey the mysterious command.

This reason for man's probation has been pithily expressed in the following terms by St. Augustine:—"It was needful for man under the dominion of God to be proved in one way or another, that through obedience he might deserve his Lord. For it may be truly affirmed that obedience is the one virtue of every creature acting under the power of God; and that the vice we call disobedience, that swelling tumour of the creature using her own power to her ruin, is the first and the greatest vice. But unless the man had been commanded something he would have had nothing to enable him to know that God was his Master." [*]
In further explanation the great Doctor says in another place: "God planted no evil tree in paradise, but He Himself was better than what He forbade to be touched. He forbade this to show that the rational soul is not in her own power, and ought to be subject to God, and to keep the order of salvation through obedience. For this reason, therefore, God called the tree He forbade to be touched the tree of the knowledge of good and evil, because, when touched despite of His command, it

[*] S. August., *De Genesi ad litteram*, lib. viii., c. 6.

2*

brought the experience of sin and the knowledge of the good of obedience and of the evil of disobedience." *

5. The fifth reason for probation is to interrogate the soul, whether she is disposed for greater gifts, and is able to respond to them with fidelity. Can she change greater trials into patience, and so become more solid? Can she transmute greater humiliations into profounder humility, and so enlarge her capacity for divine things, and be more perfectly subject to God? Can that soul transform greater manifestations of the divine love into greater acts of charity, and so become more closely united with God? "The Lord your God trieth you, that it may appear whether you love Him with all your heart, and with all your soul, or not." Trial alone, observes St. Augustine, can show to each one what gifts are hidden in him. To leave other examples, the virgin may be solicitous for the things of the Lord, and how she may please God, but how does she know but that some secret infirmity leaves her unprepared for martyrdom? Yet some poor woman over whom she prefers herself may be already prepared to drink the cup of the Lord's humiliation, the cup He gave His disciples, those true lovers of His sublim..y. How does that virgin know that she may not be ready to become a St. Thecla, whilst that poor woman is ready to become a St. Crispina? She has assuredly no proof of this gift before trial.†

The deeper regions of the soul are searched for their purification by keener and more secret trials, which cleanse away the latent inclinations of self-love, and prepare the mysterious recesses of the soul for the entrance of the Holy Spirit with a diviner light and purer flame of charity.

Why God proved the angels Himself, and proved them with good, is obvious on a moment's consideration. There was no evil in the universe until through occasion of their trial a portion of the angels fell. But why God ordained that man should be proved through the temptations of those fallen spirits is one of those profound mysteries whose highest reason is beyond our knowledge. Yet He has not left the children of faith without light to know that in this permissive part of His providence He contemplates the greatest amount of final good. It was essential that man should be drawn out of himself to enable him to enter

---

* S. August., *De Naturi Boni*, c. xxxiv.
† *Ibid.*, *De Sancta Virginitate*, c. xliv.

into better things, and trial is ordained to bring him forth from himself. But as he is of a different nature from the angels, he must have a different probation. The angels are pure activities, and only require the right direction of their unceasing contemplation and action to be perfected, whilst the human soul is encumbered with a body inclined to earth and earthly things. Made lower than the angels, yet for the same divine end as they, man has to acquire the spiritual virtues that bring him to God in an earthly body upon an earthly scene, and has to keep that body obedient to his spirit. It is evident, therefore, that he will require not only a different but a more protracted trial than the angels, owing to the gross elements with which his spirit is combined, the slower speed of his operations, and the natural obstructions that retard his development. He will require such a trial as will make his soul active, animated, and vigilant in spiritual things, notwithstanding the corporal organs through which the spirit acts, and their tendency to those sensual attractions that impede the free ascent of the spirit to things invisible and divine. But this will be best accomplished by a life of labour on the earthly side, and a conflict with spiritual powers on the invisible side. Adam was therefore placed in the garden of paradise, not merely to enjoy its beauty, but "to dress and keep it"; * and after receiving a prohibition for the exercise of his obedience, Satan was permitted to tempt him, that through combat against a spiritual adversary his spiritual powers might be awakened and brought into vigorous exercise.

Thus, in the words of Job, is "the life of man upon earth a warfare, and his days as the days of a hireling," † because of labour. When the exigencies of warfare call for labour and peril, the commander spares not his soldiers, but when the victory is gained he gives the greatest honour to the bravest. The master of the household gives the chief work to the best workman, but when the toil is over he rewards them the best. So also is the providence of God. He spares not the good from toils and conflicts, but rewards them beyond all measure in the end.

We have come into the midst of perils that are awful to human weakness and fears, and most terrible in their effects upon the cowardice of unbelief. This dark side of the universal plan can only be lighted up by contemplating the grand finale to which

* *Genesis* ii. 15.   † *Job* vii. 1.

the whole drama of life is moving. The bright side illuminates the dark side of the divine arrangements—that bright side from which the sovereign light of the supreme goodness of God is shining upon us. The dark side comes, like that of the earth against the sun, from our own limited mind and feeble will, which God would have to be intelligent and strong; for which reason He gives us light and grace, and with them labour and conflicts, that we may grow strong in light and virtue. It belongs to His magnificence to raise up the lowly and strengthen the weak; but if the lowly refuse to be raised and the weak to be strengthened in the combats of grace against evil, God does no violence to their freedom, but they must sink lower in being vanquished, and become weaker, and encounter great darkness.

If there be an unchristian error, an unbelief that is widespread, scornful, desolating, withering to souls in this sensual age, it is the disbelief in the power of evil spirits to tempt man to evil. After the belief and experience of all ages and races of men, pagan, prophetic, and Christian, in the malignant activity of those evil powers on the earth, it has now become a distinguishing mark of the faithful Christian man to act upon the conviction that the devils have powers of seduction in this world against which he has to guard and protect himself. Even the weak in faith are too apt to slumber under the heavy atmosphere of the sensual world, and to forget the apostolic admonition: "Be sober and watch; because your adversary the devil as a roaring lion goeth about seeking whom he may devour. Whom resist ye, strong in faith; knowing that the same affliction befalleth your brethren in the world." *

Wide and far men are ready in their pride to think, if thought it be, to their own ignominy, that all their evil thoughts, their sensual movements, and their malicious acts, come of their own original instigation, rather than allow that they have been tempted by any power beyond themselves. This is a pride of egotism in evil, of independence in wrong, like that of the evil spirits themselves. It is true that we are more conscious of our adversaries when our will is opposed to them than when they hold possession of the will, but the proud take a dark honour to themselves in claiming the whole origin of their evil deeds, as though this could make them independent of the tempter. But those who will not

* 1 *Peter* v. 8, 9.

allow that Satan moves them to evil are seldom disposed to feel that God moves them to their good. It is true, again, that Satan and his angels are not the grotesque creatures of their imagination, except as all evil is grotesque from want of true form and just proportion. They are spirits with the swiftness and subtlety of spirits, and therefore, except in symbolical shapes, they cannot be imagined, more than angels can. But they are spirits in terrible disorder, and their wills are distorted with fearful malice. Were they alone in the midst of us, where would be our safety? But God and His angels are nearer with help to the man of faith—so near that the gross veil of the body alone intervenes between our soul and the presence of God and our guarding angels.

As it regards our probation, we may consider this conflict with evil spirits on three sides : on the side of God, on the side of man, and on the side of the evil spirits themselves.

On the side of God, we may reflect that His great design is to show forth the power of His grace. This is accomplished by overcoming evil with good ; by exercising His providence in the highest degree in overruling the conflict between good and evil, and directing the final issue to the order of justice, rewarding the virtues brought out in the conflict, and punishing the evil that sought their destruction ; by drawing a vast amount of good out of the conflict, to the honour of His grace and the glory of souls ; by causing the pride and independence of those souls that reject His divine help, whereby they might have overcome, to be revealed ; and finally, though first in the divine intention, to crown His creation by the intervention of a Divine Combatant to repair the losses of man in the conflict. When all seems desperate, because human pride has discarded the help of God, the Almighty sends forth His Eternal Word in the feeble panoply of human nature, and by His humble obedience Satan and his angels are conquered and put to shame, pride is shown to be weak in presence of humility, man and the creation are restored to God, and the mercy of God shines through the grace of Christ in unspeakable majesty.

On the side of man, we have already given five reasons why he should be proved ; and to these we may add, that what he most stands in need of is to be advanced in humility, because upon this advancement all his gifts and virtues depend. But nothing can be more calculated to humble him than the assaults of evil spirits and the fear of being brought beneath their power, or more suited to awaken him to care and vigilance than the sense of always living in the presence of his enemies. Yet all our temptations are not from those evil spirits; many have their beginning in the promptings of our self-love, in the concupiscences of our inferior nature, in our evil thought and lax will. But the sense of being always in the presence of malignant adversaries, ready to take hold of our weaknesses, is a cause of humility and fear that prompts us to be vigilant in watching over the precious treasure of grace and virtue at every point. The custody of the thoughts and senses, the protective arms of prayer and self-discipline, and the resting patiently on the inward strength of God, are the true and safe means of guarding the soul from the hostile incursions of our spiritual enemies. As we have no strength but with God, we have a double motive for keeping nigh to Him—the love of God and the fear of our enemies.

St. Maximus the Martyr has summed up the traditional reasons prevailing in his time why God permits this conflict. "Five reasons," he says, "are affirmed why God grants us the conflict with the demons. The first, they say, is this, that in combating their attacks we may learn to distinguish the vices from the virtues; the second, that the virtue gained by laborious conflict may be firm and invincible; the third, that in advancing to virtue we may not become proud or high-minded, but may obtain the practical wisdom of humble things; the fourth, that through these very temptations from spirits so vile we may be led to hold the vices in abhorrence; and the fifth reason to be added to these is, that after our affections have been purified we may never forget our infirmities, nor the power from on high that helped us through the conflict." *

On the side of the evil spirits themselves, those "mediators of pride," as St. Augustine calls them, have an intense hatred of God, whom, nevertheless, they strive to imitate, seeking to establish in the world a dominion through pride that God establishes through love and beneficence. They have also a special hatred of man because he bears the image of God, and because by their revolt against God in the form of man they fell. In their disorder they have a certain imitation of the good angels, having their chiefs, their offices, and special ministries, in which they are

---

* S. Maximus, *Centuria*, 2ª, n. 67.

active day and night. They lay snares for our senses and watch our weaknesses; now violent, now cunning, now crafty, using their great subtlety and great experience of human nature. They are keen, versatile, accommodating, persevering, even condescending, that by little and little they may gain their ends. They have great power over the proud and the impure, who may be justly called their imitators. In their dark insinuations they caricature the light of grace, and affect to show as angels of light; in their wicked instigations and allurements, and their deceptive promises of good things, they grotesquely imitate the operations of grace. They seek to draw the worship of God to themselves in idols, charms, spirit manifestations, witchcrafts, and other superstitions. They inspire proud and subtle minds, eager with curiosity for the unknown, with false and proud philosophies, that imitate their own revolt from God and worship of themselves. They may be truly called the apes of God.

Yet God has set bounds to their action beyond which they cannot go; were it otherwise, there would be nothing safe from their destructive power. David calls them "the strong ones"; our Lord calls their chief "the strong one armed"; and St. Paul, "the prince of this world" and "the god of this age," whilst he designates their whole host as "the rulers of the world of this darkness". Yet they can do no violence to the soul; they can compel us to nothing against our will. They can tempt us, as they are permitted, through the bodily senses, and so through the imagination, but have no licence to touch the soul unless by her own will she gives herself into their power. This is fully shown in the extreme temptations of holy Job. "God is faithful," says St. Paul, "who will not suffer you to be tempted above that which you are able, but will make also with temptation a way of escape, that you may be able to bear it." * But when a soul abandons God, and the will takes to pride or to luxury, in the absence of grace and good-will the devils have great power, the dire results of which are seen in the heathen world, both ancient and modern; but they assume the most injurious aspects when human culture lends its sharp weapons to a soul immersed in egotism. The devils are strong through human unbelief and through vicious self-love.

"Resist the devil," says St. James, "and he will fly from

* *1 Corinthians x. 13.*

you."* Set your will in the right direction, and though he may be troublesome, he cannot hurt you. He can seldom even be troublesome unless you give him your attention. Give your mind to better things, and your body to better employment than awaiting his pleasure in idleness; hold yourself to God in patience and prayer, and his temptations cannot lay hold of you. Tempt not the tempter, and then his offensive importunities will inspire you with a disgust that will turn you round to those better things. It is the fostering of minor troubles till they swell to a flood of sadness and discouragement that gives the devil a turbid pool in which to cast his nets. "Take my counsel," says the illuminated Taulerus, "if those minor troubles befall you, let them drop. Be not disturbed; turn your heart to God. Do not look at them; do not dispute with them; answer them not a word. Only turn your mind from them and let them drop."+

The words of St. James are profoundly instructive: "Every man is tempted by his own concupiscence, being drawn away and allured".‡ Our own uncontrolled inclinations and propensities supply the fuel, and the devil sets the match and blows the flame. He weaves seductive pictures for the imagination and infuses a false sweetness into the senses, and so allures to sin. Where does he find the materials? In our own concupiscences, senses, fancies, and memories, and to our own self-love he adds his own peculiar sting of pride. Then, when concupiscence has brought forth death, he changes his policy; the joy of sin is changed to gloom and sadness, and he suggests the fear and dread of returning to God. There is a shame, a confusion, a reluctance even to look towards God, and he urges the victim in his power to recklessness, that he may escape the cries of conscience. Yet all this comes less from the devil's power than from our own want of virtue and vigilance.

Everywhere the Sacred Scriptures enjoin the cultivation of faith and a watchful eye against the approach of danger as our safe defence against the evil powers. Take the celebrated description by St. Paul of the full-armed Christian: "Put ye on," he says, "the armour of God, that you may be able to withstand the deceits of the devil. For our wrestling is not against flesh and blood; but against principalities and powers, against the

---

* *S. James* iv. 7.   + Taulerus, *Serm.* 1, *Dom.* 3 *post octav. Trinitatis.*
‡ *S. James* i. 14.

rulers of the world of this darkness, against the spirits of wickedness in high places. Therefore take unto you the armour of God, that you may be able to resist in the evil day, and to stand in all things perfect. Stand, therefore, having your loins girt about with truth, and having on the breastplate of justice, and your feet shod with the preparation of the gospel of peace; in all things taking the shield of faith, wherewith you may be able to extinguish the fiery darts of the most wicked one; and take unto you the helmet of salvation, and the sword of the Spirit, which is the Word of God. By all prayer and supplication praying at all times in the spirit; and in the same watching with all instance and supplication." *

The whole defensive armour of the Christian against the evil spirits, which the Apostle elsewhere calls "the armour of light," † is here reduced to faith, justice, and watchfulness in prayer. They dread the light of Christ, tremble at His power, and fly at the sound of His name. Conquered by His divine humility, those proud spirits cannot stand His presence, nor the presence of those who invoke His name with faith. His cross put forth with faith has the same power; it is the altar of His sacrifice, the sign of His conquest, the memorial of His humility, the creed of the devout Christian, the terror of all proud spirits. When heathenism possessed the world, and the power of the evil spirits was at its strongest, the Fathers tell us that the Christians signed the Cross upon every occasion, as their armour against the powers of evil; and Tertullian gives us this remarkable testimony to the confidence which the Christians had in the power of faith over the evil spirits. In his famous Apology for the Christians, addressed to the heathen authorities of the Roman Empire, he declares that their gods are evil spirits, and offers to prove his assertion by a public and judicial test. "Let any one," he says, "be brought before your courts of justice who is known to be agitated by a demon or possessed by a god." He then describes the usual signs of such admitted possession. Then he says: "Let any Christian command that spirit to speak, and if he who pretends to be a god does not confess in truth that he is a demon, not daring to lie to a Christian, let that audacious Christian be put to death on the spot ".‡

---

* *Ephesians* vi. 11-18. † *Romans* xiii. 12.
‡ Tertullian, *Apologeticus*, c. xxiii.

The loathing mixed with dread evinced by unbelievers against the symbol of humility and salvation is as mysterious in its cause, if well considered, as the terror that it inspires in the evil spirits. It is the symbol of self-denial as well as the symbol of humility. For "they that are Christ's have crucified their flesh, with the vices and concupiscences".* "It is neither wonderful nor unjust," St. Augustine observes, "that the unclean man should be subject to the unclean spirit, not because of nature but of uncleanness. . . . The stronger nature of the angel captivates the weaker nature of the man because they are associated together in vice. Yet the pride of the conqueror is destroyed by the humility of our Redeemer." + When the eyes of St. Antony were opened to see all that is commonly invisible in this world, he beheld it covered with snares and pitfalls laid for souls by the evil spirits, and exclaimed in astonishment: "Lord, how can all these be escaped?" And the answer came: "By humility". The humility of faith is clear-sighted; the humility of charity is quick to feel the present danger, and quick to turn to Christ for help. Humility has nothing on which the evil spirits can lay hold. The spirit of God dwells in the humble, and guards them from the approach of evil. God hath chosen the weak in their own estimation for the dwelling of His strength, and He perfects His power in their infirmity. The illusions with which those spirits, strong in pride but weak in power, provoke the humble servants of God, fall back and strike themselves, and augment the crown of glory for those who by humility avoid the snares laid for their ruin. St. John Chrysostom says to his flock: "If any one asks you why God allows the devils to be here, give him this answer: So far from injuring those who are alert and watchful over themselves, they are positively useful. They don't mean it; their intention is wicked; but fortitude knows how to use their malice." ‡ If the elect are sometimes touched by their infectious breath, and for awhile pine under the blast, they gird themselves with the arms of penance, and after this experience of their turpitude, they return more humble and secure to the conflict; whilst those vanquished spirits fall back upon themselves to feel the horrors of their malignant condition. Be it ever remembered,

---

* *Galatians* v. 24.

+ S. August., *De Gratia Christi et de Peccato Orig.*, lib. ii., c. 4

‡ S. J. Chrysost., *Hom. contra Ignaviam.*

however, in practice, that the true and safe law of combat is to
turn away the mind and heart from their temptations, phantasms,
and foul suggestions, which is only done effectually by raising
the mind to some better object and the heart to some better
affection, and in turning the whole man to his duty in the sight
of God.   For we are so made that the soul cannot be taken hold
of except by that to which we give attention ; and the certain way
of delivering our attention from evil is to turn the mind and
affections right round with a vigorous will to the opposite good.
Hence our Lord has taught us to pray that we may not be led
into temptation, that is, that we may not give to it our mind and
will.

We must now conclude this exposition of the divine law of
probation.   Creation is weak ; the grace of God is strong ; the
end we have to reach is high above us.   Only the power of God
can bear us up to God.   Our will is free, and if we follow the
divine attraction, the grace of that attraction will bring us to His
presence.   But if we choose the attraction of these base and low
things among which we are placed for our probation, and prefer the
sordid limits of our nature to the heights of the divine goodness,
we remain in the bonds of our disordered existence, distressed in
spirit and far from God.   The whole plan of our happiness is
defeated from our want of generosity.   What does God ask of
us ?   Not that we should be stronger than we are, but that we
should confess our weakness and accept His strength.   For God
has provided all things for us in great abundance.   Nothing is
wanting but our will.   If we are in a low position and short of
sight, He has sent forth His light and His truth to lead and guide
us.   If we are weak of will, He sends His grace to strengthen
and lift up our will.   If we are uncertain of His ways, He has
sent His Son in our likeness to teach us His ways, who has
ordained His Church for every place and time, that His truth
and will may be always at our doors.   Our will may be weak,
very weak ; He asks for that will that He may make it strong.
Our abuse of our will may have defiled our soul ; He asks for
that will that He may make us clean.   All that God asks of us
is our will ; when given to Him, in whatever condition, He will
make it good.   But without our will, every provision to help and
strengthen us is in vain ; they cannot be ours.

For the further helping of our will God has established a great order of probation, as an external force to awaken our will into action and help it to enter into His inward light and grace. This order of probation He has varied and changed to suit the different states and conditions of His intelligent creatures. He has employed fear. as well as grace, has given outward commands as well as inward light, and has ordained a visible authority to enforce His inward voice. He has set evil before us to inspire the dread of evil, and has brought us into conflict with the evil spirits that we may know how fearful it is to fall from the living God. The order of probation was also directed in its provisions to bring out, exercise, and fortify the will through the vigorous virtues produced by conflict with our evil inclinations as well as with the evil powers. With the law of redemption and grace came the laws of humility and self-denial in the clearest terms and through the divinest example, that by exhausting the fuel of sin and extinguishing the flame of selfish desire, the heavenly gifts may work upon our will with less and less resistance, and attract our affections to follow their leading to the God of all goodness from whom they descend.

LECTURE II.

ON THE NATURE OF CHRISTIAN VIRTUE.

"Whatsoever things are true, whatsoever modest, whatsoever just, whatsoever holy, whatsoever lovely, whatsoever of good report, if there be any virtue, if any praise of discipline, think of these things."—PHILIPPIANS iv. 8.

PLATO has said that were virtue to appear in visible form to the eyes of men she would awaken in them a wonderful love. Virtue, however, is not a goddess but a gift of God. St. Paul knew a diviner virtue than Plato could imagine, and saw that virtue with the attributes of truth, justice, and purity, of modesty, holiness, and loveliness, as commended for the praise of discipline, and as most worthy of our thoughts. But when virtue in all perfection did appear in visible form to the eyes of men, when Christ, "the wisdom of God and the power of God," was seen, and heard, and touched by men, the humble alone were drawn to Him with wondering love. The sensual and the proud scorned and crucified Him. Something more than human eyes is required to love that virtue which descends from God. We cannot love that of which there is no element within us; and as the divine grace is the principle of Christian virtue, we first require the grace of humility to open our eyes to the divine beauty of that virtue which alone is worthy of God.

Christian virtue differs so widely from natural virtue that its power begins from God; it is an active reflection of the moral attributes of God, and a certain partaking, such as the creature can receive, of the virtue of God. Giving the soul an active resemblance to her Creator and a divine attraction to unite her spirit with Him, this virtue begins in faith and is perfected in charity, and is the true nobility of the soul. Its atmosphere is the divine light, its principle the divine grace, its final object God

Himself. As the infinite virtue of God and the supreme beauty of His eternal action are beyond our imitation, reach, or comprehension, He has given us the form of virtue that is proper to our nature in the human life and example of His Incarnate Word.

The subject of virtue is the human will. It is of great practical importance to understand this clearly. It may be defined in general terms as the disposition of the will to conform the soul to truth and justice. The Latin word *virtus*, from which the word virtue comes, is derived from *vir* and *intus*, signifying the inward force or energy of man. The Greek words *arete* and *dynamis* are used in much the same sense as the Latin word *virtus :* and in the Sacred Scriptures these words almost invariably signify interior vigour, power, or force of soul. It must be remembered that the soul as a spiritual substance is simple and one, but it is susceptive of spiritual light and force in proportion to its purity. As it receives the light of truth, it is mind ; as it is an active power, it is will. When St. Paul tells the Thessalonians that "the work of faith is in power," he uses the word that signifies both power and virtue ; and so in many other places. The word virtue still retains with us the sense of power or effective strength, as when we speak of the healing virtue of certain plants. The object of these remarks is to impress clearly on your mind that virtue always implies a habit of force in the will either to act or to endure. But although force of will is the foundation of virtue, it is not actual virtue of itself, because that force may be given either to virtue or to vice. Virtue is the right direction of the force of the will to its right objects. The will is a free cause exercising the forces possessed by the soul from its own elective choice. In short, virtue is the strength of the soul, because it acts in order ; and vice is the weakness of the soul, because it acts in disorder. But Christian virtue is much more the strength of the soul, because in it the will is helped by the supernatural power of divine grace. The virtues are the interior fountains from which our good actions spring, like fruit from a well-sunned tree ; but the vices are the sources from which our evil acts break out, like corruption from a festering wound. Both are habits of the soul, and both habits are increased by exercise ; but our virtuous habits incline us to good, and our vicious habits to evil.

Virtue has been defined by St. Thomas, after St. Augustine, to be a good quality or habit of the soul, by which we rightly live, and which cannot be put to an evil use.* But this last clause requires a distinction. As a good habit of the soul, no virtue can be put to an evil use; but we may make that virtue an object of the mind or of the imagination, and as such it may be evilly used, as when any one despises that virtue, or treats it with pride or with levity. But it cannot be put to an evil use as it is a habit of the will. The most accurate thinker among the heathen philosophers has beautifully explained the nature of virtue as being "a certain force productive and conservative of good".† For the effect of virtue is to make the person good as well as his work, and to perfect the soul according to the quality and degree of the virtue exercised. Virtue, then, is not a sentiment or a feeling, or any conscious enjoyment of one's own goodness, as some people are blind enough to imagine; the pleasure of virtue is derived from its object and is a result of its exercise, whilst the reward of Christian virtue is neither the virtue itself nor the enjoyment of it, but the God of virtue. As St. Ambrose says: "He who quits himself and cleaves to virtue, loses his own and gains what is eternal".‡

Although the virtues are not created or born with us, but have to be acquired, yet we have the preparation for them in the image of God and the powers of the soul, in the fundamental appetite for good and in the light of reason. These are the preparations for the virtues of the natural man; their light is from the natural reason, and they go not beyond the bounds of nature, nor exceed the powers of nature. They grow into habits by exercise, which strengthens all good inclinations. But although the natural man is capable of knowing God as the Creator and Ruler of the world, and the Judge of consciences, giving natural rewards to the good and punishments to the evil, his natural virtue can never bring his soul into union with God. This is the work of supernatural and infused virtue. Here begins the marvellous difference between the natural man and the Christian man.

So enormous is the distance between created good and divine good, between the imperfect creature and the all-perfect Creator, and so infinite the difference between the natural qualities of the soul and the divine attributes of God, that no natural power in

---

* S. Thomas, *Quæst. de Virtutibus*, q. 1, a. 2.

† Aristotle, *Rhetor.*, lib. i., c. 3.

‡ S. Ambros., *Super Psalm.* cxviii., *Serm.* 11.

the creation can possibly raise the soul to God. To effect this great object a divine power must ascend from God, and enter the soul of man, purifying and sanctifying his nature, illuminating him with divine light, strengthening and attracting him to ascend above himself in will and desire by the infusion of a divine virtue, which by the acceptance and co-operation of his will he makes his own. This is the mystery of grace. This sanctifying influence is the root and force of those divine habits in man which we call the theological virtues of faith, hope, and charity, whereby the soul holds direct communication with God. These infused habits, given first in baptism, are the seeds of a divine life above the life of nature, and the principles of all the Christian virtues. They enable us to give our mind, heart, and works to God, as to the Supreme Good, and the final end of our life and being. They are habits because, so long as they are not rejected by the vices, they abide permanently in the soul, and incline us to exercise the virtues of which they are the principles; and these habits are perfected by the actual grace which constantly feeds them and gives them activity, and by the co-operation of the will.

All virtue is in the will as in its human cause. It is necessary to repeat this simple truth, because some minds are so confused that they almost fancy that each virtue and each vice is a separate will. The other powers of the soul are the subjects of the will, and the will acts through them and puts them in motion. The intellectual virtues, for example, such as faith, understanding, knowledge, and wisdom, dwell in the mind as the subject in which they reside, but the powers of the mind are moved by the will, and decided by the will, upon which they wholly depend for their free action. As it is our will that moves our corporal eyes, that fixes their attention when we wish to see, and turns them away when we wish not to see; so are the eyes of the understanding moved by the will, which searches for the truth through them, adheres to the truth when found, refuses its consent to falsehood, and suspends its assent when the truth does not appear. Hence the folly of the vulgar saying, that a man is not responsible for his thoughts or his opinions; for the will is responsible for the whole action of the mind as far as it is voluntary. There are intellectual vices as well as virtues, vices that destroy all soundness of judgment; but the will is the cause of those vices, which are always allied with pride, sensuality, or passion. Virtue, therefore, as St. Augustine remarks, is the good use of the free-will.* If we would understand the right management of the soul, this cannot be too much insisted on, that in all its branchings virtue is reducible to the good use of the will. The will moves all the other powers, and moves them with ease and vigour in proportion to the force of the will and its habitual exercise in virtue. But as the Christian virtues go beyond the scope of nature, in them the force of the will depends upon the divine gifts that assist our natural weakness, and the prosperity of these virtues comes of the subjection of the will to the powers of grace, that its action may be illuminated and sustained by the light and power that descend from God.

Another point that should be clearly understood is the essential simplicity of the will. What looks on the surface like multiplicity in the will is caused by the number of different objects with which the one simple will is engaged, each one succeeding the other. But as in a dissolving view one picture still lingers for a time on the canvas whilst another is growing over it, so in the will the last object with which it has been engaged may still quiver there whilst attention is being directed to another. When the will leaps rapidly from one thing to another, and especially when those things are at discord, the action of the will becomes confused, perplexed, and troubled; but when the will acts tranquilly, without hurry or hasty flitting from object to object, and especially when it is steadily engaged on some one good course of action, it is concentrated, strong, and peaceful, and we realize its beautiful simplicity.

The exercise of every habit of virtue includes five distinct elements. These are the object of the virtue, the motive, the law of the virtue, the decision, and the action. The object of a virtue is that upon which, or towards which, or against which, it is exercised. This object decides the nature of the virtue, and gives the name to it. Each virtue is distinguished from all the rest, and obtains its special character from its object. The object of faith, for example, is the invisible truth revealed to us by God, and in adhering to that truth the will adheres to the God of truth. The object of justice is to give to all what is their due. The object of temperance is to hold back the will from whatever is noxious, excessive, or dangerous to the soul.

* S. August., *Retract.*, lib. i., c. 9.

3*

The motive is the end we have in view, and the considerations that influence and determine the decision. The stronger the motive, the more firm, animated, and determined will be the decision that leads to action. The object of the virtue may also be its motive, and especially is this the case with the theological virtues, where God is both the object of the virtue and the chief motive, although that motive may be strengthened by various considerations. For several motives may be entertained, and may combine to help us to decide upon our chief motive, and to act upon one or more motives. This is the secret of raising the lower virtues into the region of the higher virtues, so that they may partake of the higher virtue by acting on its motive. For it is the motive that gives value to the virtue, because it is the final end to which the virtue is directed by the will.

If a man helps the poor because it becomes his station in life, or because he accounts it honourable that no one in distress should leave his door unrelieved, this man has no higher motive or end to his virtue than his own honour, which is the heathen virtue of self-respect, beginning and ending in the man himself. If another assists the poor from the natural feeling of sympathy and kindliness, and looks to no higher motive, this is the natural virtue of benevolence, but nothing beyond. If the Christian helps the helpless not merely from kindliness but for the love of God, the motive is charity; and whilst his object is to help his suffering neighbour, his final motive is the love of God.

As all the virtues, whatever their object, can be directed to God as to their chief motive and final end, they can all be commanded and ruled by the love of God. Thus every virtue may be raised to the dignity and excellence of a divine virtue by accepting its motive, and what rises no higher than a natural virtue, when done from natural motives, may ascend to a supernatural virtue when, under the influence of grace, it looks to a divine motive. The intention is the face of the soul, says St. Bernard, and a different intention constitutes a different fact. "A work is then truly excellent," says St. Augustine, "when the intention of the workman is struck out from the love of God, and returns again and again to rest in charity."* What a prodigious waste of value is caused to the virtues by exercising them on low motives and with low intentions, when they might be exercised

* S. August., *De Catechizandis Rudibus,* c. xi,

on the very highest motives! The higher the motive, the nearer the soul is carried towards God; and this is true even in the lowest occupations.

Man sees in the face, but God in the heart. Man looks to the present value of the virtues as they affect this life, but God looks at the inward motive and intention as it regards eternity. The soul may draw near to God whilst the body is humbled down to the lowest toil; but this the world cannot see. There is a sublimity arising from the high flight of the intention above the meanness of the work, whilst both unite in the will of the work-man, which angels may admire, but which the world, that sees but the mean work, can never understand. The poor man, rich in faith, who toils for the love of God and is generous of the little fruit of his labours, is much nearer to Heaven than the rich man who spends a fortune in good works from no higher motive than his natural inclination to benevolence.

The light in the mind presents the law of virtue to the will as well as the motives for its exercise, but the object of the virtue may be presented to the mind or to the senses according to the nature of that object. Thus we have the object of the virtue, the law of the virtue, and the motive of the virtue; all these are external to the will, although their influence is exercised upon the will to set it in motion. But without the free judgment and decision of the will, which is the beginning of action, and the carrying out of that decision, which is the perfecting of action, there is no virtue. The two formal elements of virtue, therefore, are decision and action. The decision of the will is that by which we judge and decide, by the light of the law upon the motives entertained, to do this or that act of virtue, or to follow out a series of acts. The chief element of virtue, as St. Thomas points out, is the decision of the will; for where there is true decision, action follows in its due time and place as a matter of course. Virtue, then, is neither more nor less than the good and right management of the will in its decisions and actions.

The strength of a habit of virtue shows itself in the firmness of its decisions and in the tranquil vigour of its actions. Restlessness and excitement betray weakness; tranquillity is a quality that belongs to solid virtue. It is one thing to see the better things, another to decide the will to seek them, and another to do them. A clear sight of the good to be done is the first but not the only requisite for decision; there must also be a wish to do them; and this wish is awakened and animated by feeling the motives that determine the will to decision. Place a dish of ripe fruit before a child, and you not only draw his attention but awaken his appetite, and so move him to desire. He feels the wish before he tastes, and it is less the sight than the appetite that determines his desire. So is it with the things of the soul; there must not only be the sight but the appetite of the beautiful things of justice. Hence our Lord has said: "Blessed are they that hunger and thirst after justice, for they shall be filled".*

Where the will is enchained to self-love, or relaxed under the influences of vanity, or is languid by reason of sensual indulgence, the spiritual habits of virtue are weak, and what are called good resolutions are feeble, and, generally speaking, ineffectual; the spiritual appetite of such persons is commonly low and queasy. It wants self-denial to give it tone, and humility to give it hunger. The phrase *good resolutions* is too often doubtful, if not painful, in the mouths of persons who pretend to piety. These "good resolutions" are often little more than weak and wavering pictures in the imagination, or words parroted by the lips, rather than decisions of the will that lead to action. Who is ignorant of those strings of "good resolutions" that lead to nothing? Who has not loathed the excuse put forward for some never-do-well, that his intentions are good? Who is not familiar with the significant proverb, that hell is paved with good intentions? These are the intentions of the imagination, fancies without reality, beautifully painted trees that will neither live nor bear fruit.

The habit of making weak and ineffectual resolutions, doomed in their birth to go no farther, can scarcely be called a virtuous habit, although sometimes truly good intentions may fail through human weakness or some other cause. But a habit of make-believes weakens our hold of virtue, enfeebles the soul by indulging in pretentious nothings, and gives occasion first to self-complacency and then to discouragement, because of constant failure. It is far better to form a few real decisions that will come to practice than to formulate a number of imaginary intentions that will have no other result than to dishearten and lower the courage of the soul. This is but playing and trifling with the virtues, as if they were not the goods of the soul, not of

* *S. Matthew* v. 6.

priceless value, but something not worth being in earnest about. If you make a promise to another person, you feel dishonoured unless you keep your promise. You are cautious, therefore, how you make such promises and how you neglect your engagement. If you make an engagement with yourself, unless some just reason prevents its fulfilment, you ought to feel equally discontented with yourself if you neglect to fulfil your engagement, for this breaks down your self-discipline. If you neglect a promise made to God, the matter is more grave. If you deliberately and formally make the promise of a better thing to God, it partakes the nature of a vow. You see then how demoralizing it is to the soul to make engagements lightly and inconsiderately with the virtues, as if in grave matters you trifled with them. As we should shrink from being dishonest either in word or deed with our neighbours, let us not use dishonest pretensions with ourselves or before God.

As the decision of the will is the essential principle in practice on which all virtue turns, it is all-important to understand by what means decision may be made firm, strong, and conducive to action. Those means may be reduced to three. When experience shows that ordinary resolutions fail, it is evident that there has been a want of decision in the will. The first thing to be done is to pray for light upon that virtue and for grace to bring the will to action, that you may obtain that force from God which you have not in yourself.

The second is to bring the will under the light of the virtue by reflecting upon it, and by considering its motives in God and before God, that the will may feel its beauty and justice, and the good that will arise from its exercise. The spiritual appetite for the good of the virtue will thus be awakened, and, touched by its motives, will gain some impulse to decide the will to act. To read some solid instruction on that particular virtue, and make that instruction a matter of thought and reflection, will greatly help to interest you in that virtue, and to saturate the will with desire of it. Great examples that exhibit the virtue in action will also do much to inspire a love and a taste for its beauty and value, and draw the heart to a veneration of its excellence, as that which is most pleasing to God. Above all, the meditating on the example of our Lord Jesus Christ, the life and perfect form of every virtue, and the fountain of its grace, will not only warm the will to decision, but bring the grace that gives decision.

The third means, invaluable for true decision, is to take counsel with yourself. The ordinary business of life ought to teach you that a vague resolution is no decision. When you have anything real to do in the matters of this life's duties, you shape out the whole line of action in your mind, you take counsel with yourself. When that is done you see your way clearly; half your work is done; you become interested in it; you feel it; it is like a part of yourself; your will is decided; you set to work, and would feel something wanting to you if you did not carry it out. But it is the same will that you have to manage in the duties of the soul, and to manage by the same methods. "Counsel shall keep thee," says the proverb, "and prudence shall preserve thee." In taking such counsel with yourself, never see small difficulties, and don't let your imagination frighten you with the contrary interests of nature, remembering that it is the object of virtue to overcome nature and make it a sacrifice to God. Counsel before resolution makes the decision clear, definite, and practical. Counsel following immediately upon resolution is the beginning of action, and the pledge that it will be carried out. For, we repeat, the soul becomes interested in what she has thought out, is encouraged by clear views of her way, and is warmed with the desire of accomplishing what she has dilligently planned. Thus every step in counsel gives its impulse to the will.

These general rules are applicable to all the virtues because they are derived from the nature of the soul. As those who first learn a language have constantly to go back to the rules of grammar, so those who first begin in earnest the noble exercise of the virtues have constantly to go back in the rules of managing the will. But as those who have acquired the habit of speaking correctly think no more of the rules of speech, but use them by habit and unconsciously, those who are well trained in the rules of managing the will can wisely exercise the virtues by force of habit without thinking of the methods upon which they act.

We have now to consider the virtues themselves, according to their distinctions, their unity, their order, and their progress.

The will is one but the virtues are many; they do not divide the will but the attention of the will. As the eye is one, but is occupied by many things in succession, so is the one will engaged by many things in succession. Each object that affects the will in a different way gives rise to a different virtue; either those objects are good and satisfying to the soul, and attract the will to desire and seek them, or they are evil or injurious to the soul, and have to be denied and rejected, or they are an inevitable trial and cause of suffering to the soul, and have to be endured. Take the three theological virtues, whose objects are the greatest good of the soul. God is the object of them all, but of each in a different way, because each of these virtues has its special object in God. The revealed truth of God is one object of the soul, and its chief motive is His divine authority; it is possessed by the mind through the adhesion of the will, and it forms the virtue of faith. The divine promises that God is all good and mighty to fulfil are another magnificent object of the soul, inseparable from God, and to trust with all our will and desire to these promises is the virtue of hope. But as God is the sovereign life and good, who loves us and has made us for Himself, to be partakers of His life and good, the love of God above all things forms the virtue of charity.

If we turn to the objects of the moral virtues, we find ourselves placed in a variety of relations both with God and with our fellow-men, and that these relations bring many claims upon us, and call upon us for many things that are due to them, such as honour, reverence, respect, obedience, duty, service, protection, love, trust, gratitude, and the giving to each his own. These and the like form the virtue of justice. We find, again, that sufferings come to the soul as well as to the body in this life of probation : they are consequently the object of the will, which exercises the virtues of fortitude and patience by enduring them in a right spirit and from elevated motives, and so preserves the soul from perturbation, anger, or any other weakness of the kind. There are other objects that bear upon us through our inferior appetites, whether spiritual or carnal, which when unlawfully or unwisely indulged are noxious to the soul, and even to the body, giving rise to disturbing, defiling, or destructive vices, such as pride, vanity, uncleanness, gluttony, inebriety, inordinate curiosity, vices of the tongue or pen, and the corrupting influence of evil communications; but these and the like are controlled or kept away from the will by the virtues of temperance, humility, and modesty. The due order, measure, and harmony of the virtues is another and superior good of the soul, which is regulated by the virtue of prudence; and it is a maxim of the wise that no virtue is a virtue without prudence. These examples will show how every virtue is determined by its object, and by the special way in which that object affects the will; and that object gives to the virtue its special character and degree of excellence, and to the will its special habit and mode of action.

When we speak of the superior and inferior will, we mean the different inclinations of one and the same will, according as it tends to superior or to inferior things. For whilst the will is solicited on the superior side by the light of justice and the attraction of divine things, it is solicited on the inferior side by the blind appetites and passions of the body, or by the equally blind appetite of self-love. St. Paul by a figure calls these appetites and passions "the will of the flesh," * although the body has not a will, but inclinations and appetites that affect the will. When the will obeys the grace of the Holy Spirit, it enters into the will of God; when it obeys the disorderly inclinations of the body, it becomes the will of the flesh. But it is the same will in a changed condition—spiritual when it ascends to superior good, carnal when it descends to the inferior appetites. Hence St. Paul says: "They who are according to the flesh mind the things that are of the flesh; but they that are according to the spirit mind the things that are of the spirit ".†

The unity of the will, in which the virtues meet and are exercised, explains the unity of the virtues with each other, and how they work together and lend their motives to each other. This uniting of the virtues in one and the same will enables us also to understand how some virtues are not only particular but universal virtues: as justice, for instance, enters into them all, and prudence guides them all, and charity gives its life to them all, and humility subjects them all to God. Thus the four cardinal virtues enter into all the rest, for prudence is the discretion of each virtue, justice its rectitude, fortitude its firmness, and temperance its moderation.

If we except the love of God, which is supreme above all, and

* *Ephesians* ii. 3.　　　　† *Romans* viii. 5.

is the end and life of all the virtues, and in which there can be no excess, every virtue holds a middle path between two opposing vices, one of which is an excess and the other a defect. Thus faith stands between superstition as an odious excess and unbelief as a lamentable defect, and hope holds on its course between presumption and despair. Prudence, therefore, guides all the virtues on their due path between excess and defect; temperance protects each virtue from what would interfere with its purity and vigour; fortitude enables each virtue to master its difficulties and to endure what cannot be overcome; and justice gives to each virtue its due conformity with the eternal order expressed in the divine law.

Not only do the general enter into the particular virtues, and also into each other, just as certain material elements are general and enter into each particular body, such as air, heat, and electricity, but the special virtues have also an intimate connection with each other, and for the same reason that their habits exist in the same will, although they do not always exist there in the same degree, because they are not always equally exercised. But from the fact of their being united together there springs this important rule, that the exercise of any one virtue influences and strengthens all the others, and especially those that are the nearest related to the virtue in exercise. The Fathers of the Church, who gave so much study to the interior operations of the soul, are of one accord on this important subject. St. Ambrose says: "Where one virtue is chiefly put forth the others are present, because the virtues are united and blended together".* St. Augustine remarks, that "although each virtue differs from the rest in character, they can in nowise be separated from each other".† St. Jerome observes that "whoever has one virtue has the others as well, not as properties of that one, but by participation".‡ St. Gregory the Great tells us that "no single virtue is a true virtue unless it be mingled with others"; § and St. Bernard notes that "the virtues cannot be separated from each other".‖ This, however, refers to the virtues possessed, not to

---

* S. Ambros., *De Paradiso*, c. iii.
† S. August., *De Trinitate*, lib. vi., c. 9.
‡ S. Hieron., *Advers. Pelag.*, lib. i.
§ S. Greg. Mag., *Moral. in Job*, lib. i., c. 39.
‖ S. Bernard., *Serm in Annunciat.*

those that are wanting in the soul; as when a person, for example, is devoid of charity.

How could the virtues in isolation encounter the conspiracy of the vices? For we know that the vices act in combination, and it is obvious that their combination can only be effectually encountered by the combination of the virtues. We have dwelt upon this point because it is a great encouragement to know that in directly cultivating one virtue we are cultivating the others, and especially those general virtues that enter into all the special virtues, such as faith, humility, prudence, justice, and charity.

Of the moral virtues, the four that are called cardinal may be considered as a quadrature, enclosing all the rest of the natural virtues, penetrating them through, and making them firm and secure on every side. But when by the descent of divine grace we rise from the natural to the supernatural virtues, we reach a higher quadrature, that embraces the first with a divine power, and lifts up the plane of the soul to the solidity of a cube, in the four virtues of faith, hope, charity, and humility. Faith brings the light of divine truth to all the virtues; hope gives them their aspiration towards the divine good, and lifts their courage; charity brings them into union with God; and humility subjects them to God with reverence and gratitude.

We may consider these divine virtues in a threefold order: in the order in which they are implanted in the soul, in the order of their excellence and merit, or in the order in which they work our reparation. The first of the supernatural virtues implanted is faith, yet not without the grace of humility, which submits the soul to faith, for we must believe before we can know what to hope or love; but in the order of excellence and holy operation charity is the first, giving life and complete form to all the virtues, and exerting its sweet empire over them. The love of God is the sovereign virtue that all the virtues serve, and under whose rule and influence every virtue rises in dignity and power. In building the soul as a habitation for God, love is the master-builder whom the other virtues serve and obey, faith holds the light and exhibits the plan, prudence regulates the work. fortitude carries it on, but charity is the chief architect.

In the order of our reparation, the first work would seem to be humility; for as the beginning of all our evil is the pride that goes before ruin, the beginning of our rectification must be humility.

In consonance with this order of human reparation, our Blessed Redeemer began both His example and His doctrine with humility: "Blessed are the poor in spirit, for theirs is the kingdom of Heaven".* But of the virtues that put us in order towards our final end, what brings us directly with all our affections to God is charity. St. Paul therefore says: "The end of the commandment is charity, from a pure heart, and a good conscience, and faith unfeigned ".†

The fear of God is so closely allied with humility that it will be well to consider how this virtue stands related with the rest. In four distinct books of Holy Scripture we are taught that "the fear of God is the beginning of wisdom". ‡ Wisdom is that sense and relish of good which the knowledge of divine things gives to the heart, inspiring us with the love of them. There are consequently two elements in wisdom—knowledge and affection. The fear of God is the beginning of wisdom as it respects knowledge, because, as the Scripture says, "The fear of the Lord driveth out sin ";§ and when the soul is cleansed from sin the eye is open to truth. In the second place, fear is the flight of evil, error, and deception. In the third place, fear is wakeful and watchful, and expels negligence, according to that of the Scripture: "He that feareth God neglecteth nothing ".‖ In the fourth place, fear disperses the tumour of pride and introduces humility, which disposes the heart to wisdom.

Although the first beginning of fear is servile, this prepares the soul for chaste, filial, and loving fear, which brings the enjoyment of truth and the sweet relish of divine things, which is the second element of wisdom. And Ecclesiasticus teaches us how intimately this wisdom depends on the holy fear and childlike reverence of God. "To whom," he asks, "hath the discipline of wisdom been revealed? and who hath known her wise counsels? There is one most wise Creator Almighty, and a powerful King, and greatly to be feared, who sitteth upon His throne, and is the God of dominion. He created her in the Holy Ghost, and saw her, and numbered her, and measured her; and He poured her out upon all His works, and upon all flesh, according to His gift, and hath given her to them that love Him. The fear of the Lord is honour,

---

* *S. Matthew* v. 3.   † 1 *Timothy* i. 5.
‡ *Job* xxviii. 28; *Proverbs* i. 7; *Psalms* cx. 10; *Ecclesiasticus* i. 16.
§ *Ecclesiasticus* i. 27.   ‖ *Ecclesiastes* vii. 19.

and glory, and gladness, and a crown of joy. The fear of the Lord shall delight the heart, and shall give joy, and gladness, and length of days. With him that feareth the Lord, it shall go well in the latter end, and in the day of his death he shall be blessed. The love of God is honourable wisdom, and they to whom she shall show herself love her by sight, and by the knowledge of her works."*

The soul begins to have this sense of God when touched by fear. Fear searches the soul, and corrects and purifies what is amiss in her. Fear expels pride. Fear opens the faculties to the influence of grace, being the forerunner of humility. The fear of God sifts the virtues clean of the earthly affections and the selfish motives that mix with them. The fear of God moves the will to many good works, and would rather abound than fail in them. For "there is no want in the fear of God," which "is like a paradise of blessing".† The holy fear of God keeps the virtues, and will not let them escape into the atmosphere of vanity, but a soul without fear is not safe from a fall. Fear shuns danger, and fences her works with the safeguard of humility.

What prompts and inclines the will to action is love. The will is love, and the object of love is good. Hence evil can never be loved except under the appearance and pretence of good. The fear of God is but a form of love, dreading to lose our greatest good, and in losing our good to suffer terrible things; but filial fear is the reverencing of the Divine Majesty with pious and affectionate awe, whom we hope to reach but fear to lose. Even the hatred of evil is a form of love, resisting the enemy of that good with the love of which we are animated. As the lover of his country resents and resists her enemies, the lover of God hates the vices that war against Him. Keeping, then, in view that the will is love, and that the principle of virtue is love, and that every virtue loves its object, we shall find that St. Augustine has given us the true and compendious definition of it in these terms: Virtue is the order of love. For it is the office of the virtues to regulate and perfect love; and when that love proceeds from the grace of charity, it is life. As there is no virtue without the choice, decision, and love of the will, every virtue regulates love according to the order of justice and prudence.

How charity gives life and unity to the other virtues will

---

* *Ecclesiasticus* i. 7-15.　　　　† *Ibid.*, xl. 27, 28.

appear if we consider that the grace of justification or charity is infused into the essence of the soul, and so passes into all her powers; and so, as St. Augustine observes, every just movement of the soul proceeds from a just love. Our Lord has therefore summed up all the virtues which are commanded us in the love of God and our neighbour. That this love is exercised through all the powers and faculties of the soul is the plain doctrine of the Gospel, expressed in the command: "Thou shalt love the Lord thy God with thy whole heart, and with thy whole soul, and with thy whole mind, and with all thy strength".* And St. Paul has shown how charity clothes herself in all the virtues, and works in them all, where he admirably says: "Charity is patient, is kind; charity envieth not, dealeth not perversely; is not puffed up, is not ambitious, seeketh not her own, rejoiceth not in iniquity, but rejoiceth with the truth; beareth all things, believeth all things, hopeth all things, endureth all things".† Thus all the virtues work to their final end in God, through the grace and inspiration of charity.

Yet every one cannot exercise all the virtues equally, because all have not the same calling, or the same state and position, or the requisite conditions, or the like occasions. Yet every one may have what is equivalent to the exercise of them all, because they are all summed up in charity. The poor man cannot be munificent, but he may be generous even beyond the munificent. The poor widow who gave her mite at the Temple gave more than all the wealthy, because she gave her all. The virtues of the virgin are not the virtues of the matron, yet the virgin may be the true mother of the destitute.

Next in order to the theological virtues in approaching the soul towards God are the virtues of religion, humility, and penance. They have a special relation to God as their object, and are in immediate subordination to the theological virtues. Then come the four cardinal virtues as their regulating principles. They are called cardinal as being the hinges upon which all the virtues turn, or the wheels upon which they move. They have been likened by the Fathers to the four corners of the spiritual house, to the four wheels of the mystical chariot in the vision of Ezechiel, and to the four chief elements of the visible world. When grounded in humility they are subject to God, and made

* *S. Mark* xii. 30.   † 1 *Corinthians* xiii. 4-7.

acceptable to Him ; and as the servants of charity, they reach their true excellence.

There is a simplicity, as Fénelon remarks, which is but a gross stupidity, but there is another simplicity which is a marvellous perfection. This perfect simplicity is the result of the unity and harmony of the powers of the soul, through the unity and harmony of the virtues in their perfect accord in charity. When the charity of God fills all the powers, and purifies and animates all the virtues, they work in their order, and work with freedom, ease, and calm decision. This is the secret of that beautiful lucidity and peace which shines from souls that are truly holy. This is the legacy which our Lord gave to His Apostles together with His body and blood : "Peace I leave with you, My peace I give unto you : not as the world giveth, do I give unto you ".* Such souls live and are made sincere by humility, just and ardent by charity ; they live in light ; and even when their consoling light is obscured or withdrawn for their probation, they have still the light of justice. The soul is calm and sweet in her operations ; and when strong things have to be done, they are not done in a tempest, but from that calm and deliberate strength that is silently collected through the habit of resting the interior man upon the infinite strength of God. Yet this calm and simple strength is such, that worldlings who live upon the excitements of the imagination will never understand it, but will ascribe this serene wisdom and clear strength to cunning and duplicity. Such holy souls, nevertheless, are always ready in their humility to say with St. Paul : "Not as though I had already attained, or were already perfect : but I follow after, if I may by any means take hold, wherein I am also taken hold of by Jesus Christ. Brethren, I do not account myself to have taken hold. But one thing I do ; forgetting the things that are behind, and stretching forth myself to them that are before, I press on towards the mark, to the prize of the supernal vocation of God in Christ Jesus." †

The Christian virtues are the feet and wings whereby the soul moves in the direction of her final end ; for even those duties that have their immediate end in this life, when directed by spiritual motives, have their final end in God. These virtues may therefore be again considered according to their advancement and progress towards God ; and upon the consideration of their

* *S. John* xiv. 27.   † *Philippians* iii. 12-14.

advancement, they have been measured by great theologians upon the ascending scale of these four degrees of progress, as they are exemplary, social, purifying, or actually purified.

Exemplary virtues are in the soul from the time she begins to look to God, whether in His divine nature or in that human nature in which He became our example. These are the forms, ideas, images, or patterns of the virtues as they are present to the soul, and the motives upon which they should be exercised, and the grace by which they are exercised. As St. Augustine says : "We must have something in the soul that virtue may be born of, and this is from God, and if we follow it we shall live well".* When we exercise the virtues according to these exemplars, we become exemplary. But even whilst the will is yet contending with the earthly appetites, tempers, and passions, we must have in us the forms of these virtues, as the rule by which we contend, and the grace through which we may contend successfully. It is one thing, however, as we have repeatedly said, to have light and grace, and another to enter into them; which can only be done through humility, prayer, resolution, and mistrust of our own sufficiency.

It is much easier to be exemplary in private than in social life. This, however, has no reference to the world's measure of what is exemplary, for the world looks to its own outward examples rather than to the inward examples which God places in the soul, and we are speaking of the will's conformity to those divine exemplars that are present in the soul. It is difficult amidst the business, the society, or the pleasures of the world to keep the inward spirit and intention pure. A great many Christians exercise their private virtues well compared with the number that can hold their soul in hand in their social life and dealings. The world's atmosphere is never very good for the Christian virtues; they breathe less freely in public than in private and domestic life; and this is much more the case where public and social life is contaminated with religious error, with luxury or with fictitious refinements. The transacting of the world's business has so many encounters, is crossed with such diversity of motives and interests, is attended with so many reservations and pretensions, that they seldom fail to checker, warp, and taint that singleness of mind and simplicity of heart which the true Christian brings before God, and even to the domestic hearth. Except, again, among intimate

* S. August., *De Moribus Ecclesiæ*, c. vi.

friends who understand each other's hearts, social life is an exchange which puts a great deal of spurious coin in circulation.
The ambition of appearing, the love of making a figure, the art
of pleasing by polished fictions, the rivalry for esteem, the suc-
cesses and the failures on the social field, with all their accom-
panying vanities, susceptibilities, jealousies, and heart sufferings,
are neither favourable to the theological nor to the cardinal
virtues. The game of conversation lends itself to subtleties of
self-love and vanity that mar the simple sincerity of the Christian
soul, and whilst the present are flattered, the absent too often
suffer. So true are the words of St. James, that "if any man
offend not in word, the same is a perfect man. He is able with
a bridle to lead about the whole body." *

Our share in the world's affairs is too apt to take us from ourselves and from the divine exemplars seated in the inward man,
and so to bring us down from supernatural to natural habits, and
from divine to human motives. It is, therefore, a great advancement in the virtues when the soul can be as simple, as sincere, as
little given to vanity, and as well habited in Christian goodness
abroad in the world as at home. This depends much upon
interior watchfulness and the keeping of the centre of the soul in
a state of calm recollectedness.

It belongs to the man who is in quest of his supreme good to
draw as near to divine things as his condition of life will allow.
To this we are often urged in the Gospel. Our Lord says: "Seek
first the kingdom of God and His justice, and all these things
shall be added to you". † And again He tells us: "Be ye perfect,
as your Heavenly Father is perfect".‡ That is to say, as your
Heavenly Father is perfect God, be you perfect man, formed
upon the type of the One Perfect Man. But this demands that
higher and diviner order of virtue which is called purgative or
purifying, which transcends the common habits of virtues, and
in purifying the soul brings her nearer to the likeness of God.
These purifying virtues, which are not without sufferings, cleanse
the soul from the predominance of earthly attachments and affections, as well as from those interior cleavings of self-love that
close the inner chambers of the soul against the better gifts of
God. Here prudence looks down upon worldly and selfish

---

* *S. James* iii. 2.　　† *S. Matthew* vi. 33.　　‡ *S. Matthew* v. 48.

things as altogether inferior to the contemplation of divine things. Here temperance refrains from the things of the body as far as nature will allow. Here fortitude admits no fear of loss in parting with the soul's attachment to the body, or in detaching our love from those inward cleavings to one's self, that the spirit may be free to enter upon eternal things. Here justice claims her noblest prerogative of approaching as near to the Eternal Justice, to its perfect order and beauty, as the soul is capable of doing.

The principle of this purification is the call of God and the seven gifts of the Holy Spirit. They lead to the love of God through the contemplation of His truth, which inclines to holy retirement whilst not neglecting the duties of life. But when duty is performed and the soul is left free, she devotes herself anew to the Eternal Truth. As the soul advances in purification she learns to measure all things by comparison with the Divine Truth, and not by her own imagination. She values their internal motives rather than their external show; she weighs their intrinsic justice rather than their outward convenience; she loves them by the charity that they serve, and not by the vanity to which they may reluctantly minister. In a word, the purifying virtues seek God in all things and self in nothing.

But when the virtues reach the divine similitude, they are called the virtues of the purified soul, where prudence is absorbed in divine things, where temperance knows the earthly cupidities no more, where fortitude ignores the passions, and where justice is in constant union with the Divine Justice through imitation. These are the virtues of the blessed, or of very rare and perfect souls, who, in whatever they may be externally employed, have their interior recollected with God. So the angels, whilst they do their ministries to men, live always in God's presence. These are the heroic virtues. Their force is in the gifts of the Holy Ghost, and in the generous fidelity of the will to their inspiration. The ordinary virtues of the Christian are transformed, and ascend with pure and energetic motion to a sublime elevation, and raise the soul with them in a singular way, directing every thought and action towards God. These are God's heroes. They have found the true use of that aspiration towards greatness which is implanted in every soul—that holy ambition inspired by the love of divine things, which, however costly in what it takes from nature, is exceedingly rich in what it gives to nature.

4*

It is difficult to draw a near comparison in detail between material imagery and spiritual things, but we will do what we can to give some picture of our spiritual nature as it becomes the subject of light or darkness, virtue or vice. The soul has been often compared to a sphere. Let us suppose it to be a globe of pure crystal resting in an earthly body. But this globe must be pervaded with light to represent the mind, and at the centre there must be a spring of action to represent the will, with a glow to represent its love and rapid movement. This transparent globe is open to subtle influences from above, from around, and from beneath. It is in the middle of all these influences. From above light and energy descend from Heaven to illuminate, strengthen, and attract the central principle of action, that the will may move in that direction towards its greater good. The middle circumference expands outwards towards the social life, and comes into contact with the external world and the social duties. The inferior region of this globe is in direct communication with the body, and receives reflected images and sensations of what passes in the body, and this forms the imagination.

Now if this central principle of love and action, which is perfectly free, turns chiefly towards the inferior side and moves towards the body, it will draw up the images and sensations of its disordered appetites and passions, and will give them countenance and enlargement ; and so the mud of sensuality, turbid with the passions, will enter the pure crystal, and will darken and disturb the whole globe. It will contend with, and obscure, and even expel the pure light that descends into the summit from Heaven. The mud of sensuality will also defile and degrade the central principle of love and action into which it becomes immersed, and the tendency of that vital principle towards higher things will either be much weakened or will cease altogether. But if the central principle of life and love be drawn and inclined to the circumference of the middle sphere, into contact with social life and dealings, it will be exposed both to good and evil, and will be opened and determined to good or evil influences according to the habit of its internal life, as that is most attracted to the upper region of light and grace or to the lower region of sensuality and passion ; for good attracts good and repels evil, whilst evil attracts evil and repels good.

But if the central principle of love is habituated to ascend into the superior region of light and grace, where God meets the soul, it becomes luminous and good through acting with the divine gifts, and the light will then descend with greater light, and the spiritual strength with greater strength, filling the central principle of the will with an ardent inclination to ascend and live in the region of God's light. And as the central love ceases to be attracted in disorder to those lesser and lower things, the obscured crystal will become more clear; the mud of concupiscence, with its turbulent commotions, will subside and disappear; whilst the purified sphere of the soul will become pervaded with the light of truth and the glow of heavenly love, and be serene and strong. Then the mid-sphere will take no harm from any prudent contact with the world, and the lower sphere, where there is a watchful temperance, will receive no serious obscuration or disturbance from its contact with the body, because the central will, by having its habitual attraction to the summit, is always gaining new light and strength and tendency to superior good.

But there is another peril to which the central principle of love and action is exposed, which, like the canker-worm in the flower, is the most injurious of all, because it lurks in the very principle of love, and may therefore corrupt the very centre of life. This is but too often found to be the case, when, instead of ascending to the greater things presented in the summit of the soul, following their attraction, and uniting with their good, the vital principle of the soul acts reversely, makes itself the point of attraction, and endeavours, however vainly, to become the superior centre of greater things, instead of submissively obeying the divine attraction to the true centre of those greater things. Then love changes its name to pride, an affection that reverses the essential order of love and the order of all things, whereby the whole sphere of the soul becomes troubled and darkened, and the will in turning upon herself loses the hold of divine things and sinks, while to herself she seems to rise, coming in contact with much defilement. For where the centre of life is corrupted, the whole sphere of the soul is contaminated, and nothing short of divine humility, expelling the canker of pride, can heal the wounded will.

What, then, can be said of the Christian virtues, especially when they live by the grace and inspiration of celestial charity, but that they emanate in their principle from the sanctity of God, are given to the soul upon the measure of her condition, and are distributed through all her powers, and worked into our life by the labours of the will ? They make the soul luminous with the light of justice, harmonious with the beautiful order of their action, noble through obedience to the Eternal Love. When God sets charity in order within us, all the virtues receive the fire of her life, and God reigns through her gentle power as the queen of the soul. By reason of her origin this divine virtue is most pure ; minds defiled cannot defile her, but she removes the stains of error whithersoever she comes. She is of such potency that anger and discontent disappear in her presence ; of such fortitude, that she grows stronger in adversities; of such liberty, that oppression only increases her freedom ; of such altitude, that no human power can reach her, but she graciously descends to the humble. By partaking of this divine virtue, what was deformed receives a beautiful form, what was dead is restored to life and love, what was depraved is rectified, what was weak recovers health, and what was averse from God in us is happily reconciled. If the beginning of the Christian virtues is from God, their path is on the way to God, and they finally rest the soul in God. The heathens imagined a heaven of gods that came to the help or the injury of man. The true God came and the false gods vanished. He brought us truth and justice and the grace of all the virtues that take His name. Become one of us, except in our sin, He practised and taught the perfection of these virtues, and they changed the world. He still teaches them, still gives the grace of them to every one who has good-will to obey His voice. Wherefore the grace of these virtues is from the bosom of God, their examples are in the Eternal Word of God made man , and their inspiration is from the Holy Spirit.

LECTURE III.

"The kingdom of Heaven suffereth violence, and the violent bear it away."—St. Matthew xi. 12.

THERE are conversions, however rare, in which God suddenly exhibits His power, changes all the affections in a moment, brings the soul into the depths of humility, and gives an ardour to the will to master the first labours of returning to her Creator, as if the soul were carried on wings. These are the miracles of grace. The holy violence with which the Holy Spirit seizes on the soul makes her swift to do violence to herself. Such was the conversion of Zacheus the publican, of St. Paul, of St. Mary Magdalen, of St. Augustine, St. Catherine of Genoa, and of other saints and martyrs. Yet after the first fervour of conversion they had trials and combats within and without before they became perfect in the virtues. After the wonderful conversion of St. Paul our Lord declared to Ananias: "I will show him how great things he must suffer for My name's sake".*

Those who begin to serve God in earnest are often taken with the fancy that nothing is easier than the cultivation of the virtues, and think they see their perfection already in prospect. In their first fervour they pass under this deception, and this is the way in which they deceive themselves. When they first turn to God in earnest, He is pleased in His fatherly clemency to give comfort and sweetness to their souls. To encourage them in their arduous undertaking He shows them the things of the Spirit in their beauty and pleasantness. He makes the severity of the virtues smooth and grateful, and quietens down the vices as with an opiate. A sweetness is infused into the virtues, and for a time the vices

* *Acts* ix. 16.

lose their insolence because they are put to sleep. When the ignorant creature finds herself in this state and feels this new happiness, she fancies herself already advanced in the virtues, and with her foot upon the first step of the ladder of perfection imagines herself nearing the top that reaches up to Heaven.   Yet this inward peace, this pleasure in the virtues, this sleep of the vices, are much more from the condescending grace of God awakening the soul to good-will and desire of the better things than from the efforts of the will to enter into the power of the virtues.   This is but a vision of sanctity presented to the soul whom God calls to Himself, a grace mixed very much with the natural sensibilities, so that grace and nature seem to go all one way; a sweet and luminous shadow thrown upon the soul of the rewards that await the toils and combats of solid virtue and a life of self-abnegation; a slight foretaste of the eternal good in exchange for which we must give ourselves up with much cost to our nature.   For God will not give us an idle sanctity; we must make the gift our own by constant labour.

St. Paul was raised to a great vision of God, and saw and heard wonders that no man can utter.   Such visions pass quickly, but leave in the soul what can never be forgotten.   But after this vision his strong, warm, and tender nature was subjected to toils, cares, pains, and afflictions; to combats without and to trials within.   He was grievously tempted, was persecuted, was calumniated; he endured perils from the people, from the magistrates, from false brethren, and from the hostility of demons.   His soul was subject to fears within, and he was exiled, imprisoned, shipwrecked, scourged, stoned, and finally slain by the sword.   But through all his labours, tribulations, anxieties, and perils, the Apostle was supported by the memory of his great vision as well as by his grace and virtue.   He was able to say : I know in whom I trust; I know for whom I suffer ; I know whom I serve.

So according to their gifts have souls called by God to a holy life received some first view and foretaste of the beauty and sweetness of divine things, the memory of which may encourage them in their future trials.   For the divine virtues are not yet gained in their strength, but only shown and accepted.   The old Adam in his weakness still sleeps within, self-love is not extinguished, the progeny of pride and vanity are not dead, sensuality has not taken its final leave ; they are all slumbering for a time, put to rest under the calming influence of the vision and sense of sanctity. But this will only continue for a time; grace and nature must come into conflict before they are conquered and removed. God will close His hand upon those sweet and consoling lights, leaving but the dry light of His justice and the dry strength of His grace, and suddenly the slumbering Adam will wake up, surprising the soul with the revelation of her weakness, and those beautiful forms of sanctity that still remain in her memory will make the revelation more complete.

This is the critical time on which the whole future of that soul depends. At first she is perplexed and troubled at her new condition, fearing perhaps that she has done some grievous wrong, though ignorant of what it may be. Grace seems to have deserted the soul, although the light of justice remains, and grace is only hidden from her sensibilities. She has hitherto been buoyant with pleasant sentiment and feeling; she has now to contend with her conscious weaknesses and repugnances, and to strive to gain those virtues by effort that she had fancied to be already her own. All this is in the order of the providence of grace; for God only gave those fascinating sentiments for a time to win the soul to the desires of solid virtue. In those first devotional feelings there was much that affected the animal spirits as well as the will, not without a considerable mixture of self-love. But God, whose government of souls is directed to the perfecting of them for their final end, according to what they are capable of bearing, withdraws this sensible light after it has done its first office, that the soul may begin to know herself, may take the way of humility, labour at her purification, and strive for solid virtue. If, yielding to discouragement, the soul slackens and recedes from her holy purpose, great mischief ensues, and she slides back into her old ways. But if that soul abides in patience, awaits the hand of God, believes in her spirit that He is near, although to her senses He seems far away, and trusts in His secret help; if, notwithstanding the waverings of nature, or even occasional lapses into weakness, she strives in the main to do her best in will and intention on the way of virtue and duty, that soul will come forth out of the cloud of trial into the light of consolation, with her spirit purified and her virtue much consolidated; and having now learnt how to bear herself under similar trials, she will go on from strength to strength, and from virtue to virtue.

Let us put the whole question of progress in the Christian virtues in a simple form at once. The end of the Christian virtues is union with God, which implies the renunciation of one's self. This requires two kinds of knowledge and two kinds of effort—the knowledge of God, which should be ever progressive, and the knowledge of one's self, which should be ever progressive. The knowledge of God teaches us not only what He is, but what He does for us; the knowledge of one's self teaches us what we are not, and what we are unable to do for ourselves without the divine help: it is the great and difficult task of getting at the truth about ourselves in which the light of God alone can help us. But these two greatest of lessons are best learnt by alternate light and trial; for in His light we know God, and in our own trials we learn to know ourselves.

The two fundamental efforts of Christian virtue are these :—The first is to leave our own selfish affections as much as we can, and to get as near to God with our will and affections as we may. The second is to get the habit of acting as much on principle and as little on sentimentality as we can. For sentiments spring from our own subjective feelings; they have no light in them; they are always changing; they are too apt to be allied with what St. Paul calls "the spirit of the flesh," to act from impulse, often from temper, and to have an element of self-love in them; and they have no wisdom in them. But principles are presented to us in the light of God; they are calm, fixed, true, just, wise, unchangeable; from God and not from ourselves; so that when indifferent to all that moves within us, whether pleasant or unpleasant, except what speaks in our conscience, where those principles reside, we act on principle, we follow the serene guidance of God, and give to Him our will. But even with good desires, it is long before many souls can reach this peaceful state of serenity, owing to the want of self-knowledge and the purification of their sense and sensibilities.

The whole labour of virtue consists, therefore, in transferring the will from the attractions of nature to the attractions of grace, and in getting out of that narrow selfishness and away from those morbid sensibilities, to reach the divine atmosphere of truth and justice. This demands inward labour and the pain of sacrifice, with sober and steady perseverance, and not unfrequent conflicts with the obstinacy of nature. David understood all the difficulty when he asked of God: "Bring my soul out of prison, that I may praise Thy name".* But the very first difficulty is that of sight. The forms of the virtues may be in the mind in a certain way, and some little of them may be known by experience, but it requires a special grace and special correspondence of the will to fix attention on their profounder sense. The light is still, perhaps, in the summit of the soul, unable to reach the interior, and reveal the condition of the soul, for it is arrested by pride or self-love, obstructing the way to the centre of the spirit. We see not what calls for correction or reform until by violent acts the old habits are broken down, when humility opens the soul, light enters, and we obtain deeper knowledge of ourselves.

Although the supernatural virtues are not acquired by human efforts, but infused, they require the vigorous co-operation of the human will before any great advance is made in them; and although the gift of charity whereby the soul lives is communicated to the other powers in which the moral virtues are exercised, yet it will happen, as St. Thomas observes, that any particular habit of virtue will encounter obstacles to its action because of certain contrary dispositions left by previous habits, so that until they are overcome there will be no pleasure or satisfaction in the exercise of that virtue. It should be observed, again, that there may also be certain impediments of constitution or temperament, or defects of instruction and training, which make the soul less active and responsive to the movements of grace, although earnest faith and ardent charity will finally master all difficulties, and bring life and vigour to the virtues. The only insurmountable obstacle is want of humility, to obtain which is the greatest labour of the soul.

The first disposition for acquiring solid virtue is undoubtedly a good will, made good by right intention. The second, not less essential, is a brave and courageous will, made brave by a resolution that never stops at imaginary difficulties, but understands that it is the very office of virtue to master real ones. Yet even then it takes time and perseverance to make the other faculties and powers prompt and responsive to the will before the virtues on which they are employed become easy and pleasant. Those virtues, again, that have been habitually exercised from human

* *Psalm* cxli. 8.

motives will have to be brought under divine motives, and referred to God as their final end, before the soul can be raised in all her powers to her just and true elevation; and this implies an habitual consciousness and realization to the soul of the presence of God.*

To soften away these truths would neither be just, wise, nor fair; it would be unjust to the truth, unwise for the interests of virtue, and unfair to the soul. Our Blessed Lord in His eternal wisdom spoke plainly and concealed nothing. He knew man perfectly, and knew that where the will is good the knowledge of difficulties awakes the soul to energy and resolution, and to the desire of the better things, for the very reason that they are costly. To the mixed multitude gathered to His Sermon on the Mount He spoke in these plain words: "Enter ye in at the narrow gate; for wide is the gate and broad is the way that leadeth to destruction, and many there are who go in thereat. How narrow is the gate and strait is the way that leadeth to life, and few there are that find it!"† On another occasion, calling the multitude together with His disciples, He said to them: "If any man will follow Me, let him deny himself, and take up his cross, and follow Me. For whosoever would save his life shall lose it; and whosoever shall lose his life for My sake and the Gospel, shall save it. For what shall it profit a man if he gain the whole world and suffer the loss of his soul? Or what shall a man give in exchange for his soul?"‡ When messengers came from John the Baptist, and the multitude around Him were filled with the thought of that austere Prophet, Jesus said to them: "From the days of John the Baptist, the kingdom of Heaven suffereth violence, and the violent bear it away".§ When the rich young man went away sad because Jesus said to him that to be perfect he must sell all that he had and give it to the poor and come and follow Him, Jesus, looking about, said to His disciples: "How hardly shall they that have riches enter into the kingdom of God!"‖ Virtue itself spoke through His mouth, and showed its difficulties, whilst pointing to its reward.

Why are the Christian virtues difficult to nature? Why do they do violence to nature? Why is that violence called the crucifixion of nature? Clearly because the principles of the divine

---

* S. Thomas, *Sum.* i. 2, q. 65, a. 3.   † *S. Matthew* vii. 13, 14.
‡ *S. Mark* viii. 34-37.   § *S. Matthew* xi. 12.   ‖ *S. Mark* x. 24.

virtues are so much greater than we are. Because the graces of these virtues make large demands upon our nature. Because the divine objects of these virtues are so much higher than our nature. Because our spiritual nature must be enlarged through humiliation and suffering to receive them, and be raised through self-renunciation to reach them. The besetting danger of souls is to imagine that they are easy to acquire and easy to keep. This comes of the habit of confusing the frailties so commonly indulged in short of mortal sin with the true and proper character of the Christian. The perfect Christian is in all things subject to God, that he may be "holy in body and in spirit". * There is an easy-going virtue, low in faith and easy in life, that is always weighing the virtues to find their lowest sum of obligation and least weight of inevitable duty, and that is always exploring the lines that divide right from wrong and sin from freedom, with no other view than that of running as near the line of danger and evil as may appear to be safe. Such a one makes his life a compromise between God and the world, and in running so close to the line of danger often trespasses beyond, for the weight of his frailty is apt to overbalance him, or at least to give him a bias on the unsafe side. But the virtues of the Gospel are not calculating; their character is generous, and their whole spirit and intent is to make the perfection of the Christian the first pursuit of life. He who does not understand this knows not the first principle of the Christian life, which is this, in the very words of Christ: "Seek first the kingdom of God and His justice, and all these things shall be added to you".

The children of the faith may be broadly divided into two classes—those who follow the routine of obligation and those who devote themselves to the cultivation of the soul. To the first the pursuit of virtue seems easy, because they make it easy; but though they scarcely know it, from their ignorance of the better things that belong to nobler virtue, they suffer internal labour from the weight and petulance of their unpurified nature, and want the light, serenity, and peace that belong to the calm joy of generous virtue. A low view is taken of the dignity of the soul, and of the grandeur of the gift of faith which gives the soul her dignity, and of the virtue that belongs to that dignity. The magnificence of that grace, not of earth but from Heaven, which the

* *1 Corinthians* vii. 34.

soul carries within her is not realized to the mind, nor what this celestial spring of life claims of the soul. A shallow measure is taken of the depth from which we have to be raised, and of the height to which we must ascend, before we can be united with God in eternal beatitude. What are all the petty interests of this mortal life, that they should absorb the soul, compared with the wonderful things above us that hang on the tree of life, and are always ready for the soul that is willing to reach up to them? Most wonderful is the mercy of God in providing a place of purification after this life, or few of the great multitude would reach the kingdom where all is pure and divine. Grace is strong, but nature is weak and blind, and though the virtues are delightful, they demand the whole man to make them delightful. Happy the man who realizes to himself the significance of life, and who devotes himself to the cultivation of life. But it is the very cultivation of spiritual life that the parables of the Gospel represent as toilsome and laborious, although rewarded a hundred-fold in this life and wholly in eternity.

The chief reasons why the real beginning and each great step in advance on the way of divine virtue are laborious may as well be here summed together. They demand self-renunciation and self-denial; they involve the breaking up of old and cherished habits to which nature clings; they require an ever-increasing humility descending further and further into the soul, pulling down the last remains of the pride of life and opening the innermost soul to the influence of grace; they have to master human respect; they have to detach the will from self-love, a detachment that rends nature to her centre, before the healing and restoring life of charity can enter thus far and close the wound of nature; they have to transfer our powers more completely from nature to grace, and to raise what still acts in us under human motives to divine motives. All this requires that we be subject to trials, for the greater knowledge of ourselves, to force our will to take refuge from our troubles in the strength and protection of God, and that the consciousness of our helpless weakness may abate our self-love, lead us to self-mistrust, and induce us to carry our affections to the God who is our only good.

Yet the difficulties to be overcome in these ascensions to better things are not in them, but in ourselves, and there is a grandeur in the enterprise, a magnificence in the venture, that is full of encouragement. What a charm to be linked and united more closely and ever more closely with the eternal mysteries ! What a help in the divine power ! What a glory for us mortals to be always approaching nearer and nearer to the Supreme and Infinite Good ! We have also a Divine Leader, not in the remote distance of history, but with us, always with us ; God in our nature, God with us, God within us, our way, truth, and life, lighting us to the virtues, giving us the force to practise them. If the Israelites had not trusted themselves to Moses, they would have remained the slaves of the Egyptians. Had they refused to follow the man of God through the forty years of their hard and difficult way, deprived of their natural comforts, they would never have entered the Promised Land. But a greater than Moses is with us. Moses came from the court of Pharaoh, and could only give them external guidance. Christ comes from Heaven, and coming to conduct us thither, gives us not only outward guidance, but inward light and help on the way.

If there were not labours calling for effort and endurance in the virtues, they would not be of inestimable value ; if they did not claim the whole man, they would not constitute the health and vigour of his life. We must either take them for our strength or consent to be spiritual invalids, or even to be infected with some mortal malady. Whatever labours or solicitudes accompany the virtues in their progress, much greater are the labours, the troubles, and even the miseries that follow the vices. Nor are they by any means absent even from those subtle interior vices which are invisible to human eyes, and which it is the work of humility and self-renunciation to discover and to remove. Not that the removal or destruction of the things denied or mortified is the destruction of nature, or of any part of nature, but it is the destruction of those propensities that soil, and encumber, and corrupt its integrity, purity, and freedom, that it may receive a divine perfection.

We must choose, therefore, between the labours of virtue and the heavier labours of vice, for there is no other alternative. We cannot stand still in one place and condition, as though we were statues and not human beings. We must go one way or the other ; and unless we strive against our downward propensities, we shall descend to what is worse than what we are. To drink a bitter draught is not pleasant at the moment, but to obtain health from the draught is pleasant to the whole man.   This is an image of the first steps in self-denial, the pain of which is soon changed into the sweetness of healthy life ; whilst vicious habits, even those that are interior, begin in a sweet delusion and end in bitterness, and if still pursued they settle down upon the vapid lees of a pleasure past and gone.   What is a harmless bitterness at the beginning compared with an evil bitterness at the end, joined to the horror of having defiled a spirit divinely created for the holiest and purest good ?

To conceal the labours of virtue from a soul is to judge her unworthy of them.   God has planted a predisposition for them in the deepest appetite of our soul, in our appetite for universal good ; and the will is more easily roused to energy and exertion in the face of difficulties where reward lies beyond them.   It is the ease and smoothness of the path that fosters indolence and indifference.   The irascible powers are strong in human nature, and love to contend with difficulties where there is an adequate motive.   Convert them to their just objects, and the evil in them when in a wrong direction will become absorbed and purified by their right direction.

When a man sets himself to make a name, a fortune, or a position in the world, the difficulties in his way become the cause of his success.   They draw forth his latent energies, increase his acuteness, and exercise his resolution, patience, and perseverance. Each obstacle augments his courage, each step gained is a reward. When there is not utter degeneration, the love of rising over obstacles is inherent in human nature, and is confined to neither sex.   What is the secret charm of those innumerable stories that never fail to interest both youth and age?   " Forsooth he cometh with a tale, he cometh with a tale, that draweth children from their play, and old men from the chimney corner."   It is always the old tale, new through a thousand editions, of some dear object to be gained that fascinates the soul, but is only achieved through the conquest of many obstacles that meet the adventurer on untried ways, and the prize that makes him happy is won by faith, courage, and perseverance.   Tales like these are the un-conscious exposition of the mystery of human life.   The Christian knight of romance goes forth in the springtide of life on his enter-prize of chivalry.   He finds some holy hermit in the woods skilled in the ways of God and of human life, who purifies his conscience, blesses his sword, and gives him the spell of faith that masters all enchantments. He proceeds on his way, and meets visions of terror that guard the enchanted castle. Horrible monsters roam about and threaten him, strong giants seem to guard every approach. He draws his sword, repeats the word of faith, strikes one blow, and the portentous vision is dissolved. He sets the captive Christians free, and they find they have been imprisoned in delusion. What is this but an exposition of the truth, that most of our fears are the work of imagination, that most of our obstacles are the delusions of self-love, and that the prison in which we are confined is raised around us by the enchantments of pride? One courageous stroke at them with the Cross in the word of faith, and they fall to nothing.

Excepting our spiritual adversaries, of whom we have already spoken, and who are easily overcome by faith and the Cross, there is nothing external to be conquered but human respect, and even the cause of this unnerving influence is within us. It exudes and flows over us from the mingled effects of false shame and fear of criticism, which have their cause in pride, and cover us like a garment of green skins, that tightens as the moisture evaporates, until liberty is exchanged for torture. Nothing cramps the freedom of the soul in a greater degree than the fear of what others will think and say ; but the ways of God's servants are not the ways of the world, and the first thing to be done after taking the narrow way is to shut the world out of consideration and look only to the approval of God. Life in the presence of God is the great safeguard against human respect, and the sense of our accountability to the Divine Majesty at every moment lifts the soul above the trivial thoughts and light fashions of human opinion.

The imagination is a great inventor of terror. There is an organic and intimate connection both of the outward and inward senses with the imagination, which may truly be called " the spirit of the flesh," as it refines, and subtilizes, and spiritualizes, and depicts in exaggerated forms everything that moves in the senses, changing with all their moods and variable humours. A soul under the dominion of this spirit of the senses is light and trivial at one moment, sad at another, full of unfounded fears at another. All this springs from the subjective man, not from the objective light of God in the mind and conscience, which is our true enlightener, our true guide, and the corrector of all that works trouble in the imagination. It is the work of spiritual direction, when we have got astray among the fancies and fears generated in the imagination, to bring us back to the truth contained in this spiritual light. For the subtle power of the imagination, when under the impulse of the blind and selfish senses, magnifies every difficulty, especially in what regards the denial of the corporal senses and the inward sense of self-love, and raises up discouraging fears without any reasonable cause.

Often, again, through this force of imagination, will the inexperienced soul mistake oppressions in the body for depressions of the soul, and thus produce a real depression and discouragement. Surrendering her liberty to these depressions, and thus drawn into them, she next gives way to disheartening doubts and fears about her state, and, absorbed in these discouragements, loses the spring of her will, and the inclination to lift up her head to the light of God in the mind, that would restore her confidence and dispel the illusion under which she labours. The imagination, again, is a great exaggerator of pain both corporal and spiritual. If what we suffer in the body, or in the labour of self-abnegation, or in the trials of the spirit, were divested of the imaginative fears that increase and multiply them, we should suffer comparatively little ; but through the fears conjured up by the apprehensions of the imagination, we anticipate greater pain and difficulty in what we have to do or encounter than we find in the reality. We exaggerate the present difficulty of suffering, and are thus alarmed and dismayed from doing what we ought to do, or from giving up what we ought to give up.

The first purgation of the soul, therefore, is the purgation from the dominion of the senses, and of the spirit of the senses in the imperious control of the imagination, so that we may rise out of them, and live in the light of God, and become gradually freed from the false alarms, delusive fears, and petulant disturbances that absorb so much of the mind and heart, and that harass the soul with frequent apprehension and solicitude. Where there is a real evil, on which the finger of the conscience can be put, let it be at once looked to, repented, and corrected. This is the first and most pressing duty of the soul, to endure no real evil or suffer it to remain. But it is those vague and indefinite fears and alarms that come not from conscience but imagination that keep the soul in a state of discouragement, fret and irritate the temper, and keep the will back from generously rising to God.

In imagining what has to be abandoned, self-love will dread the pain and loss without seeing the divine compensation in the good that will come in its place.   In imagining what is to be overcome, the same self-love will enlarge the obstacle, augment the labour and pain of the effort, and close the eye to the grace that strengthens the will, and to the high motives that encourage its action.   Making such a future for us as will never come, the imagination will burden the duty of the present hour with that fantastic future, and give rise to broodings and fears of obstacles to perseverance that will never arise as they are anticipated ; and which, in whatever shape they may arise, will not come without the divine help to conquer them.

This indulging of the imagination upon one's self is very weakening to the soul, obscures the present light, absorbs and troubles the force of the will, takes it off from working generously with the grace of God, diverts its attention from its true object, relaxes the virtues, discourages the soul with vain and useless alarms, and weighs the spirit down with sadness.   Thus the soul makes her own fears, very far from the fear of God ; her own difficulties, such as God has never made ; and her own disheartenments, where God would have her lift her heart to Him. This is neither humility nor the way to humility : it is all the vapour of self-love.   It is not self-knowledge, but delusion.   One stroke of light from God will pierce through the whole mist, reveal the soul to herself, show her how she has been nursing her self-love, and compel her to confess that she is nothing without God, and must go to Him for light and strength.   Take off your imagination from yourself, and nine-tenths of your difficulties will be removed.   You will then become subject to the light of God ; you will lift up your mind to the great motives of your enterprise, and pray with clear intention for the divine help to advance with courage on the way to God.

Instead of looking back where there is nothing to be done, or forward where nothing has yet come ; instead of inventing obstacles that nowhere exist except in the unmortified senses, in self-love, and in the imagination ; let the soul be assured that she has nothing to overcome but herself, and that every time she

5*

overcomes herself, the next step will be easier. When the imagination is brought under discipline, and made the servant instead of the master, it will come over to the service of our good habits; unreasonable fears will cease with its opposition, and holy habits will be loved as those discarded habits never could be loved.

All that we have said shows the value of a well-informed and experienced guide, who can explain to the soul what is really amiss in her, remove unnecessary apprehensions, teach her how to use her powers aright, and inspire her good-will with courage and confidence. Amidst the clamour for universal education, for progress in the arts and sciences, for the sound training of every man and woman in their own art, duty, or profession—all excellent things when under the dominion of the moral order ordained by God—the votaries of the world, who know all wants except those of the soul, exclaim against spiritual direction. They cannot realize to themselves, what they never think of, that all things are for the soul and the soul for God; and that there is a science, an art, the very first of all arts, an education and a training of the soul whereby knowledge removes ignorance, experience provides against inexperience, prudence removes perplexities, medicinal remedies give health, and wisdom teaches the way to better things. Is the body to be trained in all manly exercises by skilful teachers, the mind to be trained to the exercise of its powers by men already experienced in the rules, and the soul, which is the very life on which all depends, to have no education? Is no one to teach her the athletics of the virtues? No one to train her to run the way of perfection? This was not Plato's view, nor that of Pythagoras, nor of any of those heathen philosophers, who considered the guidance of souls the first duty of the wise. Yet they had no divine system resting on inspired authority, such as Christ has left to us.

When a virtuous habit is forming it inclines to the good of its object, feeling after that good in proportion to the earnestness of desire, until the will acts with promptitude and firmness, and moves to its object with ease and rapidity. Every virtue is proportioned to its generosity, and this generosity is the spirit of self-sacrifice, doing a willing violence to self-love or self-interest. For the object to which a virtue moves is neither ourselves nor any part of ourselves, but a greater good of which we desire to partake, so that the will must go forth out of one's self to embrace that good. The will that seeks the highest good draws all things to God, and the love of God makes the way of virtue sweet and generous.

With respect to the management of the imagination, our Lord has given us a rule that is applicable to many things. "Be not solicitous for to-morrow; for the morrow will provide for itself. Sufficient for the day is the evil thereof." * Although the literal sense of this admonition relates to the things of the body, the rule is equally applicable to the things of the soul. Do not imagine difficulties before they come. To imagine them is to make them. You have the light and help of the present hour and duty, but not of the future. "You know not," says St. James, "what to-morrow will bring forth."† To-morrow will have its providence as well as to-day. The trial of to-morrow is not the trial of to-day, and the light and help of to-day is not the light and help of to-morrow. To lay the burden of the future on the present is what God never intended. He gives to each day its duty, and to each day its help; to each hour its duty or trial, and to each hour its help. To load the present hour with the burden of the future, that never comes as anticipated, is both to encumber the present duty and weary the mind, and to derange the order of Divine Providence in your conduct. Thus that is made heavy which God has made easy.

There are persons also who burden the present with the past, calling up past errors, not as subjects of present humiliation or penance, but to judge them anew by present lights, troubling the present peace of the conscience, as if those things had not been judged by the light of the time, and were responsible anew to the greater light received since they were brought in sincerity to the tribunal of penance. This greater light undoubtedly increases their deformity, and makes them a great subject for humiliation; but they were judged and condemned in the light of the time, and if every new light upon them is to bring them anew to the tribunal, the soul will never have peace or security. This loading of the present hour with the past and with the future destroys freedom, simplicity, and peace. What you have now to do, do with all your heart and strength, and remember that the best preparation for duties to come is the

* *S. Matthew* vi. 34.　　　　† *S. James* iv. 14.

careful performance of the duty in hand. This does not, however, exclude what is really foreseen and must be now provided for, for that is an actual duty of the present hour.

There are not a few people of whom it may be said that they scarcely ever live. They are always away from themselves in some direction. They moon over the shadows of things past and gone, or over possibilities to come, or over things distant from them, or over what they fancy they would like better than what they have or are. They dream more than they live. God is the eternal present and the eternal life. In Him there is no past, distant, or future; and the secret of life is to live in the present with God, and to fulfil the duty of the present in the presence of God. This gives patience, strength, and peace.

The other rule which our Lord has given us for conquering our difficulties is sharp and effective, and happy are they who realize its full significance. "The kingdom of Heaven suffereth violence, and the violent bear it away." Of what kingdom of Heaven is He speaking, but of that of which He said: "The kingdom of Heaven is within you";* of that kingdom for which He taught us to pray: "Thy kingdom come; Thy will be done on earth as it is in Heaven"?† It is the reign of God within us that is obtained by doing violence to ourselves. This violence consists in the denial of our sensual appetites and in the renunciation of self-love. By the first we remove the fuel that feeds the fire of concupiscence; by the second we destroy the fuel that feeds the blinding vices of pride and vanity. By removing these we not only weaken the vices in their causes, but overcome our repugnance to the way of the Cross, the true path of the Christian soul. For our Lord Himself explained this law of generous violence when He said: "If any one will follow Me, let him deny himself, and take up his Cross, and follow Me. For whosoever will save his life shall lose it." ‡ This is the first condition of Christian progress: we must part with the old to receive the new. The first step is the venture of faith, and this venture is a sacrifice in the confidence that we shall receive a great return. St. Justin the martyr, a native of Palestine, made diligent search for the unwritten words of our Lord, and tells us that He often said,

---

* *S. Luke* xvii. 21.   † *S. Matthew* vi. 10.   ‡ *S. Mark* viii. 34, 35.

"Be ye good traffickers". This corresponds with His parable of the merchant who gave all that he had to purchase that precious pearl, which is the kingdom of Heaven.

He also gave us the promise, which for nineteen centuries He has fulfilled to His servants, that instead of proving a bitterness, this self-denial, when accompanied with humility, would lighten every burden and sweeten every labour. "Come to Me, all you that labour and are burdened, and I will refresh you. Take up My yoke upon you, and learn of Me, because I am meek and humble of heart; and you shall find rest to your souls. For My yoke is sweet, and My burden light." * The burden of our life is from ourselves, its lightness from the grace of Christ and the love of God. Humility takes off the weight of the burden, for it overcomes that attraction to ourselves which hinders our ascent to purer things. When we receive the light and grace of Christ with humble subjection to their celestial influence, and the seeds of eternal life are already within us, in the act of submitting ourselves to their light yoke we pass from our troubles to His rich and tranquil life. This, in sum, is the violence we have to do ourselves, according to those never-to-be-forgotten words: "He who will lose his life for My sake shall find it ".

Three things are required for the cultivation of the virtues. The first is to know what we must believe; the second, what we must desire; the third, what we must do to obtain what we desire. Faith exhibits the motives of the virtues, their Divine Example, and their law. And that our faith may be secure Christ has deposited its whole truth in His Church, and has invested her with His authority to teach the Faith with unfailing certainty; among other reasons, that in hearing the Church we may have the beginnings of humility, and in obeying the Church we may progress in humility. He Himself also helps the interior man with light and strength to see and cleave to the unchangeable truth which He has given to His Church. This is the wonderful proof of His continued power on the earth, known only to the faithful, that the inward light that He gives to souls accords in all things with the outward teaching of His Church, and that His inward gift of sacred force agrees with the outward commands to obedience.

We are brought from the pursuit of evil to the desire of good

* *S. Matthew* xi. 28-30.

by two mighty influences.   The first wakens up the conscience to
the fear of God, the dread of His judgments, and the terror of
His punishments.   The fear of God represses the force of concupiscence, brings down the elation of pride, shakes us out of our
self-confidence, drives sin away, and awakens the desire to return
to God.   The fear of God brings down those selfish, guilty, human
fears that make us shrink from approaching the justice of God.
The fear of God fills the heart with contrition, breaks up the
habits of evil, disposes the heart to trust in God's mercy, and prepares it for the seeds of good.   The fear of God humbles the soul
and prepares her for chastisement; but though fear refrains the
soul from evil it will not make her just.   After the spiritual being
has been ploughed and harrowed by fear, it must be cleansed before it can be planted and made fruitful with better things.   How
is this spiritual being to be cleansed?   By penance and the blood
of Christ in His sacrament of reconciliation.   Humility must go
before charity, because "God resisteth the proud, but giveth His
grace to the humble ". *   Love and pride are incompatible things,
and divine love can never consort with human pride; they essentially exclude each other.   Whilst yet under fear, we are in a
servile condition, incapable as yet of any good that can bring
a heavenly reward; but when the sacrament of reconciliation
brings the grace of charity, we are set free and are made the
children of God.

The second mighty influence, therefore, which succeeds the first,
is the most gracious gift of charity, the grace of justification, which
restores the soul to the friendship of God.   The whole object and
intention of the law of God is that we should adhere to Him, and
this adhesion is chiefly through love.   There are two things in
man by which, when divinely helped, he is able to adhere to God—
by his mind and by his will, for by his inferior nature he is not able
to adhere to God.   Through his mind he adheres to God by faith,
but by his will he completes his adhesion to God.   But the will
may adhere to God in either of two ways that are very different—
from fear or with love.   To adhere to God from fear is to adhere
to Him for a reason different from Himself: this reason is to
escape from impending evil.   But to adhere to God with love is
to adhere to Him for His own sake.   The love of God is therefore the most powerful way of adhering to God, and is therefore

* S. *James* iv. 6.

the whole intent and final end of the divine law. The end of the law is also to make men good. But a man is good when his will is good, for his good will brings all the good that is in him into action. His good will is that in him that desires to be united with good, and especially with the greatest good, which is his final end. The more he wills this good the better he is; but what he wills from fear has in it a mixture of unwillingness, as when a man parts with his goods to save his life.

The love of God, as He is the Supreme Good, is that therefore which makes the soul good; and as that Supreme Good has no limit or measure, the law of this good is to love God without stint or measure. And as this love is the end of the whole law of justice, upon which every virtue is formed, all the virtues, to be perfect, should be the servants of the love of God. Hence we are taught that "the end of the precept is charity"; * and that "this is the greatest and the first commandment: Thou shalt love the Lord thy God with thy whole heart, and with thy whole soul, and with thy whole mind".† Hence, as the law of Christ is the perfect law, it is called the law of love, and as the imperfect law, the old law is called the law of fear. ‡

From the presence of the love of God in the soul four wonderful effects will follow. The first is spiritual life, derived from God and pervading the soul; for the grace of charity is a certain participation of God; and St. John says: "He who abideth in charity abideth in God, and God in him". § It is the nature of charity to change the affections of the soul into the affections of Him who is loved; hence the true love of God makes us like to God. For which reason St. Paul tells the Corinthians that "he who adheres to the Lord is one spirit". || As the body can neither live nor move without the soul, the soul has neither divine life nor anything that reaches to divine life without the charity of God.

The second effect of charity is the keeping of the divine commandments; for the justice of charity moves us to fulfil all justice; it penetrates all the powers to make them the instruments of justice. "The love of God is never idle," observes St. Gregory; "wheresoever it is, it works great things: if it refuses to work, it is

---

* 1 Timothy i. 5.   † S. Matthew xxii. 37, 38.
‡ See S. Thomas, Sum. contra Gentiles, lib. iii., c. 116.
§ 1 S. John iv. 16. || 1 Corinthians vi. 17.

not love."* Love therefore fulfils the whole law, and, as our Lord says: "He who loveth Me will keep My word".

The third effect of charity is to keep us from evil. No adversities can injure those who love God; on the contrary, they help to increase the flame of charity. Charity is strong to heal injury, but not to inflict injury; it is faithful to eternity, but not to vanity. Adversities detach the loving soul from all that is not God, and concentrate the affections with greater earnestness in the exercise of charity. As external trials augment the intensity of human love, they much more increase the intensity and sweetness of divine love.

The fourth effect of charity is to bring us to our beatitude in God. This is only promised to those who love God above all things. "There is laid up for me," says St. Paul, "a crown of justice, which the Lord, the just Judge, will render to me in that day; and not only to me, but to them also who love His coming."† As the grace of charity is the foundation of the grace of glory, the degree of glory will be proportioned to the degree of charity; for the greater works are done from greater charity, and "he who loveth much, to him much will be given". The blessed vision of God is promised to love by our Lord Himself: "If any one loveth Me, he shall be loved of My Father; and I will love him, and manifest Myself to him".‡ Great love, moreover, kindles great desire, which gives the soul a larger aptitude and disposition for the light of glory.

There are other effects of charity that ought not to be forgotten. The very first of these is the remission of sins. There will be no difficulty in understanding this, if we only reflect that even among men, if one has much offended another, and afterwards regrets the offence and devotes himself with love to the person offended, the good heart readily forgives the offence. But God is infinitely good, and has no desire to see our sins estrange us from Him, but gives us His love that we may return to His friendship. St. Peter therefore tells us that "charity covereth a multitude of sins"; § whilst Solomon says in the Proverbs that "charity covereth all sins". ‖ But should any one think this a reason why he should not do penance for his sins, let him reflect that not only must penance prepare the soul for the love of God,

---

* S. Greg. Mag., *Hom.* 30 *in Evangel.*　　　† 2 *Timothy* iv. 8.
‡ S. *John* xiv. 21.　　§ 1 S. *Peter* iv. 8.　　‖ *Proverbs* x. 12.

but that there can be no real love of God without most bitter regret and repentance for having offended Him who is worthy of all love; and that the more we love God the more grieved we must be that we ever displeased His divine goodness and lost His love.

Charity also illuminates the heart with wisdom, and gives us the sense of God. For where is charity there is the spirit of God, whose unction teaches us of all things. By nature we are in darkness as to the good we ought to pursue, but the Holy Spirit of love is the Spirit of wisdom and understanding, and when He dwells in us and spreads abroad His love in our hearts, He suggests to us whatever we need for our sanctification. Hence Ecclesiasticus says: " Ye who fear the Lord, love Him, and your hearts shall be enlightened ". * Charity perfects the joy of the heart. No one knows of what joy the heart is capable who knows not the love of God. To be without charity is not to have God in one's life. To have great desires, and to have nothing proportioned to those desires, is the cause of weariness, restlessness, and discontent. But to have the charity of God is the first beginning of beatitude, the present pledge of the future joy, the commencement of union with God, and the happy expectation of more perfect union.

Consequently charity gives peace to the soul. For whoever loves God above all things rests his heart on the eternal peace. " God is greater than our heart," He can fill all our desires; and when the heart knows this, the nearer it draws to the Divine Fountain of good, the more it finds repose. Charity also gives dignity to the soul, making her the living temple of God, wherein the Spirit of God dwells to work our sanctification. In the words of St. Paul: " The Spirit Himself beareth witness to our spirit that we are the sons of God: and if sons, heirs also; heirs indeed of God, and joint-heirs with Christ; yet so if we suffer with Him, that we may be also glorified with Him ". †

All these considerations unite in commending the inestimable value of charity, as the gift above all gifts that does all things for the soul. Our one work in this life, to which all things else are secondary, is to obtain, to augment, and to perfect within us the love of God. But we must keep in mind that charity can never come from one's self; it can only come from God. St. John

---

* *Ecclesiasticus* ii. 10.   † *Romans* viii. 16-17.

expresses this truth in most clear and definite terms. " Every one," he says, " who loveth is born of God, and knoweth God. He that loveth not, knoweth not God : for God is charity. By this hath the charity of God appeared towards us, because God hath sent His only-begotten Son into the world, that we may live by Him. In this is charity : not as though we had loved God, but because He hath first loved us, and sent His Son to be a pro- pitiation for our sins." *

Charity is the greatest of divine gifts; but to receive this gift, or any large increase of it, requires certain dispositions on our part. Two things especially dispose us to receive the gift of charity, and two things dispose us to receive it in greater abundance. The first thing that disposes us to receive the divine gift is the diligent hearing and reflecting upon the Divine Word. For we only desire the good that we know, and we desire it the more the more earnestly we reflect upon it. The Sacred Scriptures compare the Word of God to an enkindling fire ; and being the Word of the Holy Spirit, it must enkindle the heart into which it enters. When after His resurrection our Lord expounded the Scriptures to His two disciples, they knew Him not at the time ; but after He had revealed Himself and departed, they said to one another : " Was not our heart burning within us whilst He spoke on the way and opened to us the Scriptures ? " †   When St. Peter preached in the house of Cornelius, " the Holy Ghost fell upon all them that heard the Word ".‡   The second preparation is to humble the soul into greater subjection under the mighty hand of God. In fear, in self-abjection, in repentance, in the cry of the heart, the soul makes known her conscious miseries and her desire to return to God, and He will exalt her in the day of visitation.

But let it be plainly understood that we cannot return to God unless we enter first into ourselves. God is everywhere, but not everywhere to us. There is but one point in the universe where God communicates with us, and that is the centre of our own soul. There He waits for us ; there He meets us ; there He speaks to us. To seek Him, therefore, we must enter into our own interior. When the Prophet Isaias called upon the people to return to God, this was his cry : " And now, ye transgressors,

---

* *S. John* iv. 7-10.   † *S. Luke* xxiv. 32.   ‡ *Acts* x. 44.

return to the heart ".* The Psalmist sings to God : "Thy law is in the midst of my heart ".† And our Lord emphatically tells us: "The kingdom of God is within you ".‡ When the soul enters into herself she begins to know herself ; her shortcomings and her wants are before her eyes, and God shows her what to do and what to ask of Him. The humbled heart is opened, the grace of God enters, and His love is desired ; for hard must that soul be, and hard with pride, that, knowing what she is and what God is to her, has no real desire to love Him who has loved her so much, and whose love is so great a good.

Two things also, we have said, are required to dispose the soul for receiving greater charity. God is always ready to augment the gift of life where He finds the soul prepared, but charity must be always proportioned to self-renunciation. In the nature of things this must be so. If the capacity of the will to love God is pre-engaged, if only one part of the affections is given to God, whilst the other part is kept back in the interests of self-love, it is evident that this second part of us is neither open nor disposed for receiving an increase of the divine gift of charity. The obstacles caused by self-love and earthly desires must be moved out of the way, that the recesses of the spirit may be opened for the larger entrance of the gift of life. These obstacles are described in the well-known words of St. John : "Love not the world, nor the things which are in the world. If any one love the world, the charity of the Father is not in him. For all that is in the world is the concupiscence of the flesh, the concupiscence of the eyes and the pride of life, which is not of the Father, but is of the world." § What injures charity, as St. Augustine observes, is the hope of gaining and the desire of holding the things of time. Diminish cupidity, and you will increase charity ; let cupidity cease, and charity will be perfect, for the root of all evil is cupidity. To increase charity you must therefore lessen cupidity. ||

The second thing required to dispose the soul for greater charity is a profounder humility, for it is to humility that charity is given ; for God can only give greater life to a soul that is empty of herself and is subject in her inmost powers to Him. But of this we shall speak fully later on.

---

* *Isaias* xlvi. 8.   † *Psalm* xxxix. 9.   ‡ *S. Luke* x. 21.
§ *S. John* ii. 15, 16. || S. August., *De Diversis Quæstionibus*, lxxxiii., q. 36.

Charity is not only the greatest, noblest, and most fruitful commandment, but is the fulfilment of all commandments whatsoever. Besides its eternal foundation in God, whom to know is to love, and whom to know more is to love more; besides its foundation in the eternal order of justice, which is the form and measure of charity; besides its foundation in the supreme superiority of the divine good over created good; besides its foundation in the relations of the soul as a living subject with God as her Divine Object, the law of loving God above all things rests upon these four considerations, arising from our human nature.

The first consideration is that of the divine benefits. We have received all that we are and all that we have, that with them we may serve the Divine Author of them, and may love Him with our whole heart. Gratitude has never a strong hold on the heart unless it springs from love of the Divine Giver of all things. When King David offered up the contributions of the people to build the Temple, it was from the deep sense of what he owed to God that he poured forth his gratitude: "Thine, O Lord, is magnificence, and power, and glory, and victory: and to Thee is praise; for all that is in Heaven, and in the earth, is Thine; Thine is the kingdom, O Lord, and Thou art above all princes. Thine are riches, and Thine is Glory: Thou hast dominion over all; in Thy hand is power and might; in Thy hand greatness and the power of all things. Now therefore, our God, we give thanks to Thee, and we praise Thy glorious name. Who am I, and what is my people, that we should be able to promise Thee all these things? All things are Thine; and we have given Thee what we have received from Thy hand." * There is no more certain proof of a great love of God than habitual and earnest gratitude.

The second consideration is our incapacity of ever doing complete justice to the Divine Excellence; for even though we love God with our whole heart, mind, and strength, we can never give Him the love that is due to His goodness. "Glorify the Lord as much as ever you can," says Ecclesiasticus, "for He will yet far exceed, and His magnificence is wonderful. . . . When you exalt Him, put forth all your strength, and be not weary; for you can never go far enough." †

The third consideration is the renunciation of worldly things.

---

* 1 *Paralipomenon* xxix. 11-14.   † *Ecclesiasticus* xliii. 32-34.

It is a great injustice and injury to God to put anything here below on an equality with Him; but we put corruptible things on an equality with God when we love them equally with God. When we say that He is a jealous God, we know that His jealousy is His justice: in justice He can suffer no rival in the love that we owe Him. If we love the creature with the kind of love which belongs to God alone, He will leave the soul, and the soul will collapse upon the creature. The love of Him is His gift, and its ardent power aspires to carry the heart back with it unto Him. Charity is also a power that enables us to love all things better in God than in themselves. To love all things in the order in which God loves them, through the virtue of divine charity, is the secret of using them as though we used them not.

The fourth consideration regards the powers with which God has provided us, that we may love Him as it becomes a spiritual creature to love her Creator, Redeemer, Provider, and Sanctifier. Our powers are our mind, heart, soul, and strength: " Thou shalt love the Lord thy God with thy whole heart, with thy whole soul, with all thy mind, and with all thy strength ". Whatever we are doing, whatever virtue we are exerting, we must make the love of God our first and chief intention, give to the love of God the full energy of our soul, enlighten that energy with the highest motives in our mind, and sustain that loving energy with the fortitude of our will against all that might weaken its ardour. Then will every virtue, as it is graced, ordinated, and ruled by charity, grow strong, pleasant, and victorious.*

Add these considerations one to another, ponder them in your heart, and they will bring you the overwhelming conviction that charity conquers all the difficulties of virtue. Every advance in charity is the mastering of some difficulty, whilst perfect charity is the conquest of all difficulties.

* See S. Thomas, *Prolog. ad. Opusc. de Decim Praceptis.*

LECTURE IV.

ON THE NATURE OF HUMILITY.

"Where is humility, there also is wisdom."—Proverbs xi. 2.

THERE are four virtues, the fruits of divine grace, which in their union bring the soul to God : these are humility, faith, purity, and charity. With the loss of the knowledge of the true God they were lost to the world, and our Lord Jesus Christ brought them down anew from Heaven to mankind. Their union in the soul is the distinctive sign of Christian holiness. When pride throws off obedience to God, humility dies. When the mind rebels against the authority of God as the Revealer of truth, faith dies together with humility. When the graceless soul allows the body to revolt and defile the soul with uncleanness, holiness is extinct. When self-love holds the place of charity, the spiritual life of man is no more. When these virtues have departed, the man is left to nature and the world, but to nature in cruel disorder, and to the world, not as God has made it in His goodness, but as man has made it in his concupiscence, to the world as it is taken up for a final end in place of God.

The men of the world have their measure of virtue, but that virtue falls short of God, and ends in this life. They measure their virtues upon the requirements of their fellow-men. A man is great in their eyes, not as he serves God, but as men serve him ; not as he loves God, but as he has gained the goodwill of his fellow-men ; not as he has accepted the supreme reason of God, but as he glorifies his own. He is a great man of the world, who by force of his own natural mind and will has obtained the ascendency over many and variously gifted minds. Truth is less his master than his useful servant, and the virtues, as the world understands them, are the docile instruments of his personal elevation. Without those four evangelical virtues, he thinks and acts on the exterior of his soul, but knows nothing of his interior. He knows little of himself and little of God.

Disguise the skeleton under whatever accomplishments, the world's virtue, as in the heathen times, is the supremacy of the natural man ; yet it was to destroy this supremacy of self-sufficiency that Christ brought these four virtues to mankind, that by humility the soul might know herself and all that God is to her, by faith she might be the humble subject of His truth and authority, by charity she might have her life in God, and by purity she might be holy in body and spirit. To have these virtues is to know them ; not to have them is to be completely ignorant of them, because they are not theories of the mind but experiences of the soul. A cynical writer of the world's school has called them " the dropped virtues " ; but where they are dropped the soul has fallen from God and all care of herself. The one least known of the four, and consequently the most misunderstood, is the virtue of humility, and yet it is the very groundwork of the Christian religion. Not only is it widely misunderstood, but often despised, and the cause of this contempt is the pride of false freedom. Putting aside, however, that ignorance which insolent pride prefers, the virtue itself is of such a hidden character, and there are so many spurious imitations of it, that to those who have never cultivated the inward conformity of the soul to truth and justice, it is not easy to distinguish true humility from its counterfeits. But where true humility exists, it seldom fails to discern its existence in another.

St. Laurence Justinian repeats the sense of the early spiritual writers in saying that " no one can well understand what humility is unless he have received from God the gift of being humble ; for there is nothing in which men are more often mistaken than in their notions of what constitutes humility ".* It is a grace as well as a virtue. It is not only a virtue in itself, but an essential element in all the Christian virtues. It belongs equally to the mind, the will, and the spiritual sense. Once planted in the heart and brought into exercise, it draws light from many fountains, moves to action from many influences, and finds its motives in all comparisons of divine with human things. It

---

* S. Laurent. Justin., *Lignum Vitæ*, c. ix.

grows upon whatever we contemplate in God or in ourselves. It is exercised in all our relations with God, in every consideration of ourselves, and in every due respect to our fellow-creatures, and even acts towards the inferior creation with a beautiful benignity ; yet so vast is the scope of this virtue, so profound its motives, so widely does it act through the other virtues, so many and so great are the evils to which it is opposed, that the difficulties are insuperable of embracing the whole virtue within the terms of a single definition. Indeed, the early ascetic Fathers who devoted their lives to its cultivation declared it to be indefinable.

On a certain occasion St. Zozimus was instructing his disciples on humility when a Sophist from Antioch was present. But the Sophist could not understand what the venerable Abbot meant. He pressed him with questions, and among other things asked how he, Zozimus, known far and wide for his sanctity and good works, could call himself a sinner. The venerable man could only smile and say that he was unable to explain further. Then his disciple, St. Dorotheus, who in earlier days had been a distinguished lawyer in Antioch, stepped forward and said : " I suppose it is like you philosophers, and physicians, and men of other professions that require great skill. You obtain your skill by study, reflection, and practice, but if any one asked you what that skill is, and how you got it by degrees, you could not tell him. So the soul obtains the habit of humility by degrees and from the constant observance of God's commandments, but that habit is unspeakable."

"Our fathers said," continues St. Dorotheus, " that we might know the presence of humility by its fruits ; but what that disposition is that is thus formed within us no man can declare in words. When St. Agatho was dying, the brethren asked him if he felt afraid. He replied that he had always done his best to keep God's commandments, but as he was a man, he knew not whether his acts were pleasing to God or not, because God judges one way and man another. This explains how we are to apprehend humility. An ancient was asked what humility is, and he replied : It is a great work, something unspeakably divine. The way to humility is to subdue the body with labour, to submit one's self to every one, and to pray to God unceasingly ; but humility itself is divine and incomprehensible." *

* S. Dorotheus, *Disciplina* 2ª, *de Humilitate.*

The celebrated Cassian, who brought the traditions of those great practical schools of humility, the Egyptian monasteries, to the West, tells us that it is based in self-renunciation and leads to charity, but neither he nor the Fathers whose instructions he has preserved ever attempt to define what it is. He only gives the ten signs of its presence, which St. Benedict afterwards expanded into the famous twelve degrees.

St. John Climacus, the Abbot of Mount Sinai, begins his conference on humility in these terms: "To attempt to explain the sense and effect of divine charity, of humility, of holy purity, of the divine illumination, or of the holy fear that it inspires, to such as have never experienced them, is like trying to explain the sweetness of honey to one who has never tasted it". The Saint then invites the brethren in conference to give their several views of the meaning of the word HUMILITY, which was inscribed upon the wall. After all had spoken, the Saint concluded in these words: "When I heard all these things, and calmly weighed them within myself, I found that I could not take hold of the blessed sense of humility from what I had heard. Humility is a grace of the soul that cannot be expressed in words, and is only known to experience. It is an unspeakable treasure of God, and can only be called the gift of God. 'Learn,' He said—not from angels, not from men, not from books, but learn from My presence, light, and action within you—'that I am meek and humble of heart, and you shall find rest to your souls.' "*

The venerable man saw the impossibility of defining the virtue without the escaping of its essence, and without such a contraction of its nature as to do injustice to its greatness and comprehensiveness. Notwithstanding all the light that has since been thrown upon this virtue from the greatest minds and holiest souls, that difficulty still remains, and is still felt, though in a less degree. When we come to treat the various definitions which holy and profound men have given of humility, we shall see it to be so many-sided that no one definition can possibly do more than give a partial view of what that virtue is.

That sinful man should be humble, through the gift of God, does not seem strange on a first reflection; but that the Eternal Son of God should take our human nature to His Person and become the humblest of men, is a fact so high and profound,

---

* S. J. Climacus, *Scala Paradisi*, Grad. 25.

that it leads us at once to see that we cannot penetrate into the sublime depths of this virtue. But our Lord is the proof that humility is essential to the perfection of an intelligent creature. Whoever imagines that the need of this virtue comes altogether from our sins, or from the necessity of conquring pride, does not understand the nature of humility. Satan fell from innocence and Adam fell from innocence only because they had ceased to be humble. Humility is therefore an attribute of innocence. Christ, as the perfectly innocent Man in perfect union with God, has the complete knowledge of what man is, and of what is justly due from him to God; and as His human will was in perfect conformity with the justice of God, in Him alone is the virtue of humility in its absolute perfection. Although the Blessed Virgin was free from original as well as actual sin, she was the humblest of creatures next to her Divine Son; she was the humblest because the most pure and innocent, and the most pure and innocent because the humblest; and her words in the Holy Scripture breathe nothing but humility: this is their wonderful charm. It belongs to the holy angels as well as to the saints, although in Heaven it is exercised in a more perfect way. For the blessed see their native nothingness, and the wonderful gifts which God gives to their nothingness, and their absolute dependence on God, as they see all truth, not in themselves, but as mirrored in the light of glory.

To understand the virtue of humility we must consider it both *subjectively* and *objectively*. By subjectively we mean the virtue itself as it exists in the powers of the soul and is exercised by them. By objectively we mean the object and end for which it is exercised, and the reasons and motives upon which it is exercised. The light and law of the virtue comes from God and is present in the mind. The exercise of the virtue is in the will, but in the will as helped by the grace of God. The feeling of the virtue is in the spiritual sense. "It is of understanding," says St. Bernard, "and comes of knowledge; it is of the heart, and comes of affection." *

Humility is in the mind when the will subjects the understanding to the divine truth which God presents to the mind, and to the Divine Author of that truth. It is in the will when the will is subject to the will of God. It is in the affections when those

* S. Bernard, *Serm. 4 de Adventu.*

affections are subject to God in charity. It is in the other powers of the soul when the will subjects their operations to God. Humility is in the judgment when we judge ourselves to be what we truly are in the sight of God. It is in the whole conduct of the soul when we hold ourselves with firmness and magnanimity in that position in which God has placed us, neither lifting ourselves with conceit above what we are, nor presuming to account ourselves for more than we are.

Humility consists, moreover, in the sense of our dependence on God, on the help of His grace and the rulings of His providence. It also very much consists in adopting the means prescribed in the Gospel and taught by the experience of the saints for making us humble. Of such means are the faithful keeping of the commandments, the following of the divine counsels of Christ, the exercising of humiliating labours and penitential devotions, the denying of ourselves both in our senses and self-love, and the taking up of our cross to follow Christ. It consists likewise, and very much consists, in living with filial reverence in the presence of God, to whom we are accountable at every moment of our lives. It also consists for its very basis in holding the will with patient fortitude in constant subjection to the strength and support of God, and refusing to be detached from our dependence on Him, whether by pride, vanity, or any other solicitation of our lower nature. Finally, humility must pervade the other virtues to make them subject to God and agreeable in His sight.

This summary account of the virtue on its subjective side will help us to understand the various definitions that give each a partial apprehension of humility. We shall consider it on its objective side in the next lecture, in which we shall treat of the grounds of the virtue.

What first led to the careful consideration of the nature of humility from the intellectual point of view was the rise of the Pelagian heresy, of all heresies the proudest, since its authors denied the necessity of divine grace for the justification and sanctification of man, and maintained that, with the preaching of the Gospel, man was sufficient for himself without the interior help of God. This was to destroy the foundation of humility.

Perhaps the first clear definition of humility is to be found in the celebrated letter to the virgin Demetriades, long ascribed to St. Prosper, but more recently to Julianus Pomerius. It was expressly written to guard that distinguished person from the wiles of Pelagius, who had addressed a letter to her. The definition is in these terms: "Humility consists in our subjection to God in all things". To this subjection all humility tends. Treating expressly of its definition, St. Thomas puts it in these terms: "As it is a special virtue, humility chiefly looks to the subjection of man to God, for whose sake he also subjects himself to others".* His great commentator, Cajetan, puts the same definition with greater precision in these words: "It is the subjection of whatever is of one's self to whatever is of God".

We must not, however, confound the subjection of obedience with the subjection of humility, although humility is at the root of true obedience, and true internal obedience fosters humility. True obedience has its chief motive in God, whilst humility has its chief motive in ourselves. Obedience contemplates the dominion of God and His sovereign right to command us, whether directly or through His representatives, and it consists in the subjection of our will to His will and law; but humility contemplates our own unspeakable inferiority, and in view of that inferiority it subjects, or more truly *abjects*, us into our just and true position beneath the infinite perfection of God. For humility is always exercised in comparing ourselves with what is greater and better than we are, and regards what we have that is less, or what we have not at all. Its essential reason lies in our native poverty and want, not as these defects are fancied or imagined, but as we see them in very truth and consciousness. For, as St. Augustine observes: "Humility holds its ground on the side of truth, and not on the side of falsehood".† Or, to put it in the plain words of St. Vincent of Paul: "The reason why God is so great a lover of humility is because He is the great lover of truth; and humility is nothing but truth, whilst pride is nothing but lying". To which we may add that God is the great lover of justice, and humility is nothing but justice, whilst pride is nothing but injustice.

On the side of God, therefore, and as the final end of the virtue, humility is the subjection of ourselves to God in all things. The Psalmist understood this when he said: "Shall not my soul be subject to God? for from Him is my salvation". And again: "Be thou, O my soul, subject to God: for from Him is my

---

* S. Thomas, *Sum.* ii. 2, q. 161, a. 1 ad 5.
† S. August., *De Natura et Gratia*, c. xxxiv.

patience. For He is my God and my Saviour; my helper, I shall not be moved." *

The second definition we shall give is that of Grossetete, the celebrated Bishop of Lincoln, and of many other theologians. "Humility," he says, "is the love of abiding firmly in that order which belongs to us according to all its conditions, as pride is the love of abiding in an order above what belongs to us." This is the definition of humility as viewed on the side of justice. By the order belonging to us is meant the rank and position that we hold in the sight of God, with all the conditions and defects that truly belong to us and determine our position. His contemporary, St. Thomas, takes the same view of the virtue. He is explaining how humility comes to be a virtue, and has the power of a virtue in repressing the appetite that aims at great things beyond just reason; he then states that "humility becomes a virtue when any one in the view of his deficiencies holds himself down in that low place that measures what he is; as when Abraham said to God: 'I will adore the Lord, who am but dust and ashes'".†

Perhaps this definition has been put more completely by another acute thinker, who says: "Humility is the virtue by which, from the true knowledge of the human state and condition, held with firmness, the man holds himself persistently in that nothingness which of himself he is, and refuses to be moved from it by any external thing". ‡ This firmness and persistency in holding ourselves to what we justly are in the sight of God shows that humility is closely allied with fortitude and magnanimity, and that it is a brave and courageous virtue. We have a sublime example of this firm persistency in St. Francis of Assissi, whom nothing could move from the lowest estimate of himself, and who was wont to exclaim: "Who art Thou, O Lord, and what am I? I am what I am in Thy sight, and I am nothing more."

We may now listen to the explanation which Bishop Grossetete attaches to his definition: "Humility is the love of abiding firmly in that order which belongs to us in all its conditions. This love may be in a man before he knows all the conditions of his state, and therefore it becomes divided from one into many exercises of humility according as he finds out those conditions. To explain by a similitude: the light of the sun in

---

* *Psalm* lxi. 2, 6, 7.   † S. Thomas, *Sum.* ii. 2, q. 161, a. 1.
‡ Lucas Opalen, *De Officio*, apud Musoco, *De Humilitate Christ.*

itself or in the air is pure light, but when it comes in contact with a colouring substance, such as a many-coloured window, the light divides into the colours through which it passes, and becomes red, yellow, or blue.   In a similar way that love which we call humility, whilst it adheres to the general principle of firmly abiding in the order that belongs to us, is a general principle, like the pure light before dividing into colours.   But as we gradually find out its several conditions, and discover what belongs to each condition, humility divides into its special kinds, as light into its special colours.   For instance, when this love discovers that it is due to our human condition to be subject to God, as the angels and saints are, and to keep the inferior creatures beneath us, humility begins to love this state in a special manner, which before was only loved in general.   So when this love begins to understand that penance is the state due to sinners, it begins to love penance in a special way, and not merely in a general way. Thus humility multiplies in man according to the number and diversity of states or habits which he discovers in himself, as light is multiplied into many colours according to the things it touches.

"As it belongs to every virtue to work and minister to that end for which it is appointed, yet no virtue can continue so to work unless there be added to it the love of abiding and persisting in its condition, it is evident that to the working of that virtue humility must be added.   And as this humility gives an abiding persistency to each virtue, and so each virtue is preserved by humility, it is likewise evident that humility is the guardian of all the virtues.   It is also the first virtue, as pride is the first vice. Again, the greater one is the more one is subject, because greatness of soul consists in the number and intensity of the virtues to which the soul ministers.   But every minister is subject to that which he serves, and this ministry is exercised by that love we call humility.   As humility, therefore, causes him who is greatest in the virtues to be all the more their minister, he is consequently all the more subject.   Yet the humbler he is in this service of the virtues, the higher will the branches of his reward ascend. Well, therefore, has the Holy Scripture said : *   'The greater thou art, the more humble thyself in all things'." +

* *Ecclesiasticus* iii. 20.
+ R. Grossetete, Ep. Lincoln, *Opusc. de Humilitate*, apud Brown, *Fascic. Rerum*, vol. ii. p. 228.

This beautiful exposition will be better understood if we reflect that the Christian virtues are in their principle the gifts of God; that man is their subject; that it is by humility he becomes their subject, and that in working with them he ministers to them as their servant; and that, in short, it is by humility that he subjects the virtues to the service of God, and secures their persistency.

According to this definition, then, humility keeps us firm in the position in which, according to our deservings, God has placed us; it measures what we are and what we deserve, and never advances to a higher position unless God advances us; and when we are by Him advanced, it never forgets from what God has advanced us. In this Spirit Abraham prostrated himself before God and said: "I will speak to the Lord, who am but dust and ashes".* In this spirit, when God had chosen Saul to rule His people, and his heart was yet as that of a little child, he exclaimed: "Am I not a son of Jemini, of the least tribe of Israel, and my kindred the last among the families of the tribe of Benjamin?"† In this spirit Peter judged himself unworthy to behold the miracles of the Lord, and on his knees cried out: "Depart from me, O Lord, for I am a sinful man".‡ In this spirit the Canaanite woman took the place our Lord assigned to her, and answered: "Yea, Lord, even the whelps eat of the crumbs that fall from their masters' table".§ In this spirit the Roman centurion declared himself unworthy that the Lord should enter under his roof. And in the same spirit of humility the publican in the Temple stood afar off, and would not so much as lift his eyes to Heaven, but struck his breast and said: "O God, be merciful to me a sinner";‖ and he went down to his house justified.

The definition to which we may give the third place is that in which humility is considered as the temperance of the soul, refraining from, and denying herself to, the adversaries of this virtue. These adversaries are self-love, pride, vanity, and vain-glory; for although inordinate self-love is opposed to charity, in another way it is opposed to humility. Self-love is opposed to humility as it is the origin of pride, of vanity, and vainglory; for if we were perfectly subject to God in mind, sense, and will, we should have no inordinate self-love. The temperance of the soul

* *Genesis* xviii. 27.   † 1 *Kings* ix. 21.   ‡ *S. Luke* v. 8.
§ *S. Matthew* xv. 27.   ‖ *S. Luke* xviii. 13.

is a spiritual temperance, refraining from those inordinate appetites that spring directly from self-love; and this temperance is chiefly concerned with humility and meekness: with humility as it refrains from pride and vanity, and with meekness as it refrains from anger.

For this reason St. Thomas considers humility as potentially belonging to the virtue of temperance, and declares it to be "nothing else but a certain moderation of spirit. For although humility is caused by the reverential fear of God, this does not hinder it from being a part of modesty or temperance." The learned and devout Suarez takes the same view. He says that although humility inclines us to be subject to God, yet, "properly, and of itself, it is not inclined to another, but moderates our affection for our own greatness, and in this way holds us subject to God, and to whatever partakes of the excellence of God". * St. Thomas therefore defines humility to be "the virtue which tempers and withholds the soul from tending immoderately towards high things". †

As opposed to the morbid appetite of pride or to the contemptible appetite of vanity, humility is the spirit's modesty, the soul's sobriety. The vices to which it is opposed are the impurities of our spiritual nature, defiling the soul with their falsehood, disordering the will with their injustice, blinding the understanding, deceiving the heart, making us contemptible, and even ridiculous, before God and His angels, as also before men. Who does not remember the withering words of the Almighty when Adam sought to be as a god? " Behold Adam hath become as one of us, knowing good and evil." Pride alone is hateful to God, and every other vice is hateful for the pride that is in it. For pride is the malignant element in every vice, the malice which rises against God in every act of injustice. Humility, therefore, may be truly called the purity and modesty of the soul, that combats every tendency to false elation, every inclination to make one's self what one is not, every movement to claim for us what is not one's own, every disposition to rise above our true and just position in the sight of God, and to combat these unjust inclinations by withholding the will from the false appetite.

We tend to true greatness by subjecting ourselves to God,

---

* Suarez, *De Statu Religionis*, lib. ix., c. 5, n. 24.
† S. Thomas, *Sum.* ii. 2, q. 161, a. 1.

because subjection is the essential condition of union with God, and this subjection is the only thing that the creature contributes towards that union. The more we are subject to God the nearer we are to Him. He is infinitely above us, but by this very subjection we ascend to Him, and find in Him whatever is truly great. But the elation of pride is a tendency to great things that are neither according to God nor to truth, but the productions of our fancy and the inventions of our conceit ; and to this humility is opposed.

The temperance of humility combats the intemperance of pride in the way in which modesty combats immodesty. It combats by withholding the mind, the sense, and the will. It combats by refraining the mind from the evil suggestion or imagination, by keeping the spiritual sense above the movement of the appetite and the will from consent. It combats by turning the mind to some nobler object more worthy of the soul, and especially by subjecting the soul with greater humility to God, and even to our neighbour for God's sake. In a word, humility effectively combats pride by withholding the will on every side and giving it some better entertainment. Nor is it amiss where temptation is urgent to remember the fact that the devil is behind every suggestion of pride as well as every instigation to impurity. But there is no more decisive way of preserving the soul from attacks of pride than to do some act of humility towards another in God's sight and for God's sake.

The Pelagian heresy gave rise to another definition of humility, which we shall put in the fourth place. As this pestilent heresy took away the foundation of the virtue by denying the grace of God, humility was defined to be the confession of the grace of God. The spirit of this heresy fills the world's literature, inspires the world's policy, and animates the world's votaries. The world deifies the human intellect and the human will. Self-perfectibility on the basis of self-sufficiency is the shallow doctrine of the world in the West, as it is the religious doctrine of the Buddhists in the East. Many, again, are they who would shrink from Pelagianism as a doctrine, yet are little better than Pelagians in their practice. They reject not the existence of grace, but they care not to have grace ; they object not to the principle of humility, but are not concerned about having humility ; they are far from denying that man is dependent on God, but they prefer to depend on themselves.

In the celebrated letter to Demetriades, after defining humility as consisting in our subjection to God in all things, the author observes that it cannot exist without the grace of God, and from this point of view he tells us that it consists in the confession of the grace of God. As the grace of God is both the cause and inherent principle of the virtue, this confession, not of the lips, but of the heart, implies the submission of the will to the grace of God, and the dependence of the soul on the divine help, and it cannot be omitted from any complete account of humility. It has therefore been adopted as a partial definition by many devout writers since the fifth century. The exposition with which the author follows the definition is so just and beautiful, that we shall here give it in substance, though much abridged.

Humility consists in the confession of the grace of God. We must therefore confess the grace of God in all its reality and integrity; for it is the first office of grace to make us sensible of the help which it gives us. And hence the Apostle says: "We have not received the spirit of the world, but the spirit which is of God, that we may know the things that are given us from God ".* Should any one imagine that he has some good that God has not given him, but of which he is himself the author, that one has not the spirit of God, but the spirit of the world; he is puffed up with that wisdom of which the Lord says: " I will destroy the wisdom of the wise, and the prudence of the prudent I will reject ".† Of these wise ones the Apostle says: "When they have known God, they have not glorified Him as God, or given thanks, but have become vain in their thoughts, and their foolish heart is darkened ".‡ Mark well the retribution of the proud, and how they receive their reward. Even when they gain the knowledge of truth, they ascribe it to themselves, and glory in their native genius, as if what they knew came not from God, was not His gift, but some production of their own intellectual faculties. When the elements of the world and those creatures of kinds so many and various are present to our sight, they reveal to us the invisible things of God. They speak as a master speaks, and as the Scriptures speak; but whatever good passes through the eyes into the field of the heart, it can never take root or be fruitful there unless the Divine Husbandman gives the force of His influence to bring what He has planted to perfection. For whether it

---

* 1 Corinthians ii. 12.   † 1 Corinthians i. 19.   ‡ Romans i. 21.

be the creature or the truths of faith that we contemplate, it is "not he who planteth, or he who watereth, but God who giveth the increase ".[*]

They who strive in their own strength take off their hope from the Lord, and set that hope upon themselves ; and in them the words of the Prophet are fulfilled : "Accursed is the man who sets his hope in man, and strengthens the arm of his flesh ; his heart hath departed from the Lord ".[†]   Pride is justly called avarice in the Scriptures as well, for both these vices are excesses beyond all right and justice.   The proud hoard up the things that belong to others as well as the avaricious, and are reckless as to whose claims they violate, looking upon all things as if they came from their own fountain.   This comes of perversely appropriating God's gifts, and forgetting who it is that gave them.   Had God given nothing to their rational nature which is sublime or beautiful, they would never have had anything upon which to extol themselves.   But their pride takes possession of what is God's, as the devil does, of whom our Lord says : "When he speaketh a lie, he speaketh of his own ".[‡]   Solomon shows the source of our knowledge when he says in the Proverb : "The Lord giveth wisdom, and out of His mouth cometh prudence and knowledge ".[§]   And St. John says : "We know that the Son of God is come, and hath given us un-derstanding, that we may know the true God, and be in His Son ".[||]   If, then, we are able to direct the attention of our soul to what is right and to what is good for us, that comes from the inspiration of God, and from His eternal and immutable will.   St. Paul therefore says : "Work out your salvation in fear and trem-bling : for it is God who worketh in you, both to will and to accomplish, according to His good will ".[¶]

The reason why we cannot discover humility in the conduct of worldly-wise people is, because this virtue subjects us in all things to God.   It is only so long as we place the care and perfection of our actions in God, rather than in ourselves, that we lose not the merit of them.   What can be so just or so becoming as that the image of God should shine towards God, and derive its grace and beauty from Him ?   This is the light of His countenance sealed upon us.   That soul is adulterous and utterly incapable of union with God that holds to the mirror of her heart any beauty which

---

[*] *1 Corinthians* iii. 7.   [†] *Jeremias* xvii. 5.   [‡] *S. John* viii. 44.
[§] *Proverbs* ii. 6.   [||] *1 John* v. 20.   [¶] *Philippians* ii. 12, 13.

is not from God's beauty, or accepts for her adornment any jewel which comes not from the treasury of the Holy Spirit.

That you, Demetriades, find yourself capable of preferring Christ to your family and fortune is a grace you can never ascribe to yourself; for He is the true humility, the true charity, and the true chastity.   And the spirit that is truly free is the spirit purified from every contamination, and that loves nothing in herself or her neighbour but what comes from God.   When the tempter fails to win certain souls to unlawful deeds because they have a high and noble spirit, he often effects his purpose by some delusive delight in themselves, that after they are lifted up he may throw them down as from a precipice.   For from the moment we cease to confess the help of divine grace, we set up ourselves on our own merits.   This pride is of the worst kind, with more folly than in other ways of elation, for if, whilst we are struck down, we still call on our Redeemer for help, He will make it easy for us to rise again; but for this ruin there is no remedy.   It is very difficult for a proud man to become conscious of his sin, and if he becomes a little conscious, it is not to his Physician that he goes for the remedy.   No cure can come of it, because he looks to his disease for his medicine.

Enter, then, into the forecourt of your soul, which is your mind, and pass into the chamber of your heart; look round there and see if you have anything that is good, useful, ornamental, or resplendent that is not the gift of God, or of which He is not the Author.   Even the good of prayer is His gift.   But whatever the gift, or whatever the increase through your labours, remember that He who gave the gift gives the increase.   Let, then, the Holy Spirit fill His organ, which is your soul; and let His finger touch His lyre, which is your heart.*

As it is of the nature of humility to confess the grace of God and to acknowledge His gifts, it follows of course that it can be no part of humility to deny His gifts, or to conceal them from our sight.   Yet St. Francis of Sales had to reason against this error as well as St. Teresa.   Lancicius found a learned religious superior so wedded to this misconception, that he was led to write a special dissertation to prove the contrary, as well from the Sacred Scriptures as from the Fathers and Saints of every age.   The mistake arises from confounding the gifts of God with our own

* *Epist. ad Virginem Demetriadem*, inter Opera S. Prosperi.

merits, which should certainly not be the subject of our reflections; or it may arise from the fear that we should appropriate to ourselves the blessings that God in His infinite goodness bestows on us; or this misapprehension may take its rise from the vague and confused notion that somehow or other it is contrary to humility to think that God has done us favours. But it is from no knowledge of God's goodness to us that the danger of elation arises. That comes from overlooking this truth, and from ascribing the good to one's self which God has given us in His generosity. Nothing can be more contrary to simplicity and rectitude of heart than to play at hide-and-seek with the mercies and graces of God, and few things are more opposite to the genuine interests of humility, whose very nature belongs to truth and sincerity. Our great protection against becoming elated over any good we receive will be found in the habit of seeing that good in the hands of God, and in constantly ascribing it to Him, still with the fear lest, through our neglecting that good, God should take it from us and give it to the more deserving.

To conceal from our heart how good God is to us is so far from fostering the sense of our unworthiness, that what most proves our unworthiness and puts us to shame is His great goodness to us. Our danger is not from truth but from falsehood; not from the sight of God's divine gifts, but from taking them for our own merits. The best protection against this is to live ever in God's presence, and to see and know how good He is to a creature so unworthy. How are such virtues as hope, charity, trust in God, and gratitude to thrive with us, if we are not to think on the bounties and favours that our good God bestows on us? Gratitude is scarce because sincere humility is rare. The want of gratitude in proud hearts is proverbial in the mouth of the human race; but a great gift fills the humble with confusion as well as gratitude, because it awakens in them the sense of their unworthiness. That is an admirable sentence of St. Theodore the Studite: "Our most clement God is so free and bountiful of His gifts, that there is danger that, through our ignorance of what He does for us, we should do an injury to His goodness".*

The first office of the grace of God is to make us sensible of the Giver. This St. Paul has taught us: "We have received the spirit which is of God, that we may know the things that are

* S. Theodor. Studit., *Serm.* 85.

given us from God". From this text St. Thomas concludes that not only do those who partake of God's gifts know what they have received, but that, without prejudice to humility, they may prefer their own gifts to those that another may appear to have received,* doubtless because they have internal proof of their own gift, and only external proof of another's, and because the gift teaches them what is best for their good. "The more thou knowest the gifts of God," says St. Augustine, "the more blessed art thou in those gifts : yea, thou art not otherwise blessed except that in having those gifts thou knowest from whom thou hast received them."† St. Bernard counts it among the impediments of grace and the effects of tepidity when we are less conscious of the good that God gives us; and he takes the failure of this knowledge for a sign of indevotion and ingratitude.‡ The celebrated Father Laynez, the disciple and successor of St. Ignatius, wrote these remarkable words : "I do not think it can be pleasing to God that humility should put an impediment to the knowledge of His gifts : this would be the effect of pusillanimity rather than of true humility". The knowledge of the divine help and the confidence which it inspires are the foundation of that Christian magnanimity which gives us courage to undertake the most arduous works because God wills them ; they are intimately connected with humility of heart, which is conscious that power is perfected in the midst of infirmity.

Blind and deceptive is the world's spirit, perverting every good gift of God to self-aggrandizement, and forgetting its Divine Author ; but secure is the light of the Holy Spirit, who teaches us the knowledge of His gifts. The knowledge that proceeds from the Holy Spirit must be useful, must be needful; for unless we know these gifts, how shall we love the Giver of them ? How shall we show our gratitude for them ? How shall we keep them with due diligence ? How shall we employ them in His honour, who has the right to their service ? How shall we breathe our confidence in that divine support which carries us through the time of affliction or of mental desolation, and upholds us in our arduous duties ? How, in short, are we to know God in His gifts ? We cannot have these advantages unless we know the

---

* S. Thomas, *Sum.* ii. 2, q. 161, a. 3.
† S. August., *De Bono Viduitatis,* c. xvi.
‡ S. Bernard, *Serm.* 3 *de Annunciat.*

spiritual good we have received. For, as the wise man says in Ecclesiasticus : * " Wisdom that is hidden, and a treasure that is not seen, what profit is there in them both ? " †

But whoever would see this subject treated with the rich fulness of profound intuition should read what St. Teresa has written upon it in the tenth chapter of her Life. The point to be guarded against is the claiming for our own what we really do not possess, which is less likely to happen if we habitually ascribe all the good we have to God. The other point to be guarded against is the claiming of more virtue than we really have, imagining we have the solid virtues of which we read or of which we think, although as yet we may scarcely have been touched with the true nature of mortification, humility, and inward patience. Nor is this confusing of imagination with fact and of sensibility with truth always limited to beginners. We must therefore judge our gifts with great moderation, never compare them with another's to our own advantage, or lose sight of the merciful and loving hand from which they come. The true tests by which to judge of the presence of the greater gifts, and of our good use of them, are these : First, if they increase our sense of the presence of God. Secondly, if they deepen our sense of the responsibility they bring with them. Thirdly, if they bring us into a profounder sense of our own unworthiness. For the higher gifts search the soul more deeply, and give cause for greater humility, which is the measure of our response to them. " The greater thou art, the more humble thyself in all things." St. Paul compares the man of grace to a frail vessel carrying a great treasure, who cannot but tremble at the disproportion between the greatness of the treasure and the frailty to which it is intrusted. There is another consideration of great moment : the greater the habitual gifts received, the greater must be the actual graces given at each moment to secure their exercise and turn them to account. In these actual graces lies the secret of our power to co-operate with the special gifts of God ; and the secret of securing this actual grace is in the exercise of humility and prayer ; for the more constant these exercises are, the more abundantly will those graces flow.

An eminent master of the interior life has put the question

* *Ecclesiasticus* xx. 32.
† See Lancicius, *Opusc.* 8 *de Humilitate Quærenda*, c. vi.

whether a soul may sometimes review her progress without injury to humility; and he replies that this may be done when it pleases God to give the soul a singular light, showing the change He has wrought in her, giving her grace as well as light to feel and know that it is not her work but the work of God, whereby she is led to confess the change which God has accomplished in her, with a deep sense of humility, gratitude, and love, and is at the same time animated with a filial fear and dread of offending the Divine Goodness.* In such a case of special light and grace there is wonder at the contrast between her present and her former state, rising into a sense of God's goodness to a creature so unworthy and incapable, and the soul clearly sees her native nothingness.

We come, in the fifth place, to the well-known definition of St. Bernard, which proves its practical value by its wide acceptance, as well by devout writers as among the faithful. "Humility," he says, "is the virtue by which, from the truest knowledge of himself, a man becomes vile in his own eyes." † This is a definition on the side of self-knowledge. As humility is the foundation of all the virtues, self-knowledge is the foundation of humility. St. Laurence Justinian emphatically insists that self-knowledge is both the ground of its existence and the condition of its growth and progress; from which he concludes with St. Bernard that without self-knowledge it is impossible to be saved.‡ How can a man have the fear of God if he knows not why he should fear? How can he have contrition of heart to break up and dissolve the state of sin if he knows not why he should be contrite? How can he have compunction if the arrows of Divine Justice have not pierced his soul with indignation? How can he be humble if he knows not why he should be ashamed? He who is ignorant of himself is most certainly ignorant of God, for it is by one and the same light imparted to us that we know God and know ourselves; and it is by entering into ourselves that we find the light that gives us the knowledge of God. That is the reason why we say of one returning to God, that he has entered into himself. The whole difference between the godly and the ungodly is this, that the one lives inside and the other outside himself.

---

* Joan. de Jesu Maria, *Tract. de Tribus Statibus*, Dub. 15.

† S. Bernard, *De Gradibus Humilitatis*, c. i.

‡ S. Laurent. Justin., *L. de Humilitate*, c. i.

But if the man who is ignorant of himself is ignorant of God, the grace of God is also ignorant of him.

In how many places of Holy Scripture does the Almighty say that He knows this or that one, but not in mercy? When Adam hid himself among the trees, the Lord God called to him : "Adam, where art thou ?"* He asked not where he was hidden, but recalled him to himself, and so to his Creator. Of the Israelites prevaricating in the desert the Almighty said: "These men always err in their hearts, and they have not known My ways".† Ignorant of the ways of their own heart, they were ignorant of the ways of God, who swore in His wrath that they should not enter into His rest. The foolish virgins slumbered, and their lamps, the light of their souls, were neglected ; and coming to the banquet after the doors were closed, the bridegroom answered from within : "Amen, I say to you, I know you not".‡ How wonderful ! The God who knows all knows not them who know not themselves. He knows their sin, but not their pardon.

"Knowledge puffeth up," but not the knowledge of one's self. This knowledge is the sure remedy against every sort of pride. It rectifies every kind of knowledge, because it puts us in the just point of view for understanding every truth and detecting every error; but without the knowledge of one's self we can neither understand one single thing correctly, nor bear one's self towards any one as it properly becomes us to do. I would have a man, says St. Bernard, to know himself above all things : reason, and order, and utility demand this of him. The right order is to start from one's self and to know what we are. This knowledge is so useful, because, instead of inflating, it humbles us and prepares us for being spiritually built up; for without a solid foundation of humility the spiritual building will never stand. The soul will find nothing so quick and decisive to humble her as to know what she really is; only she must dissemble nothing, must have no guile in her spirit, must set herself plainly before her eyes, must allow of no cheating, nor be frightened away from seeing clean through herself, whatever pain this may bring her. As she looks into herself with the clear truth, she will find herself in a region of unlikeness, will sigh over the miseries she is sure to discover, and will be disposed to cry to God like the Prophet:

* *Genesis* iii. 9. † *Psalm* xciv. 10, 11. ‡ *S. Matthew* xxv. 12.

7*

" Thou hast humbled me in Thy truth!"* How can she be otherwise than humbled when she finds the load of her sins, the oppression of her mortal body, the earthly cares that entangle her, the carnal desires that stain and enfeeble her soul? She will find herself perplexed with error, exposed to danger, disturbed with fear, encompassed with difficulties, teased with suspicion, grieved with trouble, inclined to some vice that she condemns, and helpless to practise the virtue she approves. How, then, can she lift up her eyes with self-reliance and her head with pride? Will she not rather turn in anguish whilst the thorn is fastened? Will she not turn to tears, be converted to weeping, and return to the Lord, and in an humbled spirit cry to Him : " Heal Thou my soul, for I have sinned against Thee "? † And after turning to God, He will console her, because He is the Father of mercies and the God of consolation.

So long as I look into myself, the eye of the soul dwells in bitterness; but when I look from myself to the Divine Mercy, the consoling vision of my God will temper and soften the bitter vision of myself, and I shall say to Him : " My soul is troubled within me, wherefore I will be mindful of Thee ".‡ It is no obscure vision of God that gives us the experience how fatherly He is, and how inclined to our prayer, which shows us in very truth that " He is gracious and merciful, patient, and rich in mercy ".§ His nature is goodness, His property to have mercy and to spare. We know by experience that this is the order in which God becomes known to us in the way of salvation, when a man enters into himself, goes into his miseries and wants, and cries from the midst of them to God, who will then hear him and say : " I will deliver thee, and thou shalt honour Me ". ‖ Thus shall thy knowledge of thyself be thy path to the knowledge of God, and through the renewal of His image in thee He shall be seen by thee, whilst thou, beholding with confidence the grace of the Lord with open face, shalt be transformed to the same image, from brightness to brightness, as by the Spirit of the Lord.¶

When we examine St. Bernard's definition closely, we shall find that it only takes the intellectual side of humility; it takes in the perception of our native vileness, but not the conduct of the will

---

* *Psalm* cxviii. 75.   † *Psalm* xl. 5.
‡ *Psalm* xli. 7.   § *Exodus* xxxiv. 6.
‖ *Psalm* xlix. 15.   ¶ S. Bernard, *In Cantic. Serm.* 36.

in the sight of that vileness. It is therefore but a partial definition, and was not intended for more. The Saint is expressly speaking of intellectual humility, and of that alone, and from other points of view he gives other definitions. He is showing that humility is the fruit of grace before it is the fruit of light, and the fruit of prayer before it is the fruit of reflection. He then listens to our Blessed Lord giving thanks to His Father, because He has hidden the secrets of truth from the wise and prudent, that is, from the proud, and has revealed those secrets to little ones, that is, to the humble; and he then concludes: "From this it appears that truth is hidden from the proud and revealed to the humble. Of humility, therefore, this may be the definition: Humility is the virtue by which, from the truest knowledge of himself, a man becomes vile in his own eyes. This belongs to those who dispose ascensions in their heart, and go on from virtue to virtue, that is, from lower to higher degrees, until they come to the summit of humility, from which, as from Mount Sion, they look out upon the whole prospect of truth." *

The mere perception of one's self and of one's vileness would reduce us to despair; humility, therefore, essentially implies the comparison of our self-knowledge with our knowledge of God, of our vileness with His goodness and mercy. For St. Bernard's complete view of this virtue we must therefore go to other of his writings. In a sublime discourse on the Canticles, for instance, he takes this more comprehensive view: "Justice is consummated in humility. There is a humility which truth generates, but it has no fervour; and there is a humility which charity forms, and it enkindles the soul. If thou look upon thy inward self in the light of truth, and look without dissimulation, and there judge thyself without flattery, doubt not but that thou will be humbled, and become vile in thine own eyes. Yet though thy self-knowledge make thee humble, even then thou wilt not perhaps endure to have the truth known to other persons, because thy humility is thus far but the work of knowledge, and comes not yet from the infusion of love. The splendour of truth hath enlightened thee, and hath shown thee in a true and healthy way what thou art; but if beyond this thou hadst been affected with the love of that truth, there is no doubt but that thou wouldst have wished all men to have that opinion of thee which thou hast of thyself,

* S. Bernard, *De Gradibus Humilitatis*, c. i.

as far as that can go.   And I say as far as that can go, because it is not proper to make everything known that we know of ourselves, because the charity of truth, as well as the truth of charity, forbids the wish to make that known to other persons which, were it known, would do them an injury." *

Here, as in many other places, St. Bernard shows that it is charity that brings humility to perfection, as an affective disposition of the heart.   And his final definition accords with our first. " The sum of humility," he says, " appears to consist in this, that our will should be duly subject to the will of God." †

It may be well to say a word here in reply to those ungodly men who look upon humility as degrading to man.   It is impossible for any man to understand what he is not disposed to see, or for seeing which he is not in the right point of view or in the right condition of mind.   No man can know himself without the means of comparison with what he ought to resemble. Humility results from self-examination in the light of God, in which light is the standard of truth and justice, whereby we measure what we are in the sight of God.   St. Paul draws this distinction between the man of the world and the man of God, that the first sees in his own light, and the second in the light of God.   He says to them who had passed from the first to the second light : " Ye were heretofore darkness, but now light in the Lord ". ‡   The first light is singularly obscure in what concerns one's self, especially where an unconscious pride prevails.   But he who knows not his pride knows not himself.   He knows not how much he takes to himself that neither in truth or justice belongs to him.   He knows not what great things are wanting to him, for which nevertheless his soul was made.   He makes great things of what are inferior to him, and looks with but little concern upon those truly great things, far superior to himself, which he might have if he chose.   He lives the life of nature—not of pure but disordered nature—and sees but the surface of things, which he is disposed to refer to himself and not to His Creator. The eye of the eagle to that of the mole is the figure of the distance between the insight of the humble Christian and that of the natural man immersed in self-sufficiency.   It is altogether another sight and a different power.

* S. Bernard, *In Cantic. Serm.* 42.   † *Ibid., Serm.* 25 *de Diversis.*
‡ *Ephesians* v. 8.

The earthly man sees not the difference between the soul in herself and the soul clothed with spiritual light, between her created existence and the good with which God can endow that existence, between the faculties of the soul and the truth and grace presented to those faculties, in the choice of which lies good or evil, life or death.   The man one calls one's *self* is the man without that divine light, without those grand objects, without that spiritual good, for which he was created.   The grand object for which we came into existence is more than the light and grace of God ; it is God Himself, and those gifts are given to guide and lead and help us to Him.   We are not our own good, nor are the things around or beneath us our good, however useful in their place and order, but God is our good, and whatever comes from God that is better than ourselves helps us on to Him.   We have but the capacity for good, and the power of working with the good we receive.   Pride is the practical denial of this truth, a truth that springs from the constitution of our nature.   And therefore it is said in Holy Scripture that "pride was not made for man ".*   It is not as compared with anything in this world that man is vile, but as compared with the justice and perfection of his Creator.

It is when considered in himself, and as he would be were God to leave him to himself, unenlightened, ungraced, unhelped even in the order of providence, vacant of all but himself, stained, too, and disordered with sin, that we say that man is nothing before God.   It is in contrast with the divine support, that saves us from returning to nothing, and with the noble gifts we receive or might receive, and with the infinitely noble end to which we were created to aspire and advance, that we say man in himself is vile and worthless.   Moreover it is the tendency of the creature sprung from nothingness to bring the gifts of God to nothing, and to debase and defile himself with things baser than himself, and to falsify himself with egotistical pride and vanity, that make him vile to very baseness.   We say, then, that without the merciful and loving grace of God, and without an unfailing co-operation with His never-failing goodness, we are needy and poor.   The Psalmist felt this when he prayed : "But I am needy and poor : O God, be Thou my help ".†   When the soul takes this just and truthful view of her infirmities, she rises from blindness to truth, and looks to

* *Ecclesiasticus x. 22.*   † *Psalm lxix. 6.*

God to raise her out of her vileness. She humbles herself in the truth because it is just, and the God who loves truth and justice exalts her.

But in our feeble and defiled origin; in the multitude and malice of our sins; in the corruption of our earthly body, blinding the soul with concupiscences, distempers, illusions, and low desires; in the subjugation of our mind and judgment to our imagination; in the petulance of our senses, given now to levity, now to gloom; in the fickle inconstancy of the mind, at the mercy of every mood of our earthly frame; in the dissensions of our heart from our mind, and of our mind from our heart; in the blinding excitements of our passions, and the unreasoning rage of our appetites; in our uncertain purposes, feeble resolves, and failures of performance; in the poverty of our acts compared with the pomp of our pretensions; in the selfish meanness, jealousy, and moral cowardice that lurk like serpents in the caverns of our pride; in our slavery to human respect; in our dissemblings with ourselves and our simulations with other men; in our slowness of faith and want of patience under trials; in the languor of our charity and our want of magnanimity; in those obscurations of the soul where pride and self-sufficiency stop the light of God from entering; in the neglect and abuse of the grace and goodness of our Lord, our Saviour and our God; in the very nothingness from which we came, and on which, unheeded by us, the creative hand of God supports us;—in these, and in many things besides, we know and feel that we are vile. And the more we contemplate ourselves in the sight of God the more vile we find ourselves. It was after contemplations like these that David exclaimed: " I was reduced to nothing, and I knew it not. I am become as a beast of burden before Thee, and I am always with Thee."* And finding that he was no good to himself, he concluded: " My good is to adhere to God, to set my hope on the Lord ".† St. Francis of Sales, therefore, gives us this well-known advice: Never to think long on our own miseries without thinking of the mercies of God, lest we despair; and never to think long on the mercies of God without thinking of our own miseries, lest we presume.

There is a sixth definition of humility, which is more profound and comprehensive, and which has originated in contemplative minds, accustomed to look more deeply into things. This defini-

* *Psalm* lxxii. 22, 23.   † *Psalm* lxxii. 28.

tion is based upon the first of the eight beatitudes : " Blessed are the poor in spirit : for theirs is the kingdom of Heaven ".* This beautitude has always been interpreted as profound humility. The poor in spirit are they who, detached from all but God, claim nothing as their own ; their heart is with their treasure, and their treasure is in Heaven. St. Chrysostom says with great justice on this text, that "as pride is the root and cause of all evil, Christ began His teaching by plucking out the root of pride and planting humility in its place, as a firm foundation on which all things else might be built. But if our subjection be lost, this foundation is destroyed, and all the good gathered upon it will perish." †

To be poor in spirit is to have nothing of one's own, nothing but what one receives from God. If, as St. Chrysostom observes, the word *poor* in the original text signifies a needy mendicant, this does not prevent him from deciding that the humble in spirit are here meant, who always feel their poverty and are always asking God for help. For true humility springs from the sense of our native poverty, and is fostered by a cheerful detachment from whatever is not ordained for us by the will of God. The voice of true humility is the voice of the Psalmist : " The Lord is the portion of my inheritance and of my cup : it is Thou that wilt restore my inheritance to me " ; ‡ and " For what have I in Heaven ? and besides Thee what do I desire on earth ? For this my flesh and my heart hath fainted away : Thou art the God of my heart, and the God that is my portion for ever. It is good for me to adhere to God, to put my hope in the Lord." §

This poverty of spirit withdraws the will of man from all self-love, and from every love that is not in God and for God, that God alone may be the one object of love, and that all things may be loved in God and for God. This full and perfect love of God generates a complete abdication of self-love, and a humility of love, that, as St. Thomas observes, has its root in the knowledge of the majesty of God, and in the most true and profound reverence of God. ‖ From this knowledge of the supreme majesty of God, and this unbounded reverence, there springs up a sense in the soul that accounts all we are without God as nothing and inspires us with self-contempt.

---

* *S. Matthew* v. 3.   † S. J. Chrysost., *Hom.* 15 *in Matth*
‡ *Psalm* xv. 5.   § *Psalm* lxxii. 25, 26, 28.
‖ S. Thomas, *Sum.* ii. 2, q. 161, a. 1.

From this point of view Rusbrock defines the virtue in these terms: "Humility is the abasement of the soul, that is, it is a certain internal and profound inclination and subjection of the heart and soul towards the Most High Majesty of God, which justice commands, and which the heart endowed with divine love and pressed by charity cannot refuse".* Speaking elsewhere of the profound reverential fear that springs from the loving contemplation of the Divine Majesty, he says that from this loving fear true humility and unfeigned self-abjection are born, whilst the soul is attentive to the greatness of God and her own littleness, to the wisdom of God and her own ignorance, to the wealth and generosity of God and her own poverty and want.†

Poverty of spirit springs from the true knowledge of our nature, and this knowledge is caused by the penetration of the light of truth and justice into the innermost recesses of the soul, where we see, without possibility of error, how our very existence rests on God, and all our light, life, and love are received from Him. Then we come to the last phase of humility, which is the expression of unbounded gratitude. This is the truth of all truths, and the law of all laws for the rational creature; this gratitude, this humble love, returned to Him who has loved us first, who has created us from love, who has preserved us with love, who has redeemed us from love, who has given us His Holy Spirit of love, and has prepared for us the kingdom of His love. In this love is our life, and the gratitude of this love is the perfection of humility. This reaction of our soul to the divine action within us, the returning of love for His love, the grateful acknowledgment from our inmost spirit that all we are, or have received, or shall receive, is from the goodness of our Divine Benefactor, is the foundation of all Christian humility and of all Christian dignity. It is the foundation of all Christian humility, which feels and confesses in every form of gratitude our absolute dependence in all things upon God, as well for our being as for our deliverance from evil and for our partaking of His good and perfect gifts. It is the foundation of all Christian dignity, which admits of no other authority over the soul than that which comes from God. To acknowledge our dependence with humble gratitude on God alone, and that His will alone ought to rule our will, is the only just way of using our liberty. To think upon the

* Rusbrockius, *De Præcipuis Virtutibus*, c. i. † *Ibid.*, c. xiv.

sovereign will of God, to feel and to love that divine will, which is the rule of justice and the source of all communicated good, and to make that will the law of our life, is that which constitutes true Christian dignity, a dignity before God as great in the poor man clothed with rags as in the prince who is robed in purple.

Humility is the just and truthful expression in our thought, sense, and conduct, of our nature, our position, and our dependence as the subjects of God; it is the order arising out of that subjection and dependence. It takes the form of gratitude in responding to the divine generosity: a gratitude that springs from all the good of which we are the subjects, deepened by all the sense of our being undeserving of that good. Yet, whilst the soul is made to be the complete subject of God, and to freely love and adhere to Him with our whole mind, heart, soul, and strength, she finds on self-examination that there is a division within her. This division, as she finds, is owing to her self-love. Her mind and heart are divided between God and herself. When she examines this self-love, she finds that it is nourished by inordinate earthly desires and by the vanities of life; and when she looks more deeply into herself, she finds that pride divides her affections with the love of God. This may not be in the summit of the soul, where the love of God may be, but on the part of the inferior soul, which divides the affections of the will and troubles her peace. What is the remedy? To denude the soul of these inordinate affections. Opening those closed recesses of the soul to the light of God, and humbling herself into subjection to a greater depth, she will take the short, sharp, and decisive way with these inordinate affections, will cut off their supplies, and deny herself the objects and the acts that foster her self-love. But after this is done there still remains the spring of self-love within the soul, which is not only tenacious, but often difficult to get at and to understand, before it can be converted and changed into the love of God. To accomplish this will cost many efforts and wounds to nature; but in the proportion in which self-love is sacrificed the will becomes free and generous, and subjects herself to the grace of God more ardently, uniformly, and consistently.

This brings us to the final expression of humility, which is sacrifice. Humility is the spiritual element in all sacrifice. It is the surrender of nature and life to God, that by His power they may be altogether changed into a better form. The one Divine Sacrifice obtained its power from the unspeakable humility of Him who offered His human nature and life to the sovereign justice of the Father of all. In His innocence He sacrificed himself in the likeness of sinful man, that, through partaking of the grace of His divine and inexhaustible humility, every sinful nature might be changed and made subject to God. Through that sacrifice we have all received the power of offering ourselves as spiritual victims to God. Humility is the interior, spiritual, sacrificial action through which, with the profoundest veneration and gratitude, we offer to God the being and life we have received from Him, with the desire and the prayer that we may die to ourselves and live to Him ; that we may be wholly changed and transformed into His likeness, detached from earth and united with God. But as we come to our God from sin and dark ingratitude, we owe more to Him than our being and our life ; we owe Him the contrition, the breaking to pieces of our sinful form, with regret and sorrow that we have defiled and defaced His beautiful work ; we owe to Him that we throw away every breath of vanity, falsehood, and evil, which, when cast out of us, is nothing. Penitential contrition must therefore be added to our humble gratitude, as an essential part of our sacrifice, that we may offer ourselves to His re-creating hand an oblation to His mercy as well as to His goodness, to His pardoning as well as to His bountiful love. We may, therefore, give a final definition of humility as the grateful acknowledgment to God of all we are and have, and as the sacrifice and surrender of our whole being to God, that He may reform it to perfection by His goodness.

Although the beginning of humility prepares the way for charity, perfect humility is the fruit of perfect charity. The more we love God the less we value ourselves. The nearer we approach to God the more sensible grows the truth that we have no foundation in ourselves. We then understand the Psalmist's words : " The Lord is my firmament, my refuge, and my deliverer ".* Finding no foundation but the being of God on which to rest, the soul seeks to enter into His power and to fill her treasury from His good. When, therefore, God touches the soul with His good, she denies herself, repudiates her own will, and surrenders herself to the gracious will of God, and that will becomes her own. And as

* *Psalm* xvii. 3.

the will of God is not only free, but is the very freedom, the spirit of servile fear is taken away, and in its place is given the adoption as of a Son of God and of a joint-heir with Christ, whereby that soul is exalted in God and humbled to nothing in herself, is emptied of herself, and filled with divine gifts. Thus the highest freedom blends with the lowest humility. He who is truly humble, truly empty of himself, is a vessel of election to God, full to overflowing with His benedictions. He has only to ask to receive still more. He is the child of all the beatitudes, poor in spirit, meek of heart, hungering and thirsting after justice.

When humility finds nothing in herself to rest upon, she finds her true centre, and that centre is God. But where the soul requires external persuasion to be humble, she is still much engaged with those phantoms of sense and imagination which she blindly mistakes for herself. But when filled with the life of God we cannot help being humble. The soul then sees two abysses—the abyss of her nothing in the abyss of God. This caused St. Paul to glory in his infirmity that the power of Christ might dwell in him, and so to denude himself of all things, surrendering them to their Divine Giver, that he was able to say: "I live, now not I, but Christ lives in me ".* This humility knows nothing of her own virtue; what humility knows of herself is her own abasement, emptiness, and unworthiness in the sight of God. Yet this true humility brings great peace and joy, because what we vacate of ourselves is filled with the charity of God, and our love of God extends to all that God loves, which puts us in harmony with all good of every kind ; so that, what we once loved in a natural way to please ourselves, we now love in a divine way, from partaking of the love with which God loves all things. Being in our true position and just point of view, we see all things in a purer light ; and as our sight is uncoloured by self-love, we see them justly and from God's point of view. For the humble soul alone has got the divine as well as the human measure of things.

* *Galatians* ii. 20.

LECTURE V.

ON THE GROUNDS OF HUMILITY.

"I know, O Lord, that Thy judgments are equity; and in Thy truth Thou hast humbled me."—PSALM cxviii. 75.

BECAUSE Humility is accused by Pride of acting the part of Vice in lowering the dignity of man, in degrading him from his worth and bringing him under a mean and timid superstition, our next duty will be to show that this virtue belongs to the dignity of truth and the nobility of justice. The fumes that ascend from the animal senses to the mind and the enchantments that are worked by self-love in the imagination obscure the vision of truth. But like the rod of Aaron, there is a divine power in humility to break the spell, restore us to sober sense, and bring back the perception of truth. Instead of lowering man from his true dignity, this virtue dissolves the theatrical allusions of mock dignity; instead of debasing his worth, humility discovers where his true worth lies, and dispels the fictitious charms of false greatness. The first office of humility is to put up with no deception, but to find out the truth respecting ourselves. When the truth is found, the second office of humility is to do justice to the discovery, and to be severe in repressing what is false and unjust in the estimate we have taken of ourselves. But we can only take this just measure of ourselves in the light of God's truth and by the rule of His justice; and this caused the Psalmist to say: "I know, O Lord, that Thy judgments are equity; and in Thy truth Thou hast humbled me".

The true dignity of man is very great: too great for anything but humility to know, for humility is the price of that knowledge. But when a man looks for that dignity where it is not to be found, and refuses to look where it is to be found, he gets himself entangled in delusions and falsehoods that disgrace him, and in his ignorance he invests his immortal soul in an unfitting robe of parti-coloured pretensions that will not suffer the light to go through them ; and missing his true greatness, he dishonours his soul and becomes little and contemptible in the sight of God. The true dignity of man is in his spiritual nature, in the image of God formed in that nature, and in the capacity of his soul for eternal good. This is the beginning of his dignity. The advancement of his dignity is in receiving the eternal truth from God that he may live in its light, and in the hope and charity that draw him out of himself, out of his own contracted limits, into the sphere of divine things. But the altitude of his dignity is in his final end, in that God who is the object of his existence and the fountain of all his good and happiness. The true dignity of man is therefore infinitely more in God than in himself, and can only be reached in perfection when he is united with God. Meanwhile it is his duty, and ought to be his ambition, to follow the truth revealed by God wherever it may lead him, and to begin with the knowledge of himself. This will bring him on the grounds of humility, and from those grounds he will hear the voice of Eternal Justice.

The first ground of humility is our creation from nothing. We are of a short time; our beginning was feeble, as became our origin, and nothing was the womb of us all. Whence are we? From the creative will of God. What are we? An existence dependent on the will of God. Whither are we going? Onwards, ever onwards, the body to the dust, the soul to the judgment-seat of God. God is the one, absolute, perfect Being; we are but existences, the products of His will, dependent on Him for all we are and have ; and all this great scene about us that fills our senses is of less value than the last soul that was created and born into this world ; for the soul is for God, but this visible universe for the service and probation of the soul. God has promised us an eternal existence, and that promise He will fulfil, but this increases instead of lessening our dependence on God. We are not only dependent on God for our existence, but for all the conditions of our existence. His will is His love, so that in love He created us, and in love He upholds us by the word of His power. The voice of the Eternal Word to St. Catherine of Sienna is a voice to every intelligent creature : " Knowest thou what thou art and art

not, and who I am? If thou knowest these two things thou shalt
be blessed. Thou art who art not, and I am who am. If thou
hast this knowledge in thy soul, the enemy can never deceive
thee, and thou shalt escape all his snares; thou wilt never do
anything against My commandments, and wilt obtain every grace,
every truth, and every enlightenment." *

Having no being of our own, none but what we receive from
God, none but what we hold of His provident goodness, we have
no ground for pride, none for self-glorification. "If any man
think himself to be something," says St. Paul, "whereas he is
nothing, he deceiveth himself." † What we are we are of God,
but nothing of ourselves. The root of our existence is not in
ourselves but in the will of God, and to this fundamental truth
we may apply the words of the Apostle: "If thou boastest, thou
bearest not the root, but the root thee". ‡ As humility is just,
and gives to God the things that come from God; and as pride
is unjust, and gives to one's self the things that come from God;
as, too, the creation of man is the glory of God, and not his own
glory; it is evident, as the Scripture says, that "pride was not
made for man". Once allow the fact of our creation, and it
must evidently follow that humility is the most creaturely of virtues, and pride the most uncreaturely of vices.

The second ground of humility is in our intellectual light.
That light makes us reasonable creatures. In that light we see
the first principles of truth, order, and justice; it is the foundation of our mind and of our conscience. Man is variable and
changeable, and one man differs from another; but the light of
truth and justice shines one and the same to all, and the chief
difference between one man and another is in the degree of his
communion with that light. But the light of reason is implanted
in our soul at her creation, and is made ours through the exercise
of our understanding and will. Yet the origin of that light is
from God, which caused the Psalmist to say: "The light of Thy
countenance is signed upon us, O Lord". § And he again says
to God: "With Thee is the fountain of life, and in Thy light
we shall see light". || And to show that the light of truth is also
the light of justice, he says in the next Psalm: "He will bring

* *Vita di S. Caterina da Siena del Beato Raimondo,* c. x.
† *Galatians* vi. 3.   ‡ *Romans* xi. 18.
§ *Psalm* iv. 7. || *Psalm* xxxv. 10.

forth thy justice as the light, and thy judgment as the noonday ".*
Often in the Sacred Scriptures is the light of God called "the
light of justice," although this is much more applicable to the light
of grace than to that of nature.

In the sublime opening of St. John's Gospel we are taught the
true origin of the light which shines into our mind and conscience : "In the beginning was the Word, and the Word was
with God, and the Word was God. The same was in the beginning with God. All things were made by Him, and without Him
was made nothing that was made. In Him was life, and the life
was the light of men : and the light shineth in darkness, and the
darkness did not comprehend it. . . That was the true light,
which enlighteneth every man that cometh into this world." †
The Word of God is the Substantial Light, the Original Reason,
from whom all men receive the light of reason in a way that is
obscure to them until the revelation of God makes it more clear.
The darkness into which that light shines is a darkness owing to
sin, which cannot see the cause of light, or the Divine Fountain
from which it comes to the mind. The light is there, but the
mental eye is turned from the Giver of the light, and the light
itself is obscured by the gross shadows of the sensual man. Let
him turn to God, receive the faith, and purge his sight, and he
will know the Divine Author of his light : "Blessed are the clean
of heart, for they shall see God ". ‡ The lovers of this world
come not to the light, to know the Author of their light, but
they who love the Word of God Incarnate know that He is not
only their light, but "the light of the world". § For He enlighteneth every man that cometh into the world with the light of
reason if not with the light of faith. Alas ! that so many should
prefer their own darkness to the Author of their light.

But our souls are the subjects of the light of God, and were that
light to cease from shining into our soul, we should be reduced to
mental and moral darkness. Yet if there is one thing of which a
man boasts and on which he prides himself, it is on the light of
his reason, as if it flowed from his own fountain, and had not its
origin in God. If there is anything which, instead of treating
with reverence, man abuses, as if it were of his own creation and
dominion to make and unmake at will, it is the light that shines

* *Psalm* xxxvi. 6.　　† *S. John* i. 1-9.
‡ *S. Matthew* v. 8.　　§ *S. John* viii. 12.

from God unto his mind, and shines to bring him to the knowledge of God, of His truth, and of His justice. But the root of these abuses is pride, which refuses to be subject to the light of God, whilst humility is the virtue that corrects this pride, and restores us to our true position as the obedient subjects of truth and justice. Wherefore both truth and justice compel us to conclude, that as humility is the most creaturely of virtues, and pride the most uncreaturely of vices, humility is also the most intellectual of virtues, and pride the most unintellectual of vices. What have the proud done that has not led to error and folly; and what have the humble done that has not led to truth and wisdom?

The third ground of humility is in our dependence on the providence of God. If we separate ourselves in thought from all that is not our self, we shall begin to understand what we are. We shall see that if we were detached from that wonderful system of provisions which God adapts to every requirement of our mind, heart, and body, we should perish instantly. From the heavens above, from the earth below, from persons and things far and near that serve our needs and desires, we find ourselves the subjects of God's divine providence. He created them, He rules them, He directs them to our help in their times and seasons. The sun gives us light and warmth, the air gives the body its vital energy, the earth renders us support and nourishment, the living creatures in every element supply us with food and clothing. God Himself gives us light of mind, the whole visible creation is our teacher, as also are our brethren. Beyond these vast provisions for our service is the ruling action of God, "reaching from end to end mightily, and disposing all things sweetly".* Separate the products of your own will from the products of the will of God, and you will understand how at every step and turn you depend in a thousand ways on the providence of God. Then may you put to yourself St. Paul's question: "What hast thou that thou hast not received; and if thou hast received, why dost thou glory as if thou hadst not received?"†

This wonderful providence with which God embraces us, and on which we so absolutely depend, makes us know what needy and perishing creatures we should be were we left to ourselves. The evidence is everywhere about us that were not God to uphold and to foster His creature with countless provisions, that creature

* *Wisdom* viii. 1.   † *1 Corinthians* iv. 7.

must return to nothingness. Look at the many things upon which our life in this world depends : a very little change in the position of any one of them would cause the dissolution of our body and send our soul into the world of spirits. Our life with all its conditions is in the hand of God.

The constant, manifold, and loving service of God to His rational creatures is amazing ; but when we turn to the recipients of this loving care and inexhaustible bounty, and see how scanty is the return of gratitude, or even of recognition, we may learn to what a state of mental and moral degradation the great mass of human nature is reduced. But this excessive humiliation of human nature is not humility. · The humble see all things in the hand of God ; they greatly revere His loving providence, and are greatly dependent on His goodness. Wherefore, receive, repay, beware. Receive the bounties of God from His hand with humility ; repay His goodness with thanksgiving ; beware of ingratitude.

The fourth ground of humility is our sins, whereby we have deformed and denaturalised our nature, ungraced ourselves before God, and incurred His reprobation. If the creature has cause to be humble, how far greater cause has the sinful creature ! The innocent creature is in a low estate by nature, but the sinner has descended to one incomparably lower by the conduct of His will. The creature is from nothing, but the sinner deserves to return to nothing ; yet the mercy of God comes in, and in justice to His eternal plans He upholds His fallen creature in existence. As the sinner has not answered the end of his being, but failed from it by his own act and choice, on his own part he has forfeited the right to that being ; but for profound reasons of mercy that dwell in the divine counsels, God does not accept the forfeit. The rational creature wants nothing belonging to his nature, and so long as he is innocent his nature is perfect, and only demands fidelity to the loving grace of God to bring him to the glorious end and happiness prepared for him ; but the sinner is a creature disordered, deformed, and defiled, who has deprived himself of the very first form of perfection that belongs to his nature. The creature is the work of God ; the sinner is his own work. God forms the creature ; man makes the sinner.

The imperfection of the innocent creature is neither an imperfection of nature, of constitution, or of due conditions ; but as

8*

that creature is the subject of God, and God Himself is the divine object of that creature, he can never come to completion until his whole nature is subject to God and in perfect union with Him. But the grievous sinner has renounced God as the supreme object of his will and desire, has put pride in the place of obedience, has thereby corrupted his nature, has made that crooked and perverse which God created just and right, has deformed all that God made beautiful in him, and made that guilty and impure which God made innocent and good.   He stands condemned by his conscience, in which the justice of God spoke to his heart, to which he has done violence.   The mercy of God may visit him, and if he discard his pride, and, repenting, avow his degraded condition and great need of the divine mercy, that Infinite Mercy may restore him to justice, and even to the friendship of God ; but the history of his fall can never be effaced, because it is the history of the unspeakable patience and condescension of God, and an everlasting ground for the gratitude and love of the pardoned sinner. But never can he recover the first bright bloom of that innocence in which he was created ; he will carry for ever upon him the ineffaceable signs of a creature made for God, lost to God, and, through the most wonderful condescension of the Divine Goodness, restored to God ; for we are redeemed in the blood of Jesus Christ and are justified by His grace.   We receive in baptism the innocence of Christ, and that innocence is more beautiful and precious than the innocence of Adam ; but the loss of that original innocence can never be forgotten, for this would be to forget the wonderful work of our redemption.   Even our actual sins, however grievous, may be blotted out in the blood of Christ, if we humble ourselves and repent, and our injustice be rectified to perfect justice by the all-powerful grace of Christ.   We may even obtain through greater humility a greater sanctity than was destined for the state of innocence, and consequently a greater glory, as the saints have done ; but never can this be less than true, that every soul of man has received the mercy of God, and that every faithful man has been raised by God, not only from his state of nature, but from a state of death and sin.

We are all the subjects of the Divine Mercy.   We are therefore subject to God, not only as His creatures, not only as the objects of His providential care, not only as illuminated by Him in our reason, but we are also the subjects of His mercy and redeeming grace. The unfathomable depths of injustice and degradation from which His mercy and grace have raised us ought therefore to be the measure of the depth of our humility, if we truly know what we are of ourselves, and what God has made us by His goodness. The pride that brought us into those depths of sin and degradation, and so near to nothing, is the most miserable and debasing caricature of just thought and good sense ; and nothing can rescue us from its absurd and malicious folly but that honest virtue of humility which Jesus Christ has brought into the world.

The sin in which we were born, and by which we became aliens from God, is a deep ground for humility, even after it is effaced, and we carry its consequences in our body and in our weakened powers. But what of those sins that we have ourselves committed after our regeneration to faith and justice ? What of this new league with the devil and his works, that we had so solemnly renounced ? What of this new abandonment of light, conscience, and God ? We have gone down into a much lower degradation than that of original sin, in which our own will never acted, and have fallen from a greater height, for the grace of Christ is greater than the grace of Adam. Why were we raised from sin to justice, from death to life, from communion with evil to communion with God, if only to fall into greater evil ? Oh, the weakness of man and the unbounded mercy of God ! Of what have we to be proud ? What have we of our own that ought not to humble us ? If neither our condition of dependent creatures, nor our mental dependence on the light of God, nor our absolute dependence on the will of His providence, nor our first deliverance from sin and death, nor the dependence of our heart on the Divine Grace for peace and happiness, are curbs sufficient on the elation of our self-love, or checks strong enough to stay our insane tendency to return to evil ; surely, surely, the sins whereby we have so far unchristianized our Christian life ought to make us humble, and to fill us with the conviction that without a profound subjection to the strengthening power of God we can never be safe.

Whether we think of their enormity or their abominable folly, our sins are our deepest ground for humiliation and shame. Their enormity is seen in breaking down the eternal order of law and justice, in preferring the creature to the Creator, and choosing a paltry amount of apparent good before the Supreme and Eternal Good. This is why God, who loves every nature He has created, hates the sinfulness that dishonours His work. "The Most High hateth sinners," * and saith, "They who despise Me shall be despised ".† The abominable folly of our sins is seen in their suicidal self-destructiveness, and in the gloomy delight taken in a fleeting joy that is at strife with all the good that is within us, and that puts an end to our spiritual life and peace. Justly have the Scriptures called this folly an abomination : " The way of the wicked is an abomination to the Lord ";‡ and even "the victims of the wicked are abominable ".§

If we are not humbled to the dust by our part in these truths, we are not yet cured of our pride. God grant that it may not have passed from an inflamed to an indurated condition, or even into gangrene, in which case it will call for the severe knife of incision. Humbling remedies alone can cure this vital disease. Blindness and spiritual insensibility begin the disorder, and develop the evil to its mortal malignancy. But the disease is in the will, and cannot be healed without the will ; and God is infinitely patient with our abominable folly, because He will not injure the freedom of the will.

Listen to the words in which St. Augustine points to the root in our weak nature of all our sin and all our misery : " The devil could never have caught man in open sin, doing what God forbade him to do, if he had not first begun by delighting in himself. This brought him to delight in the words, ' Ye shall be as gods,' ‖ which would have been better realized had they adhered to the Supreme Principle of all things, instead of trying by pride to exist upon themselves as a principle. The more they thirst in their self-love to be sufficient for themselves, the less they are, because they fall from Him who is all-sufficient for them. The evil whereby a man delights in himself as though he were his own light turns him from that light, the delight in which makes him to be light. But this evil begins in secret before it appears openly ; for it is truly written that ' pride goes before destruction, and the spirit is lifted up before a fall '.¶ Secret ruin is completed before open ruin, though the soul may not think it to be ruin. Who thinks that his self-exaltation is ruin ? Yet by this failure the Most High is abandoned. And who sees not the ruin after God's commandment has been openly transgressed? God therefore

---

* *Ecclesiasticus* xii. 3   † 1 *Kings* ii. 30.   ‡ *Proverbs* xv. 9.
§ *Proverbs* xv. 8.   ‖ *Genesis* iii. 5.   ¶ *Proverbs* xvi. 18.

gave an open prohibition, that it might be impossible to justify its violation. And I venture to say that it is sometimes useful for the proud man to fall into some open and manifold sin, that as he has fallen already through inward delight in himself, he may begin to be displeased with himself. Peter was in a much healthier state when he wept in his displeasure with himself than when he gave way to presumption through delight in himself. And the Psalmist prays to God, ' Fill their faces with ignominy, that they may seek thy name, O God'.* That is, that they may delight to seek Thy name, who before delighted in their own."†

The wise and experienced Saint is not advocating the usefulness of sin, but of its manifestation to the sinner. What he would have us to understand is this : that all sin originates from internal elation or pride, and acts from the pleasure to be found in that self-elation ; but this delight within one's self is so secret and self-binding, that the elation of pride often corrupts the soul, and separates her from God without the evil being seen or realized ; so that there is pleasure where there ought to be great displeasure. Then, says the Saint, with great truth, it may sometimes be useful that the internal evil should manifest itself in an external and open fall, that the soul may be thoroughly humbled and brought to shame, and so find out the evil disposition within that has caused the outward sin. What a revelation of human infirmity is this ! and what a ground for humility and fear of ourselves ! Owing to the neglect of cultivating humility, the ferment of evil elation is often so hidden from ourselves that our eye can only be opened by some visible and disgraceful fall, that at last awakens us to displeasure with one's self.

The fifth ground of humility is in the weakness, ignorance, and concupiscence that we have inherited from original sin, and have increased by our actual sins. On our moral weakness we spoke in the last lecture as of a chief ground of humility, whilst explaining St. Bernard's definition of humility ; but our corporal weakness has an enormous influence in causing our moral weakness.

We speak not of weakness of health, but of weakness from loss of order and subjection to the soul. There is nothing more humiliating to our life than that we carry about with us in our earthly frame the testimony of our sin, and the testimony that God resists the proud ; and carry it in a body that is proud without intelli-

---

* *Psalm* lxxxii. 17. † S. August., *De Civitate Dei*, lib. xiv., c. 13.

gence—in a body that is disordered in its members, on fire with concupiscence, rebellious againit the spirit, and lusting against the law of God.   This sensual body. with an unruly flame in its nerves and blood, drags the spirit down to partake of its blind egotism, and stimulates the unguarded will to an inordinate, ungenerous, debasing self-love, that develops into the elation of pride.   For this is the ordinary generation of evil : concupiscence stimulates self-love, self-love joins with concupiscence in stimulating the soul with elation, elation swells the imagination with images of our self-importance that obscure the light of truth and act delusively upon the will ; the will thus excited and deceived accepts evil for good.   Hence the vast importance of watching the first movements of elation, and of being humble in the truth that we may be sensible of the first movements of pride.

This concupiscence is the inordinate appetite produced by the disordered senses and powers.   "Every man is tempted," says St. James, "by his own concupiscence, being drawn and allured. Then when concupiscence hath conceived, it bringeth forth sin."*   St. Paul calls this concupiscence "the will of the flesh," † which, he says, "is not subject to God, nor can it be". ‡ To the three concupiscences enumerated by St. John all the rest are reducible.   These are sensual concupiscence, curiosity, and pride : "The concupiscence of the flesh, the concupiscence of the eyes, and the pride of life ".§   Of these, the one that is the least considered, but should be the most, because of its immense influence on the other concupiscences, is the cupidity of curiosity. Of all cupidities it is the most destructive of innocence.   It awakens the senses to unknown evils, sets the imagination at work upon them, and enkindles the flame of desire to taste and try the unknown.   From our first parents to their last descendants, that curiosity which St. John calls the concupiscence of the eyes has acted keenly on our mental faculties as well as on the imagination, producing a thirst to obtain the sensible experience of what is forbidden ; and, what is worse, the very prohibition provokes curiosity.   Let any one examine what has passed in his soul when he has been for some time inwardly drawn by a strong temptation towards evil, and he will be surprised to find how large has been the influence of curiosity.   Nor is this concupiscence of curiosity

---

* *S. James* i. 14, 15.   † *Ephesians* ii. 3.
‡ *Romans* viii. 7.   § 1 *S. John* ii. 16.

limited to the senses; it acts with most subtle influence upon the pride of life, especially in what regards strange doctrines of error, heresy, and infidelity, all which St. Paul, with his inspired insight, has not hesitated to connect with the concupiscence of the flesh, by reason of its attraction for the imagination. In these days the perils of curiosity are immensely increased, not only because of the unguarded manners of social life, but because the cupidity of curiosity is fed by the purveyors of every kind of information, good and bad, as well as by the professed entertainers of the imagination, who write with little regard for innocence and purity. The habitual indulgence of curiosity, like the habitual indulgence of pride, is very apt to grow, until we are unconscious of being possessed by a passion so weakening to our moral strength.

The three concupiscences are the more blinding when they are morosely kept working within than when they are manifested externally, and thus become more visible. Every one knows something of the blinding effects of sensuality and pride; but only the pure-hearted can see and understand how sensuality brutalizes the soul, and pride associates us with the spirit of darkness, and not only falsifies the soul, but puts her in a point of view to see all things in a wrong light. But that cupidity of curiosity which so much deranges the soul is not to be confounded with the just desire of knowledge, and of being the enlightened subjects of the calm truth as it is in God. Evil curiosity is a passion that serves our evil appetites and concupiscences. The just desire of knowledge looks straightforward to truth; cupidity has a backward glance to the interests of selfishness.

Ignorance of God and ourselves is the great sign that we have least cared about what most concerns us. We are born in ignorance, and receive the rudiments of knowledge with reluctance; when we reach a greater knowledge of God and ourselves, it is only through labour of mind and heart, with the help of self-denial, for our sensual nature works against the light and grace of God. Our sins, again, burn up the nerves of the soul, break the spiritual bones of the mind, and darken the light of the heart. The visible world, with its glorious show, was made to lead our mind to God, but through the predominance of sensuality over mind it takes us away from God. We know not by any experience what it is to be born innocent and free, and to have the light of God as the open sun of the soul. We know not what it is to have a body at all times obedient and responsive to the soul, and a soul at all times responsive to God. The remedy for this painful and defective condition of our life is hard to nature, for there is no other than mortification and self-denial; yet the world denies and refuses the remedy, because where there is question of freeing the spirit by denying inferior things and ascending to things superior, the spirit of the world is not only ignorant but cowardly. Even those who have the light of better things too often pursue the worse.

These undeniable features of the weak side of human nature are most humiliating, but they are chiefly humiliating when they do not make us humble, as in the nature of things they ought to do; and not only ought they to humble us, but to show us the prodigious power of that divine grace of humility which is able to free the soul, and keep her free, from such a complication of snares and entanglements.

The sixth ground of humility is in the open perils and hidden snares with which we are surrounded. St. John did not express himself lightly or without inspiration when he declared that "the whole world is seated in the wicked one";* that is to say, it is seated within the power of the evil one. The Apostle is speaking of the heathen world, but it is unhappily an undeniable fact that a great part of what once was Christendom has returned to the thoughts, manners, and corruptions of the heathen world. Through a social atmosphere beflecked and begrimed with the contagious influences of cupidity, sensuality, vanity, and pride, the devout Christian must walk his way to God. Error in all its forms, unbelief in all its modes and varieties, move in their motley shapes through nearly every grade of life, with the apparent unconsciousness that truth is one and comes from God. The widespread evil of modern life is the amazing indifference to the well-being of the soul. The energies of the soul are thrown outwards, where they are absorbed in restless activity upon material interests, upon the pursuit of natural and secular knowledge, and upon abstract speculations. An intense activity outside the soul pursues its many ways in the name of progress, although the object or ultimate aim of that progress is neither thought of nor spoken. But it is

---

* 1 S. *John* v. 19. Such is the sense of the Greek and the Vulgate. Our own version puts " in wickedness ".

chiefly a progress, not to, but from the soul, not to, but from God; and it mainly consists in making and expending money, in political and social rivalries, in licence under the name of freedom, in hiving the results of natural science, discovery, and art, in the enjoyment of literature and the world's news, in the pursuit of pleasure, in everything that begins and ends in this world; whilst the interests of the soul and her sublime relations with God, with His eternal truth and infinite good, are either made of but secondary interest, or are held in indifference, or are locked in a deadly paralysis.

The self-sufficiency of the heathen times has consequently returned as a sort of practical philosophy, supplanting the sense of dependence on God. The self-reliance that springs from the notion of self-sufficiency is a species of self-worship as grotesque as it is contrary to the truth of things. It practically ignores the intervention of God in the affairs of His creatures. But where the divine law of the virtues is made to give way to the humanly invented law of self-sufficiency, still beset with the three concupiscences, the divine virtues disappear, and the natural virtues, as in the heathen times, are left to work upon the unsubstantial basis of pride. Pride, with a gloss of politeness, takes the place of humility; a cluster of human opinions, of the vague and hazy kind, become the substitute of faith; and the laws of modesty and purity are exchanged for manners and fashions that lead to boldness and licence.

The literature of the world is the reflection of the world. It has become so aggressive on the Christian mind that one scarcely knows which of its books or periodicals to open in which there may not be some open or covered assault upon the truths of faith, some attack upon the foundations of religion, or some insidious invasions upon the purity of moral principles; whilst not unfrequently there is an advocacy, direct or indirect, of one or more of the three concupiscences. Here the faithful soul has to guard against the cupidity of curiosity, or she is thrown into danger without defence. A grave statement of evil is one thing; a seductive painting of certain evils is altogether another. The first is calmly addressed to the calm intelligence; the second is an allurement to the excitable imagination, through which it stains and corrupts the soul. Again, the spirit of the world is pride and the love of novelty, whilst the spirit of the Christian is humility and the love of those eternal things that are unchangeable, yet always new and always wonderful, and the newer and more wonderful the nearer we approach to them. But the pride of the world is contagious, and the love of novelty is an incessant distraction and a continual diversion from the better things.

Such are some of the open perils that surround the earnest Christian, and against which he must guard his walks and ways. Where evil is everywhere, it falls upon us like dust from the air, and calls for constant purification. It is a great humiliation to live in such an atmosphere, but a much greater to be exposed to its infection. Yet what are we by nature but of this common mass of sinful humanity? We have contributed of our own to the common evil, and this is our greatest humiliation before God; and where we have been preserved we have nothing to boast of, because this is not from anything better in ourselves, but of the infinite mercy of God. And this gives us a great and special ground for humbling ourselves the more in His presence, that we may be safe under His divine protection.

Besides these open perils there are the hidden snares of the evil one, who secretes himself behind our concupiscences to do his hidden work. This is the significant sense of St. John when he says that the world with its concupiscences is "seated in the wicked one". Of these hidden perils we have treated fully in the first lecture; what we have here to note is the ground for humility that we have in being surrounded and beset by those spirits of evil, from whose insidious temptations humility alone can save us. For the works of pride can only be encountered by humility; and as the humble soul is under the protection of the Most High God, the weapons of pride cannot prevail against her. Hence the Apostle warns the Christian flock of Ephesus to arm their souls with faith and justice, that they may "extinguish the fiery darts of the most wicked one".*

The seventh ground of humility is in the special odiousness and deformity of pride. We are assured on divine authority that pride was not made for man. We have unhappily made it for ourselves. It is the disease of devils, and has made them monsters of iniquity and misery, and we have contracted the life-devouring leprosy from them. It is the vice of all vices, the sin of all sins. A shrewd writer has observed that men have a natural

* *Ephesians* vi. 16.

curiosity for monsters, but that pride is a monster that is too
familiar and too much akin to us to be stared at as a curiosity.
Our unhappy familiarity with the vice prevents us from realizing
its monstrous deformity and excessive ugliness. What can be so
humiliating as to be the subject of a vice that perverts and blinds
our spiritual nature to its centre? Even to men, when it appears
externally in other men, pride is both odious and ridiculous;
and what must it be, seen in all its interior deformity, before God
and His angels? It is only when seen in the light of humility
that we begin to understand how it eats into and undermines
all truthfulness, honesty, and justice. No cancer can eat its way
more destructively into the soundness of the body than pride eats
consumingly into the health of the soul. The very best gifts fall
under its deadly influence, and feed its voracious appetite.
Like the cancer, it works inwardly, and corrupts the circulation of
the spiritual life. Pride is the one and only enemy of God, the
malignant root and virulence of the vices, the consumer of the
virtues, the falsification of the man. Pride is the lying spirit
that sacrifices good to evil, and even invents the semblances of
good out of evil to augment the evil sacrifice, making the man
who sacrifices the good things of God to his own lust of self-
exaltation contemptuously false and radically unjust. Pride
affects independence and self-sufficiency, and that in contradiction to all the facts in Heaven, on earth, and in the nature of the
man, all proving with one voice that without innumerable depen-
dences and providences he must perish, soul and body. Thus
pride is the most ungrateful and cruel of vices—ungrateful to
God and cruel to one's self.

Beyond every other vice, pride is in direct opposition to the
order, reason, and truth of things, and withstands the whole
reason of humility. We see, then, why God hates pride above
all other evils; why His chief punishments fall on pride; and
why it penally blinds the mind to truth, and of its own malignancy corrupts the soul with injustice. Pride turns all things
from God; humility turns all things to God. Pride is the
radical disease of the soul; humility the radical health of the
soul. There is no neutral ground between these two; and one
of the greatest grounds of humility is the escape which it gives us
from the most detestable vice of pride.

The eighth ground of humility is in the consideration of what this virtue does for us.   It is the essential foundation of all Christian faith and charity, and consequently the foundation of our salvation.   It is impossible to imagine a Christian without humility, or a perfect Christian without profound humility.   For the very notion of Christianity is founded in humility, as the very notion of infidelity is founded in pride.   It opens the soul to the truth of Christ, and the heart to the grace of Christ.   Christ chose it for all strength, and taught it for all strength.   What is pride but utter weakness and moral dissolution?   Yet what pride can be healed except through the humility of the Son of God?   What light can reach us from Heaven, or what charity can quicken the soul unless humility prepare the way for it?   "You can make no road to the truth," says St. Augustine, "but the one constructed by Him who knows, as God, how feeble are our steps.   This road is, in the first place, humility; in the second place, humility; and in the third place, humility.   For although other precepts are given us, unless humility go before the good we do, and accompany that good, and follow after that good; unless humility is before us that we may see it, and is brought to us that we may cleave to it, and is laid upon us that we may be kept within due bounds; whilst we are rejoicing in the good we do, pride will wrench it altogether from our hands." *

We have hitherto considered but those grounds of humility which are in our human nature or that environ us in this world; but the ninth ground of humility is first and supreme, and that ground is the knowledge of God and His divine perfections.   The knowledge of God is either acquired or infused.   Acquired knowledge is obtained with the help of divine grace by study and meditation.   When we reflect on God, as He is the Supreme Majesty, Infinite Goodness, and Almighty Power, we feel our own littleness, weakness, and vileness.   When we look to Him as the Divine Holiness and Purity, we become conscious of our sordidness and uncleanness.   When we meditate on Him as the One, Infinite, Unchangeable Truth, we learn to know our extreme ignorance and inconstancy.   When we open our souls to God as the Bountiful Giver of all that we stand in need of, we find ourselves but as poor and needy mendicants before His generous throne.   When we draw nearer to Him as to the Supreme Object of our life and desire, we find ourselves to be nothing without His presence and

---

* S. August., *Epist.* 118 *ad Dioscurum.*

His love, nothing of ourselves, but everything in Him. For what are we without the light that proceeds from Him and the charity that flows from Him ? The God of unbounded excellence, dignity, and glory grows upon our subject soul, diminishing her to her true proportions, and discovering to her wondering heart that without Him she is reduced to nothing. Then the soul finds that to herself she is nothing indeed, whilst God is all things to her ; and that what she can best do for herself is to subject herself to God with all the reverence and veneration of which she is capable, and to depend wholly on His sovereign will.

Infused knowledge comes when God draws near to a soul, and gives her some wonderful manifestation of His majesty and divine perfections. Suddenly the vision comes ; brief is its stay, quickly it departs, doing more in that moment than ages of study and meditation could accomplish. The soul is struck with stupour and amazement at the glorious revelation, and shrinks into her own littleness, fully conscious of her weakness and nothingness. Or perhaps that soul is divinely enlightened in her contemplation to behold the most sweet and wonderful affluence of God as it descends upon His intelligent creatures, and her inward eye is opened to look upon His inestimable benefits as they flow in streams into souls to convert them or to sanctify them ; and this causes her affections to melt and flow like wax in fire, and to merge her love and gratitude into the abyss of the Divine Goodness. At such a moment the soul cannot but enter into her own nothingness, especially as she is stricken with the sense of her ingratitude, and with the unfaithfulness and thanklessness of so many other souls, who, like herself, have been the unworthy recipients of great and generous mercies. This and the like infused knowledge can never be obtained by study, meditation, or any effort or labour ; it is given by God where He chooses, and given to the clean of heart, who fervently persist in prayer and in self-denial, and who unceasingly lift up their minds and hearts to divine things. We read in the lives of many saints and holy persons how they were thus favoured with divine illustrations, to the immense increase of their humility, although God often conducts the holiest souls by paths more obscure all the days of their mortal pilgrimage.

As it is the nature of the Divine Goodness to communicate and impart of His goodness when He finds a soul capable of such grace and illumination without its being injurious to humility, and where it will be helpful to that delicate virtue; when that soul is eager to accept the Divine Wisdom, He infuses a light that opens a view of the divine perfections that entrance the soul whilst it strikes her with the sense of her own vileness and unworthiness in a greater or less degree, according to the divine will and her own disposition.   But the more the soul is humbled and abased, the more she exalts and praises God, as we find recorded in those dialogues between God and the soul, so full of wonder at the divine goodness and condescension, and so profound in humility and self-abjection, which some of the saints have left us.*

The tenth ground of humility, most wonderful of all, is the secure rest provided for the soul in the unspeakable benefits of our Divine Redeemer.   It had been of little use to be born, had we not been redeemed.   By the infinite mercy of the Most High God, through the humiliation of His Son, we have been purchased from death, snatched from the evil one, and restored to the inheritance of that beatitude for which we were created.   Lost to God in the first prevarication, and lost anew by every grievous sin we have committed, each time we have been pardoned has been to us as a new redemption; for we have been called to repentance through the mercy, grace, and blood of our Lord Jesus Christ, who has taken our sins into His atonement, paid their price, blotted them out, and reconciled us to His Father.   He has paid for them with His humiliations, His griefs, and His tears; with His prayers, His stripes, His wounds, and innumerable sufferings; with His unspeakable humility, with His obedience to death on the Cross.   We are therefore the purchased servants of Christ, for which reason we bear His name, and by every law of justice we ought to be the humble servants of our humble Redeemer.

"Behold, O Christian soul," exclaims St. Anselm, "behold the power of thy salvation! Behold the cause of thy liberty! Behold the price of thy redemption! Thou wast a captive, and in this way Christ purchased thee; thou wast a bondsman, and in this way He set thee free; thou wast an exile, and He brought thee home; thou wast lost, and art restored; thou wast dead, and art brought to life.   Feed thy heart on this, drink thou of this, when thy mouth receives the body and blood of thy Redeemer, for by

* See Thanner, *Vallis Humilitatis,* c. xviii.

this alone wilt thou abide in Christ and Christ in thee, and in thy future life thy joy shall be full. But as Thou didst suffer death, O Lord, to give me life, can I enjoy liberty at the cost of Thy bonds? Can I enjoy my salvation at the price of Thy griefs? Can I glory in a life obtained by Thy death? Ought I to rejoice in Thy sufferings, or take pleasure in the cruelties that made Thee suffer? Had thine enemies not been cruel, Thou wouldst not have suffered; and hadst Thou not suffered, I should not have had all these good things. If I grieve over their dire cruelty, let me grieve the more over my sins, that brought Thee under them; for had there never been the cruel pride of cruel sins, Thou wouldst never have been subjected to their cruelty.

"How shall I rejoice over all the good that had never been but for these cruelties? Yet their wickedness could not have prevailed hadst Thou not allowed it to prevail. Thou wouldst not have suffered hadst Thou not devoutly willed to suffer. Whilst, then, I detest their cruelty, and the cruelty of my sins that brought Thee to these sufferings, let me enter into them with compassion by imitating Thy labours and death. With the humility of gratitude let me love Thy devout will, and so safely exult in the good things Thou hast bestowed on me. O poor little creature! Leave their cruelty to the judgment of God, and think of the benefits thou owest to thy Saviour. Think on what thou wast, and what thou art; think on Him who has done all this for thee, and on what thou owest Him. Look on thy great needs, and on His goodness. Understand what gratitude thou owest Him, and how thou oughtest to love Him. Thou wast in darkness, and in a slippery condition on the decline to hell. An immense weight, as of lead, was on thy neck to weigh thee down; an insufferable burden pressed with its load upon thee; and invisible enemies drove thee onwards. So wast thou, not even knowing it; for so thou wast conceived, so born into the world. Whither wast thou going then? The remembrance of it is a terror; the thought of what thou wast makes thee tremble.

"O good Lord Jesus! I was in that condition, and thought of nothing else, when Thou didst suddenly shine upon me like the sun, and showedst me what I was. Thou didst cast off the leaden weight that bore me down, and all the burden that oppressed me, and didst drive away the evil spirits that forced me on, setting Thyself against them for my sake. Thou didst call me by a new name received from Thee, and didst lift up my face from the evil on which it was bent, that I might look on Thee.   And Thou saidst: Have confidence in Me: I have redeemed thee, and have given My soul for thine.   If thou cleave to Me, thou shalt escape the evil out of which I have raised thee, and shalt not fall into the abyss from which I have delivered thee.   And I will lead thee to My kingdom, and make thee the heir of God, and a joint-heir with Myself.   From that time, O Lord, thou didst take me under Thy protection, that nothing might hurt me against Thy will. And lo! when I adhered not to Thee, as Thou didst advise, Thou didst not suffer me to fall into the pit, but didst wait for my return to Thee ; and Thou didst what Thou hadst promised.   Yet not only did I not follow Thee, but I committed many sins ; and Thou didst wait for me, and didst all according to Thy promise.

"Consider, my soul, and let all that is within thee understand, how thy substance is due to thy Lord.   Assuredly, O Lord, I owe my whole self to thee in humility and love, because Thou hast made me.   I owe my whole self to Thee again, because Thou hast redeemed me.   I owe my whole self to Thee once more for all Thou hast given me and promised me.   And I owe an infinitely greater love to Thee than to myself, because Thou art infinitely greater than I am, for whom Thou hast given Thyself, and to whom Thou hast promised Thyself." *

The eleventh ground of humility is in our distance in this vale of suffering and tears from the Supreme Object of our soul, and the risks we run in the meanwhile from our infirmities ; for although God is not far from each one of us, we are still far from the possession and security of the pure vision of Him.   And if we humbly descend into ourselves, we shall find too much reason for this delay.   We shall find that we are still far from what our conscience demands of us ; still far from what the inspirations of grace require of us ; still far from the perfect form of the virtues set before us.   There is much, very much, in our self-examination to humble us, not to speak of those hidden defects and weaknesses that faintly loom, or scarcely loom to us out of the secret recesses of the soul.   Yet "nothing defiled can enter Heaven". †   There is still much to renounce, much to place on the altar of sacrifice, much not yet made subject to God, much to rectify by the labours of humility, much to purify in the fire of

* S. Anselm., *Meditatio* 11ᵃ *de Redemptione Humana.*   † *Apocalypse* xxi. 27.

charity. Meanwhile we have to fear and humble ourselves for the evil inclinations that we know, and for the infirmities still concealed from us to pray : "From my secret sins cleanse me, O Lord ".* The completely humble and pure soul can alone see God. So long as we are not completely humble, there is always a certain amount of insincerity and hypocrisy mixed with our virtues ; and even after a certain degree of interior progress, it is difficult, as St. Gregory observes, to keep our exterior actions straight. The tongue, for example, is slippery enough to betray the incontinence of the heart, and even our gifts and virtues are so apt to endanger humility, that God in His loving care of us often leaves to us a certain amount of weakness to keep us from conceit, and only removes it in the end. St. Paul did not account himself perfect, but forgot the things behind him, and stretched forward to lay hold of the perfect things before him. Upon which St. Jerome remarks, that there are various forms of perfection, so that we cannot know that we are perfect. Where we have yet to lay hold, we have not yet received, and have not yet become perfect from imperfection. What we really know or ought to know is, that we are still imperfect, and to confess our imperfection. This, concludes St. Jerome, is the true wisdom of man, to be sensible of his imperfection, and to know that even the perfection of the just, whilst still in the body, is imperfection. † This wisdom is not a dry knowledge of the head, but a sensible and affective knowledge of the heart, with a profound contempt of one's self.

The twelfth foundation of humility is the holy fear of the judgments of God. For unless we shelter ourselves well in the humility of Christ, do penance, and use the world as though we used it not, we are not safe. Unless, again, a humble dependence on God be the foundation of our life and the love of God be our ruling affection, we know not in what state God will find us in the hour when we shall pass from this world.

There is another and a very broad ground of humility, open to all those who have the interests of God at heart, and who love Him truly. They cannot but be deeply humbled in witnessing the alienation of such a great number of souls from God, whereby His majesty is dishonoured, and the Divine Sacrifice of redemption is made of no effect ; whereby the world is filled with maledictions, and the most merciful designs of God are brought to

* *Psalm* xviii. 13. † S. Hieron., *Dialog. adversus Pelagianos*, lib. i., c. 14.

nothing.   If a whole family may be brought to humiliation through the evil conduct and ingratitude of one of its members, how ought we, who are members of the human family, to be humbled before God, when we see our Heavenly Father insulted and dishonoured by so many of His children !   Whilst, therefore, we have first to give up ourselves to God in all humility and self-surrender, because this is just and due on many grounds, and especially because this humility is of the very essence of love, we cannot be true lovers of God without mourning, and grieving, and humbling ourselves for the iniquities, many and grievous, of our brethren of the same human family.   Abraham humbled himself down to dust and ashes to entreat mercy for the five criminal cities ; Moses offered himself a sacrifice to God in an ecstasy of grief and humiliation for the great sin of his people ; St. Paul was ready to become an anathema if so his brethren might be saved.

The humble have great solicitude for the honour of God, and the more advanced they are in light the more they humble themselves before God for every sin whereby He is dishonoured.   This is the humility of the saints, always ready to see the first cause of sin in themselves, always ready to offer themselves as victims to suffer for all the sin whereby God is offended.   It is this humility of the servants of God that saves the world from destruction. Few are they who understand how much of the lightning of divine indignation is turned away from the sinful world, or how much of the grace of repentance is brought down from Heaven upon obdurate hearts, through the supplications of even one truly humble soul.   Such power has humility with God.   Not to speak of Abraham, David, and the Prophets, the lives of the saints are the undying records of this wonderful power.   When there is no more humility in the world, there can be no more charity, and therefore no more salvation.   What remains of human nature will be but waste and refuse that has failed of its end, and the destruction of the world must follow.

But whilst there is humility on the earth God has His cause in the world and Christ His power.   A few truly humble souls will change the hearts of many, and will prevent much sin, if only by their prayers ; for "God hath had regard to the prayer of the humble, and hath not despised their petition".*   They are the

* *Psalm* ci. 18.

hinges upon which God turns the providence of His mercy, the lightning conductors that avert many a storm of divine anger from their erring brethren. All power is with God and with His humble servants, who are never far from His mercy-seat, whose sole solicitude is for His honour and glory, and who often move Him to the exercise of mercy, though themselves unconscious how much blessing they bring down far and wide around them. Having no power of their own and always confessing this truth, God exercises His power through them, knowing that they will not take it to themselves. The whole history of sanctity shows that the great things of God for the salvation of mankind have been worked through humble souls, who have never claimed the work as their own, or dreamed that it could be their own. The salvation of all that are saved is first and chiefly from the humility of the Son of God, and secondly through the instrumentality of His humble ones, whose number is the safety of the world.

LECTURE VI.

ON HUMILITY TOWARDS OUR NEIGHBOUR.

"Be ye subject to every human creature for God's sake."—1 St. Peter ii. 13.

IF the virtue of humility is so often misunderstood when directly exercised towards God, the same virtue is liable to still greater misconception when exercised towards our neighbour. All error in the human mind arises either from confounding together things in their nature or properties distinct, or from separating things that are in their nature or intention one. We have a marked example of this second mode of error in the vague and confused notions that prevail with respect to the nature and intention of that humility which is exercised towards our neighbour, and it will be the object of this lecture to disentangle the confusion.

God is the ultimate object of all humility whatsoever. For the invariable office of this virtue is to subject the soul to God, either in Himself or in His gifts; or in His word, power, or authority, wherever He may place them. Every living image of God, every communication of His grace, every delegation of His authority, represents His beneficent action, and brings before our mind its Divine Author and Giver. Wheresoever or in whomsoever God is represented—in His likeness, His gifts, or His authority—there the faithful heart passes beyond what represents Him to give honour and reverence to the Sovereign Majesty from whose generosity every good and perfect gift descends. There also the light of faith enables us to perceive the immense inferiority of our nature in comparison with His divine gifts.

There are two things to be considered in every man, and these two things have to be well and carefully distinguished from each other: what the man is of himself, and what he is by the super-added gifts of God. What is of the man's self belongs to defect and failure; what is of God belongs to justice, to salvation, and to perfection. God declared through the Prophet Osee: "Destruction is thy own, O Israel: thy help is only in me". * Humility looks to the reverence that subjects man to God on account of his inferiority and dependence; and for the same reason every man ought to subject what is purely his own to what is of God, whether that which is of God is in himself or in another. For the order of justice demands that what is inferior and defective be subject to what is superior and perfect, and consequently every man ought to subject what is of his own weak nature to the more excellent things that come from God, wherever they may be. The law of humility, therefore, which belongs to justice, requires that we should submit our nature to the gifts of God with reverence, whether those gifts are in ourselves, or are, or are presumed to be, in other men.

This is the principle of humility in its exercise towards our neighbour: it is not a reverence given to human nature, but to the gifts of God within that nature, and to whatever represents His divine superiority over human nature. The man ought to bend his own nature in act or in spirit, in the sense of his inferiority, to what descends from God. This inward spirit of humility, born of grace, inspires those habits of mutual respect and reverence so conspicuous in the manners of a truly Catholic population, although persons without faith can see nothing beyond an unusual politeness. But where the gift of faith is neglected or lost, the man of nature reappears in all his rudeness, and self-assertion takes the place of humility.

It by no means follows that we are to submit what is of God in us to what is of nature in another person; that would not be humility, but a preposterous perversity. Nor does humility require, as St. Thomas remarks, that any one should submit the gifts of God in himself to what appear to be the gifts of God in another, since those who partake of those gifts are not without knowing that they have received them. St. Paul tells the Corinthians: "We have not received the spirit of the world, but the spirit which is of God, that we may know the things that are given us of God ".† We may therefore prefer the gifts we have ourselves received to

* *Osee* xiii. 9. † *I Corinthians* ii. 12.

those another may have appeared to receive, and this without any prejudice to humility.* So far from this, we have all the greater reason to be humble on account of the greater gift received, especially when conscious that we have not corresponded to those great favours as we might have done. The exceptional gifts of St. Paul were made by him the ground of the greatest humility. "By the grace of God," he said, "I am what I am; and His grace in me hath not been void, but I have laboured more abundantly than all they; yet not I, but the grace of God with me."† When the humble St. Francis was asked how he could consistently with truth call himself the greatest sinner in the world, he replied: "Had God given to even the most wicked man the graces and favours He has bestowed on me, he would have been far better and more grateful. Nor do I doubt but that, were God to withdraw His hand, I should do things more absurd and monstrous than all other men, and be the greatest of sinners. For this reason I judge myself to be the most ungrateful of mortals."‡ This spirit is common to the saints, who, having a profounder intuition into their nature by reason of their greater light and humility, were always ready to place themselves in their own judgment among the last and lowest of God's intellectual creatures.

But though we are not called upon by humility to submit the gifts of God in ourselves to the gifts of God in another, this does not stand in the way of our submitting to the judgment of the Church respecting those gifts, whether they be or be not of God, because the Church acts from the authority of God, and the Holy Spirit presiding in the Church judges of all things. Hence St. Paul says that "the spirits of the prophets are subject to the prophets".§ And St. John gives us this admonition: "Believe not every spirit, but try the spirits if they be of God, because many false prophets are gone out into the world". ||

This, then, is the great principle of humility, that we ought to revere and to subject ourselves most profoundly to God in all things; and to revere what is of God in every one, yet not with the same reverence with which we are subject to God. Whilst, therefore, we exercise humility in the sense explained to all our neighbours, always presuming some good gift of God in them,

---

* S. Thomas, *Sum.* ii. 2, q. 161, a. 3. † 1 *Corinthians* xv. 10.
‡ *Chronicle of S. Francis*, lib. i., pt. 1, c. 68.
§ 1 *Corinthians* xiv. 32. || 1 *S. John* iv. 1.

and certain that they bear the image of God and are capable of divine gifts, we are not to exhibit that worship to them which is only due to God. But where the gifts of God are great and manifest, a greater internal reverence and veneration is due, although its external manifestation is not always expedient. And where the authority of God is represented, there a special reverence and submission is due, proportioned to the nature and extent of that authority; not to the man as he is man, but to the power and dignity of that authority which is inseparable from the man. In giving the rule of humility towards our neighbour, St. Peter first gives the general law as applicable to all, and then the special law as applicable to authority. " Be ye subject, therefore," he says, "to every human creature for God's sake ; " and then he adds, "Whether to the king as excelling, or to governors as sent by Him for the punishment of evil-doers and for the praise of the good; for so is the will of God ".* As St. Peter gives the law of subjection to the temporal powers, St. Paul gives the law of subjection to the spiritual powers. " Obey your prelates," he says, "and be subject to them. For they watch as being to render an account of your souls : that they may do this with joy, and not with grief. For this is not expedient for you." † Here is a double precept, the one of subjection, the other of obedience to the pastoral care.

But with respect to the general law of humility to our neighbour, this should be well noted, and we give it in the language of the prince of theologians. " Humility requires not of any one that he subject what is purely his own to what in another person is purely his own, but only that he subject what is his own to what is of God in another person. Still a man may account something to be good in his neighbour that he has not himself, or may find something evil in himself that is not in his neighbour, and on that account he may subject himself to another person." ‡ This exposition ought to remove many errors and prejudices, as it clearly shows that all humility is directed to God, either directly or in His gifts.

But the same humility forbids the unreasonableness of judging another man's soul. We can only act on what we know, and we always know much more of our own internal weaknesses and defects

* *1 S. Peter* ii. 13-15. † *Hebrews* xiii. 17.
‡ S. Thomas, *Sum.* ii. 2, q. 161, a. 3.

than we can know in the case of another person, we also know much more of our own inward lights and graces than we can know in the case of any other soul; we likewise know of our own interior, what we can never know of another's interior, how far the soul has been true or untrue to her interior gifts; we have therefore the proper grounds for judging our own soul, but we have not the proper evidence to enable us to judge the soul of another person. Even the Church judges not of things purely internal, but only of things openly manifested. "It should be understood," observes St. Augustine, "that there is no one that may not have some good, however hidden, that you have not. There is strength in this thought to beat down pride, and to bring it under. Do not imagine because you have good gifts which are visible, that another may not have good gifts in secret; possibly theirs may be better than yours, though you do not see them. The Apostle had no notion of flattering or deceiving when he said: 'Let nothing be done through contention, neither by vainglory: but in humility let each esteem others better than themselves'.* This way of thinking subdues pride, stimulates charity, and makes the bearing of one another's burdens an equable and a willing duty. No one can judge another unless he be known in the intimacy of friendship, where defects are borne with for the sake of the good gifts that hold friends together and give them consolation." †

Reflections like these are of great value where there is question of comparing one soul with another, for we have no key to open any one's soul but our own, and the only key to open that is humility. We see the external but not the internal facts of others' souls, and we have our Lord's command: "Judge not, and you shall not be judged. For with what judgment you judge, you shall be judged: and with what measure you mete, it shall be measured to you again." ‡ But there is higher ground for the prohibition than our incapacity to judge; it is a usurpation of the divine judgment. "Who art thou," asks St. Paul, "that judgest another man's servant? To his own master he standeth or falleth." § Excepting the judges He has appointed to judge in His name, God alone is the judge of souls. Our brethren are invaluable to us for the exercise of humility, but to judge them is to reveal our own pride.

* *Philippians* ii. 3.   † S. August., *De Diversis Questionibus*, lxxxiii., q. 71.
    ‡ *S. Matthew* vii. 1, 2.   § *Romans* xiv. 4.

Every great Christian virtue has its hundredfold reward in this life, but few persons perhaps reflect on the beauty of the reward we receive for humility to our neighbour. This humility opens the soul to all the good that God has planted in other souls, and by subjecting our nature in reverence to that good, it brings us under the influence of a vast amount of good beyond what we ourselves possess. We are always partaking of that which we love and reverence, and the humility which is ever opening the door to charity brings us into communion, and consequently to the sharing of all the good gifts of God that we see, or may presume to find in those around us. Little do the proud, the censorious, and the self-sufficient understand from how much good they isolate themselves from want of humility to their neighbours. Those are the happy, sunshiny souls that are open to see all the good influences of God around them, and that receive into themselves the reflection of the divine good which God has given to other souls. This is one of the great privileges of a truly religious society where humility and charity are the dominant virtues, that each soul is always receiving a beautiful and powerful influence from all the rest of the community. The very spectacle gives a light to the words of our Lord, that "where two or three are gathered together in My name, there I am in the midst of them ".*

Undoubtedly there is a natural humility, or rather modesty of mind and heart, that even in the light and order of nature prefers what is superior to what is inferior, and what is enlightened to what is unenlightened, although that inferiority be one's own. There is also a certain natural humility of well-conditioned minds, often conspicuous in men of genius, who, by humbling their intelligence to the facts and truths of nature, make great discoveries from the loving observation of what appear to be small and humble things, such as prouder minds disdain or never notice. What is genius but the carrying of the child's simplicity, intuition, and susceptibility into the matured man? Such a mind was Newton's, who compared himself to a child gathering shells on the shore, whilst the great ocean of truth lay all undiscovered before him. Such was Linnæus the botanist, who, on first seeing an English common covered with the golden bloom of the gorse flower, uncovered his head, went on his knees, and thanked God for the

* *S. Matthew* xviii. 20.

beautiful spectacle. Such was Fergusson the astronomer, who, when a shepherd boy tending his nightly flock, with his untutored strings of beads mapped out the heavens. Such also was Cross the electrician, who, though he could rail against priestcraft, was yet so modest, that, to use his own expression, he verily believed that the door of Heaven was guarded by the angel of humility. But when God is in nowise contemplated in His creatures, this is natural modesty rather than true humility, because humility implies the subjection of the mind and heart to God, either in Himself or in His communicated gifts.

Let us ascend higher to take a larger view of the action of God in providing us with such ample means for the exercise of a virtue so essential to our peace and happiness. St. Isaac the Syrian, Bishop of Ninive, gives us this excellent advice: "Read those books," he says, "and with frequent assiduity, that wise men have written on the works of God's providence. They will enlarge and strengthen your mind, and enable you to understand how God acts towards His creatures, and how He regulates them. The contemplation of God's providence in action is a great help to humility of soul." * This is one of the great features of the Holy Scriptures, that they everywhere exhibit the movements of God among the affairs of men, and reveal His divine action and that of His angels to mortal sight. So when saints and holy men write history, they see God everywhere, not only providing and blessing, but instructing, correcting, humbling, and trying the souls of men. They never forget that "whom God loveth He chastiseth,"† to make them humble or to keep them humble. It is one of the great distinctions between the servants of God and the votaries of the world, that whilst the first see all things overruled by the hand of God, the last see nothing but the powers of nature. The first look to the Sovereign Cause in all things, whilst the last see but secondary causes which they mistake for the first, and, engaged with intermediate ends, they forget the final end.

It is the will of men acting apart from God, and preferring in their pride to see the evil rather than the good in their fellow-men, that so bitterly entangles this world of human nature. It is the myriads of self-wills, impelled each by its own self-love, that produce the knots, the ravels, and interminable complications that make this world such a wearying perplexity to thoughtful

---

* S. Isaac Syrien., *De Contemptu Mundi*. † *Hebrews* xii. 6.

minds devoid of the wisdom that descends from God. Even David was perplexed in his musings on these things until he remembered the judgments of God.

The tragedy of human life is not that strife of free-will with fate that the ignorant pagans imagined, but it arises from the collision of pride with the providence of humiliation, of self-will, destined always to defeat, against the will of God. There is such an enormous distance between what we are by nature and what God would have us to be by grace, that we may pass from misery to happiness; and the obstacles within us that hold us back or throw us the other way are of such a kind, tending to seek false instead of true greatness, in the exaltation of ourselves, and not in ascending to things greater than ourselves, that this alone shows what a great part humility must take in replacing us on the path that leads to God.

Happy are they who have eyes and light to see the exterior as well as the interior operations of God that bring us help and opportunities for the gaining of a humble spirit. The whole order of probation and the whole providence of humiliation are directed to the repression of pride and the subjugation of our hearts to God and to His gifts, whether imparted to us or to our brethren. Never will it be known until the day of judgment what a prodigious amount of external as well as internal help and provided occasion has been offered us to assist and even to provoke us to the exercise of humility; and never until that solemn day will it be known what an enormous provision of both external and internal help has been neglected or abused. This reflection alone is enough to humble us to the dust. But then it will be seen how the action of God moved supreme in its simplicity over all the complications and entanglements produced by the perversity of human wills, making all things work together for the good of His elect.

Pride is so great an evil, such a root of disorder, such a falsification of our nature, such an enemy of God, that nothing ought to be neglected that can contribute to its destruction; and humility is such a good, and such a cause of good, that nothing ought to be omitted that can help to its perfection. God has, therefore, given us not only interior helps, but many exterior ways to humility. When we have once the foundation of this virtue in ourselves, both the good and the evil in our neighbours will serve its growth.   To the good we see that God has given them we open our hearts with respect and reverence, revering God's goodness to them and receiving edification ; whilst the evils we cannot but see remind us of our own infirmities, which not only tend to humble us, unless we are like the Pharisee, but often bring us humiliations that we have only to transmute into humility.   Thus our social life is an exercising ground where we have ample means at our disposal for carrying on the conflict between our higher and lower nature. As our mortal senses have much to do with pride, and are, indeed, as St. Paul points out, the chief cause of our spiritual elation, it is of great importance that they should be brought into the service of humility; nothing can more effectually contribute to the rectifying of our nature.   It is one of the blinding results of pride to fancy that we may be completely humble before God in our interior without being externally humble to our neighbours ; but our soul is so accessible through our senses, and we are so inclined to be influenced for good or evil by other souls, that if we are not humble with them we shall be the contrary.   And however much the truly humble keep their interior gift a secret, if it exists in the soul, the spirit of humility can no more be withheld from our neighbours than the spirit of charity, not for ostentation, but from true interior reverence.

Our converse with our fellow-creatures is too often a comedy of vanity, vainglory, or pride.   For more characters are acted on the stage of the world than on the stage of the theatre.   It is more difficult to be simple before men than before God; yet even before God how much there is in many souls that come before Him which is far from simplicity and near to vanity.   For instance, when you wish to show the Eternal Majesty, who sees every fibre of your poor nature, what fine speeches you can make to Him in your prayers.   We are constantly managing our reputation with our neighbours either by fictitious presentations of one's self, or by suppression of one's true character, or by in some way or other being one thing to one's self and another to one's neighbour, playing the comedy of vanity in one way to one person and in another way to another.   Self-love moves us to act these parts, although the actor most commonly appears through the character.   The social life is, therefore, the difficult field for exercising the sincerity of humility; for it must never be forgotten that humility is the truth in sense and action; and if this be difficult, it is the great means of perfecting our interior humility before God. But unless we are truly humble towards our neighbour we are sure to act some vanity, although it wear the dress of politeness or even the costume of humility. But when this more difficult exercise of the virtue proceeds from true humility of heart, there goes from that heart a reverence towards the image of God and to His gifts in our neighbour, that, whilst directly given to him, is reflectively given to God Himself; and He, beholding the soul pursuing this lower path of humility, will be pleased with that soul, and will give her a share of the gifts that she venerates.

On higher grounds, but from the same virtue, we give honour and veneration to the angels and saints, the spiritual tabernacles of God's light and perfect gifts. We venerate those holy spirits in whom God dwells, who are the greatest works of His grace, and who are in the divine sanctuary of the beatific vision of God. We read the lives of those saints upon this earth with delight, how humble they were before God and man, what evil they resisted, what great works they did in the power of God, and how they were the servants of their fellow-men. This veneration of the spirits dwelling with God, this reliance on their prayers to support our supplications to the throne of mercy, this communion of saints, is a magnificent help to humility as well as to charity. The man who comes out of a solitary cell, where he has pined in lonely isolation, and weariness, and gloom, to breathe the free air and feel the reviving sun, to behold the wide prospect of earth and Heaven, and feel the good sympathy of affectionate friends, is an image of the soul delivered from the dark and narrow prison of her pride, to find herself free in her humility to commune open-hearted with all the good that is in Heaven and on earth.

Although the light that descends to us from God is the chief principle of our self-knowledge, the watching of our conduct towards our neighbours also helps us very much to know ourselves. That conduct, when examined, gives us many revelations of our real inward spirit, whether it show itself in vanity, in vainglory, in pride, in duplicity, in humility, or in charity. Thus our external conduct is a weather-glass that indicates the interior temper and condition of the soul. The words of St. John are as applicable to humility as to charity : "He that loveth not his brother, whom he seeth, how can he love God, whom he seeth not?"* Our brother is before us, visible to our eyes, present to our sympathies, and cannot be forgotten; we are compelled by his visible presence to have some kind of feeling towards him; and when we love him for God's sake we have the palpable proof that we love God. So if we are humble to our neighbour whom we see, which is more difficult, we have the sensible proof that we are humble before God. But if we fail in humility before our neighbour, we have the certain proof that it is not perfect before God; and if this failure shows itself in any serious degree to one who represents the authority of God, even the commonest exercise of that virtue must be wanting in the sight of God.

Humility of one to another has a mystery in it like that which belongs to obedience. We see one thing and subject our nature to another. What we see is a mortal like ourselves, what we reverence and obey is the gift of God in the one case, and the authority of God in the other. The charity of God inclines us to love all that God loves; the humility of Christ inclines us to humble ourselves to all men, as Christ humbled Himself to all men. For not only did the Son of God subject His human nature to God the Father without reserve, but to do all justice in doing His Father's will, He was subject both to the good and to the wicked. He says to His disciples : "You know that the princes of the world lord it over them; and they that are the greater exercise power over them. It shall not be so among you, but whosoever will be the greater among you, let him be your minister; and he that will be first among you shall be your servant. Even as the Son of man is not come to be served, but to serve, and to give His life a redemption for many."† This is the law of Christian humility; it belongs equally to those in authority and those in subjection, except that humility in authority is the most laborious, including as it does obedience to the law, and the service of the law as well as of those who are under the law, and the ministering to them of the good things of God according to prudence.

Another great provision, therefore, for the exercise of humility is the order of authority and obedience; for humility is the

---

*1 S. *John* iv. 20.   † S. *Matthew* xx. 25-28.

soul of obedience, as obedience is the expression of humility. Obedience subjects the will to the will of God, humility subjects the whole man to God. These are the two wings that balance the body of the virtues, whereby we ascend to the placing ourselves under the divine excellence and sovereignty of God. If either of these wings fail, both must fail, and the whole body will come to the ground. For, as St. Laurence Justinian observes: "Obedience and humility live with admirable accord in the mutual service of each other, so that you can never find humility without obedience, nor true Christian obedience without humility ".* This union was in its absolute perfection in Christ: " He humbled Himself, being made obedient unto death, even to the death of the cross ". † What the Son of God has so absolutely united in Himself, let no man put asunder.

This intimate connection of humility with obedience has been well explained by St. Augustine in treating of the first prevarication. " Evils," he says, " begin in secret, and then break into open disobedience. The evil will goes before the evil act. What begins this evil but pride ? For, 'pride is the beginning of all sin '. ‡ And what is pride but the appetite for false greatness ? This appetite for false greatness comes of the soul's deserting the true principle to which she should adhere, and from endeavouring to make a sort of first principle of herself. She does this through delighting too much in herself. She takes this excessive delight in herself after she has failed and fallen from that unchangeable good in which she ought to have more delight than in herself. But this defection is the act of the will; had the will but firmly persevered in the love of the Supreme Good, whereby the soul is enlightened to see and enkindled to love, she would not have turned from the Supreme Good to delight in herself, thus becoming chilled and darkened. Then Eve believed that the serpent spoke truth, and Adam preferred the will of his wife to the command of God, imagining it no more than a venial transgression to keep to the companion of his life even in sin. They transgressed not by eating what was forbidden until they became evil ; and the tree became evil, contrary to its nature, because their vicious wills made it evil. When the man failed, he ceased not altogether from being, but he was altogether changed from what he had been when

---

* S. Laurent. Justin., *De Humilitate*, c. xix.   † *Philippians* ii. 8.

‡ *Ecclesiasticus* x. 14.

he adhered to the Supreme Being, through his inclination to himself. For although to abandon God, to be in one's self, and to delight in one's self, is not to become absolutely nothing, yet it takes us back towards the nothingness from which we came, and is the reason why we turn from God and become a failure. For this reason the Holy Scriptures give the proud the expressive name of self-pleasers.

"It is excellent to lift up the heart to God, not to one's self, which is pride, but to God, which is obedience, and which belongs to the humble. There is something in humility that wonderfully lifts up the heart, and there is something in self-elation that brings down and debases the heart. And although it sounds like a contradiction that elation should bring us down and humility lift us up, yet it is the piety of humility that subjects us to our superior; and there is nothing higher than, nothing superior to, God, and in subjecting us to God humility must necessarily exalt us. On the other hand, the vicious exaltation of one's self, by the very fact of refusing subjection to God, must of necessity fall away from Him, than whom there is nothing higher, and so come to what is low and mean, fulfilling the sad words that are written: 'Whilst they were lifting themselves up, Thou hast cast them down'.* It is not said *after*, but *whilst* they were lifting up themselves, because in the very act of lifting themselves up they are cast down. For all this reason," concludes St. Augustine, "in this city of God from which we write, whilst serving in this world, humility is chiefly preached and chiefly commended by Christ her King, whilst the vice of self-exaltation domineers, as the Scriptures teach, in the devil, and works in opposition to this virtue. This great distinction separates the city of God from the city of the world, the society of the devout from the society of the profane, each with its own angels going before, the one in the love of God, the other in the love of self." †

Obedience belongs to justice, and is both a special and a general virtue. For God has not left us in the hands of our own counsel to do whatever we choose, but to act rationally and freely in choosing the wiser and the better things which are expressed in the will of God; for the will of God is perfect reason and justice. From this it follows that the first rule of an intelligent creature is to regulate his will upon the will of God. By obedience

---

* *Psalm* lxxii. 18.   † S. August., *De Civitate Dei*, lib. xiv., c. 13.

to the sovereign will of God we exchange our ignorance for the
divine wisdom, and accept the divine justice to make our own
will just, and all the virtues become the instruments of obedience.
Through obedience, therefore, we receive wisdom and understanding. Ecclesiasticus says: "If thou desire wisdom, keep justice,
and God will give her to thee ".* And he says again: "Great is
the power of God alone, and He is honoured by the humble.
Seek not the things that are too high for thee, and search not for
things that are above thy ability: but the things that God hath
commanded thee, think on them always." † And the Psalmist
says: "By thy commandments I have received understanding ".‡

As a special virtue obedience has for its object the precepts of
a superior. As the first rule of obedience is the will of God manifested in His commandments and prohibitions, the second rule
is to obey the precepts of our lawful superiors, who in the order
of their position represent an authority ordained by God. The
chief qualities of Christian obedience are reverence, promptness,
and prudent exactitude. Reverence is the element of humility
in obedience; promptness is the habitual vigour of the virtue that
shows the degree of its perfection; and prudent exactitude exe-
cutes the command in the full spirit and intention of the directing
authority according to the circumstances of the case. There is
no greater error than the vulgar notion that a life of obedience is
a life without freedom. What authority does is to mark out a
sphere of action; what obedience does is to fill up that sphere
with free intelligence and judgment. There are fifty ways in
which any precept may be executed in a loyal spirit, and it depends
upon the free intelligence and judgment of the person appointed
in which of those ways it shall be done. The will of every one is
strong and decisive, and consequently free, in proportion to the
degree in which they have been trained to prompt obedience.
This is an important truth, so little understood in this day of laxity,
that it will be well to examine it a moment.

Moral freedom is the power of bringing up the will to act with
promptitude and judgment in whatever direction it is wanted.
This is the one thing required in every virtue and duty. But the
habit of obedience trains the will to act with promptitude and
vigour; and as the one who exercises obedience is responsible

* *Ecclesiasticus* i. 33. † *Ecclesiasticus* iii. 22. ‡ *Psalm* cxviii. 104.
10*

for the judiciousness of his acts as well as for his spirit of obedience, this compels thought, and obliges the obedient one to act with the judgment of which he is capable, to be corrected when in error by a superior judgment. This promptitude of will and striving after judgment is wonderfully helped under obedience, because another will, strong and firm through authority, acts upon the weaker will, and helps it to exertion through the power and sanction of authority. Thus two wills are engaged in bringing one into exertion. And as the will in authority is wiser by position and experience than the will in obedience, the one improves the judgment of the other. When the weaker will—that of a child, for instance, under a parent, or of a pupil under a master—has obtained the power of acting promptly at the call of duty, that will has obtained freedom. Who are the strongest willed men in this nation? I suppose, as a class, we may point to our naval commanders. And why? Because from early youth, and through their course of advancement, they were trained and habituated to the promptest obedience. A strong will is a calm will, self-possessed as well as prompt and prudent. The license allowed to the young in these days, instead of promoting, is destructive of moral freedom.

Take it from another point of view. Our faculties are limited, and consequently work with most freedom and intelligence when their sphere of action is limited. Put a cannon-ball on a heap of loose powder; when fired, the action communicated to the ball will be trifling. Put the charge in a cannon, and the ball will go to its mark with prodigious force. What makes the difference? The limitation given to the action of this force. So is it in the moral order of obedience: authority circumscribes the sphere of action, and obedience fills up that sphere with free force and intelligence. Hence the strength of armies and the great works done by religious communities, and the weakness of mobs except for destruction.

The humility of spiritual creatures one towards another preserves the just and due order of things, and provides for the amenities of charity; it also preserves us from the offensive intrusions of pride. God has, therefore, largely provided for it in His divine economy. He has established that diversity of gifts whereby one is superior in one respect and another in another; and by this order of help in one and receiving of help in another, the members of the human corporation are mutually helpful and dependent, to their greater union. But besides this order of mutual help and mutual dependence, whereby the master depends on the servant as well as the servant on the master, and the employer on the workman as well as the workman on the employer, and those who have less gifts on those who have greater of the same kind, God has also ordained, for the perfecting of humility, authority in one and dependence in another, yet in such a manner that each one begins by subjection, and by the exercise of subjection is trained to the exercise of authority. But to him who has the light of Christian faith, this subjection rises in its motive to the authority of God placed in the creature; and he who holds authority finds but a more laborious obedience, for he is the servant of the law of God, and the servant of those under his authority, and is responsible to God for all his acts as a superior.

In the human race God has established three orders of authority—the parental, the religious, and the civil authority. Man is no sooner born than he finds himself under the parental authority, which has great beauty and security, especially in the Christian family, where it is known to emanate from God, and to represent His providence in the spiritual as well as in the temporal order. The young have their first training to humility in their loving submission to their parents.

In all times since the Fall God has delegated His religious authority to chosen men, thus providing for a more certain and definite subjection to Himself. This divine authority committed to mortal man, to teach, to minister to, and guide souls to Him, rests upon, and is a partaking of, the mystery of the Incarnation of the Eternal Word, as either promised or fulfilled. For the one and only religion whereby man is subjected to God, one in substance from the beginning, though developed and perfected with time, is no invention of man, but is imposed on him by God, and has its whole substance and foundation in the humanity of the Son of God, the Redeemer of man through His humility, and the Mediator between God and man. This ministry of the mysteries of God through men is a wonderful provision for quelling pride and helping us to humility. As pride is the radical disorder of man, and humility is its remedy; as pride is the one obstruction to the light and grace of God, and humility removes this obstruction; God has shown His most benignant and merciful consideration for our weakness in giving us a great visible and external help to assist us in obtaining His inward help for the overcoming of our pride and the bringing us to a humble temper; whilst the very necessity of submission to a visible authority, adverse as it is to our natural inclination, gives us a security for our inward subjection to God Himself.

Our Christian faith, whose light transforms everything, gives a divine motive even to our subjection to the civil authorities, and brings that subjection within the scope of Christian humility. This more exalted view of the legitimate ordinance of temporal authority has not escaped the mind of St. Paul. " Let every soul," he says, " be subject to the higher powers; for there is no power but from God, and those that are, are ordained of God. Therefore he that resisteth the power, resisteth the ordinance of God. . . . For he is God's minister to thee for good. But if thou do that which is evil, fear; for he beareth not the sword in vain, for he is God's minister; an avenger to execute wrath upon him that doth evil. Wherefore be subject of necessity, not only for wrath, but also for conscience' sake."*

All true obedience is founded in the spirit of reverence towards the authority to which we are subject, according to the quality and dignity of that authority. Thus obedience to parents rests on the reverence of piety; obedience to civil authority upon the reverence of honourable respect; obedience to religious authority upon the reverence of religion; and obedience to God upon devotion, which is the greatest act of religion. † And, like every other virtue, obedience is perfect in the degree in which it moves from humility and tends to charity, and in its own habits is perfect in proportion to its reverence of authority, its promptness to action, and its prudent exactitude in execution.

Here we must offer an instructive remark, made equally by St. Gregory and St. Thomas. As the object of obedience is not our own will but the will of a superior, which may be either written law or rule, or the spoken will of the superior—in short, the will of a superior however indicated—obedience is generally more perfect when it is not only cheerfully complied with, but where there is least of our own will, way, or inclination in it, and most of the will of the superior. The reason is, that such an obedience has

---

* *Romans* xiii. 1-5. † S. Thomas, *Sum.* ii. 2, q. 104, a. 3.

a greater renunciation of self-love and self-will, and calls for greater effort to overcome adverse inclinations and external difficulties. Whilst, on the other hand, when everything goes our own way, we may rather be inclined to look to our own will than to the precept for our motive. But this is to be understood as it outwardly appears; for God, who sees the heart, may find a devoted obedience to the will of the superior which is not less praiseworthy in one whose inclination goes with obedience than in another who has to overcome an adverse inclination.*

Humility and obedience are the two keys that open the soul to freedom. For humility opens the spirit of man to the liberating light and grace of God, and obedience opens the will to the wisdom and will of God. These two virtues are the grace of youth, the dignity of age, and the crown of those who happily depart from this life of probation to a better. Humility is the invisible spirit, and obedience the visible body of that self-renunciation which the Saviour of men and the nature of things demand of all who would live with God. Christian obedience cuts up the roots of evil to their centre, and humility removes them from the soul. They conquer us from spiritual death and are the heralds of our spiritual life. For, as the proverb says: "The obedient man shall speak victory".† What is that victory? St. Gregory will tell us: "Whilst we humbly subject ourselves to the voice of another, we conquer ourselves in our own heart".‡ Obedience removes the cause of sin and death, humility opens the way for the grace of reparation; for God gives His grace to the humble. How great is the virtue of humble obedience in the love of Christ! It has power to open Heaven and to close the gates of hell. Obedience is the tree of life producing the fruits of salvation, and it is planted in the ground of humility.

So rich is the divine economy in ordaining superiority and dependence, that the two are never wanting even in the same person; for every one who exercises superiority on the one side is subject on the other; and when we reach the highest authority in each order, the head of the state is bound to the constitution, the law, the counsels of the prudent, and the lights of conscience; whilst the head of the Church is subject to the divine constitution of the Church, to the doctrine and law of Christ, and, like all its

---

* S. Thomas, *Sum.* ii. 2, q. 104, a. 2 ad 3.
† *Proverbs* xxi. 28.   ‡ S. Greg. Mag., *Moral. in Job*, lib. xxxv., c. 14.

members, is personally subject to another in what concerns his conscience.

There is no humility so full of instruction as that which is perfected in authority. How rare yet how exquisite is that perfection! How abundant the resources that God puts in the way of Christian superiors for perfecting humility! I speak of superiors in every order of superiority, whether domestic, secular, ecclesiastical, or religious. The Sacred Scriptures everywhere exhibit authority in man as derived from God, as dependent on God, as responsible to God, and as only rightly exercised according to the law and will of God. The subject has but a single dependence; the superior is in a state of twofold dependence: on the law of his position and on the exigencies of his subjects, and must prudently conciliate the two. This he must do, not by his own sole light, but by the light of God and by the counsel of the wise and experienced. Hence to govern according to God is the most dependent of positions.

Well and wisely says the proverb that he who has never learnt to obey is never fit to govern; for superiority cannot be better expressed in a few words than as a humble but magnanimous obedience to the best lights of what is best to do and to direct under each circumstance as it arises. But this implies a thorough renunciation of one's own spirit to the spirit of duty, and that spirit is imbibed from the whole objective character of the law, work, and commonwealth over which the superior presides. The substance of Christian superiority is service—service to those who are subject, service to higher superiors, and service to God. The honour of superiority is the commendation and protection of authority: it is rendered to the superior because of the office. As all authority comes originally from God, the chief honour is referable to Him. Then the superior represents the dignity of the body as gathered in the head. Again, the old proverb is *Honor propter onus :* the honour is because of the burden. And Selden, in his learned book on the subject, shows that all titles of honour originally expressed the onerous responsibility of some office or service. Honour is a grace added to authority that gives it strength and reverence, but the true Christian superior will refer that honour to God.

Besides the usual honour paid to superiors, which in Christian souls is proportioned to their humility, there is a superabounding honour that is willingly given to those superiors who minister well, and do great or extraordinary services to their subjects. This singular honour is given to the special gift of the Spirit of God, who chooses that superior to be the instrument of special graces and favours, so that what is chiefly honoured is the singular communication of the Spirit of God. For it should always be remembered by superiors, and especially by those who are the instruments of God's goodness to souls, that the graces of which they are the channels are not the graces given for their personal sanctification, not the *gratiæ gratum facientes*, but the graces given them for others, the *gratiæ gratis datæ*. This distinction pervades the Sacred Scriptures, is strongly marked in the teaching of the Church, and is habitually felt by those who are humble in authority. Yet God chooses truly humble souls to be the channels of His greatest favours to men, and from their own light and sanctity great blessings are derived, in addition to those greater things for which God makes them His instruments. Then the humble are wise and clear-sighted, and are not inclined to mix the interests of self-love with their authority.

To one who is well founded in humility nothing can be more humbling than the exercise of authority. It discovers to him his weaknesses and limitations, and reveals to him his defects and shortcomings. This is especially the case where spiritual authority is concerned, because he has to deal with eternal interests, and the responsibility is tremendous. The light he seeks for others may turn to his own rebuke, and the simple and perfect who are under his care teach him many a silent lesson, whilst his froward and difficult subjects give him many a humiliation. The burden of responsibility makes him sensible of infirmity, and his failures reveal to Him his deficiencies and the great need he has of help from God. Undeserved praise strikes his soul with reproach. He will feel the need of humbling exercises; but these must be in secret, because he ought not so to lower himself externally as to injure his authority with the proud, the dull-hearted, or the weak; but whilst loved, feared, and reverenced as the superior and servant of all, in his silent spirit, as St. Augustine says, he must be at the feet of all.

No office demands greater humility to God and to men than the office of the preacher; for the preacher is the intermediator of truth between Christ and the souls He has redeemed. Like the Prophets, he has to put forth Christ, and not himself, and the man should disappear behind the voice of God. The true preacher is not a repeater of words, not a rhetorician, but a messenger of grace. His soul should be filled with the living Word of God and with the energy of grace ; the first obtained from study of the Holy Scriptures and the traditional wisdom of the Church, the second from prayer and meditation, that the Word within him may be filled with the life of grace. Such were the voices of the Prophets ; such, with more ardour, the voices of the Apostles ; such the preaching of the Saints. They were humble ; their spirits were subject to the Spirit of God, and the Holy Spirit spoke through the organ of their souls, and filled their voices with the grave music of truth, all vibrating with the energy of grace. St. Paul has told us the secret of his apostolic preaching, and has shown us how the power of God worked through the humility of the man. "We preach not ourselves, but Jesus Christ our Lord ; and ourselves your servants through Christ. For God, who commanded the light to shine out of darkness, hath shone in our hearts, to give the light of the glory of the knowledge of God in the face of Christ Jesus. But we have this treasure in earthly vessels, that the excellency may be of the power of God, and not of us." * The Apostle had no other notion of the preacher's office than to be the humble subject and the intelligent organ of the light and grace of the Holy Spirit. And although he had to encounter the pagan philosophies and the heathen mythologies as well as the incredulity of his brethren the Jews, his one subject was Jesus Christ ; for he knew that Jesus Christ is the one and only conqueror of every error and of every vice, and that the Holy Spirit is the spirit and the power of Jesus Christ.

The great Apostle has left for our instruction a yet more ample description of the humility of his preaching. "And I, brethren," he says, "when I came to you, came not in loftiness of speech or of wisdom, declaring unto you the testimony of Christ. For I judged not myself to know anything among you, but Jesus Christ, and Him crucified. And I was with you in weakness, and in fear, and in much trembling. And my speech and my preaching was not in the persuasive words of human wisdom, but in the showing forth of the spirit and power ; that your faith might not stand on the wisdom of men, but on the power of God."† It

* 2 Corinthians iv. 5-7. † 1 Corinthians ii. 1-5.

may be said that the Apostle was inspired, but his humility made him the fruitful subject of the divine inspiration, and every one will be nearer to the source of inspiration the more humbly he is subject to the light and grace of the Holy Spirit. For what gives the preacher power is the vibration of the light and grace of the Holy Spirit in his soul. There are a few words written by Roger Bacon, the celebrated friar of Oxford, addressed to Pope Clement IV. on this subject, which are worthy of grave reflection. "Words," he says, "have great power; and when they are uttered from profound thought, great desire, right intention, and strong belief, they have great virtue. When these four qualities unite, they forcibly move the substance of the rational soul, convey the virtue of the soul into the voice, and this virtue is received by the hearer. According as that soul is holy or sinful, of a good or evil will, will be the quality of power generated in the voice. Thus the quality of power in the soul is multiplied and imprinted, and incorporated in the voice that passes through the air, and is formed and figured in the listening soul, and is able to effect great changes." *

These words will help us to understand the type of the true preacher, such as God has given the Church in His saints. Humble must he be, that his soul may be open to the divine influences, and may not obstruct them. Humble, also, that he may have a clear discernment of what souls require. Humble again, that he may have that true love of souls which becomes the second inspiration of his preaching. His earnest charity gives earnest action to his mind and to his will, so that by right intention, great desire, profound thinking, and strong belief, the light and grace of God may vibrate in his soul, and reverberate in the souls of his hearers. Then may he make the greatest truths clear to the simplest souls endowed with faith. Of this capacity we have ample proof in the way in which children lay hold of the sublime truths of religion in the first lessons of the Catechism. Yet ordinarily he will speak to the requirements of his people.

On the other hand, due conditions are required in the souls of his hearers, of which the chief is humility of heart. For a sermon is a grace, and grace is given to the humble. The hearer is the disciple of the preacher, and the spirit of a disciple is that of humility and reverence. Humility opens the soul, pride shuts it up. The moment the hearer changes the posture of his soul from

* Fr. Roger Bacon, *Opus Tertium*, c. xxvi.

that of a disciple to that of a critic, he assumes superiority, ceases to learn, and ceases to profit. Even St. Paul had to rebuke his babbling critics among the Greeks, who in their vanity discussed the man instead of taking his inspired words to heart. Here comes in the great principle of humility to authority, that we submit what is of nature in ourselves to what is of God in another, with a reference of the final motive to God. The true mental posture of the hearer of the Word of God is to collect himself within himself, forgetting all around him, and applying to himself with awakened conscience the truth delivered to his soul. There are two communions in the Church of God : the communion of the word of Christ and the communion of the body of Christ. The communion of the word of Christ is through preaching and meditation of the Gospel; this is the spiritual communion with Christ as He is the eternal truth, whereby He purifies and enlarges the soul with His light, and prepares her for the substantial communion of His body and blood, which is the consummation of grace.

It is a divine rule in the providence of grace that God accomplishes His great spiritual works through weak instruments, made conscious of their weakness; and St. Paul gives the reason : "That no flesh should glory in His sight " : and " that, as it is written, He that glorieth may glory in the Lord ".* In making the instruments of His great works conscious of their weakness, He makes them truly humble, as He did His Apostles and saints, that they may put no obstacle of their own to the working of His grace and power through them ; and that the work of His power may be plainly seen to be the work of God, so that both he who is the channel of the work and they who are its objects may give the glory of the work to God.

In conclusion, you may wish to understand more clearly how it comes that holy and humble persons account themselves more vile and unworthy than other persons, even than those who may be open and manifest sinners. This humility is a scandal to the proud, but only to the proud and ignorant. Take St. Paul for example. He calls himself the chief of sinners, whom Jesus Christ came into this world to save ; and " the least of all the saints," and " the least of Apostles," and " unworthy to be an Apostle " ; although he admits that he has " laboured more abun-

* *1 Corinthians* i. 29-31.

dantly than all they". Does not humility spring from truth? How, then, are we to reconcile these convictions with the truth? Having a great light from God to see themselves, the saints see much more of themselves than of any one else, and so in accounting themselves vile through humility they injured not the truth. But, as St. Dorotheus observes, they often could not themselves understand by what way they had reached this sense and judgment of themselves.*

It must be first observed that the truth to us depends both on what we see and on what we do not see. It must be observed, in the second place, that what we do see depends for its amount upon the clearness and force of the light with which we see, and what we feel depends on the nearness to ourselves of what is felt. In the third place, it must be remembered that what is really vile in us is our native nothingness as opposed to God and His divine gifts, and our sinfulness as opposed to the divine purity; the knowledge of which is not obtained by comparison with man, but by comparison with God and with His pure gifts. The light thrown on a dunghill reveals its foulness by comparison with the purity of the light that shines upon it. Throw a robe of resplendent silk over a mean person clothed in dirty rags, and you make his vileness doubly vile. The humble soul is under the divine light, and sees far more of herself than she can see of any one else; and as she is also filled with the divine charity, she feels far more in her own case of what she would be without that charity than she can possibly feel with respect to any other person's soul. The more humble that soul is, the more she sees her natural weakness and defects, and the less she sees them in other persons, whom she does not judge, and whose interior can never be seen or felt by her like her own.

St. Gregory explains this by contrasting the habits of the humble with the habits of the proud. It is the habit of the proud to keep what is weak or evil in them and their ways out of their sight, but to keep the good they have, or imagine they have, in full view. For such a one looks to what is flattering and gratifying to himself, and to what he thinks will most commend him to other minds. It is also a habit of the proud to look keenly into other men's vices and defects, and to think but little of their virtues or good qualities, as being matters of little interest to their

* S. Dorotheus, *Disciplina* 2ª, c. 5.

pride. And as the proud are not free from envy, they are inclined to magnify the evil they see in others, and to lessen the good in them. It is also a habit of the proud man to claim more good than he has, and less evil than belongs to him; and as he ascribes more evil and less good to others than they have, he easily makes himself out to be of greater worth than they.

But humility takes the contrary way. It is the habit of the humble to forget the good they have done, or to make little of it, whilst thinking much of the good they ought to do. They keep before their eyes their sins and their natural weakness, and as they become more enlightened take a growing view of them and of the shame that belongs to them. It is also a habit of the humble not to look for the sins of other people, but when seen to forget them, and as far as they can to excuse them; whilst their good eyes are drawn to see what is good in others, and their good hearts to commend that good, and to take it as a sign of greater good within than outwardly appears. In consequence of these habits, the truly humble think less of themselves than they are, and better of others than they appear. This leads them to think less of themselves than of others, and to put themselves in their own estimation at the feet of all.* Moreover, the truly humble are not ignorant of what may be still reserved in the converting and sanctifying grace of God, whereby the very sinner to whom you prefer yourself may become better than you, and may go before you into the kingdom of God. Nor do you know but that this very day the change may come, whilst you know not what hidden weakness may bring you to a fall. In the hour of St. Paul's conversion Ananias was saying of him: "Lord, I have heard by many of this man how much evil he hath done to Thy saints in Jerusalem; and here he hath authority from the chief priests to bind all that invoke Thy name". And the Lord said to him: "Go thy way, for this man is to Me a vessel of election, to carry My name before the Gentiles, and kings, and the children of Israel. For I will show him how great things he must suffer for My name's sake." †

When a man suffers from some severe internal complaint, it comes far more home to his sensibilities than the greatest sufferings of other men, and to himself his sufferings are the greatest. So

---

* See S. Greg. Mag., *Moral. in Job*, lib. xxii., c. 15.

† *Acts* ix. 13-15. See De Ponte, *Dux Spiritualis*, Tract. iv., c. 5, § 3.

he who feels his own sins and infirmities feels them more deeply than he can feel the sins and weaknesses of other men; but he also feels them more deeply because he is keenly conscious of the many titles that should bring him to God, and is therefore more conscious of his own ingratitude; and he cannot but judge from this deeper sense and knowledge of himself that his sins are greater than theirs, and himself less worthy by nature than they.

St. Dorotheus will illustrate what has been said. Holy men, he tells us, the nearer they approach to God, and the more closely they adhere to Him, know all the more that they are sinners, and account themselves the more unworthy. I remember that whilst discoursing on this point of humility, a certain distinguished man from Gaza was present. But when he heard it said that one who is nearer to God finds himself more vile and sinful, he was utterly astonished, and asked how that could be; for he was ignorant and wished to learn. I then said to him: "Tell me, honoured sir, what position you hold in your own city". "A great one," he replied; "I am the chief man in my city." "But suppose you went to Cæsarea," I asked, "how would you stand there?" To this he replied: "I should be the last man in that city". "What, then, if you went as far as Antioch, who would you be there?" "I should be looked upon as little better than a rustic and half a pagan." "But what," I asked, "would you think of yourself in the imperial city of Constantinople?" "I should deem myself," he replied, "to be little better than a mendicant." Then I said to him: "So it is with holy men: the nearer they approach to God, the more vile they see themselves, and the more sinful. When Abraham deserved to see God, he called himself dust and ashes. When Isaias beheld the vision of God, he called himself a man of unclean lips. When Jeremias was visited by God, he said, 'I am a child'. But how this humility comes into the souls of mortals and is born in human hearts cannot be expressed or understood in words."[*]

But we are loitering in external views instead of entering into the humble heart to find the clear explanation. This humility is the effect of celestial light and the first fruit of contemplation. It comes with the power of a magnifying glass to bear upon our inward condition; so that when our sins are seen under this celestial light, and no one's but our own, and are seen in the root

[*] S. Dorotheus, *Disciplina* 3ª.

of evil derived from Adam as well as in our own native inclination to nothingness, we judge only from what we see in ourselves. For whilst we see into the depths of our own evil, we can only see the external acts of others, and not their internal malice. But this profound sense of our own vileness comes not from the industry of reasoning; it is an insight obtained through ardent affection. It comes of great knowledge and love of God, and from His divine gifts within us, in comparison with which we find ourselves to be altogether vile and unworthy. Experience also teaches us that the more we descend in self-abasement before God into the truth of our unworthiness, the more deeply does the charity of God enter into us, to purify our nature and to enkindle us with desire to belong wholly to Him, and in nothing to ourselves.

LECTURE VII.

HOW HUMILITY RESPONDS TO THE BENIGNITY OF GOD.

"Be ye therefore perfect, as also your Heavenly Father is perfect."—S. MATTHEW v. 48.

IT has been said that God has all the virtues except humility, not as we have them, but in the pre-eminent way of absolute perfection. God has not humility because He is absolutely perfect, is supreme over all, and all things are dependent on Him and subject to Him. How then do we receive the grace of humility from God? And as all the virtues are an imitation of God, in what respect do we imitate God in the virtue of humility? If there were not a power in this virtue that is altogether different from that defect of inferiority and corruption with which it has to combat in human nature, we should be unable to find any possible resemblance in it to the God whom it imitates. But in truth, although all the virtues imitate God, God Himself has not our virtues, but He is one infinite virtue and perfection. Our virtue is a struggle against frailty, a progress to better things, a triumph over weakness, and is perfected, as St. Paul says, amidst infirmity. It is the effort of good-will, helped by the grace of God, to bring us near to God.

We can never be like to God in His absolute being, might, and majesty, as He dwells in unapproachable light; but we should ever remember that, to use the words of St. Augustine, "God unspeakably transcends every similitude of Him in any creature whatsoever that comes near our sense or understanding".* We can only imitate God in what He is pleased to manifest and communicate to His creature. But what He manifests of Himself He condescendingly lowers to our powers of understanding;

* S. August., *Serm.* 118 *de Verb. Evangel. Joannis.*

what He communicates He lovingly diminishes to our capacity of receiving. Not then as in His glory He is, but as He makes Himself known to our thoughts and sensible to our affections, is He the object of our imitation. He has set an image of this truth in the heavens; the sun in his substance is both invisible and inaccessible to us, but he sends forth rays of light, warmth, and energy, which are tempered to our condition in the atmosphere through which they pass, and we thus know the sun and feel its influence. Our Lord said on the Mount: "I say to you, love your enemies; do good to them that hate you; and pray for them that persecute and calumniate you; that you may be the children of your Father who is in Heaven, who maketh His sun to rise upon the good and the bad, and raineth upon the just and the unjust. For if you love them that love you, what reward shall you have? Do not even the publicans this? And if you salute your brother only, what do you more? Do not also the heathens this? Be you therefore perfect, as also your Heavenly Father is perfect."* Here the actions of God towards man, His dealings with His creatures, are put before us for imitation. St. Paul uses the same argument: "Be ye kind one towards another, merciful, forgiving one another, even as God hath forgiven you in Christ. Be ye therefore imitators of God as most dear children, and walk in love, as Christ also hath loved us, and hath delivered Himself for us an oblation and sacrifice to God for an odour of sweetness."† Thus in proposing the conduct of God towards us for the object of our imitation, the Apostle follows his Divine Master: "Because it behoveth the children to be in all things resembling the Father".

But the reason why God lowers Himself in His manifestations to us is not on account of His defect, but on account of ours; and this very conduct belongs to the perfection of His goodness. This lowering of Himself to us is His divine condescension. It is an emptying, so to speak, of Himself, a certain vacating of His glory that He may communicate to our littleness what we are able to receive of His greatness, demanding humility for humility as well as love for love. There is no cause for humility in God; the ground of His condescension is in us. There is a humility that descends to what is inferior, which is incomparably greater than the humility which is subject to what is superior. A great preacher

* *S. Matthew* v. 44-48. † *Ephesians* iv. 32, v. 1, 2.

of our time arose amidst a vast audience of intellectual men in Paris, and thrilled them through with this astounding proposition : "God is the humblest of all beings".* This language is not new in the Church. St. Augustine says: "We are always aiming at great things, but to be truly great we must take hold of little things. Deign to be humble for your own sake at least, even as God, who was never humble for His own sake, condescended to be humble for your sake." †

God is not humble more than He is penitent of His acts, or wrathful, or inclines His ear to listen, or descends to behold the works of men, or to converse with them. These descriptions express not what He is or does, but they figure His communications with His creatures. He is not even good, mighty, or merciful, as we understand these words, but in a way that is infinitely beyond our comprehension. Our God is not this, but of such perfection as neither eye hath seen, nor ear heard, nor heart conceived. All His attributes are one simple perfection, and His whole being one pure and perfect action. He hath perfect society in His Three Persons, which are the interminable terms and unimaginable relations of His divine life, and the happy consummation of His unity.

If God has not the virtue of humility, or any virtue such as ours, but something infinitely more perfect, yet in Him is the type of humility as of all the virtues, and the fontal energy from which the power of all virtue is derived. What is humility when divested of its human accidents but the just and sincere estimate which any intelligent being takes of himself? What is it but the perfect accord of the mind and will with what that being truly is, and with the position in which that being stands towards every other being? It is the absence from that being of everything that is false, unjust, or inordinate, and consequently of all inordinate self-love. The essence of humility is unselfishness, and its action to reverence all that is superior or equal, and to descend in benignity to all that is inferior and in want.

Is not this the perfection of God? Man may aim at a like perfection; God alone possesses it. For is it not God alone who perfectly knows Himself, and most justly and truly estimates Himself for what He is? Is it not God alone who justly, truly,

---

* Lacordaire, *Conference* 21.
† S. August., *Serm.* 118 *de Verb. Evangel. Joannis.*

11 *

and perfectly loves Himself as He deserves to be loved? He loves not Himself covetously, enviously, or exclusively, or at the cost of that love which others desire of Him, or are capable of receiving from Him. His just and perfect love of Himself as the perfect good and beauty is so far from impeding His love of His creatures that it is the very fountain of a love, a benignity, a condescension, and a bounty that far exceed our deservings. God alone, holding ever His true position, descends in the communication of His goodness to all that is less and lower than Himself.

In the most adorable Trinity, which is the perfection of the divine nature, the Father gives His whole being and glory to the Son; the Son gives His whole being and glory to the Father; the Father and the Son give their whole being, glory, and life to the Holy Spirit; the Holy Spirit gives His whole being, life, and love to the Father and the Son. In this sublimest of divine acts, that we see darkly through the glass of faith, we behold the Eternal Goodness, Truth, and Love, infinitely giving, infinitely receiving, infinitely returning all that is received. This is not only the divine type of all goodness, but the divine type of all humility. The Son receives all from the Father, and gives all to the Father. He said on earth: "The Son cannot do anything of Himself, but what He seeth the Father doing: for whatsoever He doth, these the Son also doth in like manner".* The Father and the Son give all to the Holy Spirit, and the Holy Spirit gives all things back to the Father and the Son. The Father retains nothing to Himself but His personality, whereby He is the Father, and in like manner the Son and the Holy Spirit. So also does the Father give all it has to every creature He has made, and to His intelligent creatures, capable and willing to receive them, things divine as well as earthly; but with them He gives the law of justice, which demands that we give them all back to Him. To do this is humility in man.

The Father created all things through His Eternal Word, but the Eternal Word gives the glory of the work to the Father. He said on earth: "I seek not My own glory. . . . If I glorify Myself, My glory is nothing. It is My Father who glorifieth Me." † The Father hath delivered all things to the Son, but, as St. Paul teaches, the mission of the Son is to restore all things to the Father. Of Himself He gives this sublime description: "The

* *S. John* v. 19.   † *S. John* viii. 50, 54.

Father who abideth in Me, He doth the works. Believe you not that I am in the Father and the Father in Me? otherwise believe for the works' sake." * And of the great work for which He came into the world He says: " No man can come to Me, except the Father, who hath sent Me, draw him, and I will raise him up at the last day ".† This is the language of a divine and perfect humility, of a renunciation of self, not based on defect, but on perfection. But if the Son of God ascribes all that He is and all His works, and the glory of them, to the Father, how can we, who have no goodness whatever of our own, do less?

The most gracious Being, without beginning, end, or limit of life, is His own object and end. He is also our good, the fountain of our life, and the object of our happiness. Sincerity and truth demand of us that we estimate ourselves according to this just order of things, and that we act upon this estimation, standing in our true relations with God, and not in any false relations. But when we say that truth requires this of us, what truth do we mean? Not our own truth, for we have none of our own, but the truth by which God shines into us, demanding the conformity of our will with its light. For, as St. Bonaventure says, humility has the same relation to truth that charity has to good. Thus humility is an obedient reflection of the truth of what we are, as we see ourselves in God's truth, and the just conformity of ourselves to the Divine Justice. By humility we judge ourselves to be no more than what God sees us to be, and to have no more than what we hold from His goodness. Humility, therefore, is nothing less than the reflection in our life of the truth and justice of God.

By humility we also imitate the purity of God. For pride is the defilement of our spirit; and by this virtue we repress and purge away the levity, elation, and uncleanness of pride, the un-principled principle of all sin, which renders us unfit to receive the pure graces of God, or to be the abode of His Holy Spirit. As the God of all purity beholds Himself with an infinite reverence, the humble soul bears herself before God with all the reverence of which she is capable, and has such a respect for the presence of the divine gifts in herself, and in all who partake of His good-ness, that she will do nothing willingly to make her unworthy of the divine benignity.

* *S. John* xiv. 10, 11.   † *S. John* vi. 44.

What some have ventured to call the humility of God is His benignant condescension towards His intelligent creatures. The benignity of God is His natural inclination to communicate Himself to His rational creatures according to their capacity. It comes of His love and of His will that they should share in His happiness. For this He made them to His image; for this He adorns them with grace; for this He upholds them from nothingness. The benignity of God, to use the words of Lessius, is the procession of His love as it goes forth to His creatures and returns again to its Eternal Fountain.* God is love, and dwells in a light unapproachable by His creatures. But He sends forth the manifestation of Himself with a love of infinite condescension. He inclines to nothingness and forms the creature. He imprints His light, goodness, and wisdom on the soul of man. He goes forth to preserve, to govern, and to perfect His creatures, and bring them to their destination. He goes forth in the profound mystery of the Incarnation: God is made man, human nature is united to the person of the Son of God, communicating His divinity to a nature like our own. This is the most wonderful of all His condescensions, the greatest revelation of His benignity and mercy. He goes forth like a farmer to sow his field: he sows the spiritual seed of life, and His field is the souls of men. But His final going forth will be to gather in the harvest, when He will manifest His glory upon the work of His grace and justice, and, separating the evil, renovate the universe. This is the glorification of the saints, whom He draws into His bosom, and to whom He openly reveals Himself.

What, then, is the benignity of God but the lowering and diminishing of Himself in the minds and hearts of His rational creatures, that He may adapt Himself to our limited understanding and contracted sense? We may truly say, that although God is not humble in the sense of subjection, He is humble in the sense of condescension. He cannot be lessened in Himself, but love causes Him to lessen Himself in His communications with His creatures, to provide for our deficiencies; and the depth to which His divine condescension descends is measured by the distance between the Creator and the creature, which is infinite. If ecstasy is the transit of love from one life into another, we may say, in figure, at least, that the love of God in its condescension to

* Lessius, *De Perfectionibus Divinis*, lib. ix., c. 1.

His servants is ecstatic, for He goes forth from what He truly is, and appears to us in created forms, that we may know Him, and inclines His love to our poor estate and humble condition, to attract our affection and to save us.

"God alone is good," as our blessed Lord has taught us. In His love He gives of that goodness to them who are in want of good. The love of God, the action of His Holy Spirit, moves with His good gifts in angelic spirits and in human souls, impressing a certain likeness of Him, "a seal of resemblance"; and being, as we say, in figure a certain ecstatic love, given from the eternal life to form our life, it makes the spiritual creature ecstatic also. For the tendency of that love given to the creature is to bring her to God, and to make her renounce herself, that her life may be hidden with Christ in God. But in this exercise of love-communicating goodness we behold the mystery of humility; for what is humility but the spirit descending to the condition of the one who is loved, which in God is His divine condescension, whilst in man it is the subjection of his life and love to the infinite goodness of God?

Love always tends towards equality, and to assume the form of the being that is loved. God descends into our ways to raise us to His divine ways, and we obtain the divine likeness in the degree in which we love Him. St. Paul tells us that the Son of God "emptied Himself, taking the form of a servant". This is divine humility, the counterpart of divine love. And when we love God truly, the gift of His love works in us the vacating of ourselves; this is the humility of the creature and the counterpart of the love of God. If we would reason on this fundamental principle of spiritual natures, all we can say is, that love is beyond reason, and that God is the perfection of love, and is, therefore, the God of condescension.

It is the well-known remark of Tertullian, that, from the beginning, God preluded the Incarnation by conversing with men as a man to his fellow-man. In visions to men He made Himself known in a variety of human forms, and spoke with our human speech, in a language clothed with our thoughts and affections. What was this but to lower Himself in condescension to our sense and intelligence? And yet He says: "My thoughts are not your thoughts, nor My ways your ways. For as the heavens are exalted above the earth, so are My ways exalted above your ways, and My thoughts above your thoughts."* After many such preludes all through the ages, came the supreme act of condescension in the Incarnation of the Eternal Word, the consummated union of God with our humanity.

If we must reason on what we cannot but call the humility of God towards His creatures, let us first get rid of the blind error that looks on humility as a degradation rather than an exaltation. In its essence humility is that absence of egotism and exclusiveness from which spring generosity and devotedness to what is beyond us. Out of humility we rise towards the good which is above us, and out of the same humility we descend to give ourselves in service and sacrifice to those who are in want or in misery, or who can be made happy through the love and generosity that we can devote to them. If our love of God when directed to our fellow-men demands of us the surrender of our self-love, and great charity will sometimes call for even the surrender of our life, we have in our heart the Divine Word: "Greater love no man hath than that a man lay down his life for his friends".† This is the principle of all virtue; it proceeds from humility and issues in love, and by its force the man grows out of himself into something greater than himself. But what proceeds from humility in man proceeds from beneficence in God, who descends to exalt His creature.

Let us hear one of our earliest theologians on this sublime benignity. "All who rightly philosophise," says William of Paris, "hold it for undoubted truth that man is made to be united with God, and that rectitude of life tends to bring him to this glory. What, then, is the wonder that God should partake of our human condition through assuming our nature, that we may partake of His Divinity in some way suited to our capacity? However far our nature may be below the sublimity of God, equally distant is that sublimity above our nature; and it cannot be less difficult for us to unite with Him than for Him to unite with us. Should any one imagine such an intimate approximation of natures so different to be impossible, let him reflect how much safer it is to have the most ample and magnificent thoughts of the power of God to do what He pleases. To think less of Him proves nothing but the narrowness of our understanding. We must believe the Mind which forms all understandings, the Power which sets limits

---

* *Isaias* lv. 8, 9.   † *S. John* xv. 13.

to them all, and must know that we can understand nothing but what He enables us to understand, and that in setting limits to our understanding He sets no limits to His own divine power.

"Solomon says : 'I understood that man can find no reason of all those works of God that are done under the sun'. * God Himself is the reason of His works, and there can be no other. But if a man presumes to say that it is unbecoming the Majesty on High to descend to our lowliness, and unworthy of Him to take that lowliness upon Himself, that man can surely not see that he is blaspheming the greatest goodness and the only good. For what is goodness but the exercise of love and mercy ? And what is the Divine Goodness but the exercise of perfect love and perfect mercy, even to the embracing with those two arms of goodness what is unworthy of it. Love is the union of the spirit that loves with the spirit that is loved, chiefly in good things ; whilst mercy is the union of the spirit that commiserates with the spirit that is commiserated, chiefly in evil things. This the very word mercy intimates, for it is *misericordia*, the compassion of one heart for the woes of another. Love is the vindication by one heart of the good that is in another. It is His very goodness, then, that moves our God to give Himself to us, and to take our woes and miseries ; He associates Himself with us to bear our woes and to remove them from us, and to give us His enjoyment. To deny that God is thus intimately associated with us in love and mercy is to deny His goodness and the reason of all goodness." †

The highest thoughts and deepest emotions of a great soul find no words to express them. Could they even be expressed, a soul of inferior life and intelligence could not comprehend them. The most intense moments of life reduce us to silence. A great moment of internal light absorbs the soul from all external things. The deepest things of a soul filled with the consciousness of God are incommunicable. It is a law arising from the limitation of our faculties as well as from the ordinance of grace, that one soul can give but a limited amount of her spiritual good to another. Yet in great souls that power of communicating is greater, as we see in David, in St. Paul, St. Augustine, St. Francis, and St. Teresa. The secret of this power is not in their intellect, but in their spiritual force, which depends on the depth of their self-forgetting

---

* *Ecclesiastes* viii. 17.
† Gulielm. Paris., *Cur Deus Homo*, c. vii.

humility and the intensity of their love.   Humility opens those souls and love sends forth their powers ; but in vain do those souls send forth the life from God that is within them to souls that are closed up with pride and hardened against charity.   Yet the holy words of angelic spirits, the words of the Sacred Scriptures, and the words of saints, breathe of their light and grace into devout and humble souls precisely in the degree in which their virtues have prepared them, and the sacred words reach our hearts with a fresher and profounder sense as often as we return to them with purer and humbler dispositions.

Who can imagine the interior life and converse of God?   " My ways are not your ways, nor My thoughts your thoughts."   In the splendour of the Holies, in the ways of eternity, the Father expresses His whole thought and life in the generation of the Son ; the Son, the whole Word and Reason of the Father's thought and life, speaks to the Father the plenitude of wisdom ; whilst the Holy Spirit is the infinite energy breathed of their mutual love. The interior Word of God is God, the image and the substance of His glory.   God has therefore the perfect, the substantial expression of Himself within Himself.   But human words are not the perfect expression of the human soul ; their very number is the proof of this.   They are only signs and imperfect symbols that even in their best use convey but little of all that the soul contains.   They are a sort of natural sacrament conveying but a limited part of what is in one soul to another soul.   When the missionary goes forth from a cultivated Christian nation to a rude and savage people, his first difficulty is to utter what is in his soul.

He must become a barbarian with barbarians, and first convert their rude tongue, devoid of elevated ideas, by infusing his soul into it, before he can obtain access to their minds.   He must humble himself to them before they can rise to him.   It is the same with children ; the parents must humble themselves to their simple and imperfect babbling to raise them in intelligence.   Yet in all this we converse with our fellow-creatures through a medium that is natural to both the teacher and the learner.

But when God deigns to converse with His human children, He must condescend to a language and to actions that are infinitely beneath His nature, and must clothe His eternal truth in earthly imagery.   He must incarnate His Spirit, as it were, in the words of mortals before His Son becomes incarnate in a human body.

He becomes a barbarian with barbarians. He babbles with His children. He speaks of Himself in the language of our thoughts, feelings, and passions. He sees with our eyes, listens with our ears, walks with our feet, smells with our nostrils. He appears with the face of a man, moved with all the alternations of human feelings. He puts forth His arm now to entreat, now to strike, now to save. He rises up and sits down, sleeps or awakes, according as He is patient or expectant, aroused or indignant. He is exalted or humbled; His heart is moved over His people; His spirit yearns for them, or He is touched with inward sorrow. He implores us to turn to Him from destruction. He descends on earth to plead His cause with men. He is now a master, now a father, now a king, now a husband, now a mother, now even the husband of an adulterous wife. He is a husbandman, and plants a vineyard; a builder, and erects a tower; a shepherd, and tends His flock; a merchant, and plies His traffic. He is a man of war, and goes forth to battle for His people; a guide, to lead the hosts of Israel; a watchman, to protect them from the dangers of the night. He is the physician of them that are sick, the comforter of them that mourn, an avenger of the helpless and the poor. He binds Himself with promises, and makes solemn oaths as though He were fallible, and enters into alliances and compacts with His people as though they had rights against Him. Awful it is to read the Scriptures, and to see the incomprehensible God take all shapes of humiliation with His unworthy creatures, to reach their minds and touch their hearts, however gross, dull, or earthly they may be.

"As a father hath compassion on his children, so hath the Lord compassion on them that fear Him; for He knoweth our frame, He remembereth that we are dust."* And how has He compassion? "Behold," says Isaias, "the Lord God shall come with strength, and His arm shall rule: behold His reward is with Him, and His work is before Him. He shall feed His flock like a shepherd: He shall gather together the lambs with His arm, and shall take them up in His bosom, and He shall carry them that are with young." + How tender is this compassion! how sweet this condescension! But hearken to yet more tender offices of affection: "And Sion said, The Lord hath forsaken me, and the Lord hath forgotten me. Can a woman forget her infant, so as

* *Psalm* cii. 13, 14.   + *Isaias* lii. 10, 11.

not to have pity on the son of her womb? And if she should forget, yet will I not forget thee. Behold, I have graven thee in my hands." * To them who bought a god with gold, and likened the God of Heaven in their idolatry to the work of man's hand, the merciful God says : " Hearken to Me, O house of Jacob, all the remnant of the house of Israel, who are carried by My bowels, are borne up by My womb. Even to your old age I am the same, and to your grey hairs I will carry you : I have made you, and I will bear ; I will carry you, and will save. To what have you likened Me, and made Me equal, and compared Me, and made Me like ? " † As the God in Heaven was patient and tender as a woman with her child, so was the God on earth. " Jerusalem, Jerusalem, thou that killest the prophets, and stonest them that are sent unto thee, how often would I have gathered together thy children as the hen doth gather her chickens under her wings, and thou wouldest not ! " ‡ The God on earth recalls His long patience and the yearnings of His tenderness in the heavens.

In the mouth of the Prophet Osee, God calls Himself the husband of Israel, grieves and complains over the adulteress, and invites her to abandon her shameful conduct with Baal and return to Him. Touched with tenderness, He declares that He will give her vinedressers and a beautiful valley, and she shall sing as in the days of her youth. " In that day," says the Lord, " she shall call Me husband," and, " I will espouse thee to Me for ever : and I will espouse thee to Me in justice, and judgment, and in mercy, and in commiserations, and I will espouse thee to Me in faith : and thou shalt know the Lord ".§

In the forty-ninth Psalm God calls on the earth from the rising to the setting sun, calls the loveliness of beauty out of Zion, calls the heavens from above and the earth from beneath to bear witness for Him and to judge His people. In the vast scene of His creation He assembles His saints as in a court of justice, and there pleads His defence against the ungrateful. In Micheas He calls on the mountains to hear the judgment of the Lord, and the strong foundations of the earth, and He will plead against Israel. " O My people, what have I done to thee, or in what have I molested thee? Answer thou Me. For I brought thee up out of the land of Egypt, and delivered thee out of the

---

* *Isaias* xlix. 14-16.   † *Isaias* xliv. 3-5.
‡ *S. Matthew* xxiii. 37.   § *Osee* xix. 20.

house of slaves."* In many places of Holy Scripture, as St. John Chrysostom observes, God uses this figure, wonderful as it is and worthy of His benignity. He lowers Himself to plead with men as in a court of justice, and shows His unspeakable goodness.

From the days of Celsus, scornful unchristian men have alleged these and like passages to prove that the majesty of God is lowered in the Scriptures. Who can deny, or wish to deny, that God lowers His majesty to reveal His goodness? To be high and glorious is God's nature; there is nothing wonderful in that. But it is wonderful, it is stupendous, to see God descend so far below His nature in His tenderness to us poor mortals. Who knows, as God in His eternal wisdom knows, that in tempering His presence to the rude apprehension of rude men He makes Himself infinitely less to them than He is in Himself? But these strong, coarse forms and figures are best adapted to save us from taking them in their literal sense; as when God describes Himself rising in His strength like a drunken man from sleep. It throws us off with the violence of terror from the figure in its rudeness to Him who thus delivers His contempt of a vice so utterly degrading. It is the inward grace illuminating the outward word that carries the soul from the letter to the spirit, from the figure to the reality; and the soul, illuminated with faith, ascends above the sublimest imagery of God and His actions in the Scriptures, above all sense, above all human thought, above the heavens to near the verge of God's inaccessible light and grandeur. The humble of heart, like God in the Scriptures, by an instinct of wisdom choose those representations of God and holy things by preference that, instead of fixing our mind on their human beauty and refinement, throw off the mind from the material and sensual symbol to the divine things that they suggest. For figures, like words, are but suggestions, that, if too full and perfect in their form, cease to do their office effectively, fixing our minds on human art rather than carrying our minds to the divine things represented.

Celsus and the rational school would either give us mental abstractions without reality, or some fastidiously finished image of a Jupiter or Apollo,—forms far too complete and rounded into the perfection of sensual humanity to suggest anything beyond

* *Micheas* vi. 2-4.

human nature. But who knows, as the God of mercy knows, that in representing Himself to His creatures in gross and vivid imagery drawn from their nature He exposes Himself to the contumely of the proud and to the derision of the vain and thoughtless? Yet He who is above all creation has deigned to trace the shadow of Himself in all His works. As St. Paul says: "The invisible things of Him from the creation of the world are clearly seen, being understood by the things that are made; His eternal power also and divinity".* He cannot be less than Himself in His own eyes, but in His benignity He chooses to be less than Himself in ours; that through this imperfect knowledge of Him we may be drawn to perfect knowledge, and finally see Him as He is. He cannot exercise the virtue of humility in Himself, but chooses to give us the image of that virtue in His conduct towards us.

We shall now be better able to understand the language of the Saints. "Why need I say," asks St. Chrysostom, "that the Son speaks humbly of Himself when the Father does the same? for He says many lowly things of Himself for the salvation of them who listen." And after giving a number of examples from the Scriptures, the Saint continues: "All these things are unworthy of God, yet in another sense how worthy they are of Him! for He is so benignant and condescending that He disdains no words or imagery that will help us to our salvation".† Listen to St. Macarius of Egypt: "As neither the early times nor the recent ages have been able to understand the majesty and incomprehensible nature of God, neither have the inferior or the supernal worlds been competent to reach the humility of God, or to understand how He emptied Himself with those who are poor, humble, and weak. His humility is as incomprehensible as His majesty."‡ What we know on the subject is expressed in such terms as St. Augustine uses: "A proud sinner is a great misery, but far greater is the mercy of a humble God";§ and in the beautiful sentence of St. Hildegard: "The charity of God has created us, the humility of God has saved us".‖ If you find a heart that is

* *Romans* i. 20.
† S. J. Chrysost., *Hom.* 64 *in Joan.*
‡ S. Macarius, *Hom.* 33.
§ S. August., *De Catechiz. Rudibus*, c. viii.
‖ S. Hildegard, *Epist.* 30.

deep in humility and high in sanctity, you will be sure to find it struck with amazement at the condescension of God. The humble and burning St. Francis, for example, composed and sung this rapturous hymn to God : "Thou art good, and all good, and the sovereign good, the only true Lord God. Thou art love and charity ; Thou art wisdom ; Thou art humility." The blessed Angela of Foligni, in her vision of light, hears God thus speaking to her soul : "'I have caused thee to see something of My power, now behold My humility'. Then I saw the humility of God towards man and towards all things. And when my soul had looked upon the unspeakable power and comprehended something of the humility of God, she marvelled, and felt herself to be very nothing, seeing nothing in herself but pride." *

The very name of father implies the solicitous service of the children and the patient endurance of their waywardness. God delights to call Himself our Father, and by that holy title He seems to preside over His human family in a homely and familiar way. He thinks for us, enlightens us, provides for us, ministers to us, protects us, and guides us, and that with such a consideration for our wants and infirmities, that His action concurs in all the good we do and discountenances all the evil to which we are inclined. In a word, it is unspeakable what service God is always rendering to us, and what benignity and condescension we are daily and hourly receiving from our Heavenly Father.

Even the heathen Seneca was conscious that "He ministers to our wants, and is everywhere present to help us".† St. Thomas has concentrated this sublime truth in a single sentence : "Another thing," he says, "that influences us to love God is the divine humility ; for the Almighty One ministers to each angel and to each soul as if He were their servant and they held the place of God ".‡ What the Prince of Theologians says in calm reflection, St. Catherine of Genoa says in the rapture of contemplation. " I saw," she says, " the sweet God taking such care of the soul, that no man, had he the whole world for his reward, would take such care. And when I saw with how great a love and solicitude He supplies us with all we need to bring us into His country, I could only exclaim : O God, Thou art our servant ! If man could only see the care that God takes of the soul, though he knew nothing

---

* *Visione* 3.   † Seneca, *Epist.* 96.
‡ S. Thomas, *Opusc* 63, c. 2, sect. 3, n. 19.

else but this, he would be utterly confused and astounded to see the glorious God, in whom is the essence of all things, having so great a care of the creature. Yet it is to us it must turn to profit or destruction, according as we make account of it."＊

This, says Isaias, is "the High and the Eminent that inhabiteth eternity; and His name is Holy, who dwelleth in the high and holy place, and with a contrite and humble spirit, to revive the spirit of the humble, and to revive the heart of the contrite".† What a contrast between these two dwellings of God! The one is above all time and space, above the angels and seraphs, the inhabitation of eternity; the other is the humble and contrite heart of mortals here below. The first is God's essential dwelling, the second the dwelling of His choice. Next to Himself God loves the humble and the contrite. The Most High loves the lowest soul, provided she knows her littleness and confesses her lowliness.

God so loved the world, notwithstanding its base apostasy from Him, that He sent to it His angels, and then His prophets, and then the Word of His truth, and then His Holy Spirit, veiling the splendours of the Godhead and tempering the consuming fire of His nature in humble forms, that man might entertain His presence without dread or fear. But the world disowned His angels, stoned His prophets, rejected His Word, and resisted His Holy Spirit. Still, God so loved the world as to give His Only-beloved Son to our nature, who was crucified by the world, that from His humility and blood, which makes this world the tragedy of the universe, our life might be recovered. What love and what humility! How deep beyond human intelligence must be the evil that called for such a remedy! That evil is pride. Hard is it for faith, but much harder for love, to say that humility is not among the divine virtues. We are in God's image that we may imitate His divine virtues, and pride is that which destroys our likeness to God. Moreover, the grace of all our virtues proceeds from the divine virtue. Yet the fulness of that infinite perfection to which nothing is wanting forbids our saying that God in Him-self is humble, or can make Himself less than all being. Yet He leaves us not without the example of a divine humility, and finds its reason in our nature, though not in His own. In all His communications with us, whether before the Incarnation of His

---

＊ S. Caterina da Genova, *Vita*, c. xii.   † *Isaias* lvii. 15.

Son or in that profoundest mystery of humility, He draws round Him a veil woven of the low and weak things of our frail humanity, in which to make Himself intelligible to us, and gives us this imposing example of humility as well as of mercy and benignity.

God is not the same to all men, but to every one according to his spirit. To the pure-hearted contemplative He is all spiritual, and His nature is more nearly approached ; but to the rude and simple He is shadowed in imaginative forms. This is well illustrated in that simple concrete-minded brother among the Fathers of the Desert, who, when he was told that God had no shape or form like man, went about weeping and crying, " They have taken my God from me, and I know not where to find Him". But this is the marvel of divine condescension, that the grosser and more carnal men became, the more grossly did God address them through His visions and His prophets, as if He were endowed with their rude passions, and was thus more humbled in the mind and sense of those who were least worthy of His condescension. To the proud He was lofty, to the domineering He was imperious, to the cruel He was terrible; but to the lowly He was humble, to the meek gentle, to the sincere open, to the tender-hearted compassionate. To the crafty He is subtle, to the hard-hearted stern, to the avaricious sparing, to the scorner scornful ; but to the merciful full of charity. The Psalmist therefore sings to Him : " The Lord will reward me according to my justice, and according to the cleanness of my hands before His eyes. With the holy Thou wilt be holy, and with the innocent man Thou wilt be innocent; and with the elect Thou wilt be elect, and with the perverse Thou wilt be perverted. For Thou wilt save the lowly people, but wilt bring down the eyes of the proud."* How will God be perverted with the perverse? He tells us in Leviticus : "If you will not for all this hearken to Me, but will walk against Me ; I will go against you with opposite fury, and I will chastise you with seven plagues for your sins".† He warns as a Father, and warns often before He punishes as a Judge. It is only when He sees that the perverse will be perverse to the end, that His provident humiliations cease from that soul, mercy stands still, and judgment overtakes. Even then the sinner is taken away in mercy, lest his sin be increased without end, and his punishment augmented without measure.

---

* *Psalm* xvii. 25-28.   † *Leviticus* xxvi. 27, 28.

Of the loving condescension of God the Incarnation of His Son is the crowning act. Man had lost everything except his fallen nature in losing humility. But through this stupendous act of divine condescension he was able to recover his humility, and through humility to recover everything. The pride that offends the Infinite Holiness must be atoned for by humility, and, as the offence is against the Divine Majesty, must be atoned for by divine humility; but glory belongs to God, humility to the creature. God can find no such humbleness in Himself as belongs to the creature; His sovereign grandeur allows of no abasement; in His own nature He must always be supreme. But, as Bossuet observes, what He finds not in Himself He seeks in an alien nature. His all-abounding goodness disdains not to go a-borrowing; and why, but to enrich Himself with the virtue of humility, who was infinitely rich in every other virtue. The Son of God comes into this world to seek a new virtue and to carry it up to the throne of God. It was a new glory to draw a virtue and a victory from the basest and most miserable acts of His creatures, and to become infinitely lowly in our nature whilst infinitely exalted in His own. The greatest product of this sinful world has been to furnish the conditions for a new and wonderful virtue in Him through whom and by whom all things were made. God hath wrought all things for Himself, and the first glory of this virtue is for Him; but the second is for us, who receive from His virtue the grace to be humble.

The essence of virtue is in the expending of one's self for a higher good. Thus it is that the families of this earth are glorified after one of their blood has painfully expended his life on the victory of some great cause. The second Person of the Godhead has glorified the whole Godhead in painfully expending Himself in a suitable nature to save the divine work of His Father from defeat and ruin. For this was He made man, that the Father might see in His person clothed in human nature God subject to God, and obedient to His will in things most alien from God. When born into the world, the first movement of His heart was the humble homage to His Father that ruled His life from the Crib to the Cross. But whilst the glory of this profound humility was for God, the need of it was for man; and He who, as the Word of the Father, had shadowed out this virtue to men's eyes in the many condescensions of the former times, became the living, human, and even divine example of this virtue to us. But it would have little availed to become the divine example had He not also become the divine source of this virtue, giving us the grace for its exercise, of which He became the fountain. The first proof He gave us that God loves the meek and humble heart was in being laid in the lap of that meek and humble Mary in the cave of Bethlehem, whilst the angels sang glory to God on high.

We obtain a profounder view of this work of humility when we reflect that the Incarnation of the Son is the work of the whole Divine Trinity. As St. Leo says: "It was of that will whereby 'He loved us and gave Himself for us,' that the Lord held back within Him the might of His majesty, and allowed the persecutor to act with violence against Him. And the Father co-operated in this self-same thing, for 'He spared not His own Son, but delivered Him for us all'. For the will of the Father and of the Son is one, as the Divinity is one." *

Christ said of Himself, "He who seeth Me, seeth my Father also". Yet whilst the God of Heaven is thus lowered in our sight, and the Word Eternal is made "a short word upon the earth" to be expended for our use, we must guard against thinking that He is lessened in Himself. Let us again hear the great St. Leo, whose words are like creeds. He says: "The unchangeable Deity of the Word fitted to Himself the form of a servant in the likeness of sinful flesh; yet towards Himself, and the Father, and the Holy Spirit His glory is nothing lessened, for the nature of the supreme and eternal essence receives no change or diminution. But for the sake of that infirmity of ours which could not otherwise receive Him, He covered the splendours of His majesty, on which the eye of man could not look, with the veil of a human body. He is, therefore, said to have emptied Himself, as if He were denuded of His own attributes, and, whilst consulting our needs in that humility, made Himself not only less than the Father, but less than Himself. Yet in thus inclining Himself, He departed in nothing from that Being which He is in common with the Father and the Holy Ghost. We, therefore, understand this as belonging to His omnipotence, that whilst He is lessened as to what is ours, He is not lessened as to what is His own. Forasmuch, then, as

---

* S. Leo, *Serm.* 1 *de Passione Christi.*

12*

being light, He looked to the blind; as being strength, He looked to the infirm; as being mercy, He looked to the miserable; it was by the work of His almighty power that He took our nature upon Him and undertook our cause, to the end that He might reform our nature and destroy the death that He never created. . . . He is in our humility, and in His own Divine Majesty, true man, true God; eternal in His own, temporal in ours; one with the Father in substance, and in that substance never less than the Father; one with the Mother in the body He created. For in assuming our nature He made of Himself a stepping-stone whereby we are able to ascend through His humanity to His Divinity."

That this was but the last of many steps whereby the Eternal Word, shrouding His glory, had descended in benignity to man, St. Leo could not fail to note; and the great Pontiff thus continues: "But the manifestation of His splendour is called the mission by which Christ appeared to the world. For whereas He always filled all things with His invisible majesty, from a deeply hidden and impenetrable secrecy He came to them who knew Him not, took away their blind ignorance, and arose, as the Scriptures say, a light to them who sat in darkness and the shadow of death. For though the light of His truth was sent forth in the former ages to enlighten the Fathers and Prophets, as David said: 'Send forth Thy light and Thy truth'; and in divers ways, by many signs, the Divinity of the Son declared His presence; yet all these manifestations and each of these miracles were but the witnesses to that mission of which the Apostle says: 'When, therefore, the fulness of time was come, God sent His Son, made of a woman, made under the law'. Let, then, the Catholic faith confess the glory of God in humility." *

All the great appearances of God were the appearances of the Eternal Word preparing the way for His incarnation. Thus after the fall of our first parents God walked as a man in the noontide air of Paradise, called them to account, and promised our redemption with a human voice. When Noe entered the ark of salvation, God closed the door upon him. After the Deluge had passed He accepted the odour of sacrifice and gave a new law to men. He was seen by Abraham at Sichem; He leaned upon the ladder at the foot of which Jacob had his vision; He showed

* S. Leo, *Serm.* 5 *de Nativitate.*

His back to Moses, and appeared to him in the burning bush ; He was seen on a throne by Isaias; to Daniel He appeared as the Ancient of Days; Ezechiel beheld Him enthroned on the luminous cherubim and burning wheels. He showed Himself to each prophet, observes St. Chrysostom, according to that prophet's dignity.

He was seen, remarks Tertullian, according to the man's capacity, but not according to the plenitude of His Divinity. How, then, is it said that "No man hath seen God at any time"? God spoke to Moses as with a friend ; and Jacob says, "I have seen the Lord face to face". As the Father He is invisible, as the Son He is visible. As God, as the Word, as the Spirit, He is invisible ; but He was visible before He was incarnate in that way of which He says to Aaron and Mary : "If there be among you a prophet of the Lord, I will appear to him in a vision, or I will speak to him in a dream. But it is not so with My servant Moses, who is most faithful in all My house ; for I speak to him mouth to mouth, and plainly, and not in riddles and figures."* Why did God speak to Moses as to no other man? The Sacred Scripture tells us : "For Moses was a man exceeding meek above all men that dwelt on earth" ; and his great humility made him capable of a more intimate knowledge and familiarity with God.

The Divine Word, continues Tertullian, came and conversed with men from Adam to the prophets, in a vision, in a dream, seen darkly through a glass, clothed in mysterious obscurity. He preludes that order of things from the beginning, and always, which He will consummate in the end. In thus rehearsing His work He prepares the way for our path in Him, that from knowing He had done things in the ages before His Incarnation which resembled that act, we might the more readily believe the Son of God when He came unto the world. † We will complete the exposition of this grave Christian apologist from his book against Hermogenes. "Whatever the unbeliever objects from the Scriptures as being a diminution of God and a human thing is the Son of God practising from the first what He was to become in the end. What seems unworthy of Him, as seen, heard, and associated with man, is the Son of God uniting man and God in Himself—in power God, in weakness man, giving all to man that He diminishes from

---

* *Numbers* xii. 6-8.

† See Tertullian, *Contra Praxeam*, c. xiv.-xvi. *per totum.*

God. God conversed humanly that man might learn to act divinely. God acted on equality with man that man might learn to act equally with God. God was found little and lowly, that man might become great and elevated. He who disdains a God like this can never believe that He was crucified." *

What can give us a more profound or a more sublime conception of the goodness and benignity of God than this lowering of Himself to the comprehension of His creatures, than this diminishing of Himself to their minds, than this shaping of Himself to their littleness and grossness, that by any means He may open their sense-bound souls, awaken them out of their ignorance, and overcome their obstinate pride? The humble ways of God in this world are His tender, loving ways. They are the sublimest of all lessons to the proud, if the proud could only learn them. But whilst they attract the humble, and fill their souls with sweetness, proving, above all things else, the love which God has for them; they repel the proud, who could not receive them without the utter condemnation of their own evil condition.

We have another sublime view of the benign condescension of God in His love and providence over all little, poor, and lowly things. The smallest creature is the object of His care as well as the greatest. Their very humbleness attracts His divine benignity. To every atom of earth, to each beam of light, He gives the energy of existence and a law for its regulation. Myriads of insects fill the earth, the air, the sea, in numbers so numberless as almost to suggest infinitude. We destroy them each moment, unconscious that we are annihilating their sense of life and existence. Yet all these little things have received a beautiful aptitude for their mode of life and their final end, and the more we study them, the more we find that their lives have an office and a function in the universe that in some way converges to the nearer or remoter service of man. The telescope is to our limited senses what faith is to our limited reason, revealing worlds to us beyond the reach of our native powers of sight. This ought not to cause pride, but humility, for it is a revelation of our contractedness. The microscope, again, is to our senses what humility is to the soul, bringing many things to light that escape our native powers of perception, and the things that humility brings to light in us are all little and poor, and not unfrequently grotesque. But the

* Tertullian, *Contra Hermogenem*, lib. ii., c. 16.

microscope opens to our mind a world as wonderful in design and aptitude as the telescope, and of incomparably greater variety. But the Sacred Scriptures teach us that every one of these little creatures is the object of a special thought and care to our Heavenly Father. It is our ignorance, narrowness, and pride that cause the greatly little things of God to be overlooked and despised by us, though nothing that He has made is contemptible in His sight. They are innocent and we are sinful ; they are pleasing in the sight of God, even when we are not ; and He often uses them with terrible power as instruments for our humiliation and punishment.

The Holy Spirit has not disdained to teach us lessons of humility and wisdom from the smallest things. He says in the Proverbs : " There are four very little things of the earth, and they are wiser than the wise : the ants, a feeble people, which provide themselves food in the harvest ; the rabbit, a weak people, which maketh its bed in the rock ; the locust hath no king, yet they all go out by their bands ; the stellio supporteth itself on hands, and dwelleth in king's houses ".* From another of these humble creatures He rebukes us in Ecclesiasticus : " The bee is small among flying things, but her fruit hath the chiefest sweetness. Glory not in apparel at any time, and be not exalted in the day of honour : for the works of the Highest alone are wonderful, and His works are glorious, and secret, and hidden."† And when God created the poor worm to prepare the earth for the food of man, He saw in it a similitude of the humilation of His Incarnate Son, which He revealed through His Prophet : " But I am a worm, and no man : the reproach of men, and the outcast of the people ". ‡

In rebuke of our incessant toils and hoardings, relying more on ourselves than on God, our Lord appeals to the little birds of the air : " Your Heavenly Father feedeth them ; are you not of much more value than they ? " And from those who from their secular solicitudes give but little time to God He appeals to the flowers under their feet : " Consider the lilies of the field how they grow ; they labour not, neither do they spin. But I say to you, that not even Solomon, in all his glory, was arrayed as one of these. And if the grass of the field, which is to-day, and to-morrow is cast

* *Proverbs* xxx. 24-28.   † *Ecclesiasticus* xi. 2-4.
‡ *Psalm* xxi. 7.

into the oven, God doth so clothe; how much more you, O ye of little faith?"* Had we the true spirit of God, and a humble trust in His benignant care of all humble things that do His will, we should never want in anything that might· conduce to our eternal good. For His special love and care is for the humble, whose sincere spirit resembles His own.

But all the arguments that the most subtle intellects might draw from the divine attributes and actions of God to show that humility in man is the nearest imitation of Him, cannot equal in force the one brief word of the incarnate God Himself: "Learn of Me, for I am meek and humble of heart". All the examples of divine condescension that we can accumulate cannot bring home to the truly humble soul a conviction equal to the loving sense within that soul of what God is to the humble. If He rejects the proud, it is because they are alien to His nature; if He receives the humble, it is because they are conformable to His life.

To take another point of view, God is the special guardian of all who are beaten down in the world, of the poor, the weak, the helpless, the oppressed, and the suffering, and He has offered especial rewards to those who help and protect them in His name. He has made them His representatives in the world, and has proclaimed that "whatsoever you do to these, you do to Me". Why, but because they are in distress of soul and humbled in their distress. It belongs to the magnificence of God to "lift up the needy from the dust and the poor from the dunghill; to make them sit with princes, even with the princes of His people". Bossuet has shown in a magnificent discourse that God has built His Church on the poor, and that the rich have come into it by a sort of indulgence; but St. Paul had exhibited this truth whilst the Church was yet forming. It would take a volume to illustrate the homeliness of our Heavenly Father with the suffering and the poor who cry to Him. The priest on his rounds, the Sisters of Charity in their visits, the benevolent in their calls upon the afflicted, meet God among them, and often marvel at their faith and consolations. God calls Himself in the Scriptures the hearer of the poor, the refuge of the poor, the enricher of the poor, the comforter of the afflicted, the consoler of the humble, and the God of the poor. Well is it for a man when he is understanding

* *S. Matthew* iv. 28-30.

over the needy and the poor; God has promised to visit him on his bed of sorrow, and to turn his couch for him in sickness. Well is it to be understanding over them, because the humble poor are great teachers of the knowledge of God.

On this subject St. Gregory says : " It is the property of God not only to make good out of nothing, but to restore to good what the devil has corrupted. The humility of God came as medicine to the wounds which the proud devil had inflicted. God would have men rise up to humility anew by imitating their Creator, after having fallen into pride by imitating their enemy. The humble God appeared as the opponent of the devil and his pride, but as the mighty men of the world were partakers of the devil's pride, because He was so humble they thought Him despicable. They despised the medicine of life exactly in the degree to which their hearts were swollen ; but whilst the proud rejected the medicine from their wounds, that divine medicine came to the humble. God chose the weak to confound the strong, and that was done for the poor on which the rich with their pride looked with wonder. They saw the new virtues arise among the poor, and were astonished at the miracles of good that appeared in the classes they were accustomed to despise. They even returned with trembling to their own hearts, and looked with awe on a sanctity so marvellously exhibited, although when it only reached their ears in formal precepts it had met nothing but their contempt. Thus did the weak things of the world put the strong to confusion, and whilst the life of the humble rose into veneration, the elation of pride fell to the ground." *

More, however, by their prayers than by their example did the lowly servants of God draw the rich and powerful into the Church. This opens another view of the divine benignity and condescension, too vast to be treated here. But as our Heavenly Father delights in using humble instruments for His great works, and as it were plays with His power, He loves to put His will into the hands of the humble and to show His power in them. Those humble spirits who look to nothing but His goodness are His true children, and He loves to yield to their prayers and expostulations. He courts their importunities, and denies them only to increase their confidence in His condescension. Our Lord

* S. Greg. Mag., *Moral. in Job*, lib. xxxi., c. 1,

showed this in His treatment of the Canaanite woman, in the parable of the three loaves that a man at midnight would borrow of his friend, and in that of the woman who bent the unwilling judge to do her right through her importunities. Nay, so great a love has God for the prayers of the humble, that He seems to fear lest they should stay His justice. He yields to the humble entreaties of Abraham if even ten just men can be found in the five criminal cities. He says to Moses : " Let Me alone, that My wrath may be enkindled against them ". But Moses persisted in his prayer, and the Lord was appeased from doing the evil to His people that He had spoken. He says to Jeremias : " Do thou not pray for this people, and do not withstand Me ". Yet the Prophet continued his supplications. God loves to be resisted in His displeasure, and to be restrained by the humble from inflicting punishment. He complains to Ezechiel : " I sought among them for a man that might set up a hedge, and stand in the gap before Me in favour of the land, that I might not destroy it ; and I found none ".* Had there been a man like Abraham or Moses to stand before God for His people, Jerusalem had then been saved. One saint will often save a nation ; so true is it that humble souls are the hinges on which God moves the world.

Humility so perfects man for God, that when the Son of God took our nature He could find no other virtue so capable of uniting that nature with God. It is the very capacity for union with God. And as the deeper the sea the more water it contains, the deeper the soul is in humility the diviner are the things it can receive. The plenitude of the Godhead entered into the humility of the manhood of Christ, so that, as St. Paul says, it dwelt in Him bodily. Emptied of himself, the man was taken into the personality of God ; and that this might be accomplished in the most suitable way, the humblest of virgins was chosen for the temple in which this union was accomplished by the power of the Holy Spirit.

This lowly virtue, pure from evil, hath in truly humble souls a certain humour of childlike affection, that smiles at one time and is awed at another at the magnificence of God and the littleness of His creature ; and gently, as with a subdued fear, rejoices in the lightness of heart that comes after the toil of casting off the oppressive load of pride, a lightness which enables the

---

* *Ezechiel* xxii. 30.

soul to ascend as on luminous wings to the God of all delight. Yet is there fear in this love, lest through want of vigilance the spirit of elation should return to defile the nest of peace.

Humility is to man what wisdom is to God. That wisdom, I mean, which speaks in the words of Solomon : " I was with Him forming all things, and was delighted every day, playing before Him at all times ; playing in the world ; and my delights were to be with the children of men ".* The creation of the world and the converse of God with men are here represented as the pastime of the Eternal Wisdom. And still the Eternal Wisdom entertains Himself with His children. He chooses the foolish in the world's estimation, and confuses the wise in their conceits ; He chooses the weak who know their weakness, and confounds the strong ; He chooses the lowly and contemptible, and brings the self-exalted to nothing ; so that nothing may glory in His sight that glories not in Him. He lifts up the humble, enriches the poor, and sends the rich empty away ; He leaves the vain to their pitiful vanities, and the proud to their blind conceits. He opens the charms of virtue to the simple, and hides them from the worldly wise. The wisdom of God plays with the children of men on the side of humility, and one of the divinely wise has said that humility is *ludus Dei cum hominibus,* the pastime of God with men.

* *Proverbs* viii. 30.

LECTURE VIII.

THE DIVINE MASTER OF HUMILITY.

"One is your master, Christ."—St. Matthew xxiii. 10.

THE scriptural sense of the word Master signifies one who teaches with authority; and this title was given to the Son of God both by His disciples and His adversaries. The Pharisees and the Herodians say to Him: "Master, we know that Thou art a true speaker, and teachest the way of God in truth, neither carest Thou for any man: for Thou dost not regard the person of man".* When Nicodemus came to Jesus by night, he thus addressed Him: "Master, we know that Thou art come a teacher from God: for no man can do these signs which Thou dost unless God be with Him".† This title was also given to Him in the prophetic days. Isaias says: "Behold I have given Him for a witness to the people, for a leader and a master to the Gentiles".‡ And the Lord Himself accepted the title for His own. He said to the Apostles on a solemn occasion: "You call Me Master and Lord: and you do well, for so I am".§ He claimed it even as exclusively His own, saying to His disciples: "Be not you called Rabbi, for One is your Master, and all you are brethren. . . . . Neither be you called masters, for One is your Master, Christ." || And the Gospel tells us how He taught with the power of a Master; the people were in admiration and astonishment at His doctrine, for He was teaching them as one having power, and not as the Scribes and Pharisees.

But this title of Master was derived from another title that is infinitely higher, holier, and most divine. He was the Word of God, He was the Light of the Father, He was the very Truth.

* S. Matthew xxii. 16.   † S. John iii. 2.   ‡ Isaias lv. 4.
§ S. John xiii. 13. || S. Matthew vii. 28, 29.

He was the Truth from whom all truth proceeds, and by whom all minds are enlightened that are enlightened.   And as, to use the words of St. Paul, " He cannot deny Himself," He proclaimed Himself for what He was.   He says plainly : " I am the Light of the world ".*   And St. John explains this declaration ; " He was the true Light, which enlighteneth every man that cometh into the world ". +   If you boast your reason, the Eternal Word is the author of the light that constitutes your reason.   But He came into the world to give a diviner light, of which He says :   " I am come a Light into the world, that whosoever believeth in Me may not remain in darkness ".‡   And again He says of Himself : " I am the way, the truth, and the life.   No man cometh to the Father except through Me ". §   When we read these things, let us not stop at the words, but pass in mind from the words to the truths, and from the truths to the Divine and Eternal Substance of that Word of God and Saviour of men from whom the truth proceeds.   For in the faith of Christ everything is fact, and the truth is the light that shines from those divine facts, and makes them known to faith.

Christ is the real Son of God and the real Son of man, united in the Divine Person of His Godhead ; in whom is the knowledge of all things heavenly and earthly ; in whom is the remedy of all human evils ; in whom is the light of all truth and the grace of all virtue ; in whom is the life of souls and the resurrection of the dead ; and by the partaking of whose gifts we are restored to God.   " I am the way, the truth, and the life.   No one cometh to the Father except through Me."

What is the mission of the Son of God in this world?   To sum up that august mission in two words, it is to destroy pride and to establish humility.   The one adversary of God is pride. The one cause of separation from God is pride.   The one evil that brings down the maledictions of God is pride.   Pride is not only the root of all evil, but the malice that lurks in all evil.   Mention whatever vice you will, the malicious element in that vice is pride. It is the virulence of this inflammatory disease that awakens rebellion against God in man, and brings him to spiritual death. It swells the man into a self-elation that will neither be subject to God nor at concord with his fellow-creatures, but is always falsifying the man until he lasciviates destructively within himself.

* *S. John* viii. 12.   † *S. John* i. 9.   ‡ *S. John* xii. 46.   § *S. John* xiv. 6.

This is our ruin.   This is the blind obstruction between man and
God.   To put an end to pride is to put an end to error and evil,
and this can only be done by humility.

The Eternal Word preached the remedy of humility through
the prophets, and promised a divine deliverance, and those who
received His humility in faith became the servants of God.
But in the great body of mankind the pestilence of pride grew
inveterate, until not only the virtue, but its very name and notion
was lost among them.   They felt their misery, but could not
understand its cause.   Their conscience receded farther and
farther from God, until the very notion that He was their Creator
was lost.   They sought for new gods and mediators, and fell among
lying angels, who had deserted the truth, and who increased the
pride which they first instilled into the human race.   Having
fallen by their own pride from God without losing their intense
zeal and activity, the demons made themselves the mediators of
pride, intruding themselves between man and God, and suggesting
their unclean pride in place of pure humility.   And having caught
man in their toils, they contrived to promote and augment the
blinding pride they had first inspired.   Spiritual and invisible,
they haunted the air of this lower world; and as the multitudes
who had lost communion with the true God looked for gods,
mediators and deliverers akin to their own nature, they were
captured by the evil spirits that first led them into pride and sin.
The world was filled with the worship of demons transfigured
into angels of light, yet with every human vice, who were worshipped with many profane and superstitious rites, sacrifices,
and vain purgations, sometimes mingled with vile obscenities, not
unfrequently with atrocious cruelties, and always with idolatry.
By such-like means the first authors of pride became its terrible
promoters, clothing the destructive vices with seeming sanctions
and solemnities of religion, of which, behind the curtains of many
illusions, the demons themselves were the real object, until pride
itself became the basis of virtue, and humility was discarded as a
degradation.   From Deuteronomy to the Psalms, and from the
Psalms to the later Prophets, the inspired Scriptures declare that
the gods of the Gentiles are demons and their worship an immolation to demons.   They might profess to inhabit the sun or the
moon; they really inhabited the lower elements, and took their
abode in the gloomy sanctuaries of idols.   What the Scriptures

proclaimed in so many of their pages, the early Fathers of the Church who had been initiated in the pagan mysteries, and afterwards converted from idolatry, not only asserted but proved.

There was a class of men who professed themselves wise, and thought to find a way to God without a mediator. These indeed obtained glimpses of the truth, sufficient to know the unity of God, but not sufficient to do Him honour. They had the form but not the power of truth. Confiding in themselves, they knew not that their mental powers were blinded and afflicted with their pride; whilst spurning the gods, they still joined in their worship; whilst speculating on the truth, they fell back upon every sensual vice and defilement. They boasted a fortitude that had no better ground than self-reliance, and a magnanimity with no foundation more solid than their pride, and which issued in the contempt of all whom they accounted inferior to themselves.

St. Augustine, who was trained in their schools and knew them well, speaks thus of them : "There are some who think to purify themselves, to contemplate God, and to adhere to Him ; but they are deeply stained with pride, and there is no vice that finds a greater resistance from the divine law, or over which the proud spirits of evil, those mediators of the vilest things, those obstructors of the way to things divine, have greater power. These men think to purify themselves with their own virtue, because some of them have power to direct their minds to a light beyond the creature, and in some way to touch some little of the unchangeable truth ; and they deride numbers of Christians who live purely by faith as being unable to do the same. But of what gain is it to the proud to obtain a distant glimpse of a far-distant country, if they are ashamed to embark on the ship that would carry them to that country ? And what loss is it to the humble not to have that distant glimpse, if they are on board the ship that is carrying them to that country, although the proud disdain the vessel that conveys them ? " *

The evil spirits are the mediators of pride, who have intervened between man and God, and by their evil influence have turned man back from God, and thrown him upon himself. The true Mediator between man and God must therefore of necessity be the Mediator of humility. He must destroy evil by destroying pride, and by overcoming the power of the mediators of pride.

* S. August., *De Trinitate*, lib. iv., c. 15.

This can only be accomplished by re-establishing humility, which is the first reopening of the soul closed up by pride, the first return to truthfulness and justice, and the first recovery of submission from the creature to the Creator. But the true Mediator, the Mediator of humility, must be God and man. If He were God alone, He could not be humble ; if He were man alone, He could not have the divine power of a mediator with God. But as God in man He clothed Himself with humility ; He made it the virtue of our redemption ; He restored it to us as the groundwork of our renewed integrity ; He brought it forward as the healing medicine of all our spiritual maladies. "There is one God," says St. Paul, "and one Mediator of God and man, the man Christ Jesus : who gave Himself a redemption for all, a testimony in due time."* Upon which St. Augustine observes : "He appeared between mortal sinners and the Immortal Just One, mortal with men, just with God; that as the wages of justice are life and peace, He might make void the death of sinners, justifying them through the death that He willed to have in common with them all ".†

When we speak, then, of Christ as the Master of humility, we speak of something pre-eminently great and excelling. The Son of God could not take the nature of man without making that nature morally perfect, and He has shown in Himself that the foundation of moral perfection in a creature is perfect humility. He could not, again, take the office upon Him of our Mediator and Redeemer without showing us in a pre-eminent way by what virtue we are reconciled to God and made open to His sanctifying gifts. This virtue He therefore manifested the most conspicuously in Himself. He took it as His singular prerogative, because it was the perfect subjection of His humanity to His divinity, because it was the virtue by which He redeemed the world, and because it is the one virtue by which every soul that He came to redeem returns to God. To this virtue, therefore, as to His great human prerogative, He especially appealed, as to the chief lesson that we are to learn of Him : "Learn of Me, for I am meek and humble of heart ". ‡ We have but to learn this of Him, we have but to acquire this from Him, and God will do all the rest. For though Christ was the Divine

---

* *Timothy* ii. 5, 6.   † S. August., *De Trinitate* lib. iv., c. 10.
‡ *S. Matthew* xi. 19.

Master of all the virtues, He claimed for Himself in a special and singular way the attribute of being the Master of humility, which from the moment of His Incarnation to the moment of His expiring on the Cross He perpetually exhibited in all His life and ways, both to His Father in Heaven and to men on earth. This truth is so admirably expressed in the words of the great St. Leo, that though we gave them in the previous volume, we here repeat them as deserving of our constant meditation.

"The whole victory whereby our Saviour conquered the devil and the world was conceived in humility and was worked out by humility. His predestined days began and ended under persecution. Sufferings came upon the child, and the meekness of the child came to the suffering man, because in one and the same descents of majesty He took a human birth and received a human death. When, therefore, Almighty God took up a cause so exceedingly bad as our cause was, He made it good by the prerogative of humility, and through this humility He destroyed both death and the author of death ; for He refused nothing of all that His persecutors brought against Him, but, in obedience to His Father, He endured with the gentlest meekness whatever cruelties His raging enemies might inflict. . . . Wherefore the whole sum of Christian discipline is to be found neither in voluble speech, nor in keen disputations, nor in the appetite for praise and glory ; but it consists in true humility freely accepted, and this, from His mother's womb to His agony on the Cross, the Lord Jesus Christ chose for all strength, and taught that strength to us." *

Who is the true Master but He who is all that He teaches and incomparably more than He teaches ? Jesus Christ was the substantive Master of humility. Our Divine Redeemer was. Himself humility, precisely as He was justice and truth. The descent of the Son of God, that infinite descent from the bosom of the Father into the lowly nature of man in this rude and sinful world, is humility. His perpetual subjection to the Father in this lowly nature is humility. His pleading for us to the Father with prayers and sacrifice and tears is humility. The voluntary shedding of His blood and surrender of His life for us is humility. All the humility whereby men have approached to God, whether before His Incarnation and Crucifixion, or since

* S. Leo, *Serm.* 7 *in Epiphaniam.*

that marvellous birth and awful sacrifice, is derived in floods of grace from the humility of Christ. Not only the mortality that He took upon Himself, not only His acts and words, His life and death, but the very substance of His Incarnation is humility. And when we thus look upon Jesus Christ, the Author and Finisher of our salvation, as the substantive humility, and feel how little of its healing virtue has yet entered our hearts, because of our unwillingness to surrender our self-love, we must at least feel deeply humiliated, even if unwilling to be humbled.

"I account humility," says a great and most humble contemplative, "as not having reached the full height of what it is even in the greatest saints. When we look at the infinite greatness of God and at His love, and then at His humility, written in His blood; when we gaze upon Him, so abject, so emptied of Himself on the Cross for our sakes; our heart faints, our mind fails, and we are beyond all expression ungrateful unless we respond with our whole existence to a love so prodigious. As His humiliations and sufferings are on His own part infinite, it is better that we keep our souls suspended in wonder for ever than to think too meanly of an abyss from which such an ocean of truth has flowed upon us." *

The Son of God could never have accepted this condition of humility but for the divinest reason of glorifying the Holy Trinity, which He did in taking the headship of humanity, in perfecting that humanity in Himself, in recovering that humanity to God when lost, and in restoring that humanity to the great and divine end for which every intelligent soul was created. He took this humble condition to drive back and destroy the huge invasion of pride that was the ruin of the human race. " Being in the form of God, He thought it no robbery to be equal with God, but emptied Himself, taking the form of a servant, being made in the likeness of man, and in habit found as a man. He humbled Himself, becoming obedient unto death, even the death of the Cross." † In which form of a servant He was less than the Father, less than Himself, unequal to Himself, unlike Himself, emptied to all appearance of Himself, in this land of misery and sorrow, that by restoring us to humility He might restore us to God.

---

* Venerabilis Joan. De St. Samson, *Theoremata*, c. i. *De Humilitate.*
† *Philippians* ii. 6-8.

Finding nothing but disorder and rebuke in their souls, men abandoned their offensive interiors, and threw themselves outwards upon visible things, with all the passion of cupidity and curiosity. But when utterly debased by things baser than themselves, God met them in a visible nature like their own, with such attractive sweetness and humility, that by accepting His humility they might again endure their own interior, and returning to themselves they might return to God. For, to quote the inexhaustible wisdom of St. Augustine once more, "The soul must be changed from the vanity of pride to the state of humility, before she can rise to what is high and solid; and this taming down of the ferocity of pride must be accomplished by persuasion, and not by violence. This could not be done more gently or magnificently than by the Eternal Word, the Wisdom and Virtue of the Father, who reveals Himself to the angels through Him, but who could not be seen by human hearts, blinded as they were with the cupidity of visible things. But He condescended to come in person and to live in man, and showed himself to men, that they might have greater fear of lifting themselves in pride, than of being humble after the example of God." *

Thus through His Incarnation the Son of God both consecrated and deified humility, making it more glorious to be humble with God than to be exalted with pride among the children of men; and giving us a more illustrious ambition than the world can offer, in associating ourselves with the virtue of the Lord God. Through divine persuasion we embrace that virtue freely to which we had once a great dislike, and find its power and sweetness. Through the sense which that virtue gives us, we have also the intimate assurance that to imitate Christ in His humility is something truly great, and that conducts to things incomparably greater; whilst even the children of this world may see how great is its power, since Christ has subjected the world to God through humility. For it is not a Christ clothed with temporal power, not a Christ rich in earthly goods, not a Christ refulgent amidst the pleasures of the world, but it is Christ crucified, who is preached to mankind. Let earthly pride, then, mark this fact, that there is nothing so mighty in the world as divine humility, which conquers nation after nation, although they fail when they fall anew from humility to pride. Nor is there anything

* S. August., *Epist. ad Madaurenses.*

mightier in man than humility, when truly derived from the humility of Christ, for it is strong to resist the ostentatious insults of pride, in whatever shape they may come against the humble.*

The humility of the Son of God is not only our example and encouragement, but it fills us with shame and reproach. For it rebukes our self-conceit, strikes our pride with reproach, and puts us to shame and confusion that we should be so foolish and perverse as to suffer so base and deceptive an evil to separate us from God, or keep us at a distance from Him; through which shame and confusion, and the repentance that follows upon it, our souls are healed. We learn from His humility to what a distance we have gone from God, and what a medicine we have in grief and repentance when we return to God through such a Mediator. It was the exceeding love of God for us that made Him humble, the inclining weight of His charity that brought Him down from Heaven. He could not have been incarnate without descending. He could not have descended but from exceeding charity, and therefore with unspeakable humility.†

When, therefore, we say that Christ is the Divine Master of humility, we speak a truth of the utmost profundity, but a truth that concerns us most intimately, even in the very highest of our interests ; and the longer and deeper we meditate upon the humility of Christ the more we shall find that it is not only a wonderful virtue, but a still more wonderful and fruitful power.

It was not the way of our Divine Master to define the virtues that He taught, or to follow the methods of science. He spoke as nature speaks, and with the simple voice of intuition. Science is a limiting method of teaching, obscure to the multitude, acquired with labour, taught with effort, and always raising more questions than it solves. But as Christ Jesus was the very truth, virtue, and life, He took the unlimited way of teaching, and taught not merely by words but by the light and virtue that went forth from Him in whatever He did, or said, or suffered. His words were most simple, transparent, and homely, filled with the light and energy of grace, yet intelligible to every humble soul.

---

* S. August., *Epist. ad Madaurenses.*
† See Thomassini, *De Incarnatione Verbi Dei*, lib. ii., c. 9.

Who can be intelligible if the Divine Truth in person be not intelligible? Hence "all gave testimony to Him, and they wondered at the words of grace that proceeded from His mouth ".* Wherever He appeared He was followed by crowds, drawn by His gracious presence, and by the wonderful things that He said and did.

There is a language of children that flows in simplicity from the heart of innocence; and there is a language of wise old men who have bid farewell to the vanities and pretensions of the world, that flows in clear simplicity from the experience of this life and the near prospect of the life to come. But the words of our Lord flowed from His spirit with another kind of simplicity—the divine simplicity of an all pure and perfect intelligence and love. He beheld all truth as it illuminates all good, and abridged and tempered that truth to the capacity of His hearers. Being in the person of the Word through whom all things were created, and by whom all intelligences are illuminated according to their conditions, He beheld all the similitudes of things earthly with things heavenly, and with the state and conduct of human souls. He therefore drew similitudes and parables at will from the visible things before His audience, and from the things familiar to their lives, with which to bring home to their bosoms the things of God and of the soul. He spoke and acted as the Master of creation, and as the Master of souls, as well as the Master of truth.

In a vast number of souls He found a dark obstacle that withstood the entrance of His grace and truth: this obstacle was pride and the concupiscence that fosters pride. Against this He opposed His humility with a gentle kindness and a divine patience. But where He found that pride or that covetousness to be not only hard and obstinate, but active and mischievous in misleading the people, He rose up against it with all the power of divine indignation. The Scribes and Pharisees who put their hard pride into the law, which in itself was sufficiently severe, and who knew no mercy in its interpretation when applied to their brethren; who, as our Lord reproached them, "bound heavy and unsupportable burdens, and laid them on men's shoulders, but with a finger of their own would not move them ";† these He rebuked with a fire of indignation that

---

* *S. Luke* iv. 22.   † *S. Matthew* xxiii. 4.

caused every one to tremble. To the covetous profaners of His Father's house, again, He not only used words but acts of indignation, and drove out the traffickers with stripes from the Temple. The two objects of His divine indignation were the proud teachers who blocked the way between God and the people, and the profane intruders who brought the world into the sanctuary of sacrifice. His humility rose against the pride that desolated God's people, and against the profanation of the divine worship.

Of the pride that closed the minds of so many of His hearers, He spoke in the words of the Prophet Isaias : " He hath blinded their eyes, and hardened their hearts, that they should not see with their eyes, nor understand with their heart, and be converted, and I should heal them ". Yet St. John adds the remark, that " Many of the chief men also believed in Him, but because of the Pharisees they did not confess Him, that they might not be cast out of the synagogue. For they loved the glory of men more than the glory of God." * He therefore chiefly sought the poor, the simple, and the afflicted, leaving the wealthy and the wise in their own opinion to seek Him.

But pride was not the only evil that withheld men from God ; the covetousness of the things of this world, and the appetite for sensual pleasures drew them with an overpowering fascination from the knowledge of God and from the love of eternal good. On this account it was necessary that we should not only have the example of humility but of self-abnegation as well, which is intimately connected with humility. Our Lord, therefore, united His humility with poverty, and His poverty with self-abnegation. Nor was this merely for our example, but because the life of humility, poverty, and self-abnegation is the most perfect of human lives, as depending on God alone, and as setting the things of this mortal life at their true value compared with the things of eternity. Yet through all the humility and poverty of Christ His Divinity shines ; as in the humility of His saints the Spirit of God shines through every abasement. He is born of a poor and humble Mother, but His paternity is a stupendous miracle of the Holy Spirit. His birth takes place in a wretched cave, a stable for beasts of burden, but the angels sing His glory in the heavens. He is wrapped in the swathings of poverty, but a miraculous

* S. *John* xii. 40-43.

star reveals His birth, and leads princes from a far country to adore Him. He works at the trade of His reputed father, industrious and obedient until His thirtieth year; but even at the age of twelve He astonishes the doctors of the law in the Temple by His wisdom. During the years of His divine mission He tells us: "The foxes have holes, and the birds of the air have nests, but the Son of man hath not where to lay His head ".* Yet He healed all infirmities, gave sight to the blind, and life to the dead. He is the sublime proof in His own person that humanity is but the instrument through which God works great things, and works them through humility and self-abnegation.

That was a solemn moment when, after His forty days of solitude, fasting, and prayer, the Son of God opened His mission to the world. St. Luke tells us that "Jesus returned in the power of the Spirit into Galilee, and the fame of Him went through the whole country. And He taught in their synagogues, and was magnified by all. And He came to Nazareth, where He was brought up; and He went into the synagogue according to His custom on the Sabbath-day; and He rose up to read, and the Book of Isaias the Prophet was delivered unto Him. And as He unfolded the Book, He found the place where it was written: *The Spirit of the Lord is upon me, wherefore He hath anointed me, to preach the Gospel to the poor He hath sent me, to heal the contrite of heart. To preach deliverance to the captives, and sight to the blind, to set at liberty them that are bruised, to preach the acceptable year of the Lord, and the day of reward.* And when He had folded the Book, He restored it to the minister, and sat down. And the eyes of all in the synagogue were fixed on Him. And He began to say to them: This day is fulfilled this Scripture in your ears." †

The calm and gentle way in which the Son of God first makes Himself known to the people of Nazareth, to those who had known Him for thirty years from His infancy, and let them know that He, whom they had only known as an obedient son and a pious working man, was the expected Messiah, and the fulfilment of the Prophets, has always appeared to me to be one of the most remarkable passages in the history of His divine life. It is not only remarkable for the calm gentleness of His bearing at so

* *S. Matthew* viii. 20. † *S. Luke* iv. 14-22.

solemn a moment, but for the humility with which He makes an announcement so startling to His audience. There is none of the excitement or fervour of enthusiasm with which mere human nature would have announced a great personal claim for the first time, especially when contrary to all the preconceptions of His hearers ; there is the calmness of God in the figure and voice of man. He reads the prophetic description of His divine mission in the ordinary course of His duty as a reader in the synagogue, and then, when all eyes are fixed upon Him, He gently drops the word to their attentive ears : " This day is fulfilled this Scripture in your ears ". All the rest He leaves to the silent inference of their own minds.

Take the wisest of the heathen sages, and compare this passage with any that occur in the teaching of Socrates. Socrates never opens his mouth without humiliating and wounding the susceptibilities of his hearers with the consciousness of his superior understanding. But the Eternal Wisdom Incarnate breathes forth the divinest truths in humility. In His ordinary conversation He calls Himself the Son of man ; and it is generally some special circumstances of objection to the divine power exhibited in His works that leads Him to assert His equality with the Father. For example, when He healed on the Sabbath, and the Pharisees condemned Him for violating the Sabbath, He says : " My Father worketh until now ; and I work ". Then they sought to put Him to death, because He said that " God was His Father, making Himself equal to God ". And now we have to observe the sublime humility of the Son of God—a humility which is always truth and always justice. He never speaks of His equality with the Father without adding that of Himself He can do nothing. On this very occasion, " Jesus answered and said to them : Amen, amen, I say unto you ; the Son cannot do anything of Himself, but what He seeth the Father doing ; for whatsoever He doth, these the Son also doth in like manner ".* And when the Capharnaites asked Him what signs He showed, and what works, that they might believe in Him ? He said to them : "All that the Father giveth Me, shall come to Me ; and him that cometh to Me, I will not cast out. Because I came down from Heaven not to do My own will, but the will of Him that sent Me."† Everywhere He humbly proclaims that He does nothing

* *S. John* v. 17-19.   † *S. John* vi. 37, 38.

of Himself, that He does no will but His Father's will, and no work but His Father's work.

When He taught in the Temple, and the people wondered at His doctrine, and said to one another: "How doth this man know letters, having never learned?" Jesus said to them: "My doctrine is not Mine, but His that sent Me. If any man will do the will of Him, he shall know of the doctrine, whether it be of God, or whether I speak of Myself. He that speaketh of himself seeketh his own glory; but he that seeketh the glory of Him that sent him, he is true, and there is no injustice in him." *

In this, as in the previous examples, we contemplate both the human and the divine side of the humility of the Son of God. On the human side, when His teaching has awakened admiration and wonder, He calls Himself but the representative of another, whose doctrine He speaks; on the divine side, as He is the Word of God, He ascribes all His knowledge to the Father, from whom it is eternally received. "What is the doctrine of the Father but the Word of the Father?" asks St. Augustine. "If Christ is the Word of the Father, He is the doctrine of the Father. As the Word He is the word of another, He therefore calls this doctrine His own, and not His own, because it is the word of the Father." † Whoever speaks from Himself, seeks his own glory; but whoever speaks from another seeks the glory of him from whom he speaks. Such a one is just and true, and therefore humble. Take away the passion for self-glorification, and the greater part of the divisions of mankind will cease. There is something most admirable and divine in this wisdom of humility or humility of wisdom with which the Son of God speaks of Himself, that puts the pride of our miserable self-glorying to shame.

Let it be further observed that in all His humble words and ways, our Divine Lord never speaks directly of His own humility but once. He lives and breathes and personifies the virtue, as what is inseparable from Him; but of His own humility He spoke but once. He spoke once because that was necessary for our instruction; He spoke once to consecrate this wonderful virtue; He spoke only once, because of the exceeding delicacy and hidden nature of the virtue, which, like purity, is far too modest to be spoken of by its possessor except in a case of

* *S. John* vii. 15-18.   † S. August., *Tract.* 29 *in Joannem.*

absolute necessity. And in this too He conveys to us a profound instruction.

It was after making one of those great declarations, of which we have quoted several, that our Lord gave that most touching instruction about the spirit in which alone we can come to Him, and through Him to His Father. "All things are delivered to Me by My Father. And no one knoweth the Son but the Father; neither doth any one know the Father but the Son, and he to whom it shall please the Son to reveal Him. Come to Me all you who labour, and are burdened, and I will refresh you. Take up My yoke upon you, and learn of Me, because I am meek and humble of heart; and you shall find rest to your souls. For My yoke is sweet and My burden light." *

Here we learn that humility is the special virtue of Christ, the virtue proper to Him, the virtue most dear to Him, the virtue that brought Him moved by infinite charity from the splendour of the eternal glories into the extremes of poverty and humiliation, so that there is nothing more illustrious in His life and death than this divine virtue of humility, whereby He redeemed the world, and with which He prepared the medicine that healeth all our infirmities, and bringeth us from all our sin and misery to rest in Him. Here we also learn from Him that that which pleases Him in souls is humility. And if He speaks of meekness as well, it is because meekness is the most exquisite and delightful fruit of humility, exhibiting the interior strength and fortitude of patience in a gentle sweetness. The yoke of Christ is the discipline of humility in self-abnegation; and the refreshment which He promises the humble is His interior light and grace, and especially that luminous and life-giving charity which dries up all sorrows, calms down all troubles, makes every labour easy, and every burden light. When charity reigns in humility Christ also reigns, and bears our trials with us. We are no longer under the yoke of Satan, no longer under the yoke of the world, no longer under the yoke of pride; we bear the yoke of Christ, whose yoke is sweet and His burden light.

"Come," He says, "to Me, learn of Me"; "I am the way, the truth, and the life: no man cometh to the Father except through Me".† He is the way to Heaven, the truth from Heaven, the life

---

* *S. Matthew* xi. 27-30.   † *S. John* xiv. 6.

that brings to Heaven; and He says, Come to Me; learn this one thing from Me, and you shall know all things; learn this one thing from Me, and you shall possess all things; learn of Me to be meek and humble of heart. There is nothing so wonderful in power as the humility of Christ, who resting the created nature of His humanity wholly upon His divine nature, ascribes nothing whatever to that human nature, which He knew so perfectly to be nothing without God. All, whatever He is and does, He attributes to the Father; and by reason of His humility, He receives from the Father an unspeakable power for our deliverance and sanctification. And when we subject ourselves to His yoke, with that mighty humility He enters our soul, and so great is its power that it carries the whole man away from the false and frail foundation of pride on which he has laboured in vain to build himself, and rests His life on God as an unfailing firmament of strength. There is a total change effected in our whole mind and thought, in all the habits and aspirations of the soul, and the divine virtues come into the place once occupied by the blinding and disordering vices, giving us a peaceful communion with God, instead of a restless and anxious dread of coming nearer to the good of divine and eternal things.

Having once learned from Christ that the great lesson He has come to teach us is His own meekness and humility, we then discover that His Incarnation, His birth, all the actions of His life, His sufferings and death, all speak to us, and breathe into us this divine lesson of humility; and everywhere, even when His voice is silent, His life and conduct say to us: " Learn of Me, because I am meek and humble of heart ".

Go to the cave of Bethlehem, and look at the desolate condition of the new-born child. At the voice of the angels the shepherds come to adore ; but what a scene of poverty and distress ! The Virgin Mother all veneration and service, Joseph all silent and attentive. Yet here, if anywhere, must the divine humility take hold of us. Our pride melts into compassion, our heart is moved with tenderness, we are disarmed by stooping to this fresh-born misery; our soul is opened by the touch of humanity, and, whilst in all outward appearance we seem to be stronger than He, the divine grace of humility passes from the heart of the Divine Child into ours, and convicts us of our weakness.

Subjected to the law of circumcision made for sinners, He

receives the name of Jesus, and pays the first forfeit of that blood which shall save the world. On the fortieth day from His birth He is offered to His Father in the Temple, and is redeemed as the first-born with the offering made for the poor. The wise men from the East find Him in abjection, the honours they render to Him bring on Him His first persecution from the powers of the world, and He escapes in His Mother's arms to Egypt, where His human ancestors so long suffered exile in slavery and misery.

At the age of twelve He is taken from Nazareth to the solemn festival in Jerusalem, where He is found "in the Temple, sitting amidst the doctors, hearing them, and asking them questions. And all that heard Him were astonished at His wisdom and answers." And He went down with Mary and Joseph, "and came to Nazareth; and was subject to them".* But from this time to His thirtieth year He disappears from the eyes of the world, and the Scriptures are silent upon Him. We have a glimpse of His supernatural wisdom at twelve, after which that long period of His life is summed up in the word *subjection.* He exercised obedience, attended the synagogue, and did the work of a labouring man. How profound the lesson of His meekness and humility! His silence instructs us to learn before we teach, to be subject under discipline before we are masters, and to be long silent and retired before we give our light to others. All we know is, that during those long years of humble obedience covered in silence, "Jesus advanced in wisdom and age, and grace with God and men".

His humble and austere Precursor was already preparing the way for His appearance. As he preached "the baptism of penance for the remission of sins," all the people took John the Baptist for a prophet. But in the truth and justice of his humility, St. John considered himself as nothing but a voice, calling on them to prepare the way of the Lord; and when the people in their hearts thought that he might be the Christ, the prophet of the humble one said: "I indeed baptize you with water; but there shall come one mightier than I, the latchet of whose shoes I am not worthy to loose; He shall baptize you with the Holy Ghost and with fire". † Then comes Jesus to be baptized by John. "But John stayed Him, saying: I ought to be baptized by Thee, and comest Thou to me?" And Jesus said to

* *S. Luke* ii. 46-52.   † *S. Luke* iii. 16.

him : " Suffer it be so now. For so it becometh us to fulfil all justice. Then he suffered Him." What a scene of humility is here presented to our contemplation ! The humble prophet of God, and the humble God of the prophet, and humility obedient in both ; the humble God ruling the humility of the prophet, that both might obey the law of justice in doing the will of the Father, in setting the example of submission. Then, as ever, came the reward of humility. "And Jesus being baptized forthwith came out of the water ; and lo, the heavens were opened to Him ; and He saw the Spirit of God descending as a dove, and coming upon Him. And behold a voice from Heaven, saying : This is My beloved Son, in whom I am well pleased."＊ The Holy Trinity is sensibly manifested in the divine mission of the Son. The Father in the voice, the Son baptized in the body, and proclaimed by the Father, the Holy Spirit in the dove descending on Him, and the mission in the words : " This is My beloved Son ; hear ye Him ".

But before He begins His mission He exhibits another great in- stance of humility and self-abnegation in His forty days of retirement and preparation. During those forty days he abides in the wild and unsheltered solitude of the desert, among wild beasts, in fasting, prayer, and the temptations of Satan. Then, after angels have ministered to His fainting humanity, He pro- ceeds to His stupendous work. As His work is to be the result of humility and charity, and His power to be exercised in infirmity, He selects twelve poor, simple-minded, unlettered men, for His disciples and companions, in whom to plant the Word of Truth that shall subdue the world. He lives in common with them, and they observe His ways, and listen to His sweet con- versation, as He forms them by degrees to His divine example. He claims no exceptional privilege, but is with them as their servant more than their master. From this time He appears before the world, gathering men together in great numbers through His attractive grace, sowing the Word of Truth among them, doing signs and wonders, and healing the infirm. Sinners humble themselves to Him, and He pardons them. He pro- claims Himself the Good Shepherd that gives His life for His sheep, searches for the sheep that are lost, and tenderly brings them to the fold.

＊ *S. Matthew* iii. 13-17.

The portrait of His meek and gentle character was drawn by the Prophet Isaias six hundred years before His appearance: "Thus saith the Lord, Behold My servant, I will uphold Him; My elect, My soul delighteth in Him: I have given My spirit upon Him; He shall bring forth judgment to the Gentiles. He shall not cry out, nor have respect to person, neither shall His voice be heard abroad. The bruised reed He shall not break, and the smoking flax he shall not quench; He shall bring forth judgment unto truth; He shall not be sad, nor troublesome, till He set judgment in the earth." * Charmed by His words and awed by His works, the multitudes followed Him into the lonely deserts by four and five thousand at a time, until they forgot to eat, and He fed them miraculously.

He opened His teaching with the commendation of humility, giving His first blessing to the poor in spirit. He never lost an opportunity of exalting and drawing attention to the humble who came near Him, as though He preferred setting forth its example in others rather than in Himself. When Magdalen bathes His feet with tears, He declares her sins forgiven, and to the murmuring guests at the table He enlarges upon her penitential and most loving sacrifice. When the heathen centurion exclaimed, "Lord, I am not worthy that Thou shouldst enter under my roof, but only speak the word, and my servant shall be healed," † He held up the humble faith of that stranger as an example to the Jews. When He repelled the Canaanite woman's petition to try her faith, and she replied in the simplicity of her heart, "Yea, Lord, even the little dogs receive the crumbs which fall from their master's table," He said to her, "O woman, great is thy faith; be it done as thou wilt ".‡ He taught humility when He called the poor and the ignorant to follow Him; when He healed the abject in body and soul; when he conversed with open sinners and with lepers; when He enjoined silence respecting His miracles, and especially respecting His glorious transfiguration. He was Himself the great model of that poverty and self-abnegation that He advised to others.

The wonderful contrast between the Divine Teacher and their ordinary instructors could not fail to produce an extraordinary impression upon the minds of the people. It was this and the claims He put forth that awakened so keen an envy in the

* *Isaias* xlii. 1-4.　† *S. Matthew* viii. 8.　‡ *S. Matthew* xv. 27, 28.

teachers and ministers of the law.   His great humility and gentleness, the wonderful power He put forth, and the divine title
upon which He rested that power, spread His fame through all
circles; whilst His tender beneficence won the souls of the
people and captivated their hearts.   The great mass of the population was with Him, and this was made one of the principal
grounds for putting Him to death.

He showed a singular love for innocent children, and St. Mark
tells us that He took them up in His arms and laid His hand
upon their heads, and was much displeased when His disciples
endeavoured to keep them from Him, and He said : "Suffer the
little children to come to Me, and forbid them not, for the kingdom of Heaven is for such".   When His disciples asked Him :
"Who thinkest Thou is the greater in the kingdom of Heaven ?"
Jesus called to Him a little child, set him in the midst of them,
and said : "Amen, I say to you, unless you be converted, and
become as little children, you shall not enter into the kingdom of
Heaven.   Whosoever therefore shall humble himself as this little
child, he is the greatest in the kingdom of Heaven."*   Mark this
act attentively.   We know that ambition had shown itself in some
of His disciples, and this very question intimates as much.   The
child is called and set among them, they little thinking that he
is to become their model.   An innocent child is simple, humble,
free from guile, conscious of ignorance, more conscious of dependence; open as the day, possessing nothing, hoping for all
things, and still relying on parental love, protection, and support.
He is submissive and obedient to His parents as the Christian
should be to God; he is full of faith, hope, and love to his
parents as the Christian should be to God.   "Whosoever therefore shall humble himself as this little child, he is the greatest in
the kingdom of Heaven."   On another occasion, He teaches them
that he who is the least, that is, in his own esteem, shall be the first;
and that he who holds the first place shall be the servant of all.

Christ must be publicly acknowledged as the Son of David and
King of Israel before He is put to death.   He therefore makes
His public entrance into Jerusalem when the multitudes are
assembling from all parts to celebrate the Passover.   The news
of His raising Lazarus from the dead four days before has filled
the whole population with excitement, and many of the friends

* *S. Matthew* xviii. 1-4.

of Lazarus have seen and conversed with him since his resurrection. See the solemn state in which the Son of God advances. On the humblest beast, covered with the cloaks of His disciples, the Saviour of the world is mounted. "Tell ye the daughter of Sion," said the Prophet Isaias, "Behold thy King cometh to thee, meek, and sitting upon an ass." * · And a very great multitude spread their garments on the way ; and others cut boughs from the trees, and strewed them before Him ; and the multitude that went before and followed after cried out: "Hosanna to the Son of David; blessed is He that cometh in the name of the Lord; Hosanna in the Highest ". + St. John tells us the immediate cause of this triumphal reception : "The multitude therefore gave testimony that was with Him when He called Lazarus out of the grave, and raised him from the dead. For which reason also the people came to meet Him, because they heard that He had done this miracle." ‡ And what was the demeanour of the Son of God amidst this universal acclamation ? "When He drew near, seeing the city, He wept over it, saying : If thou hadst known, and that in this thy day, the things that are to thy peace ; but now they are hidden from thy eyes." § He is still the Master of humility, and His acts still say to us : "Learn of Me, for I am meek and humble of heart ".

He leaves us His testament of humility before He gives His testament of blood, and this testament is very solemnly recorded by St. John. "Knowing that the Father had given Him all things into His hands, and that He came from God, and goeth to God, He ariseth from supper, and layeth aside His garments, and having taken a towel, girded Himself. After that, He putteth water into a basin, and began to wash the feet of the disciples, and to wipe them with the towel, wherewith He was girded. . . . Then after He had washed their feet, and taken His garments, being sat down again, He said to them, Know you what I have done to you ? You call Me Master, and Lord : and you do well, for so I am. If then I, being your Lord and Master, have washed your feet, you also ought to wash one another's feet. For I have given you an example, that as I have done to you, so you do also. Amen, amen, I say to you : The servant is not greater than his lord : neither is the apostle greater

* *Isaias* lxii. 11 ; *Zach.* ix. 9.   + *S. Matthew* xxi. 8, 9.
‡ *S. John* xii. 17, 18,   § *S. Luke* xix. 41, 42.

than he that sent him. If you know these things, you shall be blessed if you do them." *

The works and virtues that our Divine Redeemer has taught in the Gospel are completed in their utmost perfection in His passion. His Cross is the end of the Law and the Scriptures; His passion is the sum of all that man can offer up to God; His death is the consummation of every word that is written concerning Him; the consummation of all humility that gives everything from man to God; the consummation of all charity that gives everything from God to man. Justly then did St. Paul sum up all in Christ crucified, and proclaim this to be "the power of God, and the wisdom of God".† To know Christ crucified is to know the open way from earth to Heaven. The four Evangelists have therefore given us more than the history, they have left us the living picture of the divine passion of the Son of God, filled in every point and circumstance with all its spirit and feeling; that the passion of Christ may everlastingly live in our souls, and we in the passion and death of Christ.

The devout man contemplates the passion of his Lord and Saviour, that he may imitate, and compassionate, and wonder, and exult, and resolve, and rest on Him.

First, we contemplate Christ in His passion to imitate the divine rule of virtue and perfection; and the more we conform ourselves to Him, the more we are strengthened and consoled.

Secondly, we contemplate to compassionate, and in spirit to suffer with Him, opening our soul to His sufferings, to His words, to His patience, to His humility, to His sorrows; turning and ruminating them in our heart, that they may make us contrite for our sins, and that we may learn their bitterness through His bitter expiation of them; and may be humbled and confounded at our ingratitude.

Thirdly, we contemplate that awful and stupendous passion with wonder. For when we realize to our minds who it is that suffers, what He suffers, from whom He suffers, and for whom He suffers, amazement takes possession of the soul. For the sufferer is the Son of God, the divine lover of mankind, who endures all that can be inflicted on body and soul, of pain, shame, and ignominy that man can invent, or God the Father impose on His obedience, for the expiation of our sins, and for our deliverance from evil.

* *S. John* xiii. 3-17.　　　　　† I *Cor.* i. 24.

Fourthly, we contemplate that wonderful passion to exult. For through all the sorrows of the Son of God we must rejoice in the deliverance of mankind. We must exult that through this blessed passion our Lord has delivered us from eternal damnation, from the ignominy of our guilt, and from the power of the devil. We must exult in seeing that God has loved us so much, even when we loved Him not; and though we take no joy in His ignominy or sufferings, but only sorrow, yet must we rejoice in their happy fruits, and in the wonderful manifestation of His eternal love. Again must we exult to see the reparation of our ruin, and in that union, brought about by the blood and sorrows of our Lord, in one fold of salvation, under one Shepherd. For this the Church above and the Church below unite in joy. Oh, how lovely and how venerable is that Sacred Passion which unites things so remote as Heaven and earth in one love, in one eternal joy! Above all must we exult in the clemency of our Lord and Saviour; for this is the highest glory of angels and just men, to enter most profoundly into the clemency, benignity, and immensity of the Divine Goodness, which shines so luminously through the tremendous passion of our Lord Jesus Christ, who raises up His enemies from everlasting death to everlasting life. Let then your heart rejoice in your reparation by the magnificent benignity and unspeakable clemency of our crucified Redeemer. What a revelation does His passion give us of the unfathomable evil of sin, of the unsearchable depths of His humility, and of the inexhaustible treasures of His love!

Fifthly, we must contemplate the passion of our Lord to reform and resolve our soul. This is effected when we not only imitate, compassionate, admire, and exult, but when the whole man is drawn to Christ Jesus, beholding Him as our Redeemer, always and everywhere crucified. Then the soul is resolved, and, so to speak, is liquidized, and flows from herself and self-love to rise above herself, quitting what is beneath her, and moving wholly towards her crucified Lord; then she sees nothing, feels nothing in herself but Christ crucified, dishonoured, and suffering for her sake. This was the sense of St. Paul: "With Christ I am nailed to the Cross ".*

Sixthly, we ought to contemplate the passion of Christ to find therein our rest and peace. This is effected after the soul has

---

* *Galatians* ii. 19.

been thus transformed, when we thirst for the passion of Christ as an inexhaustible treasure of goodness, and an ever-flowing fountain of grace and love, wherein we find sweetness, rest, and peace. There the more we give up our love and devotion to ourselves, all the more we cleave to Him who died to give us life, and find our life and peace in Him. When thus we enter into the passion of our Lord, we receive from Him these six affections: of imitation to purify and enkindle our souls, of compassion to unite us with Him in love and gratitude, of wonder to enlarge and elevate our mind, of exultation to expand our heart, of resolution to confirm our soul in His perfection, and of peace to preserve our devotion.*

The passion of our Lord presents all the great virtues in their perfection for our imitation, whether self-denial, poverty of spirit, obedience, silence, humility, purity, patience, prayer, resignation, contempt of the world, or charity. But among all these virtues He pre-eminently appears as the Master of humility. His passion is the book of humility, His Cross is the throne of humility, the terrible way from the Mount of Olives to Mount Calvary is the substantive exposition of the words: "Learn of Me, for I am meek and humble of heart".

Who shall sound the depths of that lonely agony beneath the olive trees? It is the oblation before the immolation of the Divine Victim, and the crucifixion of the spirit before the crucifixion of the body. "The Lord hath laid on Him the iniquities of us all."† As the salt and flour fell on the sacrifice of the law, and the hand of the priest laid the sins of the people on its head, the Father laid the sins of the world upon His Son, and His innocent soul is charged with the guilt of mankind, and with its terrible expiation. The cup of human iniquity, all its pride, uncleanness, and infidelity, are mingled in the horrible draught, from the first to the last drop of malice that the earth has seen, or shall see that Heaven has reprobated, or shall reprobate; and especially that original sin which all the rest have followed. With this foul and fearful burden laid upon His pure nature He exclaims : "My soul is sorrowful, even unto death".‡ And He began to fear, and to be weary, and to be heavy, and to be sad. And falling flat with His face to the ground, He prayed, that if possible this hour

* Cisnerius, *Exercitatorum Spirituale*, c. lvii.
† *Isaias* liii. 6.   ‡ *S. Matthew* xxvi. 38.

14*

might pass from Him.   A struggle had arisen between His human nature and the divine will, and he prayed : "Father, all things are possible to Thee ; remove this cup from Me, yet not as I will, but as Thou willest ".* He comes to His three disciples, finds them asleep, and returns to make the same prayer.   His struggle has become a dreadful agony.   What is that agony ? The agony of a dying man is to retain the soul escaping from the body.   The agony of Christ is to subject His innocent soul to responsibility for the foul load of human sin, and to undergo its expiation, because though His nature shrinks with horror from it, it is His Father's will.   "And His sweat became as drops of blood trickling on the ground." †   Then He prayed the third time in the self-same words, and gave up His will to the will of His Father.   Then He arose with resignation to accomplish that will. What hear we throughout this terrible agony but the words of the Divine Master : "Learn of Me, for I am meek and humble of heart "?

Mark the traitorous kiss of Judas, and hear the gentle reproach of Jesus.   Before the chief priests and their council He holds a mysterious silence.   But when the High Priest adjures Him in the name of the living God to say whether He is " the Christ, the Son of the Blessed God," Jesus said : "I am.   And you shall see the Son of man sitting at the right hand of the power of God, and coming in the clouds of Heaven." ‡   He defends not Himself ; such is His Father's will, to whom He is in all things subject. But when He is adjured in His Father's name by him who sits in the chair of Moses, He spoke the truth, and on that truth was condemned to death.   All that night the Divine Victim was salted with sufferings, and saluted with spittings, with mufflings of the face, and buffetings : "Learn of Me, for I am meek and humble of heart ".

In the morning the chief priests call the High Council of the nation to consultation, and, binding Jesus, they led Him away, and delivered Him to Pilate.   His meek silence under every accusation awakens the wonder of the Roman governor.   Knowing the envy of the accusing priests, Pilate seeks to deliver Him, yet only exposes Him to deeper ignominy and greater sufferings. For all that was written of Him must be fulfilled ; He must be "reputed with the wicked," that the sins of the world may be

* *S. Mark* xiv. 36.   † *S. Luke* xxii. 44.   ‡ *S. Matthew* xxvi. 63, 64.

expiated superabundantly. "He was wounded for our iniquities, He was bruised for our sins; the chastisement of our peace was upon Him, and by His bruises we are healed." *

Pilate declares His innocence, and appeals to the people. But urged on by the priests, the fickle multitude cry out: "Give us Barabbas, and crucify Jesus. If thou dismiss Him, thou art no friend of Cæsar's. His blood be upon us and on our children." After this awful imprecation, Pilate commands Jesus to be scourged. After suffering all night from the Jews, He must now suffer from the Gentiles. The Evangelists have omitted all the incidents of the scourging as though too fearful to relate, but they have been precise upon the ignominious mockery of His royalty. The soldiers of the governor took Jesus into the hall, and calling the whole band, they put on Him a robe of purple, and platting a crown of thorns, they put it on His head, and a reed in His right hand. And bowing the knee before Him, they mocked Him, saying: Hail, King of the Jews, and spitting upon Him, they took the reed, and struck His head. O divine patience! O eternal love! O unspeakable profundity of the humility of the Son of God! "Despised, and the most abject of men, a man of sorrows and acquainted with infirmity; His look as it were hidden and despised, whereupon we esteemed Him not. Surely He hath borne our iniquities, and carried our sorrows: and we have thought Him as it were a leper, and as one struck by God and afflicted." † Now doth He expiate the pride of man that shuts out the truth of God, and refuses entrance to His love: His heart is a furnace of humility and prayer. Every mock, each stripe, and every sigh of supplication that ascends from His lowly heart, is a call upon us to give up and punish our despicable pride. He is the humble, beaten, down-trodden way to God: "Learn of Me, for I am meek and humble of heart".

And they took Him away to crucify Him. In the sight of the whole nation assembled at the Passover, contemplate the dolorous way of the Lord of life under the load of His Cross from Pilate's house by the Temple through Jerusalem to Calvary. All along that path of blood He is perfecting the power of salvation in infirmity. Upon that desolate hill, where, according to ancient tradition, lay the body of the first sinful man, the Lord of life was stripped to nudity, stretched out on the prostrate Cross, nailed

---

* *Isaias* liii. 5, 12,   † *Isaias* liii. 3, 4, 7.

with cruel nails to its cruel wood, and lifted up as the sin-offering of the God on earth to the God in Heaven. "He was offered because He willed it." Adam stretched his hands to the forbidden tree, and his feet hurried on to complete his condemnation. Christ gives His hands and feet to the tree of obedience, fastens the decree of condemnation to His Cross, and blots it out with His blood. Abel is slain by His brother; Isaac is offered by Abraham; the brazen serpent is lifted up by Moses; the Paschal Lamb is immolated by the law; God is crucified by man. Sin sacrifices innocence, pride immolates humility; God overrules these evil instruments to His sovereign will, that humble innocence may destroy both pride and sin.

Oh, soul redeemed by that fast-flowing blood, look well to thy redemption! In that bowed head, so venerable; in that sweet face, so livid; in that august brow, so wounded; in those lightsome eyes, so worn with weeping; in those authoritative lips, so pale with thirst and suffering—contemplate the cost of thy salvation. In that virginal body bruised with buffets, rent with scourges, wet with the slaver of the wicked, worn and wan with pain and labour, behold the expiation of thy sensual sins. In those gaping wounds on which thy Saviour hangs, see the open doors through which the ruddy price of thy salvation streams upon thee. The life exuding with that blood is thy life. Pass through those wounds to the heart from which the stream of life is flowing. See how that heart is abandoned by an interior crucifixion, not of man, but of God, to darkness and desolation of spirit, for the expiation of all sins of the spirit. How far more terrible is this interior expiation! Listen to the cry of that afflicted heart: "I thirst!" However great the corporal thirst, far greater is the spiritual thirst for the souls of men! Listen again to the cry of charity: "Father, forgive them, they know not what they do". Listen once more, and listen with awe, to the cry of desolation from the heart of the Sacred Victim: "My God, My God, why hast Thou abandoned Me?" The dreadful expiation is hastening on, the sacrifice is burning out, burning in the furnace of humiliation, consuming in the fire of charity. With a strong cry, full of the power of His will, the Victimal Son cries to the Father: "Into Thy hands I commend My spirit," and all being consummated, He expires. David heard that last cry of his Son a thousand years before, and proclaimed its solemn import to mankind "Into Thy hands I commend my Spirit; Thou hast redeemed me, Lord God of truth ".*

The Cross is the instrument of contrition upon which the earthly man is broken to be reformed upon the heavenly man. The Cross is the divine school of patience; the school of self-abnegation; the school of penance; the school of charity. The foot of the Cross where Mary stood with John, and where the prostrate Magdalen wept her loving grief, is the great school of humility, where the soul is purified and brought to God. There for ever sounds the great command of the Divine Master: "Learn of Me, for I am meek and humble of heart".

The resurrection of our Divine Redeemer from the grave, His ascension from earth to Heaven, His seat in our human nature at the right hand of the Father, with all His wounds glorified, and His power over the souls of the humble, who draw their humility from Him, are the crowning of His sacrifice, the sublime demonstration of His divinity, and the encouragement of all who love and suffer for His sake. "He humbled Himself, becoming obedient unto death, even the death of the Cross. For which cause God also hath exalted Him, and hath given Him a name which is above all names; that in the name of Jesus every knee shall bow, of those that are in Heaven, on earth, and under the earth. And that every tongue should confess that the Lord Jesus Christ is in the glory of God the Father."†

* *Psalm* xxx. 6.   † *Philippians* ii. 8-11.

LECTURE IX.

ON HUMILITY AS THE RECEPTIVE FOUNDATION OF THE DIVINE GIFTS AND VIRTUES.

"God resisteth the proud, but to the humble He giveth grace."—1 St. Peter v. 5.

IT is impossible to imagine holiness in any of God's creatures without humility and purity. For as chastity is the body's purity, humility is the soul's purity, and purity is the first condition of sanctity. Humility prepares the way for holiness, and holiness deepens the grace of humility; so that the higher the holiness the deeper must be the degree of humility. But humility, like purity, is an extremely delicate virtue; it is the soul's purity, the spirit's modesty, the will's continency, as it refrains the soul from self-elation, from pride, and from vanity, which defile the spirit with inflation, falsehood, and injustice. As acids dissolve the lustre of the pearl, as the rude hand brushes the bloom from the flower, the breath of its revelation melts away the graces of humility. Like the virtue of modesty, and because it is the spirit's modesty, humility is a silent virtue that only reveals its presence unconsciously. With a delicate perception of this truth, St. Francis of Sales thus writes of it to his friend the Bishop of Bellay: "There are two virtues that, whilst we never cease to exercise them, should be kept under perpetual silence. If we speak of them, it should be on some very rare occasion, so that it may pass for unbroken silence. These two virtues are humility and chastity. The reason of this is, that it is difficult to touch them without leaving some tarnish on them. No tongue can express their value, and to speak less of them than their value is to lower their excellence. Even if we praise humility in itself, we awaken the desire of it of self-love, and thus draw the man to

seek it by the wrong door. For the more a man finds the reputation of humility, the more he will be tempted to think himself humble, and the more he thinks himself humble, the less
humble he will be."

As the miser shrinks with a sense of danger from the least
allusion to his wealth, as the modest virgin blushes with conscious
apprehension at the slightest reference to her purity, the humble
soul is pained at the smallest commendation of her humility.
Equally fine is the instinct of both these virtues. To breathe on
them is to offend them, to speak of them is to hint a peril. A
word in their praise sounds as a reproof, and is felt like a wound.
When they are strong, this arises from no queasy scrupulosity
or false delicacy, but is owing to the fact that they are not the
becoming subjects for self-reflection, or of direct self-consciousness
on the part of their possessors, and any direct allusion to them is
an appeal to that self-consciousness which invades their integrity.
The more humble and pure a soul is, the more she looks away
from herself into the perfect type of holiness, in whose light she
sees nothing in herself but the gifts of God and her own defects.
She knows, frail creature that she is, that her treasure is from
God, and is only safe when hidden from mortal eyes. For however true, however beautiful, however sublime may be the praises
of this virtue, self-love is all the more inclined to take that to
herself which belongs only to the virtue. St. Bernard felt this,
when one day sounding the commendations of humility, he felt
certain movements begin to rise in him that caused him to fly
from the pulpit in dismay.

Although our Blessed Lord was the perfect form of humility,
and the fountain of its grace, yet, as we have seen, He only
referred to His own humility once, and that for the instruction of
all ages. Are we then to abstain from the praises of humility?
In due season, and to souls well disposed to the virtue, most
certainly not. We must rather draw the distinction between the
virtue in itself and in those who are safe with God, and the same
virtue as it may exist in souls still exercised in this world of trial
and temptation. For no virtue has received greater or more
frequent commendations in the Holy Scriptures, and from the
Fathers and Saints of the Church, unless it be the virtue of charity.
As it is the rarest of virtues in its perfection; as, nevertheless, its
perfection is essential to the perfection of the other virtues; as it

is also the most hidden, as all the roots of life and growth are hidden ; as it is also a virtue that costs much labour and sacrifice to our nature, and therefore requires encouragement, both the interest of God's cause and the interest of the cause of souls requires that it be enlarged upon. There is the more necessity for this, because of the many spurious imitations by which deluded pride caricatures this virtue ; and because it is so little exercised by the world at large, that of all virtues it is the least known and the least understood. But as it dwells in living souls, silence belongs to its essential modesty.

To the living man, therefore, these words of St. Maximus are especially applicable : " The Scripture says : ' Praise not a man during his life '. Praise him after death ; magnify him after all is finished. For two reasons ought he to be rather exalted in remembrance than in life : that his sanctity may be honoured when flattery can no longer move the speaker, and when elation can no more tempt the man who receives the praise." * St. Francis therefore concludes : " Yet must we not be scrupulous about praising these virtues when occasion demands it of us. Never can they be sufficiently praised, esteemed, or cultivated ; yet what does this signify ? All the leaves of praise you can heap together are not worth a handful of the fruit that grows of practice."

Why does God love to see His rational creatures humble ? Why does He endow the humble, and only the humble, with His gifts and graces ? Why does He save the humble alone ? The answer to this is hard to flesh and blood, and still harder to pride. For humility is not the highest or most dignified of virtues, its place is very low. St. Paul sums up the highest virtues in faith, hope, and charity, which have God for their direct and immediate object, and the greatest of these is charity. But humility more directly concerns ourselves ; its first office is to disbelieve, mistrust, and renounce self-love. Justice again, and especially justice to God, is a very high and noble virtue, with its perfect type in God ; and it dwells in all the virtues, to conform them to the perfect law of justice ; but humility is the virtue that measures our failures from justice, and our distance from the Eternal Justice, and that labours to make and to keep us truthful and honest within ourselves and before God. Re-

---

* S. Maximus, *Hom.* 59 *de S. Eusebio Vercellen.*

ligion also is an elevated and an elevating virtue, whereby we
worship God and give Him honour and adoration ; whilst humility is much expended in keeping us from the insane folly of
honouring and worshipping ourselves. Religion therefore is far
more glorifying to God.

We need scarcely bring in St. Thomas to show that humility
is inferior to many of the virtues as it respects their elevation and
dignity. Yet the Sacred Scriptures overflow with the doctrine
that what God seeks in man, what He loves in man, what He
rewards in man, is humility. And the Fathers and Saints proclaim with the united chorus of their minds and hearts that
humility is the root and foundation of all the virtues that are
born of grace. It is the condition on which they are received,
and the attraction that brings to the soul those nobler gifts of
God ; the measure of their reception, and the nurse of their
prosperity. No soul that follows interior ways is ignorant of the
fact that humility is the indispensable foundation of Christian
virtue ; but only a limited number trouble themselves to understand how and why it is the indispensable foundation which no
other virtue can supply. Yet to understand this well gives great
light to the interior man, and to many things.

The comparing of our spiritual operations to the construction
of a building is so frequent in the Scriptures, and so familiar to
our minds, that it is become natural to our spiritual language.
We speak of edifying, of laying the spiritual foundation, and of
building up the soul, scarcely noticing the fact that we are using
material images from the builder's art to express spiritual operations. But though there is a resemblance between material
and spiritual building, there is a great difference between them.
For example, we speak, with St. Paul, of building on Christ as
our foundation ; and in so far as we rest on Him, are sustained
by Him, and draw our strength and support from Him, this
image is correct. But in so far as a foundation is beneath and
exterior to the building, it is incorrect. For Christ is above us,
and we rest on Him by subjection and dependence, as the fly on
the ceiling ; yet though this image relieves us from the literalness
of the former one, it cannot itself be taken literally, because the
action of Christ is first external, awakening us, and then internal,
abiding within us. Christ Jesus is our true foundation when the
centre of the soul rests on Him. This may serve to explain how

by spiritual insight we rectify the figurative language that we use to give more vivid expression to our spiritual acts.

The spiritual founding of the soul, like the material founding of a building, requires three acts. We have to remove the unsound foundation to come at the true foundation, and to lay upon that the positive foundation, or the foundation-stones. The first preparation for building the spiritual temple in which God may dwell is to remove what is unsound and insecure. This is the self-love and pride on which the soul has hitherto rested. The removal of this weak and unsafe foundation brings us to the rock or solid ground, which is Christ, and the positive foundation upon which the structure must rise is the faith of Christ. Humility, therefore, is neither the solid rock, for that is Christ, nor the foundation built upon it, which is faith; but it is the clearing and preparing of the ground in ourselves. We shall recollect this the better if we remember that the word *humility*, from the Latin *humilitas*, comes from *humus*, the soft, moist earth, and *unitas*, which implies connection with the earth. Humility is the vacancy made in the soul by the removal of our unsound and unsupporting self-love, and of the unsubstantial inflation of pride.

By thus evacuating ourselves as a most untrue foundation, we come to the rock, which is Christ, upon whom the whole spiritual building rests with firmness and security. "For other foundation," says St. Paul, "no man can lay, but that which is laid, which is Christ Jesus." * Thus we see that humility is not the positive but the negative foundation, the emptying ourselves that Christ may dwell in us, and the resting on Him through subjection to Him. But Christ dwells in us by faith, hope, and charity; these therefore are the true foundation-stones, whereby the whole building rests on Christ. The first is faith, of which St. Paul says: "Without faith it is impossible to please God. For He that cometh to God must believe that He is, and is a rewarder to them that seek Him." † Next to faith St. Paul places hope, which rests on faith. "Continue," he says, "in the faith, grounded and settled, immovable from the hope of the Gospel which you have heard." ‡ But of the most precious of the three foundation-stones, the Apostle says: "Being rooted and founded in charity, you may be able to comprehend, with all the saints, what is the

* *I Corinthians* iii. 11.   † *Hebrews* xi. 6.   ‡ *Colossians* i. 23.

breadth, and length, and height, and depth. To know also the charity of Christ, which surpasseth all knowledge, that you may be filled unto all the fulness of God."*

Not to adhere too closely to the architectural images of divine things, humility prepares the way for receiving the Christian virtues as St. John the Baptist prepared the way for Christ. His office was to cast down pride and to purify with water. His cry was: Let the hills be brought down, the valleys be filled up, and the crooked ways made straight. Everything about him breathes humility, and the mortification and self-renunciation that produce humility. He is nothing of himself, he is but the voice of another, whose shoes he declares he is unworthy to untie. Having done his work, he disappears in the sacrifice of martyrdom, and Christ comes into his place.

St. Paul calls the true Christian God's building and God's husbandry. He lays in us the foundation of faith that we may know Him, of hope that we may desire Him, and of charity that we may love Him, serve Him, and rejoice in Him. But this can only be done in a soul that is duly disposed. For God cannot build a divine edifice on an earthly foundation, not upon self-love, not upon self-elation, not upon self-seeking, not upon hollow, delusive, revolting pride; not upon animal concupiscence. A building upon such quicksands would soon be swallowed up. All this creation of our own, if anything so vain ought to be called a creation, must be swept away. And why? That God may find His own creation, and not a mere falsified creature made into a lie by vanity and pride, but His own creature as He made it, pure and simple, and duly subject to Him, that He may work what is good and holy on His own foundation.

We are not created with virtue, but with nature; we are not created with grace; that must be given to our nature. But as we are born in pride and sin, and have suffered and even encouraged these evils to grow in us, they must be removed by the labours of humility. What we have by nature is a large capacity for light and grace, and for the good they bring to us. But this capacity has been grievously contracted and defiled by the pride of sin, and humility must open it, and contrition must cleanse it. But if we draw our affections in upon ourselves, we narrow them down to things less than ourselves, we still more contract our capacity

* *Ephesians* iii. 17-19.

for divine things, and close up ourselves against them. The soul thus closed in and pre-occupied cannot receive them; thus pre-engaged, cannot work with them. Sin is no foundation for the divine virtues to rest upon; the pride that repels God is no receptacle for the charity of God.

When the force of affliction came, and allayed the inflammation of evil, David returned from his sin to God, and, humbled to the dust at the sight of his condition, He thus mournfully speaks of what he discovered in himself: "As the dream of them that awake, O Lord; so in the city Thou shalt bring their image to nothing. For my heart hath been inflamed, and my reins have been changed: and I am brought to nothing, and I knew it not. I am become as a beast of burden before Thee, and I am always with Thee." The Psalmist saw his nothingness when his sin had parted Him from God; but when he had entered into himself, and humbled himself in the truth, He was able to say: "Thou hast held me by my right hand; and by Thy will Thou hast conducted me, and with Thy glory Thou hast received me. For what have I in Heaven? And besides Thee what have I on earth? For Thee my flesh and my heart have fainted away: Thou art the God of my heart, and the God that is my portion for ever. For behold they that go far from Thee shall perish: Thou hast destroyed all them that are disloyal to Thee. But it is good for me to adhere to my God, to put my hope in the Lord God." * The humility of the Prophet abandons his self-reliance as an empty and worthless thing, and subjects his soul to God as the one and only source of his good.

How is this accomplished? The Almighty tells us through the same Prophet: "Empty yourself, and see that I am God".† In proportion as the soul vacates herself by humility, God fills that soul with light and charity. For God is all around us with His light and charity, and only requires a humble and an open soul, subject to Him, that He may enter with His gifts. When the inhabitants of Jerusalem were full of pride and luxury, so that God could do nothing for their souls, He sent them in captivity to Babylon. But in their humiliation and sorrow by the waters of Babylon, their souls were humbled and their hearts were opened; then they recalled the prayer of Edom over their beloved city: "Empty her, empty her, even to the foundations

* *Psalm* lxxii. 20-28.　　　† *Psalm* xlv. 11.

thereof ". * Jerusalem was emptied, and with what result? The souls of her exiled people were emptied of their vanities, and they returned in humility to God.

When our Lord said, "Blessed are the poor in spirit," He spoke of those who are conscious of the native poverty of their souls, and of their utter indigence without the help of God. This is that vacuity of self which the Fathers call the place of God in the soul, and the place of the virtues, and the treasure-house of the virtues. They also called this open receptive virtue of humility the hive in which the heavenly sweetness is deposited, the vase that receives the divine unction, the mouth enlarged with spiritual hunger, the garment that enfolds the grace of Christ and the secret operations of His Spirit; and St. Paul calls the humble spirit the habitation of God in· which His Spirit dwells. Or we may call it the thirsty ground craving for the gifts of Heaven. St. Bridget has another figure, and compares the humble soul to the rapid wheel that moves beneath the Almighty, seated in His chariot upon the cherubim, and moving over the world, whilst the hollow centre of the wheel rests on the axle of divine power as the principle of its progress. In short, humility is the animated capacity of the soul, vacated of self-seeking, and looking to God with desire to be filled with His light, grace, and goodness. But this vacating of self leaves no void, it receives a fulness. For, to use the words of William of Paris, grace will never allow the soul that vacates her own nature to be left void of its own presence ; the divine gifts flow into what nature vacates with a powerful inundation, and fills the void of the soul as fast as it is made. †

The first work of humility is to open the soul that pride has closed, that the light of divine truth may enter and reveal you to yourself. When we feel that all is not well with us, when there is not peace but trouble and remorse, the sign of God's displeasure and of our own spiritual indisposition, then we begin to look for a remedy. Humiliated in the sense of our misery, we turn to God and pray for mercy. This prayer is mingled with the sense of our misery and want. The seven penitential Psalms of David are the expression of this state of soul. The more contrite the cry of the heart, the more intense the desire of return to God, the more the soul opens and the light enters, but it enters to discover to us our wretched condition and awakens us

---

* *Psalm* cxxxvi. 7.   † Gulielmus Parisien., *De Moribus*, c. x.

to shame and sorrow. All this while pride is receding and humility is coming into its place; and as pride relaxes its hold of us and begins to move away, we see its folly, injustice, and deformity, and a hatred of it begins to rise within us. This hatred is the work of humility, beholding that deformity in the light of justice. As Christ draws nearer to the penitent soul, the soul becomes more humble and takes the side of God against herself.

Suppose yourself shut up alone in a dark room, you imagine a great deal though you see but little, and what you imagine is anything but the truth, of which you see nothing clearly. This is not a state of peace. Some one enters bearing a light before him; that light effects two things: it is a light cast upon you, it is a much greater light on him who brings it to you. Such is your condition when left within the dark shadows of your pride; you see nothing clearly and nothing rightly, because you are under delusions of the imagination, which affect your vision in all that affects you personally. Christ approaches you with His light, which breaks through your delusions and opens your soul to see two things, yourself and the Divine Bearer of the light. In Him you see the perfect humility, purity, and beauty of all justice; through the light which proceeds from Him you see in sad contrast the deformity of your own pride, defilement, and iniquity. You see this in the light that shines into you and awakens your conscience; you see it much more in the light that brings your Divine Redeemer before you. The more you meditate on Him, the more you gaze on Him, the more you are humbled; and the more you look into yourself with eyes filled with His light, the more empty and vile you find yourself and the more ashamed. What can you do but cast yourself at His feet and implore His mercy, recall what He has done for you, and hasten to the tribunal appointed for the purification of your soul?

The very setting of your sins before you, the bringing of the hidden things of pride into the light, the consciousness that you are putting them before God, before the pure hosts of Heaven, and before His minister on earth, brings a deepening of your humiliation and contrition, and helps the opening of the soul. Then descends the healing grace of purification and forgiveness on the soul in her abjection at the foot of the Cross, receiving into her heart the cleansing blood with the spirit of mercy. You are once more the child of Christ, who has endowed you with His charity and raised you to a quicker faith and a surer trust in Him. Your heart is enlarged, you have recovered peace, and a certain sweetness has entered your soul. But what opened your soul to these divine gifts was the exercise of humility, and what will preserve them is the same virtue of humility.

Solomon says in the Proverbs: "Take away the rust from the silver, and there shall come forth a most pure vessel".* But if the vessel be not clean enough to be made cleaner, if it be too foul to receive what is pure; if it be not ample also to receive what is so great; God will not throw away His noble gifts upon those who cannot be made worthy of them even by the gifts themselves. Again, if the soul is not subject to God as well as open, she cannot receive the grace of the Christian virtues. You may carry your vessel where else you like, but it can only receive water when placed under the fountain; you may place it under the fountain as long as you choose, but unless the lid be opened no water will enter into it. Humility opens the soul which pride had closed, and subjects that soul to God which pride had taken away from Him.

When the Divine Author of health and life gave sight to the blind, soundness to the leper, and feet to the lame, He always required a humble faith and trust in Him as the condition. The humility of faith subjected their souls to Him, and the humility of confidence opened them to His health-giving action. Two things must always concur: the humility of the patient and the ability of the physician; if either fails there is no cure. St. Mark tells us that when Jesus came to Nazareth, His own country, "He could not do any miracles there, only He healed a few sick, laying His hands on their heads". And he gives the reason: "He wondered at their unbelief". †

Humility, then, is the forming of capacity for receiving the gifts of God, and profound humility is an immense capacity, capable of receiving the greatest gifts. The saints were always labouring to enlarge this capacity by deepening their humility. This was the real secret of their obtaining so great a sanctity. No cost of self-abnegation or humiliation was spared that might contribute to the emptying of themselves, or to the spirit of ascribing to God whatever they were and whatever they received; and

* *Proverbs* xxv. 4. † *S. Mark* vi. 5, 6,

every gift they received and cultivated enlarged their capacity by enlarging their humility. For although humility is the receptive virtue, every Christian virtue increases humility in proportion to its right and due cultivation.

The inexhaustible gifts that dwelt bodily in Christ, dwelt in the unspeakable humility that subjected His human to His Divine nature. Of this David says, "Thou hast made Him a little lower than the angels; Thou hast crowned Him with glory and honour; and hast set Him over the work of Thy hands ".* And that this taking the lower place, this abasing Himself to the Cross, was the receptive foundation of His honour and glory, St. Paul explains: "We see Jesus who was made a little lower than the angels, for the suffering of death, crowned with glory and honour, that through the grace of God He might taste death for all ". † As he says elsewhere: "He humbled Himself. . . . Wherefore God hath exalted Him". ‡ The gifts and prerogatives conferred on the Blessed Virgin were all given to her humility; this she expressly declares in her Canticle of gratitude. Whosoever shall often meditate on that sublime yet most simple outpouring of the gratitude of humility, will find a light in it to illuminate the deeper mysteries of this hidden virtue.

What do we mean when we say that of ourselves we are nothing? Or rather, what do they mean who through great humility make this discovery, and see and feel its truth habitually? What did Job mean, what did Abraham mean, what did David mean, what did St. Paul mean, what did St. Francis mean, what did St. Catherine mean, what did so many of the saints mean, when they declared, with the clearest and most solemn conviction, that they found themselves to be nothing before God? They meant far more than that vague and obscure notion of the truth which is more or less in all religiously disposed minds. They saw, and they felt, and they realised that their existence rested on God; that they were made for God, and not for themselves; that their whole life depended on the providence of God, and their interior life upon His divine grace. They saw clearly that God was their object, their light, their life, their good, and their happiness; that they were incapable of any good without the help of God; and that of themselves, because of their origin from nothing, they were inclined to evil and to nothingness. Without God we must

---

* *Psalm* viii. 6, 7.   † *Hebrews* ii. 9.   ‡ *Philippians* ii. 9.

return to nothingness; without the help of God we must remain contracted in soul, feeble in will, darkened in mind, closed against the light of Heaven, defiled with pride and concupiscence, and chilled to death in all our spiritual powers. With such a view of ourselves as apart from God, truth, justice, and humility require us to admit and to confess that without God we are nothing.

Father Thanner, the Carthusian, has ingeniously illustrated the relation of humility with the other virtues from the figures of arithmetic. Place a cipher, o. This represents nothing but capacity. Add one cipher to another, and every cipher added to the first expresses the deepening of capacity and nothing more; thus, o,ooo,ooo. The first cipher represents a certain degree of capacity, that is, of receptive power or humility. Every cipher added to this expresses a multiplied growth of capacity, that is, of humility. But to the first cipher of capacity add the first positive virtue by the figure 1, this will make 10, faith resting on the first degree of humility. Add the virtue of hope and it becomes 20. Add charity, the first vital virtue, and it becomes 30. But these virtues deepen humility, and the more humility is deepened, the more these virtues increase in us, and grow in proportion. The first great deepening of humility will raise the 30 to 300, the second to 3000, and so onwards; because the more the soul is opened and enlarged by humility, the more amply she is filled with faith, hope, and charity. The same may be said of all the Christian virtues, and it will serve to illustrate the well-known maxim of St. Augustine, that the higher you would raise the structure of charity, the deeper you must sink the foundation of humility.

This mode of illustration is capable of a sublime application. Father Gratry, the Oratorian, has employed the same method to represent the degree of union of God with our nothingness. But we must remember that greater numbers often represent smaller things, and lesser numbers greater things. For example, 50,000 grains of earth can never equal 1 soul. The figure 1 includes the essence of all numbers, and represents the perfection of Being. It may stand as the symbol of God, who is the perfect Unity. We took the figure 3 to represent the theological virtues; we take the figure 1 to represent God. We take the cipher again to represent the capacity of the soul for God, which is formed by humility. The soul is the subject of God; God is her supreme

15*

object and good. The more you increase capacity through the labours of humility, the more you are able to receive of the power of God. Represent the growth of this capacity of soul by ciphers, thus, 0,00,000,0000 ; let this capacity be united with the perfect One, with the divine object of your soul, and you will see how the communicated power of God increases to 10,100,1000,10,000, according to the degree of humility which vacates us of ourself and subjects us to God. This will help you to understand how humility is the receptive foundation of the divine gifts, and to see the force of the Divine Word : " Empty yourself, and see that I am God". This was the perfect humility of Christ as described by St. Paul : " He emptied Himself and took the form of a servant," " in whom the fulness of the Godhead dwelt bodily ".* His human nature was totally given up to the divine nature.

The rind comes before the fruit, embraces it, protects it, and expands with its growth. In like manner is humility the receptive and protective counterpart of every Christian virtue ; and as the soundness of the rind secures the soundness of the fruit, the grace of humility is inseparable from the grace of the other virtues. As pride is the virulent element in every vice that gives to it its malice, humility is the element in every virtue that subjects it to God, and makes it acceptable to Him. With his acute discernment of internal things, St. Gregory the Great has marked those singular functions that belong exclusively to this virtue, and has so classed the virtues as to group all the other virtues on one part, and, on the other, humility as their counterforce and indispensable complement as well as foundation. "The signs," he says, " of the great grace of Christ are the virtues and humility ; if both completely meet in the soul, there is clear proof of the presence of the Holy Spirit." † In another place he gives the reason of this : " When we use the virtue we have with a view to our own transitory praise, that virtue becomes the servant of vice, and ceases to be a virtue. The reason of this is, that humility is the origin of virtue, and virtue can only germinate and expand when it remains in its proper root of humility. If you cut your virtue away from that root it must wither up, because it loses the vital sap of charity."‡

---

* *Colossians* ii. 9.   † S. Greg. Mag., *Dialog.*, lib. i., c. 1.
‡ S. Greg. Mag., *Moral. in Job*, lib. xxvii., c. 27.

In further illustration of this great truth it may be here observed that, as we are instructed by that learned Pontiff, Benedict XIV., in his great work on the Canonization of Saints, the first step taken in investigating the virtues of the person proposed for canonization is this, whether humility has been practised in the heroic degree, for if that fails the rest must fail as a matter of course.

We have chiefly considered humility as it is the receptive virtue under three similitudes : as a vacant vessel made void of self to receive the gifts of God ; as a tree on which the virtues are engrafted ; and as a foundation in which they are securely placed. This virtue may also be compared with the all-receiving, all-fertilizing mother earth, from which its name is derived ; which is subject to the heavens, is opened by the labour and toil of lowly men, is softened by the rain of Heaven, refreshed with the dews, warmed by the sun, and becomes through these descending influences the nourishing mother of every plant that our Heavenly Father has planted. So far from having anything in its nature to exalt us, it is the death of self-glorification ; should it fail to be that, self-glorification becomes its death. Yet what can this virtue yield to self-glorification, since it only removes what is unsolid, ignoble, and disgraceful from us, and brings us down to our nothingness before Him who is all things to us. The most unreasonable, then, of all unreasonable things is to take pride in humility, which both destroys this virtue and withers up the rest. Yet even this folly will often arise in demonstration of the utter weakness and perversity of human nature.

Let us turn for light to the Holy Scripture. Through the Prophet Isaias thus saith the Lord : " Heaven is My throne, and earth My footstool ; what is this house that you will build for Me? and what is this place of My rest? My hand made all these things, and all these things were made, saith the Lord. But to whom shall I have respect, but to him that is poor and little, and of a contrite spirit, and that trembleth at my words ? " * You give me what is My own, says the Almighty. Vacate Me a temple in the lowly places of your spirit, and there I will rest in you. As the flowers planted in the ground are stirred by the gentle south winds to yield their perfumes, so is there a tenderness in humble souls that is sensitive to every breath of grace, and is tremulously alive to every

* *Isaias* lxvi. 1, 2.

ray of light and every inspiration. This delicate sensibility to the breathings of grace raises up the affections to meet the low-voiced call of God that comes to the soul like the murmuring wind upon the flowers, whilst her spiritual veins receive His whisperings. If the soul is but half opened, and half closed upon herself, she will not find full peace, unless the eternal truth, like a keen and searching wind, cut sharp into the hidden tumours that close up the secret ways to the inmost sanctuary of the spirit. But when humility has entered so far, its unction gives a yielding temper to the very centre of the spirit, that frees her to go forth from her poor self to meet the attraction of divine charity, and to her very centre she finds herself in peace. "What is this place of my rest?" It is the soul subject to God's will from her very centre.

St. Bernard does not hesitate to say that humility is the con- summation of all justice; and as it subjects the whole man to God, to His truth, to His will, and to His commandments, it cannot be less. "Who," he asks, "is just, except the humble man? When the Lord bent Himself down beneath the hand of John the Baptist, and John feared to act because of the Divine Majesty, the Lord said to him, 'Suffer it now, for so it becometh us to fulfil all justice'. This was assuredly to place all justice in humility."* Hear what the Apostle says: "We brought nothing into this world, and certainly we can carry nothing out of it".† This plain truth is justice, but the justice of humility. We take nothing to God but what we have received from Him. And what will He accept of us? "A contrite and humble heart, O God, Thou wilt not despise."‡ Hear what the humble Prophet says: "My soul hath cleaved to the pavement, quicken Thou me according to Thy word. I have declared my ways, and Thou hast heard me: teach me Thy justifications. Make me understand the way of Thy justifications: and I shall be exer- cised in Thy wondrous works."§ The humility of the Psalmist is just to evil, and just to good, which is the consummation of justice. He is just to evil, which he confesses and condemns in himself; he is just to good, confessing that his justification is from God, and in nowise from himself.

If the basis of humility fail, all the virtues born of grace come

---

* S. Bernard, *In Cantic. Serm.* 48.   † 1 *Timothy* vi. 7.
‡ *Psalm* l. 19.   § *Psalm* cxviii. 25-27.

to ruin. Faith loses its vitality, hope sinks into despondency, charity is destroyed, prudence loses her sight and her balance, justice is turned into injustice, fortitude is loosened from her strength, and temperance melts into dissipation. Take humility from the learned man, and losing his true position and just point of view, he will put imagination in the place of truth. Take it from the prudent man, and his wisdom will evaporate in conceit and vanity. Take it from the man in authority, and ambition will succeed to moderation, and he will overstep the lines of his just power. Take it from the devout man, and either to escape his interior desolation, he will break into open evil ; or will give way to a wasting melancholy ; or, whilst keeping the resemblance of his lost piety as a mask, his hypocrisy will make ravaging additions to his inward corruption.

What page of Holy Scripture resounds not with the proof that "God resists the proud, but gives His grace to the humble " ? One page proclaims the precept, another shows the effects in men of its observance or neglect ; another rebukes the proud and encourages the humble. A history of humility, drawn from the Sacred Scriptures, would be the most instructive of books, and to continue it through the history of the Church would complete a most wonderful record of the way in which God at all times blesses the humble and repels the proud. Then would it be seen as in two great processions of the human race, the one advancing towards God, the other departing from Him, supplying an overwhelming evidence, that from the beginning of the world to our time God has always resisted the proud, and always given His grace to the humble ; has always turned the work of the proud to barrenness, and the work of the humble into a marvellous fertility of good. Line upon line, precept upon precept, example upon example, one great universal law has been incessantly proclaimed by command and by example, as the condition of human salvation. As in the Book of Job : " He that hath been humbled shall be in glory ; and he that shall bow down his eyes shall be saved ".* And in the Psalm : " Thou wilt save the humble people ; and wilt humble the eyes of the proud ".† And : " He hath looked on the prayer of the humble one ".‡ And again : "The Lord is nigh unto them who are of a contrite heart ; and He will save the humble spirit ".§ Solomon also says in the

* *Job* xxii. 29.   † *Psalm* xvii. 28.   ‡ *Psalm* ci. 18.   § *Psalm* xxxiii. 19.

proverb: "Humility goeth before glory ".* And again: "Glory shall receive the humble of spirit ".† Our Blessed Lord sums up the teaching of the prophets in these words: "He that exalteth himself shall be humbled, and he that humbleth himself shall be exalted ".‡ St. Peter continues the same teaching with all the Apostles: "Be ye humbled beneath the mighty hand of God, that He may exalt you in the time of visitation ". §

It is the constant similarity in the form of the precept and of the reward attached to its observance, running through the Old and New Testaments, that gives it such a fixed, unchangeable, and eternal character, resting on the immutable order of things. And in every repetition of the fundamental law of humility there is attached to it, and to it alone, the promise of exaltation, of salvation, of the kingdom of God, or of glory. And why, but because humility is that which God rewards with His grace and justification. As the Psalmist says, God will "justify the humble and the poor ". ‖ There may be many virtues, but the reward is promised to the humility of those virtues. For God never changes the rule of resisting the proud, and giving His grace to the humble.

The voice of the Apostles has no sooner ceased, except that of St. John, when St. Clement, "whose praise is in the churches," gives this emphatic advice to the Corinthians: "Let your children be bred up in the instruction of Christ; and let them especially learn how great a power humility has with God". And through three chapters of his beautiful Epistle to the Corinthians, the disciple of the two great Apostles illustrates the power of humility. The Epistle of St. Barnabas is entirely based upon the history of humility in the Old Testament.

It would take many volumes to repeat what the Fathers and Saints have written in exposition and enforcement of this their favourite virtue. The chief points on which they dwell are these: 1. That humility is the distinctive virtue of Christ, and of the true Christian. 2. That it is the very groundwork of sanctity and salvation. 3. That it is the essential condition upon which the divine gifts are received. 4. That it is the mother and the nurse of the virtues. 5. That the depth of humility measures the greatness of the gifts received by the soul. 6. That the more they strove with great labour to cultivate this virtue, the nearer

---

* *Proverbs* xv. 33.   † *Proverbs* xxix. 23.   ‡ *S. Matthew* xxiii. 12.
§ 1 *S. Peter* v. 6.   ‖ *Psalm* lxxxi. 3.

they found themselves to God, and were the more amazed to see how little it was understood or prized among Christians, except those who aspired to perfection. 7. In short, that the want of steady and persevering labour in this virtue was the cause of all failures in the supernatural life.

St. Cyprian has expressed the whole force of the virtue in one short sentence: "We Christians," he says, "have no occasion to strive for exaltation, we grow to the highest things from humility". * When Celsus, representing the pagan mind, threw his sneers at the very possibility of such a virtue as humility, Origen showed its depth and grandeur, from the fact that no mere man on human authority could have obtained a hearing for such a virtue; it required to have God for its teacher, and not only God, but God made man. † When St. Pacian had to reprove the heretical pride of Novatian, he sharpened his reproach by contrasting the deformity of his obtrusive spirit with that beautiful innocence which he had lost in losing humility. "All humility," he says, "even that of the sinner, even that which gently tempers the sinner with its spirit, is innocence." ‡ This accords with St. Augustine's doctrine, that "humility exercised among evil works is more pleasing to God than pride among good works". § This truth was taught by our Lord Himself in the parable of the Pharisee and the publican.

We may take Cassian as representing the great spiritual schools of Egypt and Palestine in the early ages of the Church. In his Institutes he says: "It is of the plainest evidence that no one can obtain the end of perfection and purity except through the means of humility. The disciple obtains the virtue in the first instance by exhibiting it towards his brethren, until he learns to exhibit it from his inmost heart to God." || In his celebrated Conferences the same spiritual writer says: "Humility is the mistress of all the virtues; the most solid foundation of the celestial building; the peculiar and magnificent virtue of our Saviour. All the wonderful things that Christ did, humility does when we follow our meek Lord, not in sublime miracles, but in patience and humility." ¶ And he quotes the beautiful saying of Abbot Pemen, that humility is the land in which God commands us

---

* S. Cyprian, *De Zelo et Livore.* † Origen, *Contra Celsum*, lib. ix., c. 5.
‡ S. Pacian, *Epist.* 2. § S. August., *In Psalm.* xciii.
§ Cassian, *Institut.*, lib. xii., c. 13. ¶ Cassian, *Collat.*, lib., ii. c. 7.

to offer sacrifice. This is beautifully true, because humility is the immolation of self-love to justice. St. Isaac the Syrian says: "You will show how deeply you have entered into the Scriptures exactly in proportion as you demean yourself humbly to the brethren". The holy Bishop of Ninive takes this as his test, because humility to the brethren is proof positive of humility to God.

For the Fathers of Syria let St. Dorotheus speak. He says: "If pride be the root of all evil, humility is most certainly the restorative medicine of all good. It is the recipient of all gladness, rest, and glory." * For the recluses of Mount Sinai let St. John Climacus be the witness. He designates humility as "the virtue that conquers all passion," as the "destroyer of all intellectual poisons," and as "a grace of the soul that no tongue can describe, and that experience alone can understand; an unspeakable gift from the treasury of God". + From the Holy Land comes the voice of St. Jerom: "Do thou hold nothing more excellent than humility, nothing more lovely. It is the preserver and chief guardian of all the virtues. Nothing else whatsoever can be so pleasing to God, or even to man, than to be great in merit of life and little through one's humbleness." ‡

We now come to the great St. Basil, whose rule has guided all Eastern religious life from his own day to ours. "A great service," he says, "is the service of God, embracing all His precepts in a net, and winning the kingdom of Heaven. But of these precepts the first is humility, the parent of every virtue, giving birth to all good things in abundance. . . . The progress of humility is the progress of the soul, whilst the ignoble failure of the soul comes from elation. . . . To know piety is to know humility and meekness; it is our emulating of Christ, as elation is the emulating of the devil." § Elsewhere he says: "As the hive receives its swarm of bees with all their sweets, humility is the recipient of all good graces and gifts". ‖ And the other St. Basil, of Seleucia, tells us that "we may know the extent of the grace that is given us by the strength of our humility". ¶ St. Ambrose considers it

---

* S. Dorotheus, *Disciplina*, 2a, *De Humilitate.*
+ S. J. Climacus, *Scala Perfectionis*, Grad. 26.
‡ S. Hieron., *Epist. ad Celanum.*
§ S. Basil., *Serm De Renunciatione Sæculi.*
‖ S. Basil., *Serm De Abdicatione Rerum.*
¶ S. Basil. Seleuc., *Orat.* 19.

as a searching light: "Can there be anything so precious as this humility? It searches thy nature through in body and soul; and whilst it subjects thy body to thy soul, it teaches thee in thy soul to know thyself." *

If there be a saint who, uniting great sanctity with amazing genius, has thrown the light of science and experience upon this wonderful virtue, it is St. Augustine, who may be called the Doctor of humility by eminence. Through the ten folios into which his numerous writings are gathered, he never loses sight of this virtue, he never relaxes from inculcating this fundamental justice, whether he is writing to Catholics, heretics, or heathens. It is the medicine of the mind and heart, the restorative of spiritual strength, the head, sum, and force of Christian discipline, the indispensable condition of all union with God. To his profound mind humility is as the bass in a chorus of music, the sustaining force of all intellectual and moral harmony in the soul. He calls it "the first and greatest gift of the Spirit". † He sees in it "the path whereby we return to life in Christ, and to the joy of God's countenance". ‡ He finds that "all strength lies in humility". § He calls it "the key of knowledge". ‖ He notes that "humble obedience goes before wisdom, and true wisdom can only follow humility". ¶ He says that "our very perfection is humility"; by which he undoubtedly means that this virtue perfects our subjective condition, that God may perfect our charity. For it is one of his maxims that "where is humility there is charity". ** And he extracts the doctrine from the Scriptures that glory is the reward of humility, and is won by the labours of humility. We may now understand what he writes to the inquiring Dioscurus: "However much you question me about the precepts of the Christian religion, although there are so many things on which I might be expected to speak, yet the best reply to all your questions would be to speak always and only on the one subject of humility". ††

Like the facets of a diamond, each passage we have quoted presents the virtue from a special point of view, deserving a special attention. And we will venture to say that whoever will ponder

---

* S. Ambros., *Serm.* 10.   † S. August., *In Epist. ad Galat.*, c. v.
‡ Id., *In Psalm.* xv.   § Id., *In Psalm.* xlii.
‖ Id., *Quest. Evang.*, lib. ii., q. 23.   ¶ Id., *In Psalm.* cxxx.
** Id., *Prolog. in Epist. Joan.*   †† S. August., *Epist. ad Dioscurum.*

sentences like these, and pass them from the mind into the heart, will be led into the profundities of the virtue from which they spring, and will find their truth blended in the deep-seated root of the virtue where it has taken possession of the soul. One or two more extracts shall be given to represent the treasures of the middle ages. St. Hildegarde says: "Faith is the eye of humility, and obedience its health, and contempt of evil the measure of its magnitude ".* Beautiful in their truth also are the words of the holy hermit Guarric: "We may certainly affirm, without any injury to our baptism, that humility is not unlike to baptism in its influences. For though it repeats not the death of Christ, it renews the death and burial of sin. It opens the heavens to us, and gives us back the spirit of adoption. The man is renewed by humility in the innocent spirit of a child, and the Father again acknowledges that child. Seven times in a humble spirit did Naaman wash in Jordan's waters, and his flesh became as the flesh of a little child." †

There are many books written on the interior exercise of prayer, and not a few persons perplex themselves with a multiplicity of rules that injure their simplicity, because they do not attend to the one essential foundation of prayer. The Sacred Scriptures require but the one condition, that prayer be humble. "He hath had regard to the prayer of the humble," says the Psalm, "and He hath not despised their petition."‡ And again in Ecclesiasticus: "The prayer of him that humbleth himself shall pierce the clouds: and until it come nigh he will not be comforted: he will not depart untill the Most High behold ".§ In short, "the prayer of the humble and the meek hath always pleased God ". ‖ Need we recall the prayer of Abraham, of Moses, of David, of Elias, or of the publican, given expressly for our example? Need we recall the prayer of our Lord Himself in His agony and crucifixion? A little reflection on the subject ought to show us that humility is the spirit, life, and very nature of prayer. For prayer is all subjection, all adoration, all exposition of our wants, or it is gratitude and humble praise to the Supreme Lord of our souls. Nor is the higher way of contemplation other than the subjection of our mind and heart to the light and divine operations of the Holy Spirit of God.

* S. Hildegarde, *Epist.* 30.   † Guarric, *Serm.* 4 *in Epiph.*
‡ *Psalm* ci. 18.   § *Ecclesiasticus* xxxv. 21.   ‖ *Judith* ix. 16.

Let us consult some of the great authorities on this subject. St. Teresa says in her life: "The whole edifice of prayer is founded on humility. The nearer we find ourselves to God, the more must this virtue be increased; otherwise all is lost, and falls to the ground." Again this great contemplative says: "Let others go by some other short cut if they please. What I have been able to understand is, that the whole of this structure of prayer is grounded on humility; and that the more the soul is abased in this holy exercise, the more doth God exalt her. Nor do I remember that He ever showed me any of those singular mercies, but when I found myself as it were annihilated at seeing myself so very wicked." *

St. John of the Cross inculcates this truth in a chapter of great clearness as well as profundity. He is speaking of the higher degrees of sanctity, but even the lower must proceed on the same fundamental principle. He warns us, however, that he is writing only for the true friends of Christ, and significantly adds that the greater number who claim this title are too well contented with their spiritual consolations to enter into the crucified interior of our Lord. "But," says this profoundly illuminated Saint, "I would have spiritual persons understand that the way of the Lord consists not in multiplying reflections, devout exercises, and fervid affections, however requisite they are to beginners. It consists in one sole and indispensable thing, and that is to know how to deny one's self in reality, both as to our interior and exterior self, surrendering one's self up to suffer, and to aim at annihilating one's own spirit in all things for the love of Christ. For this one exercise comprises in itself all, and more than all, that can be found or accomplished in all other exercises whatsoever. But if we fail in this, which is the root and sum of all virtue, in other methods we are but following paths that turn aside, instead of going straight to the mark. . . . David said, 'I am brought to nothing, and I knew it not'. And so does the truly spiritual soul understand the mysterious way and the door through Christ, that leads to direct union with God. But when, resting in nothing that she can call her own, she gains the state of sovereign humility, then is her union with God perfected; and that, not through the medium of her spiritual delights, but of the

* S. Teresa, *Vida*, c. xxii.

living crucifixion and death of her own self, whether sensual or spiritual, in her interior or exterior."

To bring the instruction of this lecture to a point, two things work together in the perfecting of the soul, the abdicating of one's self, and the influx of light and charity into the soul, always in that degree in which she abdicates her own spirit. The first of these is gained by great labour and effort; the second is divinely given to those labours. By no labour of ours can we give ourselves one single ray of light or one spark of charity; these are purely the gifts of God. But we dispose our souls to ensure these divine gifts by self-abdication and humility, which, though founded on grace, can only be perfected by great effort and the persevering toil of the will. This has been admirably expressed by St. Mary Magdalen de Pazzi. "The soul," she says, "becomes possessed of the divine love with the greatest ease, if she be perfectly exercised in humility. Nor is any other exercise required than that of humility to gain this love. For what wins the divine love for us is the much abasing and lowering one's self before God, upon which His love enters into our humbled souls. What invitation can be so influential to the love of God as to offer Him a soul that is really humble? There never was and there never will be a human heart filled with humility, that was not, or will not be, as full of love. And through this love the soul is united perfectly with Thee, O my God, and becomes in a measure one with Thee, by partaking of Thy love." †

Frail as man is, humility will make a foundation in him strong enough for God to raise an edifice upon it that shall last for eternity, an edifice to receive a celestial life whose magnificence exceeds our present power of comprehension. Strong is this foundation to hold the divinest treasures in security; strong to carry our frail vessel, with all its precious freight, over the troubled waters of this life into the haven of peace. Upon a foundation so strong as this humility, resting on God and not on us, we bend safely under every storm, pass securely through the darkest hours of trial, and endure what we may have to suffer with peaceful magnanimity.

---

* S. Juan de la Cruz, *Subida del Monte Carmelo*, lib. ii., c. 6, Lewis's translation.

† S. M. Magdalen de Pazzi, *Opere parte* 2ª, c. xvi.

In his pride of science Archimedes asked but for a point outside the world on which to rest his engines, and he would undertake to remove the world from off its course. What the great mathematician asked for in vain, the humble Christian has found. His point of rest is in God, his moving power is prayer, and its force is in the humility of his heart. For however little known to the world at large, it is well known to the humble, that the God of Heaven and earth, in response to their prayers, changes the issues of the world's affairs, despite of all human policy. The supplications and good works of His servants are a motive with Him to increase His merciful and beneficent action in the world. Pride puts everything wrong in the world; humility moves God to put many things right, though not all by a long way, because pride is still predominant in the greater number of souls.

We have already quoted the profound saying of an ancient Father, that humble souls are the hinges on which God moves the world. At their supplication God changes the hearts of rulers, the action of the elements, the issue of counsels, and the direction of events. Such is the power of humble souls, whose prayers obtain their efficacy through the divine mystery of humility in the crucified Son of God. It is prodigious to think what evils are stayed, and what good is begun or advanced, through the prayers of the humble servants of God. For proof we have only to pronounce the names and recall the history of Abraham, Moses, David, and Elias; of St. Paul, St. Antony, St. Benedict, St. Francis, St. Bernard, St. Catherine of Siena, St. Teresa, St. Charles Borromeo, St. Francis Xavier, or St. Vincent of Paul. Hidden as the power of such as these may be from the great world around them, the heavenly spectators behold the secret springs of that power, and we who are familiar with their lives know the immense blessings that came of their presence wherever they might move.

When this world will come to an end our Lord has declared to be a secret reserved to the Father. But what will bring the world to an end is a less difficult question. When it no more produces humble souls, there will be no longer a divine reason for its existence. When "all flesh had corrupted its way," * the deluge came to purify the world, that the human race might begin anew from the just man Noe. When a like corruption of pride and sensuality so pervades the world that God is no longer able to find humble

* *Genesis* vi. 12.

souls on whom to bestow His grace and admit to His kingdom, what remains of human nature will be useless for its end, useless for the eternal purpose of its creation, and will be cast away as refuse, and the world be purged by fire. For all things are for the elect, and the elect are the humble.

Humble souls may be compared to the wheels beneath the glowing cherubim, that form the chariot of God, but of God in the form of man, in the vision of Ezechiel. They have eyes for contemplation, and there is life in them; and whithersoever the Spirit goeth, thither they go responsive to His will. They return not back when they go, because they seek not themselves; and in their going they depart not from their subjection to the throne of God. In their repose as in their activity they are equally actuated by the Spirit of God, and equally on fire with His charity. In all their actions, whether interior or exterior, they recede not from the guidance of the Divine Presence under which they move, and meditate, and glow; on whom reposing, amidst the sounds of their prayer and praise, the power of the Almighty goes forth into the world to do His work of mercy and good-will to man.

LECTURE X.

ON THE MAGNANIMOUS CHARACTER OF HUMILITY.

"It is He that giveth strength to the weary: and increaseth force and might to them that are not."—ISAIAS xl. 29.

HOWEVER excellent it may be, what we do not know we cannot love. This is the special difficulty that stands in the way of recommending the virtue of humility, that its power and its excellence are hidden from the proud and from the sensual man. To the natural man it is unknown, to the proud man it is repulsive. Yet what so many persons look upon as the mere result of weakness and timidity is in fact a great self-conquering force, which places the four cardinal virtues on their true basis, and employs them in vigorous action. No man can be so prudent, just, firm in endurance, or temperate in life and conduct, as he who is blessed with sincere humility. But to unlock this truth to minds that are unprepared is no easy task, for it chimes not with the inclinations of the sensuous and the proud. The subject is in its nature severe, and requires to be unveiled in its simple truth, rather than to be clothed with attractive colouring. Of what use is a golden key if it will not open what we want? And why should we refuse an iron key if that will suit our purpose? All that we seek is to open what is locked from sight.

Among the cardinal virtues and the virtues included in them, we have chosen magnanimity as the one in which all the rest are exercised in their highest degree. It was the noblest virtue of the heathens, and is still looked upon as the noblest virtue of men of the world. And our object will be to show that this virtue of magnanimity, which is the noble outcome of the cardinal virtues, has its true basis, not as the world imagines in self-sufficiency and pride, but in the humility that rests all virtue on the grace and power of God. And further, to demonstrate that it is exercised in an incomparably higher degree by the servants of God, in whom it springs from humility, than by the servants of the world, in whom it springs from pride.

Magnanimity, or greatness of soul, is opposed to pusillanimity, or littleness of soul. It is the virtue that inclines the will to arduous and generous acts in every kind of virtue, and is classed with the cardinal virtue of fortitude. But Christian magnanimity contemplates more elevated motives, and aims at higher objects, and is consequently of a much nobler character than either the magnanimity of the heathen or that of the admired man of the world. The magnanimity of the heathens, as explained by their philosophers, and especially by Aristotle in his Ethics, and Cicero in his Offices, contemplated human honour, the shunning of dishonour, and the conquering of those difficulties that stand in the way of honour. They rested their greatness of soul on self-sufficiency and self-esteem; and as their chief object in life, they looked to the elevation of the man before his fellow-men of the honourable class. For they professed to despise the multitude as dishonourable, although they were always ready to humiliate themselves to the multitude in outward show when they sought their suffrages for public employments. The magnanimity of the heathen had no connection with his religion, and but little with his moral conscience; it sprang from a public unwritten law, with the opinion of the honourable class for its sanction. It began and ended in the man, and had its sphere in his reputation. Honour was to these men what God is to the Christian, the chief object and end of their life. When honour failed them, their pride could not endure dishonour, and most of them were ready to commit suicide in order to escape from dishonour, a clear proof that they considered honour to be the final end of their existence.

As the code of honour is not the code of conscience, it allows of many exceptions from the dictates of conscience. And in this respect the modern man of honour is not unlike his pagan predecessors, for he is but too apt to put honour before conscience, and to sacrifice his conscience to his honour. Yet there is a spirit of honour which the good Christian ought to cultivate, a self-respect from high Christian motives, that, as a habit will often restrain him from ill-manners, imprudence, folly, and even worse, at times and under circumstances when conscience moves but languidly, or not at all. But the love of honour, as cultivated by the heathen and by the modern man of the world, holds the same position with them as the love of God holds with the true Christian: it is their first of virtues, to which all the rest are subordinate. Yet, when measured by the Christian law, it is a vice rather than a virtue, because its motive is the contenting of pride in obtaining human glory; and Tertullian does not exceed the limits of justice in calling these men of honour " the animals of glory ".

I take up the first modern book that comes to hand, in which the virtue of magnanimity is treated in the old pagan spirit, and I read its description as follows: " Perseverance, firmness, fortitude, constancy, courage, and calmness, manfulness, dignity of mind, *self-esteem*, and consistency, are each the same principle, and only different terms applied to a different degree of intensity or different relations and circumstances, or they stand to each other in the relation of principle and application, or, lastly, they are very nearly akin to one another, and one can hardly be imagined to exist without the other ".* Here the political or public virtues are all identified with self-esteem, as their obvious basis; remove this, substitute humility, and you will have the description of Christian magnanimity. For the essential difference between pagan and Christian greatness of soul is this, that the one rests on the self-sufficiency of man, and the other on the insufficiency of man without God.

Christian magnanimity is a most generous virtue, because it is essentially opposed to selfish considerations; it moves the will to great efforts in seeking the greatest good, and in valiantly overcoming the obstacles that stand in the way of that good, whether those obstacles be interior or exterior. It is intimately concerned with hope, because without hope we cannot aspire to great things. It is also closely allied with confidence, because without great confidence in the help of God we cannot ascend to a good that is so far beyond our nature. This confidence is a certain promptitude of will acting on the trust that God is with us, and will enable us to master all difficulties in doing what we know He wills that we should do, in order to obtain the arduous

* Lieben's *Manual of Political Ethics*, book iii., c. 2, sect. 13.

16*

good that we seek. This hope and this confidence are themselves a generous and magnanimous exercise of the soul, for there is a greatness of soul in giving up the fears and misgivings of nature, and in resting more trust on God than at the moment we see reason for, by acting in generous faith. It is considered a mark of greatness of soul in Alexander, that, despite of warnings, he trusted his life to his friend and physician; great also must be the soul that transfers her whole trust from self to God. This made the martyrs, the confessors of the faith, and all the generous heroes of God.

Magnanimity is also concerned with security or tranquillity, which rests with a sincere conscience on God. This removes all unnecessary cares, and clears away superfluous anxieties, which only encumber and impede the soul, fret her powers, and absorb her energies in a useless way, so that the will cannot give itself whole and undivided to the great objects to be aimed at, and much power goes to waste and worry within the man. This is quite as improvident as any other kind of waste or dissipation, for it is a waste of our moral power, and the cause of inward trouble and confusion. The security of the soul comes of concentrating herself upon her true supporting centre, upon the God who sustains all things, and belongs to the soul that trusts herself to Him. Have you never found that, when you rest your troubled soul on God, there comes a calm, and serenity follows? There is no spiritual strength but what is from God. "The Lord is my firmament, my refuge, and my deliverer."* And "the strength of the upright is the way of the Lord". †

A soul loses her sense of security, and consequently her tranquillity, when she gets restless and impatient because of the obscurity that surrounds some present difficulty, or some difficulty in prospect, through which at the moment she sees not her way. This often arises from not habitually living in the higher and serener light of the mind, but in the lower sphere of the inferior nature, so that imagination gets the start of intelligence, and soft, sensuous fear puts in its influence. Then patience should wait with calmness until light comes to clear the subject, or until prayer obtains a serener light. But the weakest way of losing tranquillity is to let the difficulty get inside of you and take possession of your feelings, which will not only trouble you, but

* *Psalm* xvii. 3.   † *Proverbs* x. 29.

will obscure the light that should fall upon it, and darken your perception; whereas if you keep the trouble outside in its objective position, your calmer mind will see through it after awhile, and how it is to be dealt with.

A great soul that is calm in her security is simple in action. But pride and vanity make a weak soul, that acts under excitement, which is always the sign of weakness, and acts more from imagination than from the light of intelligence. He who acts from humility is calm and strong, because he rests his powers on the eternal tranquillity. The sculptor understands how calmness is strength when he represents his heroes in the tranquil balance of their powers. The ocean is the symbol of strength when calm, but when agitated by the winds it shows weakness, and like a passionate man it becomes destructive.

The first motive for security is the concurrence of God, who helps all natures to do their offices, and withholds not His general co-operation even from sinners, that the appointed order of things may not fail or come to a stand. But how much more powerfully does He keep His servants who labour in justice to do His will. Nor will He suffer them to be vanquished by the difficulties that beset their path to Him. Trusting therefore in God, and not in ourselves, we ought to seek the things that are above with the calm valour of a tranquil spirit. For " those who trust in the Lord shall renew their strength ".*

The second motive for security is a good conscience. This wonderfully strengthens the confidence of the just man, and confirms the hope and belief of a successful ending to all his labours. Listen to the wisdom of holy Job : " If thou wilt put away from thee the iniquity that is in thy hand, and let not injustice remain in thy tabernacle ; then mayest thou lift up thy face without spot, and thou shalt be steadfast, and shalt not fear ". † " There is nothing," says St. Bernard, " more secure in this life than a good conscience, nothing that we can possess more joyful. The body may oppress the soul, the world may betray us, the devil may frighten us, but a good conscience is always secure." ‡

The third motive for security exists, when with a calm solicitude we do all in our power to accomplish every good we under-

---

* *Isaias* xl. 31.   † *Job* xi. 14, 15.
‡ S. Bernard., *De Consideratione prope finem.*

take to do in a magnanimous spirit, not rashly or imprudently, but knowing that God will help us to do what He wills us to do, if we trust in His mercy. St. Cyprian has admirably expressed for us this source of security. "From God it is, from God it comes, whatever we can do. From Him we live, from Him we have power, and whilst still upon earth we receive vigour from Him to know the signs of the future things. Only let fear be the keeper of innocence, so that the flow of heavenly influence which God sends may be received by the delighted soul with hospitality and just co-operation, and the security thus obtained may neither give occasion to negligence, nor suffer the old enemy to creep in." *

Christian magnanimity is opposed to pusillanimity, or littleness of soul, and to softness, as defects from this noble virtue, and to presumption, ambition, and vainglory, as excesses beyond the true objects, right motives, and just temper of the magnanimous soul.

Pusillanimity, or littleness of soul, is a vicious diffidence and mistrust of the powers that God has given us, making this mistrust a reason for escaping the good work set before us, and shying and shunning the duty we ought to accept and to do; and so weakly giving up the spirit of devotedness under the plea that it is beyond our strength. This weakening vice comes of excessive and superfluous timidity, disordering, dejecting, and saddening the soul, and greatly hindering her from serving God, and from employing those means whereby the virtues are obtained and preserved. It is a vice that greatly displeases God, is very ignominious to the soul, and utterly opposed to the divine goodness and sweet providence which God ever shows to those who are willing to serve Him. It is therefore condemned in the Holy Scriptures, and commanded to be cast out of the soul. "Be not pusillanimous in thy soul," says Ecclesiasticus. † "Say to the fainthearted," says Isaias, "Take courage, and fear not: behold, God will bring the revenge of recompense: God Himself will come and will save you." ‡ When Christ walked on the troubled sea, and His disciples, tossed in the boat, were troubled and afraid, He said to them: "Be of good heart; it is I, fear ye not". §

This feebleness of soul may sink from one degree of pusillanimity to another, until it reaches a settled despondency. St. Bernard

---

* S. Cyprian. *Epist. 2 ad Donatum.*   † *Ecclesiasticus* vii. 9.
‡ *Isaias* xxxv. 4.   § *S. Matthew* xiv. 27.

has shown the degrees of this descent: "As in the holy and elect of God," he says, "tribulation worketh patience, and patience trial, and trial hope, and hope confoundeth not ; in the reprobate, on the contrary, tribulation worketh pusillanimity, and pusillanimity perturbation, and perturbation desperation, and that worketh ruin ".* The severest punishment that God inflicted on the Israelites in the desert was for their pusillanimity. When the spies reported to them the strength of the inhabitants of the Promised Land, and of their walled cities, they lost all heart and courage ; and of the six hundred thousand men that had left Egypt, God decreed that, except Josue and Caleb, all should perish in the wilderness.

The remedy for this faint-heartedness is to put no trust whatsoever in one's own strength, and not to listen to flesh and blood, but to cleave with faith and trust to the divine help and strength alone, because God never fails those who trust in Him. So He has promised, and His promises are firm and faithful. " It is He that giveth strength to the weary : and increaseth force and strength to them that are not. Youths shall faint, and labour, and young men shall fall by infirmity. But they that hope in the Lord shall renew their strength, they shall take wings as eagles, they shall run and not be weary, they shall walk and not faint." †

There is a kind of pusillanimity that insidiously relaxes the soul, and is often very enfeebling, especially in those who have not yet reached the experience of solid piety. It may be described as a habit of fostering inward discomforts on unreasonable grounds, and of nursing them into discouraging fears. The subjects of this habit may be compared with those sensitive people who are unreasonably anxious about their health, and keep themselves shut up in a close and unhealthy atmosphere rather than face the fresh open air ; they weaken their health by too much care of it in a wrong way. Such people have all manner of discomforts and timidities, and are too much occupied with themselves to do anything that is large and generous. If asked the radical cause of this spiritual infirmity, the answer is clear and certain, but the difficulty is to get the answer understood by those whom it most concerns. It comes of a self-love that is always wanting to feel one's self, and with the subtle feelers of this self-love the will is entangled and held down from rising to what is greater and better

* S. Bernard., *Epist.* 32.   † *Isaias* xl. 29-31.

than one's self, and that would free the soul and strengthen her powers by lifting her out of these unreasonable troubles and fears.

After a soul has done penance for her more serious sins and is happily free from them, she finds herself subject to venial sins, and various defects. Undoubtedly we ought to do our best to correct and amend them, but neither to be surprised at them nor lose our peace ; and above all not to suffer our hearts to faint or our courage to sink on account of them, or suffer them to relax our efforts to advance towards our Divine Good. We ought thoroughly to realize that we are weak and infirm creatures, with a natural proclivity to evil ; to be exceedingly grateful to God that He keeps us from the greater evils that destroy His friendship ; and to take the generous way of correcting those infirmities. This is the vigorous way, to work at the abnegation of self-will, and at obtaining a solid humility, which go to the roots of our weakness, on the one side ; and at generously loving and serving God, on the other, which will bring the strength required to conquer our infirmities. In short, the effectual way of self-correction is the magnanimous and not the pusillanimous way. We must have some infirmity to keep us in mind of our weakness, and preserve us from elation and self-conceit, the worst of all spiritual evils next to separation from God. But to sink down into one's weaknesses, to make much of them, to indulge the imagination with exaggerations of them, and give one's self more or less to sadness on account of them, is to waste no small amount of spiritual strength in a vain and foolish way upon one's self. This is not the strong and cheerful way to God, but the weak and melancholy way back to self-love.

The first faults of those whose chief aim in life is to love and serve God are commonly surprises and results of weakness and infirmity, without anything in them of deliberate malice ; they are consequently venial or pardonable, and every generous act is effacing them. The Council of Trent teaches that there is not even an obligation of confessing them, although that is commendable, because they are constantly being effaced by every pious act and good work. The worst evil in those of whom we speak is not their first, but the second committed upon the first, in making a trouble about it, taking it to the bosom of self-love, there nursing it, and making much of it, and murmuring over it with the murmurs of mortified pride. This kind of nursing is very weakening to the spiritual constitution; it is accompanied with a constant imbibing of mistrust, and draws hope away from the soul as well as courage. It comes of fixing our eyes upon ourselves rather than on God, and of sinking our hearts into our infirmities rather than lifting them up to the Divine Source of help and strength. Not so did the magnanimous Psalmist manage the weakness of his soul. He says: " I have lifted up my eyes to the mountains, from whence help shall come to me. My help is from the Lord who made Heaven and earth."* And repeatedly in other psalms he says: " To Thee, O Lord, have I lifted up my soul. In Thee, O God, I put my trust, let me not be ashamed." † When we lift up our hearts out of ourselves to God, and keep them lifted up, these self-made miseries drop off for want of nutriment.

There are two children in one family, of whom the one is weak and impulsive, and often committing faults, but this child is open, cheerful, self-forgetting, and always trusting to his father's love and forgiveness, even though punished for his faults; the other commits fewer faults, but is morose and fretful over his failures, mopes in the fancy that they are still remembered and unforgiven, however assured to the contrary, and still goes on curling himself up round his wounded self-love. Which of these children will the father love most? Assuredly the one who trusts in his father's love and forgiveness. So will your Heavenly Father do to you.

There is another kind of pusillanimity to which women are more liable than men. I can only describe it as a want of courage to stand on their own spiritual feet. They remind one of dolls : they have neither nerve nor strength of joint to keep themselves up without external support ; and this nerveless habit grows with indulgence. In grave difficulties and trials, advice and direction must of course be sought ; of these I am not speaking. But there is a class of persons that have a real desire of better things, yet are always in a relaxed and helpless state of soul, because they give up the habit of acting from themselves and of using their own judgment. This is the vice of softness. The result of the habit is a weakness and flaccidity of soul, that will not take the least step, or encounter the least difficulty without external help and guidance. This defect of spiritual vigour stays all solid progress, and causes an habitual timidity

* *Psalm* cxx. 1, 2. † *Psalm* xxiv. 1.

and uneasiness that is very injurious to the soul's health, leaving the languor of an invalid. Yet these same persons, who through this self-indulgence, but too often fostered by injudicious treatment, become utterly incapable of acting with decision in their internal affairs, will often act with vigour, judgment, and decision in all the external duties of life. Some few souls are by nature and constitution scrupulous and perplexed, and require frequent though judicious help, but in the majority of cases this pusillanimous indulgence is a serious enfeeblement that can only be corrected by requiring the soft soul to rise to her responsibilities and stand on her own feet.

Softness is a vice that in a foolish and disheartened spirit holds back from being generous through languor and weariness of soul, arising from fear of the difficulties and long labours of generous virtue. Self-love, cowardice, and sloth have each their share in this ignominious vice. Imagination has also much to do with it, bringing together into one point of time, and so frightening the soul with what, in fact, is distributed over a long period, each hour of which has its own help and grace, as well as its own burden, and thus overwhelming the mind with a delusion, as if the whole burden of the future came on the present hour and the present help.

Presumption is an excess arising from over-estimating our own powers, and from attempting, in a conceited spirit, things that are above and beyond us, because God has not called us to them, nor given us light and strength for them. Ambition is an inordinate appetite for exercising power over others, and for being honoured by others. Vainglory is an inordinate appetite for praise, fame, and glory. These are the puffings of an inflated soul, preferring the show of things to solid good.

After this rapid review of the vices opposed to magnanimity, or greatness of soul, if we compare them with the solid goods of the soul, we shall see at a glance that they are weak and ignoble deficiencies, or else unworthy passions of the soul, requiring only to be noted to be shunned as unworthy of the generous soul. Wherefore, in the words of Dante, we will not stay to reason upon them, but look and pass them by.

As a universal virtue, magnanimity is the brave and generous element in all the virtues, in so far as the soul aspires to great things. St. Thomas has drawn the features of magnanimity and humility as they are special virtues, and so distinguished from each other, but he by no means excludes the one from the other, for every Christian virtue, as he teaches, has its foundation in humility, and there cannot be great humility without magnanimity. "There is something," he says, "that is great in man which he possesses from God ; and there is a defect in him that comes from the infirmity of his nature. But magnanimity is that whereby a man makes himself worthy in great things, in consideration of the gifts that he possesses from God. Thus, if he have great vigour of soul, magnanimity will direct that vigour to the perfect works of virtue, and in like manner to the use of every good ; to the use of knowledge, for example, or of the external goods of fortune. But humility will dispose a man to hold himself of little account, because of his defects. In like manner will the magnanimous man despise every great failing from the gifts of God in others, because he cannot so much value those who do what is unworthy of them. But the humble man honours others, and accounts them superior, in so far as he sees the gifts of God in them." * Here Christian magnanimity is shown to coincide with humility in despising that within us which is unworthy of the gifts of God.

Great generosity gives to every virtue the quality of magnanimity, because generosity proceeds from greatness of soul : great in aiming to please God, and to do Him honour. But generosity is not exercised in the imagination alone, that is idle fancy ; nor in shortcoming resolutions and promises, but in vigorous acts of the will, and in doing what we undertake with a great spirit. The other part of magnanimity is to trust ourselves freely to God's help in overcoming difficulties. It is on this part that magnanimity belongs to fortitude, which is a firmness of soul derived from resting on the strength of God, that makes the soul of invincible firmness. The fable of the giant who could not be conquered on his native earth, but only when lifted above it, may be taken as the figure of the soul which, born of God, cannot be overcome until separated from God. This part of magnanimity is fortified by habits of endurance, as we see in the Saints and Martyrs. But when the adversary to be overcome is the domestic enemy, the greatest strength is shown by flight, because this pulls contrary to the attractions of nature.

* S. Thomas, *Sum.* ii. 2, q. 129, a. 2 ad 4.

The special virtue of magnanimity looks to honour for its object, and to the doing of great acts that are accounted worthy of honour, as also to the shunning of dishonour.   But, as the Christian religion is the conversion of man from the love of self and of the world to the love of God, and from acting on worldly and selfish motives to acting on divine motives, the magnanimity of the true Christian seeks not the honour or the approval of man, but the honour of God and His approval.   St. Thomas has therefore defined the special virtue of Christian magnanimity to be, a virtue that does great and generous works, worthy of honour, for the ends contemplated by Christian virtue, whilst unambitious of receiving human honours on their account, and despising such honours when offered.*   The reason assigned by St. Thomas for this contempt of human honours is the one obvious to a Christian soul, that there can be no proportion between the value of virtues exercised for God's sake and the human honours with which men would reward them.   When these virtues are honoured and rewarded by God Himself, to seek, or to value, human honours for what God Himself is pleased to honour, would not only be to divide the heart between God and the creature, but to detract from that divine and eternal honour by accounting human honours of the least value in its presence, as if a rushlight were of any value in the sunlight.   Moreover, the principle of the Christian virtues is the grace of God, with which we are only the co-operators, and, therefore, their chief honour is due to God and not to us.

The mere natural man, without faith or knowledge of himself, will attach much greater value to human honours, and will seek them with greater avidity than Christian truth permits, or than such honour deserves ; but what the true Christian looks to above all is the glory of God, and the eternal honours and dignities that God alone can give.   The magnificent objects presented to us in the light of faith are so infinitely superior to the things of this world, that, before the things of Heaven, these human honours and rewards shrink to nothing.   The lofty motives also that are given to the contemplation of the Christian soul reduce all earthly motives to vanity.   The sense of God, again, always present with us, and ever within us, attracting and moving us to aspire to His glory, ought to give us a great spirit, in some degree, however

* S. Thomas, *Sum.* ii. 2, q. 129, a. 3.

humble it may be, yet in some degree worthy of the great things to which we are called.   But it is on the contempt of these lesser things which the world values so much, that we rise in a spirit greater than the spirit of the world, to those greater things above the world.

God alone is great, and it is a great thing to be His servants, and still more to be His children.   Great is His love for us, and greatly has He shown that love, giving us His only beloved Son for our redemption, and His Holy Spirit for the sanctification of our hearts.   Great is His power, and great are His gifts, "who redeemeth thy life from destruction, who crowneth thee with mercy and compassion".   It hath also pleased Him to give us a kingdom that is far greater than the kingdom of this world.   Who, then, can doubt but that the servants and friends, the sons and daughters of the Eternal King, ought to have great souls?   Who can hesitate to think or to say that they ought to be ready to do great things for His honour and glory?   "God has taught us great things," observes St. Gregory, "and has commanded us great things, that after doing them He may give us great things."*   Even in this life He presents magnificent gifts to those who serve Him in a generous spirit, such as purity of heart, divine consola-tion, firmness under difficulties, security in dying, and a quick transit to Heaven.

He is magnanimous who rudely mortifies his senses, giving no more to the body than it needs, that the spirit may hold command, and be free, and the soul filled with good things.   He is magna-nimous who will not let his soul be ruffled by offensive words or violent deeds.   He is great-minded who has his chief conversation with the Eternal Truth and Justice.   Why should that truth be always near us, and we commonly far away, unless from our little-mindedness?   He is great-minded who keeps himself in the Divine Presence, and is never long away from the sense of the Eternal God.   God is always with us, why should we not always be with God?   The great souls of all ages have walked with God, not only the great ones of history, but many of the poor and unknown who were wise in God, though counted for ignorant in this world; who were honoured by God, though despised by the world.

Soft and pusillanimous souls are too weak to walk steadfastly before God through the pilgrimage of life; but the great-souled

* S. Greg. Mag., *In 7 Regum*, ad cap. 17.

are subject from their inmost heart to God, accounting that nothing can be greater for them than to be in the hands of God. To be great-souled is to be full of faith, of a faith that so lights up the eternal world to them, that the mortal things of this world fade before their eyes like dying flowers. The great-souled are magnanimous in sacrificing the love of self to the love of God, until all their strength flows into charity. Happy they who are released from bondage to themselves, that they may be large and free in the generous atmosphere of light and grace. All that we require is that the soul be open and generous. Humility opens the soul ; charity makes her generous.

Put yourself in Plato's position, to whom even the shadow of Christianity was a blank. Take the position of that heathen philosopher at the moment when he declared to Alcibiades that no one knows what to ask of God, until a Divine One come to teach him. In such a state of mind one might naturally reason in this manner : Man is evidently in an unsatisfactory state. Though he dares not look closely into his soul, yet he feels that he is not what he ought to be. Something has gone wrong with him, one cannot say what it is, but something very serious. He longs to be what he should be, at least the right-minded man does so, but he does not know what he ought to be. He therefore knows not what to ask of God, for in his ignorance he may ask for what will make him worse instead of better. It is evident we are on a wrong line, and are going further away from the right line : one has only to look into one's self to see that people are dying every day, dying with the full consciousness of immortality, yet not knowing what is to become of them.

If the God who made us would only come and tell us what we ought to be ! It is an audacious thought, but who knows the power, or the goodness, or the condescension of God ? God is not proud, as we are. His thoughts are not like ours, nor His ways like ours. We are certainly His children despite our errors. Yet were He to come, could we see or understand Him ? He is the Eternal Spirit, and we are wrapped up in mortal clay. It is a stupendous thought ; but what if God were actually to come, as He has so often been imagined, in a mortal form, and to live with us, and to teach us what we are, and what we ought to be ? It is an astounding supposition for mortal men to raise who know so little of God, but we should then have with us a perfect man, whom we could see, to whom we could listen, and who being God as well as man, would tell us what we are, and show us what we ought to be, and what He would have us to be. Oh! what an infinite relief would this be to us distracted mortals, with our consciousness of immortality!

Well, this astounding fact has came to pass. For nigh two thousand years the world has known the Son of God in human nature. The great event was preparing from the beginning of the world; the rumour of its approach grew into expectation, and He came. Yet when He came the world knew Him not. The world had its own great men, sages and heroes of renown, whose chief virtue was their magnanimity; and the world expected that a perfect man would be a hero and a sage of its own type, completing its own ideal of a perfectly magnanimous man, as drawn by Plato, Aristotle, and Cicero. Christ Jesus was the Perfect Man in perfect union with God, the model of manhood to all men, most perfect in magnanimity as in all the virtues, yet the world could not understand Him; so very different is the divine from the human view of magnanimity. For the Perfect Man was wholly turned to God; whilst the great man of the world was wholly turned to the affairs of this mortal life. The Perfect Man was wholly subject to God; whilst the great man of the world was chiefly ambitious of dominion over his fellow-men. The Perfect Man denied Himself the honours of the world and the gratification of Himself; whilst the great man of the world made its honours the chief end of his life, and the gratification of his pride his main pursuit. The Perfect Man was humble and His life hidden with God; the great man of the world rises in the spirit of self-elation and self-reliance to subject to his rule the children of pride. The Perfect Man did nothing of Himself, but looked in all that He said and did to the will and wisdom of God His Father; but the great man of the world stepped forth with unbounded confidence in himself, in his own wit and wisdom. The Perfect Man looked above all to the perfect end of man, and sought to draw all men to their perfect end; but the great man of the world only sought a deathless fame among perishing mortals like himself. The Perfect Man built upon eternity, and His works are glorified eternally; but the great man of the world built on himself, and his work could not endure.

Such is the contrast between the magnanimous man of the

world and the magnanimous man of God, that the first principles of
the man of the world are completely reversed in the first principles
of the man of God. The one rests everything on himself, uses
everything for himself, and draws everything to himself; the
other rests everything on God, obtains everything from God, and
draws everything to God. The difference between the interior
states of these two men is so absolute as to establish a fundamental
opposition in their thoughts, their desires, and their actions, and
to such an extent that St. Paul calls the one darkness and the
other light. To the converted heathens he says: " Ye were darkness, but now light in the Lord ". *

In nothing is this fundamental difference more strikingly shown
than in the different way in which the virtue of magnanimity is
understood and exercised, which entirely depends on the view
taken of what constitutes true greatness of soul. But as the true
greatness of the soul is not in herself except in capacity, but arises
from the truth and the good which God communicates to her
nature, it is obvious that the heathen's notion of the soul's greatness as derived from herself, and from her own native resources,
is utterly false ; and that it gives a false foundation to the virtue
of magnanimity. Christ gives it its true foundation in resting
it upon the humility of the man dependent in all things on the
divine communications of God. This foundation rests in the
truth and justice of things, and gives the soundness of justice to
all that is built upon it.

It is impossible, therefore, to express these two kinds of magnanimity under one name without adding some specific terms of
distinction to things so opposite in their nature, and we must call
the one heathen magnanimity and the other Christian magnanimity. For although some few Catholic writers have gone so far
as to maintain that the magnanimity of the heathen is the humility
of the Christian, the question will not stand a moment's examination, for the exposition of magnanimity by Aristotle shows clearly
that it rested on pride and self-sufficiency. When the learned
though eccentric Raynaudus urged the point in a dry dissertation,
by inserting the contrary arguments of Lessius, he unconsciously
refuted himself. The pagan Celsus maintained that the Christians had stolen their humility from Plato, but by his admiration
of Plato and his loathing of Christian humility, he contradicted

* *Ephesians v. 8.*

his own statement.* Cajetan, the great commentator on St. Thomas, declares that the notion of any identity between heathen magnanimity and Christian humility " is a new fantasy, a novelty undiscovered by all past doctors, to be exterminated from the precincts of the Church and of moral philosophy ".†

Although both heathen and Christian magnanimity aim at making the soul great, and that, by seeking great things and despising little things, there is an immeasurable distance between them, which is still visible in the man of the world as compared with the servant of Christ. That distance will be discovered in the answer to the two questions: What are the great things that make a man great-souled? And what are the little things that make a man little-souled? The things of this world are certainly little in comparison with God. To be honoured by this world is little in comparison with being honoured by God. Time is little in comparison with eternity. Man himself is little in comparison with God. The man, therefore, who prefers himself to God, or the things of this world to the things of God, or the interests of time to the interests of eternity, or the being honoured by men to the being honoured by God, is not great-souled, but little-souled. Such a man is poor in his reason, small in his aim, and low in his aspirations. For even reason teaches that we ought to be subject to God, to do His will, and not to estimate ourselves above what we are, or anything beyond its true value. When the heathen thought that he was all sufficient for himself, he first defied himself, for his pride led him to pantheism. It is evident that the soul is not great in herself, but only capable of greatness; if the soul were great in herself she would have no occasion to seek for greatness, and to seek it with much labour and contention. But when men sought for greatness through human opinion, and it failed them, they could no longer endure themselves, an evident proof that the greatness of the man was not in himself.

It is also evident that the soul is a middle good, placed between superior and inferior good, and capable of either the one or the other; so that the soul becomes great by attaching herself to what is greater than she is, and little by attaching herself to what is less than she is. In the first case she rises to the virtues, in

---

* Origen, *Contra Celsum*, lib. vi.
† Cajetan, *in Summam*, ii. 2, q. 192.

the second she sinks to the vices. The soul, therefore, becomes great, good, and elevated, in proportion to the greatness, goodness, and elevation of the objects at which she aims, and to which she attaches herself. If she receives a great truth from God, she is greater by all that truth. If she receives a great gift of grace and virtue from God, and works faithfully with the gift, she is greater by all that gift. If she has a great sense of God, and that sense inspires her with a great love of God, she is the greater by all that love which unites her with God. By that love the soul aspires to the greatest of all things that can give her excellence, she aspires to an eternal union with God, and in thus seeking God with her whole mind and heart, at whatever cost to herself, the soul ascends to the sublimest act of Christian magnanimity.

The soul is one and simple, and the will that moves the soul is one and simple. When therefore the will moves the soul with a sovereign movement of affection towards the Supreme Object of her existence, she must of necessity move away at the same time from the less things beneath her, and must even give up herself to what is greater than herself, which is the greatest act of magnanimity.

Our Divine Lord has taught us this grand truth in His Sermon on the Mount. He says: "Lay not up to yourselves treasures on earth, where the rust and moth consume, and thieves break in and steal. But lay up to yourselves treasures in Heaven, where neither the rust nor moth consume, and where thieves do not break through nor steal. For where thy treasure is, there is thy heart also." * Then He gives us a beautiful illustration of the conduct of the will from the conduct of the eye, and of the intention of the will from the attention of the eye. "The light of thy body is thine eye. If thine eye be single thy body will be in light. But if thine eye be evil thy body will be in darkness. If then the light that is in thee be darkness, the darkness itself, how great shall it be!" The eye of the will is compared with the eye of the body. If the eye is in an evil condition the whole body is left in darkness, and if the intention of the will be in an evil condition the whole soul is in disorder. If the will looks to the real treasure of the soul, the whole soul partakes of that treasure; but if the attention of the will is taken up with inferior things, the whole soul suffers deterioration. Those lesser things

* *S. Matthew* vi. 19-21.

become the treasure of the heart instead of the greater things, and through abiding in little things the soul becomes little.

Our Lord then applies this instruction: "No man can serve two masters. For either he will hate the one, and love the other, or he will sustain the one, and despise the other; you cannot serve God and mammon." The soul is no more her own object than the eye; it is made for something else, and to her object the soul is subject, as the eye is subject to what it looks upon. Either the eye of intention is subject to God, which makes her great-souled, or is subject to what is less than herself, which makes her little-souled. To be subject to God is the magnanimity of humility, and this brings her near to God, which is a very great thing. Wherefore, after further showing that it is the vice of the heathens to seek after those little things, our Lord concludes: "Seek ye therefore the kingdom of God and His justice, and all these things shall be added to you". * And to show that whatever we attach ourselves to enters into the soul, and makes it great or little, good or evil, He says elsewhere: "A good man out of a good treasure bringeth forth good things; and an evil man out of an evil treasure bringeth forth evil things". †

In this divine instruction we have the two sides of Christian magnanimity presented to us: the one on which the soul seeks the true honour and greatness in God, and the other on which she renounces herself and whatever is less than herself for God, whereby she contends against dishonour, and refuses degradation. As she aspires to God she is great by charity; as she refuses to be attached to herself, to any false idea of herself, or to things less than herself, she is great by humility. S. John Chrysostom therefore asserts the principle, and argues it through a discourse, that he is magnanimous and sublime who is truly humble. This virtue, he says, makes the soul healthy and elevated, enables a man to do great things, makes him sweet and gracious to all men, and peaceful within himself, whilst the arrogance of pride comes of a debased mind and an illiberal soul. But whoever has the sense of moderation is not high-minded even in great things, whilst the debased soul thinks in a high-minded way even of little things, and makes much of them. To reach sublimity from the ground of humility we must take the true measure of human things, that we may be enkindled with the desire of

* *S. Matthew* vi. 22, 33.   † *S. Matthew* xii. 35.

divine things, because we can be humble in no other way than by the love of divine things, and the contempt of present things.*

But as to face the true knowledge of one's self, to pursue it thoroughly, and to act upon that knowledge faithfully, is the most difficult of all things, demanding great courage and a great sacrifice of our natural inclinations, it is undeniable that true humility demands great magnanimity. And on this view of the virtue a distinguished spiritual writer has defined it in these terms : " Humility is the courage which applies the truth to ourselves in its rigour and completeness, and which carries it out into all its consequences ".

The magnanimous character of humility is shown in its long and stubborn conflict with pride, that most subtle, secret, tenacious, and destructive evil to the soul, the first evil to enter the soul, and the last to be exterminated. This is the greatest of all human difficulties, only to be mastered by the most arduous efforts to overcome one's self, and to accomplish the destruction of one's pride and self-love. The first part of this difficulty is to know one's self, a work demanding great courage and perseverance. The second is to bring what is wrong in us to judgment and conviction. The third is to execute justice and to apply reformatory punishment. The last is to devote one's self to the reformation of the criminal. But when this criminal is not another but one's very self, this is a difficulty so great, and so liable to recur, that it demands a most magnanimous humility.

In a well-known literary work, Dr. Johnson gave a voice to this side of human nature that is terrible in its truth. "Very few," he writes, "can boast of hearts which they dare lay open to themselves, and of which, by whatever accident exposed, they do not shun a distinct and continuous view ; and, certainly, what we hide from ourselves, we do not show to a friend."† The natural man shrinks from entering into himself ; he has neither the light nor the courage to explore the weaknesses that he would there discover ; he is inclined rather to censure such self-introspection as a morbid disposition of mind, confounding the morbid things discovered there with the eye that sees them. There may unquestionably be a morbid habit of self-introspection, when the mind is under the dominion of fancies and delusions, but this is

---

* S. J. Chrysost., *Hom.* 1 *in I. ad Corinthios, per totum.*
† Dr. Johnson's *Life of Pope.*

an abuse, and not the legitimate use of self-knowledge. That true knowledge of one's self on which humility is founded is the result of co-operation with the light and grace of God; but to obtain this self-knowledge effectually, and to rectify the evils discovered, demands great courage and magnanimity, especially if the evils that spring from self-love, vanity, and pride are to be vigorously pursued to their extermination. For this cannot be accomplished by any powers of our own, nor in a short period of time, nor without arduous labours in conjunction with the light and grace of God. For pride cannot correct pride, nor vanity expel vanity, nor self-love overcome self-love. This can only be done by a brave and vigorous siding of the will with the light and help of God. But the first difficulty is to see ourselves as God sees us, which can only be done by taking the side of God against ourselves.

A routine examination of conscience is one thing, and quite a shallow proceeding; a vigorous effort to track our evil thoughts, inclinations, and acts to their origin in self-love, sensuality, or pride, and to follow these down to their cause in our weak and changeable nature, and our native nothingness, is altogether another thing, which brings us to the deep ground we have for being humble. This will discover to us that all our weakness and defilement comes of separating from God, the source of all strength and purity. We then see how far we are on a false foundation, and can only recover our true one through the most complete subjection to God. But except in rare and miraculous conversions, resulting from a great and sudden gift of humility from God, this great transfer of the soul from self to God is not accomplished at once, nor without long and persevering efforts of the will. For after the pardon of grace and justification has been received, many inclinations of nature must be sacrificed, and this is only done at the cost of conflicts, and through patience under humiliating failures; not losing confidence in God because of them, since it is not He, but we, who have failed; and making a generous application of the means at our disposal before the great work is so far accomplished as to give habitual peace and security to the soul.

It is very difficult for a man to bring his spiritual eyes into the depths of his soul, and to see the true springs of his actions. This is the work of interior reflection, and interior reflection is difficult to most people. But God is a strong helper to good-will. Yet those who go below the surface of the soul or the concrete acts recorded in their memory are not very numerous. The plants shoot through the soil, but their roots are invisible, yet the quality of the roots determines the quality of what springs up from them. So it is with the roots of evil; until we get at them, we can have but a shallow surface knowledge of ourselves, and can deal only with the effects and not with the causes of evil. Of two souls that take account of themselves, one sees but the facts that remain in the memory, the other sees the secret movements towards evil in the deep region of the soul. The last has self-knowledge, the first but remembrance.

The magnanimous character of humility is also shown in the fortitude with which we persevere in holding ourselves down to that just and true position which belongs to us, never advancing until God advances us, and that in spite and contempt of every natural impulse to false elation, or the assumption of a place or character that does not belong to us. Pride has a certain ferocity of self-assumption even in its more subtle ways, and this is false and weak; but humility is gentle, just, and sincere, which are the attributes of power. Understand from this that nothing is strong out of its true place.

Humility must also be brave and magnanimous in holding herself steadfast to her height above the opinions of the world. For her true place is under God. The world's thoughts are not His thoughts, nor the world's ways His ways, but far beneath them. To suffer the soul to be touched or influenced by the vain opinions of the world is to expose her to deterioration. The humble soul must, therefore, despise the levity of remark, the offensive satire, and the ironical flattery in which the thoughtless world is apt to indulge out of insolent pride against the ways of humility. These, however, are but external trials that have no real influence over solid humility. There is another danger that is internal, and consequently far more serious, and that is the fascinating influence of human respect, which is apt to run kindness into compliance, and fear of offence into compromise. This gives occasion to many subtle falls from consistency; but true magnanimity knows how to make the gentle sacrifice of human respect to the sincerity that belongs to humility; and calm courage is the shield that protects this delicate virtue from the tremulous movements of human respect.

But we rise to the sublime heights of humility, and hold to them with firmness and constancy, when we adhere to God, and abide in subjection to His sovereign dominion, knowing that our good is from Him, and not from ourselves; trusting in Him that He will fully fulfil all His promises; and humbly conversing with Him in prayer as a child with a loving father. It is a noble part of this magnanimity to follow in obedience every grace and inspiration that moves us to acts of generosity, and invites us to self-sacrifice. It is another part of magnanimity to receive all things from the hand of God, and to use them only according to His will, as Abraham refused that any one but God should enrich him. For this is the sublime way of humility, that a man be poor in himself and rich in God.

We will conclude this lecture with a solid instruction drawn from a rare book that is seldom met with.*

The mightiest shield against our adversaries is humility. St. John Climacus calls it the tower of strength against our enemies. To be effective it must have certain conditions. First, it must not be mean or pusillanimous, but high and magnanimous. The humble man must distrust himself altogether, and wholly trust in God. He must "enter into the powers of the Lord," and partake of His fortitude and constancy. Then he will not only resist sin and temptation, but will become in a certain way unconquerable by sin. St. John affirms this: "Whosoever abideth in Christ, sinneth not"; and "Whosoever is born of God, committeth not sin".† And St. Paul exhorts us: "Let no temptation take hold of you, but such as is human. And God is faithful, who will not suffer you to be tempted above what you are able";‡ that is, beyond what you are able to resist.

The Holy Spirit counsels us to unite this magnanimous humility in a firm adhesion with the love of God, as a security against all temptation. "Son, when thou comest to the service of God, stand in justice and fear, and prepare thy soul for temptation. Humble thy heart, and endure. . . . Wait on God with patience; join thyself to God, and endure, that thy life may be increased in the latter end."§ Separate thyself from thyself by humility; join thyself to God in the bond of charity. Bound in this chain of charity, St. Paul was certain that nothing whatever could separate

* Sideri, *De Evincendis Tentationibus*, c. iv., *de Medio Humilitatis.*
† 1 *S. John* iii. 6-9.   ‡ 1 *Corinthians* x. 13.   § *Ecclesiasticus* ii. 1-3.

him from the love of God; neither tribulation nor anguish; neither height nor depth; neither things present nor things to come.

Humility must also be magnanimous in despising the temptations of evil spirits, and in making little of them. They are fallen creatures, overpowered by Christ through His death. He suffered them to tempt Him, and then overcame them in Himself, that, as St. Peter Chrysologus says, "Having been once conquered by Christ, they might give place to every Christian who invokes the name of Christ against them"; * and that, as Jerome says, Christ might hand them over to His disciples to be trodden on; which, in fact, His Apostle exhorts us to do: "Be wise in good, and simple in evil, and the God of peace crush Satan speedily under your feet".†

Let magnanimity, then, be the just condition of your humility, for this is a holy combination. Magnanimous humility, humble magnanimity; as much as to say, humility and charity. These are the two wheels of the sacred chariot on which you ascend to God; charity carries you up, humility keeps you safe from falling.

The third condition of humility is to mortify the passions; this wrenches them out of the power of the adversary, and turns them into instruments of good.

The fourth condition of humility is to be grateful for all blessings received; for, as the Fathers say, true humility is not blind, but enlightened to know and acknowledge the gifts received from God, to give their honour to the Divine Majesty, and to be grateful. But it is a very great benefit to conquer temptations, because this comes of the effective grace of God.

The fifth condition of humility is for the soul to keep herself in a lowly state through self-knowledge, that she may justly ascribe the glory of victory over her enemy to God, and may attach nothing of it to herself.

This is the perfect humility that not only protects the soul from evil, and makes her safe under temptation, but which conquers in every hand-to-hand conflict with the enemy. Humility, then, is magnanimous in courage, and ardent in charity; is mortified in the passions, and grateful for blessings; is elevated in the light of divine truth, and lowly in self-knowledge. This armoury, with its five weapons of perfect humility, was possessed by the Blessed Virgin Mary, who celebrates its power in her sublime canticle. It made her mighty against the powers of evil, and sinless.

---

* S. P. Chrysolog., *Orat.* 21.   † *Romans* xvi. 19, 20.

LECTURE XI.

ON THE DETESTABLE VICE OF PRIDE.

"The beginning of the pride of man is to fall off from God; because his heart is departed from Him that made him; for pride is the beginning of all sin; he that holdeth it shall be filled with maledictions, and it shall ruin him in the end."—ECCLESIASTICUS x. 14, 15.

A S pride is the root of all evil, the vice of vices, and destruction of the virtues, it is the chief enemy of God and of man. The right order of every being is its perfection; order gives to each being its virtue, justness, and strength; its beauty, harmony, and value. Virtue is the moral order that perfects free and intelligent beings. Destruction is that which breaks up the just order of things, and brings it to ruin. But what breaks up the just order and destroys the virtues of the soul is pride. Hence the Scripture says that "pride goeth before destruction; and the spirit is lifted up before a fall ".*

We have already shown from many points of view that humility is the fundamental law of the rational creature : that it holds him in his just and true position; that it establishes him in his due relations of dependence on his Creator; that it founds him on God as his solid firmament; that it settles him in just order within himself; and that it places him on his due bearings towards his fellow-men. But pride contradicts the whole reason of humility, and is the most irrational as well as the most destructive of vices. It is the most irrational, because it is opposed to the whole light of reason, whether human or divine; for that light springs from the order of truth and justice, and pride destroys the order of truth and justice in the rational creature of whom it takes hold. The pride of the creature reverses not only the foundation of his

* *Proverbs* xvi. 18.

nature, but of his creation. It is not only irrational, therefore, as all sins are, but it is an uncreaturely sin, which other sins are not, except as they contain in them the malignant venom of pride. But he who sins from great pride virtually disowns his creation, as the heathens did altogether, for he affects to be something great and independent of God, beyond his state and measure of a creature. Lucifer aspired to be like the Most High in power and Adam in knowledge; and all pride has something of this, enough to show its descent.

The proud man does not behave like one whom God has recently created from nothing, and whom He may summon to His presence at any hour. He acts as though he were not dependent on God, and as if what he is, and has, were not altogether owing to the divine will and bounty. He turns from God with the insolence of an upstart, forgetting his mean origin, and who made him what he is, and endeavours to establish himself in opposition to his Creator. He will not have His dominion, however benignant; he will not have His law, however just; he will not have His wisdom, however divine; he will not have His will, however much directed to his good; he will not have His good, although the great good for which he was created. For pride is the love of one's own excellence independently of God; and when a man trusts to himself and to his self-sufficiency, when he commits himself to his own independent resources, he separates from God, and the more he separates himself the greater is his pride. "The vice of pride springs up," as St. Augustine observes, "when a man trusts above all to himself, and makes himself the head and principle of life. In thus acting he withdraws himself from the Fountain of life, at which alone he can drink of that justice which is life; and he equally withdraws himself from that unchangeable light, by partaking of which the rational soul is in a certain way enkindled so as to become herself a created light. By this impiety he ascribes to himself what belongs to God, and is driven into his own darkness, made by his iniquity." *

If the proud man so far forgets himself and the law of his being as to behave as though he were a god rather than a creature, how much more unreasonable and absurd will his behaviour appear from the fact that he is a fallen creature, whose fall from truth

* S. August., *De Spiritu et Littera*, c. vii.

and justice has come of the pride that has already brought him to ruin. If pride is utterly disgraceful in the creature, it is absolutely shameful in the sinner, whose degraded condition ought rather to be clothed with humility than with the fig-leaves of vanity. This vice, in short, is so thoroughly opposed to the nature and condition of man, as well as to the rights and claims of God, and is so destructive of all spiritual good, that God has proclaimed to us this warning in His Scripture: "Pride was not made for men".*

In its general character pride is defined to be an inordinate appetite for one's own greatness. But an account of its generation in the soul will much better help our understanding of it than a definition. To do this effectually we must take a large scope. What is not made for itself but to receive something better is a very imperfect creature until it has received the nobler existence for which it is made. A garden made to receive flowers and fruits is not worth the name so long as it grows nothing but weeds. A house is made for man, and is desolate without his presence. Our body is made for the habitation of our soul, and without the soul it is but corruption. The soul is made for the living God, whose light and grace prepare her for His inhabitation. In the very centre of our soul is an instinct that urges us to seek after the Supreme Good for which the soul is made; and St. Thomas notes the terrible truth, that even the lost are not without the sense of that higher good on which our good is founded, or they would not have remorse for having neglected it.

A soul, then, without the Spirit of God, is an existence without its object, a mere failure from the reason of its existence; like a house that is never inhabited, or a body that is never animated. Yet with this grievous difference, that the soul without God is conscious of misery, and of being herself the cause of her desolation; if she is not so conscious, it is because of a blindness and insensibility which is the bitter penalty of her sins. As a moral or intellectual being, again, is only perfect as far as the will acts according to the perfection of order, and as the rule of that order is founded in the light of that justice which proceeds from God as the Eternal Justice, the soul can only be perfected according to the completeness of her conformity with the eternal law of justice that God reveals in her. As that, again, which is the living image of another can only be perfect in so far as it has the life of that

* *Ecclesiasticus x. 22.*

other, even so only can the soul be perfected, as the very constitution of her nature is an image of God, in so far as she possesses the life of God. In one word, the greatness of the soul is her capacity for God ; and therefore the degree of her union with God is the real measure of her perfection. But the essential condition of each degree of this union is, that the creature who receives the blessing be subject to the Supreme Giver of the blessing. For by no strength of our own, by no effort made by our mere nature to rise, can we ever ascend to union with God, who is infinitely above every creature He has made. And therefore, as St. Augustine so frequently remarks, for a creature to ascend nearer to God, means the same thing as to be more subject to Him, and it is through that subjection that we ascend beneath His Divine Majesty, and receive the heavenly influences descending into us.

If, then, it be the truth of all truths for us, that we are made for God, who alone can perfect our nature by adding what is divine to it, what is it that separates us from God? what keeps away from us His gifts by which He desires to perfect us? what, again, is the effect upon us of this separation from God?

It is of the last importance that we should clearly understand this subject, and that we should give it all that patient attention which ensures intelligence. It is pride that separates the soul from God, the setting up of the soul upon herself, the rivalry with God in His own domain of independence, the practical assertion of our own sufficiency independently of God. The other vices are the stimulants of pride, the instruments of pride, and the servants of pride ; but pride itself is the element of revolt and independence in all the vices. Pride is therefore not only a special but a universal vice. It precedes all other sin, generates all other sin, and is the malignant virus in all sin. The Holy Scripture says that "pride comes before a fall " ; that " pride is the beginning of all sin " ; and that "pride is the root of all sin ". Pride not only precedes the other vices in time, but is the cause and principle of evil. Sin is an aversion from God and a conversion to the creature, accepted as a good in place of God against all reason and justice ; and pride is the aversion from God in all sin. It is the revolt from subjection to Him, the arrogance that claims to act in independence of His law, and arrogates to be what He is, as though one were a god to one's self, assigning to one's self the gifts received from God, and using them against the rights of God. Hence the Divine Wisdom says through Ecclesiasticus : " The beginning of the pride of man is to fall off from God, because his heart is departed from Him that made him ".*

Pride begins, then, by a fall from God into ourselves, and continues through that elation by which we swell ourselves into something greater and higher than what in truth we are. How is this brought about? Through self-love. For inordinate self-love is the cause of pride. Here we must explain what inordinate self-love is, and how it generates pride. But to do this satisfactorily, we must first state in what the true love of ourselves consists. St. Augustine asks this question in his book on Christian Doctrine, and he answers, that the just love of ourselves consists not in any enjoyment of ourselves as originating from ourselves, but in receiving enjoyment from God, who is our good. When we are enjoined to love our neighbour as ourselves, it is in God, and for God, that we are to love him. This, then, is the order, so fruitful in felicity, in which we are to love ourselves. The love of God is dominant in all true love, even in the love of what is inferior to God. This is that charity towards our soul, and towards other souls, and towards all God's creatures, which is priceless, pure, and animated by a divine principle. And so we love not alone, not even ourselves, but the Holy Spirit by His grace loves also with our love. For charity is not of one, but of two, of God and of ourselves. This love of ourselves is the spiritual ground in which is planted the grace and virtue of divine hope. And as our soul is not her own good, but the recipient of that good for which we hope and pray, it is evident that the true love of our soul cannot be separated from the love of God, which is the good and salvation of our soul.

When we reflect on this, and on what we have been, and on what we now are, and on what this charity makes us to be, there can be nothing so beautiful, nothing so strong, nothing so wonderful, as this charity of God in a soul that is subject to Him. What the soul loves in herself is her happiness, but this happiness she finds not in herself, but in the union of her spirit with the good that is unchangeable, and therefore, as St. Augustine remarks in a celebrated sentence, " That man is the truest lover of himself who devotes his whole life to gaining hold of the unchangeable life, and cleaves to God with every affection of his

* *Ecclesiasticus* x. 14, 15.

soul". He turns not his desires to himself, but to Him in whom all desires find their contentment and their end. But if we only love ourselves truly as far as we direct our love to God, our neighbour ought not to be discontented if our love of him repose more on God than on himself. Such a love ought even to give him greater content, since it is that love of charity which is not mere human love, but a love that the Holy Spirit prompts and inspires.

Inordinate self-love excludes the love of God, and makes one's self the first and chief object of affection; and as we have nothing of our own that is worthy of this devotion, by a habitual delusion and self-deception practised through the imagination, the self-love of the soul appropriates many things to herself that do not belong to her, which, though they may be true in their right place, and with their right owner, are not true in the soul that lays claim to them. "Does any man doubt," asks Lord Bacon, "that if there were taken out of men's minds vain opinions, flattering hopes, false valuations, imaginations as one would, and the like, but it would leave the minds of a number of men poor shrunken things, full of melancholy indisposition, and unpleasing to themselves?"* The light of truth, which God makes to shine into the soul, she will make her own light; the rules of justice, that she sees in her mind, she will make her own justice; the good things and beautiful qualities that she has anywhere seen or fancied she will make her own qualities. Into all that self-love thus gathers in fancy to herself she will put her own feelings and affections; and though there is nothing solid in them to build her into being, nothing but fiction and imagination, nothing but the amorous affection with which she embraces these shadows in place of substance—all this affection swells the soul with conceit of herself, and of her assumed superiority. Thus looking to a self that is not real but imaginary, and flattered by the fiction, the true self, with all its poverty, want, and weakness, is lost sight of; and the more this self-love is indulged, the more is the soul blinded to her real condition, and to the sense of her real good.

This self-love is not only fed by unjust appropriations that make her thoroughly dishonest, as well as deluded; it is also fed by grosser and baser elements, by the animal senses and the appetites that move in them, by temptations from the evil one,

---

* Lord Bacon's *Essay on Truth.*

and by many external acts and things from which self-love borrows flattery. Thus that consciousness of ourselves that is given to establish our individual nature and personality and for the sense of responsibility, so that through our consciousness of our great wants, and our appetite for what is better than we are, we might move from ourselves to seek our true good in our true centre, is turned, by an enormous abuse of our faculties and free will, into a disposition to make ourselves our centre, and the centre and end of many things, which, like ourselves, have their true centre and end in God. Thus inflated and inflamed by self-love, and by the things that feed self-love, this inflammation bursts into pride, into the inordinate estimation and love of our own excellence, that aspires in its blind folly to a false freedom, and swells against the law and will of God, against dependence on Him, against the authority He has constituted, and, in its excess, even against God Himself, ignoring Him, and setting up this poor, needy, blinded creature as a god in His place. " The beginning of the pride of man is to fall off from God ; because his heart is departed from Him that made him." Such was the fall of Satan, who was spiritually inflated with himself. Such was the fall of Adam, who was both spiritually and sensually inflated with himself.

The result of this virulent inflammation is blindness in the mind, disorder in the faculties, internal confusion, and the loss of the divine gifts. For "God resists the proud," and "knoweth the proud afar off ". He can allow of no arrogant rivalry in a creature that depends on Him for everything, of no turning of His gifts against Himself, without leaving that creature to the desolateness of his disordered nature. Charity loves all good, and through the love of the Supreme Good unites with all good ; pride separates from all good by separating from the Supreme Good. Hugo of St. Victor has explained this very clearly. These are his words : "As all good is derived from the Supreme Good, the good we have exists less in the soul than in God, from whom the soul derives that good. But he who seeks his delight in some detached part of what is good, as if it were exterior to and independent of the Supreme Good, whilst he perversely strives to separate that part from the whole, for the sake of making it his own exclusive possession, he incurs the loss of all. The proud will that, in the perverse affection of appropriating what she can to herself, would cut off the part communicated to herself from the whole Supreme Good that is so infinitely beyond her reach, destroys its life and beauty." * Like separating a faculty from the mind, a limb from the body, a ray of light from the sun, or a streamlet from the fountain, the part dries up, ceases to shine, or expires. Or more truly in this case, the gift of God is withdrawn, and its former influence dies out by degrees, if not all at once.

Amort has very accurately defined pride as an inordinate appreciation and false estimate of our own excellence. It is an excess above and beyond the measure of what we are, against all truth and justice. It is more than an appetite for perverse exaltation, as St. Augustine observes, it is a perverse imitation of God. The proud man not only claims an excellence he does not possess, but he dislikes the dominion of God, and hates equality with other men, loving to assert his own dominion over them in place of God's dominion. † Pride therefore is equally opposed to humility and to magnanimity,—to humility in refusing subjection to God, and to magnanimity in aiming at great things in a false and disorderly way. Notwithstanding its brave show, pride is really pusillanimous, and especially so in spiritual things, because it is hollow within, having no spiritual support, whilst the humble are brave because they have the inward support of grace and justice. The proud can swell, but not endure, they have a fear of spiritual power, and, from their very hollowness and imaginativeness, are easily intimidated.

Pride not only refuses subjection to God, but turns from God, and is adverse to God, whilst claiming an excellence that belongs to God alone, and a primal dominion over His creatures that essentially belongs to God. We see, then, how pride is a perverse imitation of God. It is therefore that *delictum maximum*, that sin of sins, that dereliction or forsaking of God from which David prayed to be free. "Who," he asks, "can understand sins? From my secret ones cleanse me, O Lord: and from those of others spare Thy servant. If they shall have no dominion over me, then shall I be without spot: and I shall be cleansed from the greatest sin." ‡ This *delictum maximum*, this greatest sin, is the pride that constitutes the malice of every sin, the first to enter

* Hugo de S. Victore, *Exegetica*, p. i., lib. ii., c. 4.
† S. August., *De Civitate Dei*, lib. xix., c. 10.
‡ *Psalm* xviii. 13, 14.

the soul, the last to leave the soul, linked in the secret depths of the soul with the fuel of all sin, so that when the soul is completely cleansed from this greatest sin, she is immaculate, because the whole malice of sin is in pride.

What makes pride the greatest sin is not the conversion to evil of the will created good, but the aversion of the will from God. This St. Thomas has explained in the following terms : " In other sins a man turns from God through ignorance, or weakness, or the desire of some other good, but pride has an aversion to God from unwillingness to be subject to Him, or to His rule. As Boetius says : All vices fly from God, but pride alone rises in opposition to God. For this reason God resists the proud. That aversion to God, which is but a consequence in other sins, belongs to pride as its first principle, and this makes its acts a contempt of God."* St. Ambrose expresses the same truth in more vivid terms. On the words of the Psalm, "The proud man did iniquity altogether," he says : " Man's greatest sin is pride, and from this as from its origin all sin has flowed. With this weapon the devil struck and wounded us ; for had man never listened to the serpent's persuasion and wished to be as God, the inheritance of this deadly guilt had never been transmitted to us. Why do I limit the case to man ? The devil also lost the grace of his nature through pride, when he said : " I will set my throne above the clouds, I will be like to the Most High ". Then fell he from the fellowship of the angels, and after condemnation to the punishment due to his crime, he sought to make man a partaker with him, and to transfuse into him the fellowship of his offence. What can be worse than the sin that begins with insulting God ? For this reason the Scripture says that God repels the proud; He repels the contumely against Himself; He takes up His special war against the proud as though He said : "This is my adversary : this sin is aimed at Me : this is My cause ". †

The antagonism of pride to God is expressed with a terrible power in the Book of Job, and its consequences depicted with a fearful truth : " The wicked man is proud all his days, and the number of the years of his tyranny is uncertain. The sound of dread is always in his ears ; and when there is peace, he always expecteth treason. . . . Tribulation shall terrify him, and distress

* S. Thomas, *Sum.* ii. 2, q. 162, a. 6.
† S. Ambrose, *In Psalm.* cxviii.

shall surround him, as a king that is prepared for the battle. For he hath stretched forth his hand against God, and he hath strengthened himself against the Almighty, he hath run against Him with his neck raised up, and is armed with a fat neck. . . . He shall not depart out of darkness, the flame shall dry up his branches, and he shall be taken away by the breath of his own mouth. Being vainly deceived by error, he shall not believe that he may be redeemed at any price." *

St. Augustine points out how even light sins may become grievous by the addition of pride. "Even upon those," he says, "who watch and are solicitous not to sin, certain sins of human frailty will creep in, and though small and few, they are sins nevertheless; but if pride gives its weight and increase to them, they become great and grievous. Still let devout humility put an end to them, and they are easily cleansed by our High Priest in Heaven." †

Pride is not only the greatest but the most blinding of sins. It puts the soul in an utterly false position with respect to herself, and consequently with respect to everything else, and she therefore sees nothing in its true light; so that whatever affects the soul is seen reversely from the divine point of view, which is the only true one. As the soul is turned from God the man is involved in his own shadow, and, resting mostly on that shadow, loses from view the serene light of truth. As, again, the will infected by pride acts upon the fictions of the imagination rather than on the understanding of truth, the soul is immersed in error. Who has not experienced this when inflated with pride against his fellow-man, and even against his friend? When the heat of anger swells his heart with pride against him, he imagines all kinds of evil and malice in him, and can see nothing that is good; but when he returns to sobriety, he is astonished to find that he has been the dupe of such a mass of error. · As pride closes the soul upon herself in a greater or lesser degree proportioned to its intensity, and isolates the mind from what is better, she looks not to God, but to herself, for the standard of truth and justice; and the mental eye plunges into the obscurity and disorder arising from the troubled shadows of her own confused and darkened nature. St. Paul has portrayed this condition of soul in de-

* *Job* xv. 20-31.
† S. August., *De Sancta Virginitate*, c. 1.

scribing the pride of the heretical man : " He consents not to the sound words of our Lord Jesus Christ, and to that doctrine which is according to godliness. He is proud, knowing nothing, but sick about questions and strife of words ; from which arise envies, contentions, blasphemies, evil suspicions, conflicts of men, corrupted in mind, and who are destitute of the truth." *

Pride is not only the blinding but the destructive sin. It is not only the venom of the vices, but the destruction of the virtues, corrupting with its putridity whatever it touches. It is both the head and the foot of sin. As the venom is in the head of the serpent, pride, inspired by the devil, is the head of the body of sin. But when conceived by man it is the foot of that infamous body, treading on inferiors, spurning equals, and aiming at bringing down superiors. David therefore prayed : " Let not the foot of pride come near me ". Every other vice is devoted to some one evil work, but pride moves in them all to make them malignant, and even besets our good works to bring them to ruin.

Vain, says St. Ephrem, is every exercise of piety, vain is all patience, vain all obedience, vain is voluntary poverty, vain is every kind of discipline, however you multiply its pressure, if you be destitute of humility. For exactly as humility is the beginning and end of all that is good, so is pride the beginning and end of all that is evil. Crafty and cunning is this evil spirit, and takes many shapes to obtain dominion over men, casting nets on every path in which they move. The wise man is caught by his wisdom, the strong man by his strength, the wealthy by his wealth, and the beautiful one by her beauty. The eloquent one is entrapped by his speech, the fine-voiced singer by his sonorous notes, the expert workman by his skill, and even the beggar by the claims of his poverty. In like manner, this spirit tempts the spiritual ; him who has renounced the world by his renunciation, him who is temperate and continent by these virtues, him who lives in silence by his quiet and solitude, him who cultivates poverty by his poverty, him who is studious by his facility in learning, him who is quick of apprehension by his quickness ; the religious man by his religious profession, and the erudite by his erudition. And yet real knowledge and true science are only to be found in conjunction with humility.

* 1 *Timothy* vii. 3-5.
18*

Thus doth Satan labour to sow his cockle in every field. Our Lord, therefore, who knows how hard it is to conquer this passion, when once it has root in us, and how completely useless it makes us, despite of all our exertions, has given us humility for a banner and a trophy, saying: "When you shall have done all these things that are commanded you, say: We are unprofitable servants: we have done that which we ought to do."* And why should we bring lightness and folly upon us, when the Apostle admonishes us: "If any man think himself to be something, whereas he is nothing, he deceiveth himself".†

As the most deadly and destructive of diseases, pride often demands the most desperate remedies. As the healing art inflicts deep wounds or takes off limbs to save the body, or administers deadly poisons as a last resource to recover life; so, when we are unwilling ourselves to apply the severe remedies required, the Divine Healer of souls will sometimes permit one to fall into some shameful sin, that through its great humiliation the soul may be recovered from her pride. We need not quote St. Augustine, St. Isidore, or St. Thomas on this point, since the doctrine and experience of this runs through the Scriptures, and the Psalmist, as well as the prophets, invokes shameful things upon the proud that they may be humbled, and so restored to health and reason. But we will give one brief passage from St. Gregory: "The man who exalts himself for his virtue, returns to humility through vice. As the surgeon makes wounds to heal, God also makes a remedy of wounds, that when stricken with pride through virtue, we may be healed through vice; we fly from humility, but after a fall we cleave to it for safety."‡

A special characteristic of pride is its utter injustice. The proud man is almost always the least entitled to be so. A man solidly just casts a veil of modesty over his acts which adorn them whilst designed to conceal them; and which, instead of effacing their lustre, but tempers their brilliancy so as not to wound the sensitive eyes of envy; whereas the arrogant is commonly a vicious man. He exacts respect because he fears that it will not be voluntarily rendered; he wishes to conquer the homage which he suspects he does not merit. He sees not that he is only

* *S. Luke* xvii. 10.
† *Galatians* vi. 3. S. Ephrem, Syr. *Hom. ad Eversionem Superbiæ.*
‡ S. Greg. Mag., *Moral. in Job*, lib. xxxiii., c. 11.

assuming one vice more which renders all the rest conspicuous. Note the man who boasts of some quality, you may be almost certain he has the opposite defect ; for boasting has almost always for its end the imposing on one's self or on others.

Pride is a vice of incredible voracity : it feeds not only on all evil, but on all good things, turning all on which it feeds to putridity. " Other vices," observes St. Gregory, " attack but the virtues that destroy them : anger attacks patience, gluttony assails temperance, and lust destroys continency. But pride is not ·content with the destruction of one virtue ; it rises against all the members of the soul, and as a universal pestilence corrupts the whole body of virtue. It bursts upon the mind like a tyrant into a city that he has besieged, and drags the wealthiest captives into the hardest slavery. For the greater the abundance of virtue, if it be without humility, the wider will the dominion of pride range over it." * " Every other vice," remarks St. Augustine, " is exercised in evil works, to do them ; but pride is exercised in good works, to destroy them." †

Following St. Gregory, St. Thomas enumerates four species of pride. The first is, when a man ascribes to himself what he has received from God, whether of spiritual or corporal good, whether in the natural order of providence or in the supernatural order of grace. The second is, when, though the man acknowledges that what he has he has received from God, yet he ascribes his gifts to his own merits, or so speaks and conducts himself as to lead others to think so. The third is, when a man arrogates some good to himself that he does not possess, or when he endeavours to establish in other persons the opinion that he has this good. The fourth is, when, with a contempt for the less gifted, the man affects to have a higher degree of some excellence of which he has but a lower degree, whether he claims this excellence in knowledge, virtue, or skill, in the gifts of nature, of grace, or of fortune.‡ There is a fifth species of pride, which, though it commonly unites with those enumerated, is yet a species by itself, and that is the pride of ingratitude. For to the proud mind, gratitude is a badge of dependence; it is the open admission that we are indebted for our good to another. But this is inconsistent with any original claims to

---

* S. Greg. Mag., *Moral. in Job*, lib. xxxiii., c. 11.
† S. August., *Epist.* 211.
‡ S. Thomas, *Serm.* ii. 2, q. 62, a. 4.

that good, or with the notion of its being due to one's merits. The proud man, therefore, would efface all traces of what has passed between the giver and receiver, and would cover them with oblivion. But the humble are grateful, and confess from whom they receive their gifts.

Owing to the many vices which pride animates, it presents many faces, and as some of these vices are in opposition to each other, it will sometimes seem to act in contradiction with itself. Yet apart from the modification which it undergoes from its union with other vices, this may be given as a portrait of its general features. The central point of the proud man's character is an intense consciousness of self, with comparatively little sense or consideration for what contributes but little or nothing to his self-love. Yet he reflects his self-love in many things, and finds it crossed and interfered with in many more ; for there is nothing so sensitive, or so sore when touched, as pride ; it is as tender as a wound. To spiritual things the proud man is shortsighted, less from defect of organ than of light, from which he is turned by his false position. Pride makes a man envious and jealous, peevish and passionate, contentious and disputatious. Easily provoked, he is hard to reconcile, especially where his self-esteem is touched ; for he is suspicious of the kindliest advances, fancying them a design to win his submission. He has a large appetite for flattery, but a queasy stomach for friendly advice, which he regards as dictation. He is rude and ungenial, self-opinionated and meddling, ambitious and aspiring. As he has no faults, or does not see them, which appears to him the same, his troubles arise from the ill-judged conduct of other persons, and especially of his friends. He is keen, however, in sighting another's faults, or in imagining them where they do not appear. He is troublesome and ungovernable, resolute against reason, and stiff against wise counsel. Contemptuous to his inferiors, he is critical of his betters, and disobedient to his superiors ; unfit to govern, he is unwilling to be governed. With all his show and pretension he is hollow within ; with all his outward bravery, the moral courage inside of him is low ; and although artificial manners may cloak much that is here described, they take nothing of it away from the inclinations of the heart.

All that we have said goes to show that pride is not only a special vice but a universal vice, not only the root of the vices but the malicious element within the vices. With the help of St. Thomas we will explain this further. As it is the appetite and affection for our own excellence, pride is a special vice, having this false excellence for its specific object ; but as it is a rebellion against God, refusing subjection to His law and submission to His will, pride is a universal vice to be found in all the vices.

Every appetite of our nature has some good for its lawful object, and that good is so far good as it has some kind of resemblance to God, nearer or more remote. We have an appetite for truth, for example, but truth has a near resemblance to God. We have also an appetite for the things of this world, but they have so remote a resemblance to God as to be only a trace of resemblance. But everything is excellent in that degree in which it resembles God. Every virtue is the right and lawful use of some appetite, whilst each vice is the unlawful use or abuse of these appetites. The rule for the right use of our appetites is the law of God in the light of reason or the light of faith, and this rule directs our appetites in their due measure to the good which is their object. When our appetite obeys the rule of reason, it is good ; when it goes to an excess beyond the rule of reason, the appetite becomes vicious and leads to evil.

But the fundamental appetite of the soul is for excellence, because what is excellent perfects the soul. When we exercise this appetite for excellence according to the divine illumination of faith and of the law of virtue, it tends to the true greatness of the soul, and, therefore, belongs to magnanimity. St. Paul explains this to the Corinthians : " We will not glory beyond our measure, but according to the measure of the rule which God hath measured to us ".* To exceed this measure in our appetite, as we do in seeking for excellence where it is not to be found, that is, in ourselves and not in God, is pride. For which reason St. Augustine defines pride to be the appetite for perverse loftiness. † Pride, then, is a universal vice in two ways, by its diffusion through the other vices, and by its effects in them. For as God is the final object of the soul, and charity brings us to God as our final object, when the love of God enters into the other virtues, and animates them, it brings those virtues to God as their final end ; for whatever we rightly love is subject

---

* 2 *Cor.* x. 13. † S. August., *De Civitate Dei*, lib. xiv., c. 13.

to the love of God , so in the opposite direction the final end of the love of one's self takes us away from the love of God, and sets us upon our own excellence, and thus everything that we love inordinately in any vice has the love of one's self and of one's own excellence for its final end.   Thus, as the love of God infuses its life and rules through all the virtues, pride infuses its malice and rules through all the vices.   It is for this reason that pride is called the root of all the vices, for by its diffusion it corrupts all the powers of the soul, and not only gives its venom to the vices, but destroys the virtues.

As sin is committed from some special affection, that disorderly affection gives to the sin its special character ; but that same sin may also produce certain effects upon the general conditions of the soul, and this makes it a universal sin.   Such in a most singular way is pride, which has an effect upon the entire condition of the soul, upon all her faculties, powers, and actions, that makes it a universal vice beyond every other.   Every sin is a sin of pride by affection, though not the special sin of pride, for some are only committed from ignorance, or from weakness, or from passion, but the malice that is in every sin is in the revolt against God, against His law or will, and this is the effect of pride.   For this reason pride is hateful to God above all other sins, because it is an aversion of the soul from God, whilst cupidity is the turning to the creature in preference to God.   There are, therefore, two elements in every sin, the turning from God, the unchangeable good, which is pride, and the turning to the changeable creature in preference, which is cupidity.*

The intensity of pride is measured by the distance to which a soul departs from God—a distance, not of space, but of unlikeness. For as we approach to God through the good love of Him, we depart from God through the evil love of ourselves.   The nearer we approach to God the more fully are we enlightened by Him ; the further we depart from God the more darkness we encounter in ourselves.   The Psalmist therefore says : "Come ye to Him and be enlightened, and your faces shall not be confounded ". †　But of those who have gone far from God the Book of Wisdom says : "These things they thought, and were deceived ; for their own malice blinded them.   And they knew not the secrets of God,

---

* S. Thomas, *De Malo*, q. 8, a. 2.
† *Psalm* xxxiii. 6.

nor hoped for the wages of justice, nor esteemed the honour of holy souls." *

The first departure from God is when one begins to lose one's gratitude, and to neglect the worship of God. The second and further departure is when one begins to neglect the voice of God in the conscience. The third is when one begins to love the creature rather than the Creator, although not yet going so far as to abuse the creature. When, for example, there is a disposition to neglect any commandment of God rather than suffer some considerable inconvenience, or lose some considerable advantage of a temporary kind. Such a one will do no visible wrong so as to give scandal, but his intention is relaxed, and the conscience is accommodated to circumstances. The fourth degree of departure from God is when the interior is neglected, and the sense of the presence of God almost lost, whilst the man gives himself more ardently to the creature. His inward light grows dull, and his recollection is lost in dissipation. His affections turn upon himself and on what belongs to him, and breaks out in concupiscence. The curiosity of the eye awakens evil appetites, these awaken the passions, and the pride of life springs into action. As the sense of God becomes lost by neglect, the sense of self, under the stimulation of cupidity, passes into its place; self-esteem swells into elation, and the man begins to fancy himself the author of the good that God has given him, for "his heart is departed from Him that made him".

The fifth degree of departure from God is when the proud man abandons the unchangeable good to give himself wholly to changeable things. His pride has perverted his spiritual appetite, and he has lost the taste for divine things. He then begins to abuse the creature of God both in himself and in others, for pride is not only blind, but destructive, and not only destructive but cruel, hardening the heart as nothing else can do. Turned to sensual tastes as well by passion as by the love of self-elation, the proud soul plunges her spirit into shameful and degrading vice. "The horse-leech hath two daughters that say: Bring, bring." † These two daughters of all-devouring pride are Sensuality and Concupiscence; the body is not sated with sensuality, when pride has sunk the soul from the better things, nor the heart with evil desire.

* *Wisdom* ii. 21, 22   † *Proverbs* xxx. 15.

The sixth degree of departure from God is when a man not only delights but glories in crime, and sins because he is proud of his licence. He takes his licence for liberty, and his licentious abuse of the creature for the superiority of dominion. The devil was first proud of his nature, although it was the work of God, and then he was proud of his crime, because it was his own work. They fall into this depth of degradation who sin of deliberate malice, and find a gloomy sstisfaction in their malicious actions. "Who leave the right way," as the proverb says, "and walk by dark ways: who are glad when they have done evil, and rejoice in most wicked things; whose ways are perverse, and their steps infamous; "* and of whom Solomon says again: "The wicked man when he cometh into the depth of sin, contemneth ". † Elated with the pride of his sins, he despises God; and, wrapped in the false sense of security, he makes light of the enormity of his crimes, being blind to their punishment.

The seventh degree of departure from God is when, through a long and studious pursuit of evil in mind and conduct, the soul is darkened into oblivion of God, and of all that belongs to the salvation of the soul. Here pride swells into a loathing of the law of God, and of the truths of faith, and of all authority derived from God. Of this state the Apostle says: "There shall be a time when they will not endure sound doctrine: but according to their own desires they will heap to themselves teachers, having itching ears, and will turn away their hearing from the truth, but will be turned to fables ". ‡

The eighth degree of departure from God is into utter darkness, when a man becomes so absorbed in self-consciousness, and so exalted in self-love as to lose sight of his creation, and of all dependence on his Creator, even to the mania of self-idolization, and the making of himself an element of divinity, and consequently the source of all he is or has. For as pride runs its course of apostasy from God, this is its final end: after denying God it comes to the denial of man, and the substitution of a human god in His place. This is maniacal pride.

The ninth degree of departure from God, and of progress in pride, is when, not content with his own perdition, a man seeks to propagate the evil that is in him, and to spread his own corruption far and wide. Even to this the world of our day has come;

---

* *Proverbs* ii. 13, 15.　　† *Ibid.*, xviii. 3.　　‡ 2 *Timothy* iv. 3.

for fiery zealots are on their destructive mission against God and His Christ, and against the faith and purity of souls. Men and even women unite the fierceness with the Satanic cunning of pride in evil communication and the corrupting of life. Like the demons, they find their pleasure in diffusing corruption, that they may have companions in evil and subjects to its power as it reigns in themselves. But from all such evils may humility guard us, and Jesus Christ protect us.

· Let those who are justly shocked with these last degrees of pride make use of them to understand what is hidden in the first degrees. For even the beginning of pride contains the germs and seeds of these portentous growths. All pride has the same general character, and as the wisdom of God warns us in the Scripture, "The beginning of the pride of man is to fall off from God"; there is some falling off from God in all pride, though that falling off may not be consummated. Yet nothing grows faster than pride when indulged without opposition or restraint. How this pride develops from the first instincts of its appetite to its riper monstrosities has been fearfully portrayed by Father Gratry in his book on Logic :

"From the instinct of his pride man proposes to act, think, and live in no other way than God Himself lives. He begins his thinking from the little he is, and has, and knows. Beyond him exists the great Source of all being, truth, and life. But in his self-sufficiency he refuses to be more, to have more, to receive more, to learn more, or to know more than he actually does know, or has received. He will not believe beyond himself, see beyond himself, or seek beyond himself. He would derive all things from himself, as God derives all things from Himself. He takes the posture of one who is always giving, not the posture of one who is always receiving. From what little he has by sense and by sight, he generalises the law of the visible universe, and dictates laws to God. From the small glimmer of light in his intellect he constructs God, and the whole order of truth, and the whole order of justice. If he were a spider, he would make the universe a great spider's web, and to him God would be as a great spider. If he were a bee, he would make God out to be a great bee, gathering honey from a world of flowers, and constructing waxen cells. As he is a man, he makes of God a being of human faculties, with the qualities and limitations of humanity.

If a sensuous man, he will make God sensuous. Is he prone to abstract speculations?—He will make God out to be a great abstraction. Is he a sentimental man?—God shall also be a sentiment. But as man is not God, he ought before all to search after life, and come nigh to life, before he attempts to explain the mystery of life."

But, to quote another thoughtful writer, rather than humble himself to the truth, or sanction what his own mind has not created, the intensely proud man prefers inventing all sorts of chimeras; for he would rather be a creator than accept what God has created. Yet when he sets himself to create, he creates but nothings, mere lying vanities that are less than nothing, and finds his punishment in the nothingness of his creations. He is constantly in the pains of parturition, and brings forth wind.* But pride cannot destroy the creations of God.

It remains for us to obtain some perception of the way in which pride acts in the other deadly sins, and how the habits of those evils react on pride and increase its intensity. The seven deadly sins are the seven ways in which our nature is corrupted and defiled. They are pride, envy, anger, sloth, covetousness, intemperance, and impurity or lust.

Vice is the corruption of our affections beyond right order and due measure; and these seven vices are called capital sins or deadly vices, because all corruption of our rational nature flows from them.

The wholeness or integrity of our corporal nature is one thing; the integrity of our spiritual nature is another. Of corporal natures, some have existence and form, but without sense, such as gold; others have sense as well as form, such as the human body. A body that has no sense is corrupted by the violating or breaking up of its unity. Thus if you break a gold cup to pieces you corrupt its form. But if corruption enters into a sensible body, like that of man, it injures, disorders, and destroys the strength of that body, and we call the person who owns it sick, disordered, or infirm, any one of which states endangers or destroys the mortal life, and so brings that body to its final corruption. But our spiritual nature, the soul within the body, is made for truth and goodness, and the right order of the soul towards truth and goodness we call justice. The soul is therefore in a state of

* Rosmini.

utter poverty and want when separated from truth and goodness; and when wilfully separated she is in a state of violence, of disorder, and disunion. For the soul grows in that proportion in which she is united with truth and with goodness, and when perfectly united with them she is in perfect unity, because there is a perfect unity between the subject and its true object, which constitutes perfection.

The integrity, therefore, of a spiritual nature like the soul consists in adhering to the truth that is made known to her, and to the good that is given to her; and it should be remembered that truth is the light of good, so that when we have more truth than good, as we have in this world, it gives us the hope of a good to which we have not yet come. This adherence consists in acknowledging the truth and in loving the good which are presented to the soul, and this adherence is an act of the free affection of the will. But the sincerity of the soul is corrupted, and her unity and integrity violated, when the affections of the soul resist the known truth, or when she does not love that good for which she was created. When the soul resists the known truth, she becomes divided, and so corrupted in mind; and when she resists the good for which she was made, or the law of order and love by which that good is reached, she becomes divided in her will, and in all her soul, and is disordered and defiled. The purity of the mind is defiled by falsehood and rebellion against the truth; and the purity of the will and spiritual sense is defiled by vice and rebellion against God's law.

The spring of this disorder is in the will, and its first disorderly movement is to turn from God, which is pride; whilst the second disorderly movement is to turn with a love of preference to the creature, which is cupidity. But before we can turn with a love of preference to what is either false or inferior, we first turn in pride from the truth of God, or from the law of God, or from God Himself, to what is low and base. In other words, pride rises in the will before the will enters into cupidity and stimulates concupiscence into sin. This was the case with Lucifer, who turned from God before he turned to himself, and abandoned the love of God before he gave his whole love to himself. This was also the case with Adam, who turned from the truth of God before he accepted the falsehood from Satan, and ceased to be subject to God before he aspired to be equal to God through independent knowledge.

The soul in her integrity is united with God in affection through the medium of His light and grace, and through that union is united in affection with all the good that proceeds from God, whether to herself or to any creature, and through this affection is ready to acknowledge and to honour that good wherever it appears. But there are seven deadly corruptions of this affection, of which pride is the first. This false and disorderly love of one's own excellence, as if it were the chief and most desirable good, disorders and deforms our whole affection, by drawing it to one poor and needy part of being and cutting it off from the whole. For, as we have already said, all good is from one Supreme Good, and the good that proceeds from God is less in itself than in Him, " in whom we live, and move, and have our being ".* Whosoever, then, puts his delight in any good apart from the Supreme Good, perversely gives himself but a part and loses the great whole of good. By this separating of the soul from the Supreme Good and source of all good, all the beauty of rational affection is destroyed, the soul is left in an evil and most absurd position, and is exposed without defence to every evil and punishment. For the six capital vices that follow pride bring grief and punishment to the soul. The punishment of pride becomes visible in the vices that follow it; for whilst pride begins all iniquity, the vices that follow punish the iniquity of pride.

Pride would have good for its own exclusive property, for the proud soul delights in having, or imagining, or wishing a good that another has not. This love of having one's own especial excellence as an individual and exclusive property is the distinctive characteristic of pride, and is the reason why the vice is defined to be the love of excellence as one's own property. But this causes a hatred of all communion in good, from which springs envy, the first daughter of pride. For you would not be displeased at another's good, unless you first wished to have it yourself, and to have it alone. What wounds and grieves your pride in another's good or happiness is the sense it awakens in you of your own deficiency, and the discovery that you are not what you imagined you were, or wished to be. In taking an unjust delight in your pride, you are justly tormented by envy ; your pride

* *Acts* xvii. 28.

makes you pleased with what you think you are, and your envy makes you displeased with what another is. The less conscious a soul is of the malice of her pride, the more deeply she is corrupted by it, and the more alluringly it has entered the more deeply has it penetrated. Its very first influence is to blind the soul to its presence, and we mostly see it when, through the dawning of humility, it begins to disappear. But envy wounds pride and inflicts pain, yet even then it is not the evil that is felt so much as the bitterness; and so this envy is the beginning of the punishment of pride.

The vice of anger follows that of envy. It is an irrational perturbation of the soul that also brings with it a certain punishment. For if the good or the happiness of another is wounding to pride, how much more is it wounded when another rises to oppose or to offend our pride! Then it will rouse up with an irrational excitement, and reason is lost in anger, being utterly unable to endure with patience. The soul becomes agitated and tormented, revealing a weakness and want of foundation, and is incapable of bearing adversity with calmness. There is a just anger, of which the Scripture says, "Be angry and sin not";* but this is that righteous indignation which refuses to accept, to countenance, to encourage, or to do evil. It is quite different from that evil anger that refuses to suffer infliction. Just anger rejects sin; unjust anger refuses the punishment of sin, and is restless and disquieted, losing all patience in the presence of opposition. Thus pride suffers misery whilst the body is tortured with anger and the soul with its grief.

These three capital vices, pride, envy, and anger, are in most vicious ways opposed to God. Pride denies Him, envy accuses Him, anger flies from Him. The man whose glory is in his independent excellence will have no superior; in envying the good given to another he accuses the Divine Giver; in taking anger to his heart he expels the Divine Lover of peace, and breaks into language that either insults God in Himself or in His creature. Pride says: "God is not my good". Envy says: "He is not my benefactor; the good I loved He has given to another". Anger says: "He has not sent me good, but evil". Thus are these three vices especially injurious to God: for pride separates from Him; envy

* *Psalm* iv. 5.

is offended with His goodness to others; and anger expels His memory from the soul.

After these three, those four other vices follow, in which God may be said to avenge the injuries that pride commits against Him; for when the soul abandons God, God abandons the soul to her own devices, and she sinks from one degradation to another. The first of these four is sloth, which is a weariness of soul arising from the loathing of interior good. For after a soul has lost her spiritual good she finds herself in a solitary and deserted state that leaves her in pain and bitterness, and without any disposition to seek what she has lost. After this follows covetousness, or avarice, which is an immoderate cupidity for external goods. For as the soul is without internal good, and is utterly insufficient for herself, she is driven to fill her appetite with external things that are far below her nature. Sloth fills the soul with weariness and pain, and avarice distracts her with incessant cares and labours upon many inferior things. But when it is taken up into the pride of possessing, the heart becomes extremely hardened; the fruits of all this toil and care are hoarded up from use, and gloated upon, and the avaricious man obtains the name of miser, or miserable. Yet this is but one base and conspicuous form of that vice of pride, which, by its selfish and exclusive claim to good of one kind or another, is miserly in everything.

After covetousness comes the vice of gluttony. The soul lost to interior solidity, and framed upon exterior things, is caught by intemperance, an ignominious passion that satiates the body whilst it obstructs and brutalizes the mind; and whilst under the plea of necessity it disorders both body and soul, it leads to yet viler things. Lastly, comes the vice of lust or impurity, to which intemperance directly leads. The pride of the spirit ends in the pride of the flesh, and what begins in rebellion of the soul ends in the rebellion of the basest part of our human nature. The first of these seven vices brings down the soul from the highest and noblest good; the last brings her down to the lowest degrees of turpitude. As the Psalmist says: "I have come down into the deep mire, and there is no substance".* The inflation of pride has no substance: reaction comes from that inflation, and, still seeking the substance of good where it cannot be found, sinks

* *Psalm* lxviii. 3.

into the shameful mud of uncleanness. This last vice is the mockery of the first, and self-elevation rebounds into self-degradation.

These are the seven vices that corrupt the whole integrity of the soul, of which pride is not only the first, but the bitter root that provides the poison of malice for all the rest of these unhallowed vices, whereby the sanctity of God is insulted. But against these seven destructive evils, God has sent His seven witnesses into all humble, holy, and penitent souls in the seven gifts of His Holy Spirit.*

From the beginning to the end of the Holy Scriptures, we shall find, if we study them attentively, one fundamental truth and one unceasing admonition. We hear it in Paradise, we see it on the Cross. It runs through the sacred histories, is loud in the prophets, frequent in the sapiential books, continuous in the Gospels, and rises in many pages of the apostolic writings. This fundamental truth instructs us to know, this constant admonition exhorts us to act on the belief, that what God accepts from man is humility, and that what He rejects is pride. His blessings are for the humble, His maledictions are for the proud. In every virtue it is humility that He rewards, in every vice it is pride that He punishes. And when we remember that it is humility that subjects the soul and the virtues to God, and that it is pride that sends the soul away from God, and inflames the vices with its malice, we shall see that it cannot be otherwise.

St. Cæsarius of Arles has left us a remarkable homily in exposition of this truth, which he has drawn from every part of the Scriptures. † The whole doctrine is summed up in a Proverb of Solomon, which is repeated by St. Peter and by St. James, that "God resists the proud, but gives His grace to the humble". ‡ This truth is so obvious to humble souls that they see it by a spiritual intuition and feel it by a spiritual instinct. It should, however, be observed that the humble are sometimes in the Sacred Scriptures called the poor, and sometimes the right of heart. For the humble are the poor in spirit, and the right of heart are those whose hearts are in just submission to God. On the other hand, the proud are often called the arrogant, or the stiff-necked,

---

* See Hugo de S. Victore, *Allegoriæ in Matthæum,* c. iii.-vi.
† S. Cæsarius Arlaten., *Hom.* 11, *apud Gallandi.*
‡ *Proverbs* iii. 34; 1 *S. Peter* v. 5; *S. James* iv. 6.

or the malignant, or by other terms denoting their insurrection against their Creator and Lord.

A few passages will show how all maledictions, evils, and punishments are denounced or directed against pride. In the Book of Leviticus, for instance, the Almighty declares to the Israelites who despise His laws or contemn His judgments: "I will break the pride of your stubbornness". * And in the Book of Numbers: "The soul that committeth anything through pride, whether he be born in the land or a stranger, because he hath been rebellious against the Lord, shall be cut off from among his people. For he hath contemned the Word of the Lord, and made void His percept: therefore shall he be destroyed, and shall bear his iniquity."† And in the Book of Job it is said: "The praise of the wicked is short, and the joy of the hypocrite but for a moment. If his pride mount up even to Heaven, and his head touch the clouds: in the end he shall be destroyed as a dunghill, and they that had seen him shall say: 'Where is he?' His bones shall be filled with the vices of his youth, and they shall sleep with him in the dust."‡ And the proverb says: "The proud and the arrogant is called ignorant, who in anger worketh pride".§ Of the impious man the Psalmist says: "The proud did iniquitously altogether".‖ Of the heretic St. Paul says: "He is proud, knowing nothing".¶ In these, and in a great number of passages besides, pride is pointed out as the malignant element in the other vices, as the cause of those vices, as that which is hateful to God in them, and as that which is punished. As the Prophet Joel says of the enemy of God's people: "His stench shall ascend, and his rottenness shall go up, because he hath done proudly"!** For as Isaias says: "The day of the Lord of hosts shall be upon every one that is proud and high-minded, and upon every one that is arrogant, and he shall be humbled".††

But whilst the God of all goodness reprobates the proud because they are the enemies of all goodness, humiliates them because they lift themselves in conceit, and brings them to confusion because they labour in their vanity to confuse all things; in what page of His Divine Revelation does He not love and bless the

---

* *Leviticus* xxvi. 19.   † *Numbers* xv. 30, 31.
‡ *Job* xx. 5-11.   § *Proverbs* xxi. 24.
‖ *Psalm* cxviii. 51.   ¶ 1 *Timothy* vi. 4.
** *Joel* ii. 20.   †† *Isaias* ii. 12.

humble? He looks down upon the humble, visits the humble, gives His grace to the humble, consoles the humble, dwells with the humble, gives His peace to the humble, sends down His spirit upon the humble, and promises His kingdom to the humble.

Why do we speak only of humility and pride, and not also of charity and cupidity, since charity is the perfection of virtue, and cupidity the root of evil? For this plain reason, that it is humility that obtains charity, and pride that gives malice to cupidity. Without humility we could not receive charity, as without pride cupidity might slumber without evil action. Humility is the human preparation for charity, the sacrificial altar on which it is enkindled; pride is the malicious side of cupidity, that awakens and excites it to sin. Pride sets fire to cupidity, and cupidity is its smoky flame. Humility is obtained with great labour; charity descends from Heaven upon the toils of humility. Humility and charity are, by the grace of God, inseparable; but cupidity and pride are the double fetters that bind the wicked to their misery. When you hear the Scriptures or the Church sound the praises of humility, you know that charity is in her company. But when you hear their execrations upon pride, you know that pride is bound up with cupidity. Whoever, therefore, would be freed from pride must labour also to extinguish cupidity. And whoever would obtain true humility must strive as well for perfect charity. Let us, then, entreat of God with our whole powers, that in His mercy He would deliver us from pride and cupidity, and would grant us the inestimable gift of humility and charity, that we may not follow the evil spirits in their pride to destruction, but Christ, the Divine Master of humility, to sanctification. Which may God in His goodness grant us now and for ever. Amen.

LECTURE XII.

THE WORLD WITHOUT HUMILITY.

"When they knew God, they have not glorified Him as God, nor given thanks: but became vain in their thoughts, and their foolish heart was darkened."—ROMANS i. 24.

THE light of reason is sufficient to teach the knowledge of God, but not to bring man into union with his Creator. For the light, naturally implanted in the human mind, bears witness to God, and the conscience in His voice. All His works speak of their Creator, and in the action of His providence He manifests His care of them. But the pride that is in man separates him from God, turns his soul from the light, corrupts his interior sense, and smites him with spiritual blindness. When that pride has gone so far as to isolate man from God, and his self-love has deluded him into the absurd notion of self-sufficiency, his understanding is drawn from the light that makes God known, and, retreating behind the fictions of his imagination, he proceeds to deify himself.

As it is the natural effect of pride to swell the imagination and obscure the understanding, the effect of this, again, is to fancy that the more independent a man is of superior truth and authority, the more liberty he gains. But to have less of truth is to have more of darkness, and darkness is the loss both of liberty and power. Those men of progress backwards, who seek light from the things beneath, and not from the things above them, cannot understand what the Incarnate Truth has taught us, that "if therefore the Son shall make you free, then you shall be truly free".

In the Scriptures and the Church we learn that the true progress

* S. *John* viii. 36.

of man is towards God, and that the path of this progress is upwards to greater truth and higher justice. But the heathen world teaches us the terrible lesson of the final end of false progress, of progress away from God through the dreary downward path by the ways of negation and false liberty. First, the sense of dependence on God is lost, and so the virtue of humility departs. Then man forgets his Creator, forgets Him until he no longer knows that he is a creature, and so the intellectual principle of humility disappears from his mind. Pride then remains master of his heart without a rival: but still wanting a God, though a God consistent with his licence, he begins to deify the creature.

Next, the keener intellects begin to theorize and philosophize apart from God, working their proud intellects under the influence of their proud imagination, and confounding the light of those eternal principles that gleam in their obscured reason with the phenomena reflected to their mind from the visible creation. But as the loss of humility is the loss of that God-given light which makes the distinction clear between what is of God and what is of nature in the mind, they confound God and nature in one, and transfer this confusion to the universe. They thus find a miserable self-flattery in bringing down God to the level of the soul, and in raising the soul to a level with God, making the material world a changeable garment of illusion to both. Pantheism is the levelling system carried into the sphere of divinity. There is but one descent lower into which the debasing tendency of intellectual pride can fall, and this is the terrible revenge that the mind takes of its own deification, when both mind and life are turned into the material results of a material cause. This is the work of minds so steeped in animal sense and matter, that they can no longer see spirit, or understand its nature. Very pitiful it is that, when these results of the defects of mental vision are put into many words, they should be mistaken for science, although nothing but a cloak for ignorance and want of light.

S. Paul describes the mental condition of the heathens whom he knew so well in these words: "The nations walking in the vanity of their minds, having their understandings darkened, being alienated from the life of God through the ignorance that is in them, because of the blindness of their hearts, who in their callousness gave themselves to luxuriant lasciviousness, to every work of uncleanness with greediness ".* This sensuous and unclean life thickened the darkness of their minds, and intensified their egotism immeasurably, blinding their heart with an ever-increasing pride.

Thus separated from God by their pride, with their minds turned from the truth and cut off from the source of light, these proudly imaginative men, like children in the dark, were subject to many fancies and illusions, which became their punishment. They made gods for themselves, whom they projected from their imagination, and whom they filled with their own life and character. For these gods of human make of necessity partook of human qualities, with such exaggerations as the poetry of the obscured mind could furnish. As the sun sheds light from the heavens, and fertilizes the earth, and is the brightest and most imposing of visible things, the man in search of the God he had lost transferred his life and intelligence to that luminary, and made it his god. As the moon predominates in the night, and mitigates the darkness, he made the moon his goddess under many names. For as he draws his types of life and action from human nature, he naturally imagines gods of both sexes. The stars become to him as minor gods, and the clouds as ministering spirits. Carnalized as he is by the predominance of sense and imagination over intelligence, the man has lost the power of penetrating beyond the material into the spiritual heavens, and of realizing to his mind and heart the purely spiritual and perfect nature of God; for his pride and sensuality combine to blind his intelligence.

But as pride grows with habit, with time, and through the constant interchange of minds divorced from God, and as the reaction of sensual elation upon mental elation increases in proportion, the imagination becomes more gross, though not less vivid. And upon this, like fanciful children, who reflect their own vivacious life into whatever interests them, whether a rocking-horse or a doll, these lost children of a larger growth began to imagine life and divinity in woods and mountains, in caves and streams, in gardens and springs, and wherever they found indications of power, beauty, or beneficence. And as fear begets the imagination of power, victories and panics, fevers and their cures, whatever things in short affect humanity strongly, were ascribed to special gods, until at last almost everything, from the visible

* *Ephesians* iv. 17-19.

heavens to the household hearth, had its peculiar divinity, each with its special character and many limitations. Behind all the chief features of nature, and in all that was useful to man, the heathens imagined the presence of deities, requiring to be honoured or feared, until almost everything became the abode of some god, and the God who made all things was alone forgotten. What is this but an enormous corruption of the truth that the action of God is everywhere? To the vague notion of a Divinity that still hung in their minds, the heathens put their own corrupt imaginations, and fancied gods innumerable that were only the caricatures of themselves. Yet still was there left in them a sense of one great, mysterious, and universal power, that filled their minds with awe and dread, a power that ruled both gods and men, and whose decrees were inevitable, into which, however, they feared to search, and to which they gave the name of Fate. Undoubtedly this was a shadow upon their mind, though lost to their understanding, of the one eternal God Almighty who rules all things, but of whom, because alienated from Him, they stood in fear and dread.

After imagining their gods, the next step was to represent them externally. This was first done in rude symbols or fetishes, that seemed to localize their influence. Attempts were next made to represent them in human forms, or in forms uniting the animal with man ; finally, with the progress of skill, they took the naked human figure with all its refinements and allurements as the fitting representation of those gods of human fashion. For ever as idolatry advanced the gods became nearer in likeness to human nature in its fallen state, as we see them represented by the poets, with not only the virtues but the vices of mankind. But the vividness of the corrupt and pride-inflated imagination stopped not here. There is testimony in the pagan writers that their idols were assumed to be inhabited by the gods they represented. Even the Sacred Scriptures declare that they were "not gods but demons" ; and certainly where pride is so great as to put the figures of mortals in the place of God, the demons cannot be far away.

Many writers have dwelt copiously upon the sensual vices of the heathen world, and upon its innumerable superstitions, but scarcely any one seems to have gone to the root of the evil which accounts for all the rest. Neither the writers on pagan morals

nor the commentators on the classics take much notice, if any, of
that terrible pride which not only separated the heathens from
God, and threw them in full reliance on their own self-sufficiency,
but so completely possessed and blinded them, that they mistook
that for the first power of their nature, which was the first of their
vices and the chief cause of all their moral weakness and superstition. Much care is taken, and justly taken, by every truly
Christian teacher, to guard the minds of youth from the impurities of the classics; but whoever thinks of cautioning them
against the false foundation of their virtues? St. Augustine, who
had such bitter remembrance of his own pagan youth, and was so
intimate with the pagan philosophies, never ceases to instruct his
hearers and readers upon the radical difference between Christian
and pagan morals as based on the opposite foundations of humility
and pride. We will here give a cluster of his maxims that pervade his voluminous writings in many forms: Man loses God by
pride; he regains God through humility, of which Christ is the
author. A proud soul is the greatest of miseries, but a humble
God is the greatest of mercies. The law of Christian life, and
almost the whole of its discipline, is the virtue of humility. In
vain shall we look for this virtue in the writings of the philosophers or in the schools of error: it is peculiar to the Sacred Scriptures and the Church of Christ. In his great work on the City
of God, to which he devoted so many years, his whole object is
to show that the pride of man explains the history of the action
of God in the world; and that but for His providential visitations
in the shape of humiliations, calamities, and sufferings, the un-
curbed pride of man would have brought the human race to
destruction. He then shows how the humility of Christ is
changing the world of his time.

The heathen sages and heroes claimed the virtues; their wise
men disputed on them; they had much to say on prudence,
justice, fortitude, and temperance, and great examples of these
virtues to allege. Yet they had nothing capable of standing by
the virtues of the Gospel, or even of the Old Testament. They
knew absolutely nothing of their creation, and as little of the
principle of grace, and were utterly ignorant of the virtue of
humility. At the root of their virtues lay the poison of pride; and
the admitted ground of them was the self-sufficiency of the man
for whatever he chose to undertake; it infected them all through

and pervaded their philosophical expositions of them. In a well-known passage of St. Augustine, who had examined all their philosophies, he says: "The confession of sin, the humbling of the heart, the saving life that subjects one to God, that presumes in nothing on one's self, that ascribes nothing to one's own power; this is not to be found in any of their books who are alien from us: not in the Epicureans, not in the Stoics, not in the Manichæans, not in the Platonists. We find excellent moral precepts and rules of conduct in them, but humility cannot be found. Humility comes from another direction: it comes from Christ. This way is from Him who was high, and came in lowliness. . . . By this humility we approach to God, who is nigh to the contrite of heart. But in the deluge of many waters that lift themselves against God, and teach proud impieties, they cannot come nigh to God.*

As Cajetan observes, one or two of the heathen sages caught a distant glimpse of the virtue for a moment, and that was all. Plato has a passage in his Laws in which he speaks of God as the avenger of those who fail from the divine law, and of the coming happiness of the man who adheres to justice with a composed and modest mind, and follows the conspicuous guidance of justice with constancy; and that He deserts the man who is inflated with pride, depriving him of force and success. This solitary passage rises far above the habitual thinking of heathen philosophy, even above Plato himself at other times, and seems to have found its way to the writer from a Hebrew source. The famous oracle of Delphi—Know thyself—makes little to the argument, unless we knew to what extent man was advised to know himself. Humility arises from the knowledge of God and one's self, and the true knowledge of one's self is only obtained in the light of God.

Some few writers, as we have observed in a previous lecture, have attempted to identify the magnanimity taught by Aristotle with Christian humility; but this will not stand even the briefest inquiry. Not to speak of the Ethics being nothing more than an exposition of political morality, we have only to examine the famous chapter on the magnanimous man to see that it is nothing more than the description of the shrewd, self-seeking, worldly,

* S. August., *In Psalm.* xxxi. *Ennarat.* 2.

ambitious man of all times, who cultivates honour as the way to social success.

"The very name of magnanimity," says the philosopher, "implies that great things are its object. Whatever is great in each virtue would seem to belong to the great-minded. This virtue, then, would seem to be the ornament of all the other virtues, in that it makes them better, and that it cannot be without them." It is obvious that magnanimity is put forth as the supreme of pagan virtues, brightening and perfecting all the others. It holds the place that charity holds among the Christian virtues. But how does it accord with humility? Let us hear further. "He is thought to be great-minded who values himself highly and yet justly. The man who esteems himself lowly, but yet justly, is modest, but not great-minded. He who values himself highly without just grounds is a vain man, though the name must not be applied to every case of unduly high estimation. He that values himself below his real worth is a small-minded man." Thus man is constituted the supreme judge of his own worth, and is high or low-minded according to that judgment. St. Paul says, on the contrary, "Be not high-minded, but fear". The great-mindedness here described is not from humility, but from pride, as it comes out more clearly in what follows.

"Honour, then, and dishonour," continues the master of heathen philosophy, "are specially the object of the great-minded man; and at such honour, as it is great, and given by good men, he will be moderately pleased, as getting his own, or perhaps somewhat less, for no honour can be quite adequate to perfect virtue; but still he will accept this, because they have nothing greater to give him. But such as is given him by ordinary people, and on trifling grounds, he will despise, because this does not come up to his deserts; and dishonour likewise, because in his case there cannot be just grounds for it." Then the philosopher tells us that "Honour is the cause of power and wealth, being worthy of choice, for certainly they who have them desire to be honoured through them. It seems, too, that pieces of good fortune contribute to form this character of great-mindedness. I mean the nobly born, or men of influence, or the wealthy, are considered to be entitled to honour."

We see, then, that the chief heathen virtue begins and ends in the man. Its foundation is self-esteem, its object human honour, and its chief instruments what we should call the advantages of fortune. It resolves itself into self-regard, worldly success, and the worship of honour received from honourable, that is, from successful men. This was the heathen wisdom, of which St. Paul says: "The world through wisdom knew not God"; and: "The wisdom of the world is folly with God". Tertullian cut this wisdom to the quick, when he called its votaries "the animals of glory". It was the proud, self-seeking, worldly wisdom philosophized into a virtue for the select few men of better fortune. It could not have been preached to the multitude excepting in bitter irony on their lot in life. The multitude were the ordinary and small-minded men, incapable of magnanimity, whose little tributes of honour were to be despised because they were unworthy the notice of the great-minded man.

That the circle of the favoured few formed the limits of this magnanimity is obvious from the terms in which the virtue is described, and is more explicitly stated in what follows. "It is the characteristic of the great-minded," concludes the philosopher, "to ask favours not at all, or very reluctantly, but to do a service readily, and to bear himself loftily towards the great or fortunate, but towards the people of middle station affably; because to be above the former is difficult, and so a grand thing, but to be above the latter is easy; and to be high and mighty towards the former is not ignoble, but to do it towards those of humbler station would be below him and vulgar."*

Compare this heathen wisdom with the teaching of the Eternal Wisdom, whose first words when He opened His mouth to instruct were these : "Blessed are the poor in spirit, for theirs is the kingdom of Heaven". This pagan magnanimity is neither more nor less than the exaltation of pride. The very reverse of Christian magnanimity, it rests on the sufficiency of man, whilst the Christian, even when employing the sources of human influence, rests his virtue on the sufficiency of God. Yet this chapter is entitled to careful study, because it anatomizes the heart of the polished man of the world of all times, whose first principle is himself, and the breath of whose life is the good opinion of his social circle.

That Plato had heard something of the divine wisdom revealed to the Hebrews is rendered probable by other passages than the one

---

* Aristotle's *Ethics*, lib. iv., c. 4, Browne's translation.

we have quoted from his writings. For example, where he says that the triangle is the figure that nearest resembles the Divinity. And, again, the famous passage in the Second Alcibiades, where he puts the declaration into the mouth of Socrates, that man knows not what to ask of God, until the Divine Governor of Man shall come to teach him. The dialogue deserves to be quoted in proof of the utter darkness and perplexity of the wisest of the heathens with respect to God and himself.

"*Socrates.* Do not you remember you told me you were in great perplexity, for fear you should pray unawares for evil things, whilst you only intended to ask for good?

"*Alcibiades.* I remember it very well, Socrates.

"*Socrates.* You see it is not at all safe for you to go and pray in the temple in the condition you are in, lest the god hearing your blasphemies should reject your sacrifices, and, to punish you, should give you what you would not have. I am therefore of the mind that it is much better for you to be silent, for I know you very well. Your pride, I say, will probably not permit you to use the prayer of the Lacedæmonians.* Therefore it is necessary you should wait for some person to teach you how you ought to behave yourself towards both gods and men.

"*Alcibiades.* And when will that time come, Socrates? And who is He that will instruct me? With what pleasure shall I look upon Him!

"*Socrates.* He will do it who takes care of you. But I think, as we read in Homer, that Minerva dissipated the mist that covered the eyes of Diomed and hindered him from distinguishing the god from man, so it is necessary that He should first scatter the darkness that covers your soul, and afterwards give you those remedies that are necessary to put you into a condition for distinguishing good and evil; for at present you know not how to make the difference between them.

"*Alcibiades.* Let Him scatter them, let Him destroy this darkness of mine, and whatever else He pleases; I abandon myself to His conduct, and am very ready to obey all His commands, provided I may be made better by them.

"*Socrates.* Do not doubt of that, for this Governor I tell you of has a singular affection for you.

"*Alcibiades.* I think I must defer my sacrifice to that time.

* A general prayer for all good and against all evil.

"*Socrates.* You have reason: it is more safe so to do than to run so great a risk."

In this singular passage, written by the most soaring mind among the Greeks, and ascribed to the wisest of them, we see what was the condition of the most enlightened heathens. After all their investigations, they were ignorant of their final end, and of the real good of the soul; in consequence of that ignorance they knew not what it was safe to ask of their gods, and confessed that the one God alone is the secure guide and teacher of man. St. Clement of Alexandria observes that Plato's writings prepared the minds of the heathen for Christianity. But though St. Augustine owed his conversion from materialism to them, he declares that their general spirit inspires the heart with pride. The social system set forth by this "divine man," as he was called, embraced the wildest schemes of modern communism, absorbing the family in the State, rejecting the marriage tie, transferring the care of all children from the parents to the State, and advocating the unnameable vices to their last extremes.

If we turn from the Greek to the Roman moralists, we find them enamoured of the proudest as well as the sternest of all systems, that of the Stoics. "The man who studies wisdom," if we are to believe Cicero, "thinks of nothing that is abject, of nothing that is humble." If the chief virtue of the Greeks was magnanimity, that of the Romans was a stern fortitude, not the Christian's fortitude, but a fortitude based on the pantheistic notion of the divinity of the soul. Yet this divinity of the soul was limited in practice to men of honour and rank, for the multitude, whether of freemen or of slaves, was looked upon with contempt. Satanic rather than humane, this fortitude implied the scornful rejection of all providential humiliations, and the presumption of an inward strength to resist and despise the chastisements of God. "Observe," says Cicero, "that although good affections take the name of virtues, that name belongs not properly to all of them. For *virtus a viro*, virtue takes its name from manliness, and the virtue proper to manliness is fortitude. This is chiefly exercised in the contempt of fear and death."[*] Again he says: "If there be any virtue, and of that Cato has removed all doubt, that virtue looks upon all adversities that befall a man as beneath him, so that in despising adversities he may scorn the trials of life, and being

* Cicero, *Quæst. Tusculan.*, lib. ii., c. 18.

innocent of criminality, he may think that nothing concerns him but that virtue ". * Yet this Cato, this model of Roman virtue, was a man of stern and cruel pride, who showed a positive indifference to his wife's purity, and, instead of enduring adversity with courage, committed suicide to escape from it.

The pagans had no consciousness of sin, for the very notion of it was excluded by the overmastering influence of their pride, and by their self-deification. They could not say with Ephraim: "Thou hast chastised me, and I am instructed. Convert me, and I shall be converted: for Thou art the Lord my God. And after I was converted, I did penance." † Left to themselves, the punishment of pride was the paralysis of their conscience.

It has been said of Seneca that he had imbibed some degree of Christian doctrine, and had even conversed with St. Paul. If this were true, the Christian teaching never reached his soul. The very root of his philosophy is the Stoic doctrine that man is all-sufficient for himself, and that he has the inherent power to scale the summit of virtue, and to set himself on equality with God. According to his teaching, reason or the soul—for he makes them one—"is nothing else than a part of the divine spirit merged in the human body ; and as reason is divine, and there is no good without reason, all good is divine. And as there is no distinction in things divine, there is no distinction between one good and another." ‡ This confounding of the objective light of reason with the subjective soul is the false foundation of all pantheism. From this view of things the philosopher concludes, that the supreme good of man is to follow nature with the will of nature, that the one virtue receives various forms according to the matter to which it is directed, that all virtues are equal, and that all men are equal by the exercise of this virtue. Joy is therefore equal to the strong and obstinate enduring of torments. § All this he educes from his first position, that the spirit of man is a part of the Divinity merged in the human body, which, when a man dies, is returned to its former elements. ‖ From this notion of the divinity of the soul he concludes that "nothing is so great, nothing so strong, as man. He

---

* Cicero, *Quæst. Tusculan.*, lib. v., c. 1.
† *Jeremias* xxxi. 18, 19.
‡ Seneca, *Epist.* 66 *ad Lucilium.* § *Ibid.*
‖ Seneca, *De Consolatione*, c. xxvi.

may become good, just, gentle, temperate, and acquire all virtues by dint of his own strength."* The pride of this philosopher goes to yet further excess. "There is something," says Seneca, "in which the wise man surpasses God. God is without fear through the good of His nature, and the wise man through his own good. Behold a great thing, that man in his weakness should have the security of God. Incredible is the force of philosophy to repel the force of fortune. No weapon finds a place in its body: it is fortified and solid, and as the weapon comes its way, the philosopher bends and avoids it; he shakes these things from him, and hurls them back on him who sent them."†

Epictetus thought that the will of man had no object beyond itself, and he taught a morality whose sole object was to concentrate the will upon self alone, with the view of seeking all things as far as possible in self alone. The philosophical Emperor Antoninus, called the delight of mankind, rendered worship to himself as being a part of the divine nature. With all the Stoics, these men professedly sought their final end in themselves. And if we take the most celebrated philosophers of the Grecian schools, one seeks his final end in health of body and mind, another in honesty, a third in wisdom, a fourth in the contemplation of ideas, a fifth in the science of numbers, a sixth in the moderation of pleasure, and so on. But not one of them, even among those who believed in the unity of God, ever dreamed that God is the final end of man. Nor can any one of them, unless it be Pythagoras, stand an examination into their moral conduct by the test of their own teaching, low and defective as that was. Cicero admits, as Lactantius observes, that the lives of the philosophers were far removed from their teaching, and that their wisdom was more for ostentation than for the guidance of their lives; and Seneca remarks that these sages did not exhibit their doctrine in themselves: "Plato, Zeno, and the rest," he tells us, "taught not how they themselves lived, but how men ought to live".‡ There was not one of them who, whilst privately teaching but one God, and secretly despising the gods of the multitude, did not offer their sacrifices to the popular gods as though they entirely believed in them.

Origen truly says of them, that their lives were so contrary to

* Seneca, *De Consolatione*, c. xxvi.   † Id., *Epist.* 53.
‡ Seneca, *De Vita Beata*, c. xviii., xix.

their knowledge, that by the just judgment of God they lost the knowledge of the true God, and of His divine providence, and fell to such blindness and ignorance as to give that honour to corruptible creatures which was due to the Eternal God.[*] It is even so, and the revolt of the intellect from God leads straight to the revolt of the animal man, and the egotism of the interior man breaks forth into the sensuous egotism of the exterior man. He who is not subject to God cannot subject his lower to his higher nature. The imagination, which is the mental seat both of pride and sensuality, becomes intensely active, and puts the intelligence under an eclipse. The sense of self-sufficiency arises in the absence of the sense of God, and when he has lost the sense of accountability to God, the man becomes accountable only to himself; but when he is only accountable to his own pride, what is there he will not do in secret, devoid of every shame? In their gods the poets deified their own vices and passions, and the philosophers quoted them without any reprehension. There were no martyrs to philosophy, not one, for they never opposed themselves to the vices, oppressions, or false opinions of those in power, or went in their conduct against the world at large.

Yet the Gentiles had the natural law written in their hearts; nor were all their acts vicious, for they did the natural works of the law, some of them more, some less. As St. Augustine tells Evodius: " Except that they did not worship God, but worshipped vain inventions according to their national institutions, serving the creature rather than the Creator; many of them led lives that were in a certain degree praiseworthy, and in the rest of their morals they were chaste and sober, and despised death for their country's sake; and they kept faith with their fellow-citizens, and even with their enemies, and these things they deservedly set forth for imitation. But when these habits are directed by no just or sincere motives of piety, but go to the motive of conciliating human praise and glory, even these virtues vanish into nothing, so to speak, and are barren to their possessor."[†]

The secret of the heathen's heart was this: by a prolonged alienation from God, pride became rooted until it was taken for an element of nature and the spring of moral strength, and from

[*] Origen, *Contra Celsum*, lib. vii.
[†] S. August., *Epist.* 164 *ad Evodium*

this the intellectual notion arose that the spirit within him was divine, and so the man was sufficient for himself. The loss of the knowledge of God led to the loss of the knowledge of sin, and to such an obscuration of the conscience that the inner soul, so little known, so far from the all-revealing light of God, was hidden from the man. This explains the magnanimity of the Greeks, based altogether on self-sufficiency, and the self-inebriating enthusiasm of the Brahmins and Buddhists based on emanative pantheism. The law of virtue became the regulator of pride. The pride rebuked by the heathen moralists and lashed by the satirists was not the principle of pride, but the offensive and excessive manifestations of it that disturbed or inconvenienced the pride of other men. No one dreamed that its roots were to be extirpated. What was to be avoided was the too great obtrusion of one man's pride upon that of another. From the virtues that moderated the exhibition of pride arose civil refinement, public usefulness, and pleasant friendship. But the true spirit that lay beneath these social virtues is amply revealed in the chapter from the Ethics already quoted. The philosopher says further, that the magnanimous man " must speak and act openly; for this is a characteristic of one that despises others; he is bold in speech, and therefore is apt to despise others; and truth-telling, except when he uses dissimulation; but to the vulgar he ought to dissemble ".* After describing the meek man as one " who is undisturbed and not carried away by passion, but who feels anger according to the dictates of reason, and for a proper length of time," the philosopher says, " but the meek man seems to err rather on the side of defect; for he is not inclined to revenge, but rather to forgive ".† This accepted exposition will suffice to show that heathen virtue was but the management of pride.

Yet God left not Himself without a witness in the world at any time. Take that period when the Roman Empire was at the worst, when either pantheism or materialism was the wisdom of the learned, and the most corrupt idolatry and vice were the practice of the multitude as well as of their masters. In that terrible period when the Roman world was contending against the advancement of Christianity, the grave Tertullian gives most remarkable evidence of the tendency among the common people to

---

* Aristotle, *Ethics*, lib. iv., c. 3.　　　　　　† Id., lib. iv., c. 5.

invoke the true God, and proclaim their dependence on Him, notwithstanding all their idolatry and superstition. In his book on the Testimony of the Soul, he appeals to the heathen world, and calls on all its men and women to bear witness that they know the God of the Christians. He declines to summon the men of letters from their schools and libraries; he will not listen to the wise philosophers; he calls upon all the rude, simple, and unsophisticated souls, from the public ways, the streets, and the workshops. He rests his cause in complete confidence upon those who have nothing but their souls to bring in evidence.

Then the great apologist of the Christians tells us that at every turn he hears this heathen people crying out quite naturally: "God grant it," or, "If it please God," thus ignoring the multitude of gods in their temples, whether Saturn, Juno, Mars, or Minerva. Nor are they ignorant of the nature of God, for they say: "God is good," and "God be good to us". And they know who is the Author of blessings, for, like the Christians, they exclaim: "God bless you". And they know that God is present, and that He judges them, for both at home and abroad, without fear of ridicule or hindrance, these poor pagans cry out: "Well, God sees all," or, "I commend you to God," or, "God reward you," or, "God will judge between us". And these things they say, even though they carry about them the symbols of Saturn, of Ceres, or of Isis. And when they execrate evil deeds, they will ascribe them to the demons, or will call those persons demons who are malignant or impure. All these, observes Tertullian, are natural testimonies to the truth. But where does he find these witnesses to the truth? Not among the learned disputers, with their wise conceits, but among the lowly, the labouring, and the suffering poor, who, as he says, have nothing but their souls. Then he offers these shrewd remarks.

Souls existed before letters, speech before books, and men before philosophers and poets. Did men never utter these speeches before there were books and theories? Did they never speak of the goodness of God, or of death, or of hell, of which they now speak so openly and naturally, before Mercury was born? Let us suppose they have learnt all these from books; yet the Holy Scriptures brought down the tradition of them long before those books were written, and from those sacred pages alone could they have learnt to speak of God. But God formed the conscience of man as well as the Scriptures, and nature also bears witness to Him. After contemplating this general testimony of souls to the Christian's God, the great apologist exclaims in an excess of fervour: "O soul, thou art by nature Christian!" After which he makes this appeal to the heathen's mind: "Every soul is both a culprit and a witness of the truth, and each soul shall stand at the judgment-seat of God, with nothing to plead in her defence. Thou didst proclaim the One God, but thou didst not seek Him. Thou didst execrate the demons, yet thou didst adore the demons. Thou didst call God into judgment, yet thou didst put no faith in the God whom thou didst call upon to judge. Thou didst admit of the eternal torments, but didst not shun the eternal torments. Thou didst know the name of the Christian's God, yet thou didst persecute the Christian." *

This instinctive knowledge of the One God, which lay deeper in the conscience than the superstitions encrusted upon it; this spontaneous crying of the untutored populations to the true God, in the habit of which their humble position preserved them, undoubtedly prepared them to receive the Gospel of Christ. Whilst those who were cultivated in the falsely grounded philosophies which they called wisdom, who held the high places of the world, and who despised humility as something utterly ignominious and contemptible, as their language to the Christian martyrs showed, remained for the most part for ages in their pride and darkness.

The frenzy of self-deification came not upon the world at once. The parents of our race under satanical temptations aspired to be as gods, but their fall quickly opened their eyes to the delusion. After pride had caused apostasy from God, the powers in the heavens were first idolized, and then the powers of nature on the earth, whether as causes of beneficence or as objects of fear. The one they invoked to their aid as children invoke the objects of their fancy; the other they strove to propitiate, much as Friday entreated the gun of Robinson Crusoe not to kill him. Then came the deification of heroes, whether of a beneficent or destructive character, such as the inventors of arts, the founders of cities, or mighty conquerors. But after deifying their fellow-men, the next step was to deify themselves.

This self-deification arose from causes that require careful con-

* Tertullian, *De Testimonio Animæ.*

sideration. In looking on things far removed, they are confounded in your vision one with another. The mountains blend with the skies, the hills blend together, the woods cannot be distinguished from the soil. The reason of this confusion is the faintness of the light reflected to the eye of the spectator from objects at so great a distance. But the reverse of this may be the case. The objects may be near the spectator, and with full light upon them, whilst the eyes are weak or diseased; he then sees all things confusedly and without much power of distinguishing one thing from another. The loss either of light or of sight is the loss of the power of distinction, and thus one thing is confounded with another.

Now what takes place in the understanding is not unlike what takes place in our corporal eyes. The understanding is the eye of the soul, and it sees its objects by the means of spiritual light. If the eye of the soul is far removed from the spiritual light, or if that eye is greatly disordered and obscured, in either case, and much more in the case of both, the power of distinguishing is to a great degree lost. Children see mental truths in confusion, and as it were blended together, but as their mind strengthens, and they are subjected to education, they learn to distinguish truth from truth, and one thing from another. The process of education is chiefly by analysis; it is the process of finding out the distinction of things that are united in one common light.

After the heathen world had departed from the true God, had lost the clear knowledge of Him, and abandoned His worship; after men had devoted themselves to the worship of the powers of nature, and to their sculptured representations, the lights of their mind became greatly diminished, although they still retained a certain vague and indefinite notion of one Supreme Spirit, as all the records of history bear witness. The image of God was still in their souls, however much obscured, and they still retained some general notion, however vague, of a first cause of all things. But with the loss of all definite knowledge of God, the knowledge of Him as their Creator was lost, and consequently they lost the knowledge of creation. The primitive relation of the creation of the world and of man had died out of their traditions. The common notion of the heathen world was that all the elements of things had existed from everlasting, although the forms of things were constantly undergoing change. With even the wisest Greeks, creation was nothing more than the fashioning and forming of things that had an eternal existence in their elements. They knew nothing of that power of God that creates from nothingness. Their maxim was that nothing is made from nothing.

But when the heathen world was brought to this obscure state of mind; when they made almost everything a god except God Himself; when the earth, made for the glory of God, was almost reduced to a temple of idols; when the human mind was brought to that state of darkness that men neither knew their Creator, nor that they and the world around were created from nothing; there came a reaction in the minds of men from the deification of the material creation to the deification of their own souls. When men began to think more upon themselves, or, as we now say, to philosophize, the keenest intellects found a spiritual force in themselves, and a principle of causation, greater and more effective than all the material forces which they worshipped. And believing all things to exist from eternity, they concluded that their own rational spirits had existed from eternity. Remote from God in mind and heart, inebriated with the love of that self which they imagined had existed from eternity, and blinded with the pride that springs from self-love; finding also in their reason certain principles that are universal and unchangeable though obscure in their light, in the intoxication of their pride, they lost the power of distinguishing between their subjective selves and the objective light of truth presented to their mind, and confounded themselves with the Eternal Light. Finding in themselves a principle of causation, they confounded this principle with the Eternal Cause. Observing in themselves an originating force, they confounded this spiritual force with the Eternal Power. In short, as they had lost all knowledge of their creation, they concluded that their souls were a portion or particle, an emanation or an evolution, from the One Eternal Divinity. They did not go so far in absurdity as to imagine that each one was the whole Divinity, but they fancied themselves to be an element of that Divinity. The deification of heroes had its influence, no doubt, in confirming this notion, for if the souls of certain men were found after their death to have been divine, there was no reason why other men's souls should not be equally divine.

The result of this self-deification is to fill the soul with a terrible egotism, elation, and enthusiasm. If the enthusiasm of the

Anomæans, against whom St. Chrysostom delivered his magnificent discourses, was so great because they fancied they saw the very light of God; if the enthusiasm of the Greek monks of Mount Athos in the eighth century was not less because they imagined they could see the same light through the navel, a delusion not unlike modern spiritism; if the enthusiasm of the false ontologists, led by Malebranche, was fervid because they thought the light of truth was seen in God; if the enthusiasm of certain sects, who imagine they have received assurance of an unchangeable justification, is attended with a dreadful spiritual and even animal elation, and with a proud contempt of others; what must have been the inebriating enthusiasm of those who first imbibed the notion that their spiritual part was an emanation of the Divinity! But this false enthusiasm lends itself with terrible force to the propagation of its own fancies, and is so exceedingly flattering to the pride of human nature, that the doctrine of pantheism was rapidly diffused through the populations of India, China, and most of the Asiatic nations. Pythagoras brought the doctrine from Syria into South Italy in the fifth century before Christ, and from him it spread among the philosophers of Greece, and invaded mighty Rome. The natural consequence of this superexaltation of the human spirit equalized with God was to look upon the material world and the human body as something utterly weak, although strong enough to detain the spirit from returning to its first principle until the body was destroyed. But they concluded that the soul alone was substantial, and the body an illusion. Such is the final result of the inebriation of self-deification.

From this came the doctrine of the soul or mind of the world, pervading all things and mingled with all, imprisoned in bodies like a celestial fire or a divine air; and of the soul of man being a particle of the divine breath, which Virgil poetized, and which was taught in the writings of Seneca, and in those of the Emperor Marcus Antoninus, in these terms: "There is one common substance distributed among countless bodies, one soul distributed among infinite natures with their individual circumscriptions, one intelligent soul, though it seems divided". How this soul returns to itself from inhabiting bodies, the imperial philosopher expresses in these terms: "As bodies after a certain time are changed and dissolved, and make way for other dead bodies, souls are also transferred to the air, where they are changed, and fused, and set on fire, and received into the seminal region of the universe, and thus give place to other souls that come into the same regions ".* Of the weakness of matter he thus speaks : "What ought we to fear from the death of the body and the departure of the soul ? Consider the brevity of this life, the immensity of our past and future life, and the imbecility of all that is material." †

Then comes the conclusion as a matter of course, that man is everything to himself: "These things," says the Emperor, "are proper to the soul endowed with reason ; she sees herself, forms herself, makes herself what she wishes to be, and reaps the fruits that she bears ". ‡ The pagan systems of morals had no other foundation than this self-sufficiency, not even the Ethics of Aristotle, or the Offices of Cicero. Aristotle himself defines happiness as a certain energy of the soul. The Gauls, Celts, and Germans believed equally in a soul animating all nature, united with all bodies, and producing all phenomena, whilst their druids or priests offered sacrifices to propitiate that spirit that he might not turn those phenomena into fearful and destructive forms.

As the civil State is the centre of mind, force, and authority, to whose dominion men look for law, government, justice, and protection ; after men had deified themselves they were led to deify the State as something much more divine than the individual man, and this deification was not unfrequently followed by religious worship. On this part of our subject we may accept the able summary given by Mr. Lecky. Speaking of the Roman Empire, he says : "We find the city itself, as the centre of civilization and seat of law, is deified by its rulers and people, and thus the laws themselves are accounted divine. To pass over the great Eastern cities of earlier civilization, the Athenians worshipped themselves in the divinity of their city. The Romans worshipped themselves under the name of Rome. The Emperors, as incorporating in themselves the social power, were elevated into divinities, and altars were raised to their worship. The Eastern nations, subject to Rome in their profound corruption, were ever the first to exhibit this idolatrous worship to the city or ruler that held them in subjection. This was nothing new to them. We

---

* Marcus Antoninus Imperator. *Commentaria*, lib. iv., c. 21.
† *Ibid.*, lib. xii., c. 7.   ‡ *Ibid.*, lib. xi., c. 1.

read that the statues of the kings of Persia were adored in Babylon. . Domitian went so far as to deify himself, calling himself
'Lord and God' in his public documents, so that no one dared
to address him otherwise."

Again, this writer says with great truth : " With the Greeks the
State was considered a divine institution, and its welfare the supreme
end of life to all and each of its members.   They belonged, body
and soul, to the State.   Justice consisted in what was profitable
to the State, and morality in doing the will of the State, and in
the worshipping of the gods of the State in the manner in which
the State commanded.   The pride of the Greek was to exalt himself in the community of freemen, to leave labour to slaves, and
to look on the rest of the world as barbarians."

Mr. Lecky justly observes that, "for some centuries before
Christianity, patriotism was in most countries the presiding moral
principle, and religion occupied an entirely subordinate position ".
But in what did that patriotism consist ?   Not in the care of the
well-being of the people, but chiefly in the pride taken in the
power of the deified State, and in a passionate love of extending
the power of the State over other countries at whatever cost and
sacrifice of blood and life.   " Perhaps," says the same shrewd
observer, "the greatest vice of the old form of patriotism was the
narrowness of sympathy which it produced.   Outside the circle of
their own nation all men were regarded with contempt or indifference, if not with actual hostility.   Conquest was the one recognized form of national progress, and the interests of nations were,
therefore, regarded as directly opposed.   The intensity with which
a man loved his country was a measure of the hatred which he
bore to those who were without it." *

These sound remarks on the broad and general facts of heathen
life and government point to certain affections, or rather defec-
tions, that belong to all strongly developed pride.   Humility is
large, ree, sympathetic with all life and good, whether in Heaven
or on earth, and partakes of all the good with which it sympathizes.
But as pride is the practical development of egotism or selfishness, its necessary tendency is to isolate and contract the affections, and to harden them towards all that it excludes.   But there
is a corporate as well as a personal pride, and this corporate pride
has a strong tendency to intensify personal pride, and to increase

* Lecky's *Rise and Influence of Rationalism,* vol. ii., chap. 5.

contempt for those from whom, whether as individuals or corporate bodies, the proud are isolated. For a man augments his pride by reason of the family, corporation, or nation of which he is a member. The heathens fed their pride on the multitude of slaves who served them, and whom they looked upon as property; on their superiority to the nations they conquered; on their being the members of distinguished families; on the rank and distinction of the corporate bodies of which they were members; and on their belonging to some nation whose State was regarded as divine. But all beyond that circle of humanity of which they formed a part they regarded with contempt. This was their corporate pride. But within those circles their personal pride had sway, and often showed itself in one towards another of the same family, rank, or corporation, in jealousy, envy, anger, isolation, hatred, or contempt. For pride is always seeking personal superiority, distinction, domination, and, consequently, isolation.

St. Paul points to one of the grand results of the Christian faith, in the breaking down of the partition walls that separated the nations, which, as faith destroyed pride, brought all men into one family and brotherhood. "For you are all the children of God by faith in Christ Jesus. For as many of you as have been baptized in Christ, have put on Christ. There is neither Jew nor Greek; there is neither bond nor free; there is neither male nor female. For you are all one in Christ." *

We must not omit Egypt out of our general survey of heathen pride, for out of that extraordinary country came the greatest abominations. Even Greece derived its mythology from Egypt, as well as its arts and civilization. Herodotus tells us that Greece in early times offered sacrifices to the gods, but had no names for them, and had never heard of their names: they simply called them gods. But after a long lapse of time the names of the gods came to Greece from Egypt. At that time there was but one oracle in Greece, which had been established by a dark-coloured Egyptian who had been stolen from Egypt. This oracle was consulted: Whether they should adopt the names that had been imported from the foreigners? And the oracle replied by recommending their use. † Such is the origin of that Grecian mythology which has fascinated the world.

On Egypt we may hear Mr. William Palmer, in his Preface to

* *Galatians* iii. 26-28.   † Herodotus, lib. ii., c. 52.

his Egyptian Chronologies. "The end of the false religion," he observes, "in opposition to the true, being to glorify the enemy by leading men and nations more and more astray from God, and enslaving them to evil lusts, this end was not only aimed at in Egypt through an outward ceremonial and a powerful priesthood, with the worship of almost everything except the true object of worship, but it was especially sought and attained by the deification and worship of the living ruler. The monarch was the keystone of the whole fabric. To him the deceiving serpent—the dragon, to whom the religions as such belonged—delegated his own seat, his own power, and great authority. That evil character of pride, ambition, selfishness, and cruelty, which the false religion naturally formed, was enthroned and deified in him. As the centre of human society, the source of that law and order without which society itself could not exist, nor consequently its highest forms of perversion be developed, the monarch was not inappropriately compared to the sun. And he was not merely so compared metaphorically, but he was actually worshipped as the Sun-god. The kings of Egypt, from very early times, took the title of *Ph-Ra*, or Pharaoh, which is the name of the Sun-god, with the articles prefixed.

"The Egyptian king meets and embraces the gods more as a brother and an equal than with any humility as a worshipper. He receives from them all that can gratify his pride and ambition. They give to him never-ending life, and the empire over all the world; they give him victory over all his enemies, and put their necks under his feet; and he, on the other hand, massacres in their presence 'his vile enemies'. And as with the people below, so with the gods themselves, who might seem to be above; the delegation of their honour to the king as their living representative or embodiment is so complete, that at the very first sight of the walls and sculptures of any Egyptian temple, the beholder is struck by the impression that the king its builder is not only *one* of the gods of Egypt and of that temple, but that he has a far greater share in it than all the gods to whom it is ostensibly dedicated, and than all the gods of Egypt put together.

"The same blasphemous titles, and the same deification and worship, with temples, altars, sacrifices, libations, and incense to their honour, passed from the Egyptian Pharaohs to the Ptolemies, and at length to the Roman Emperors in the time of Herod, under whom Christ was born. At that same time the development of sin in the world, Jewish and Gentile, had reached its height. . . . Not merely were the characteristics of the old Egyptian kings, their tyranny, cruelty, and pride, too faithfully repeated, and on a vaster scale, by the Roman people, whether under a popular or imperial government, but in the emperors the concentrated profligacy of the heathen world, boasting itself in enormities unheard of before, and almost inconceivable, publicly enacted, and even surrounded with the forms of legality, was enthroned, and deified, and worshipped."

Such, on a general view, was the world without humility. It was not merely a world without God, but a world antagonistic to God, to His dominion, to His light, to His law. Leviathan, the monster apostate, is " king over all the children of pride," * who, through his numerous satellites, ruled the fallen world of man. He elated their souls, inspired them with the mutual hatred that broke up the brotherhood of mankind, hardened them into cruelty, sensualized them into the worship of the creature rather than the Creator, suggested they should be as gods, and took all the honour to himself. But the Prophet Isaias proclaimed the day when " the Lord with His hard, and great, and strong sword shall visit Leviathan the barring serpent, and Leviathan the crooked serpent, and shall slay the whale that is in the sea ".† Then was the weakness of the king of pride made visible before the power of the humble King. " God hath overthrown the power of the proud princes, and hath set up the meek in their stead. God hath made the roots of proud nations to wither, and hath planted the humble of those nations." ‡

Pride crucified Humility, and Humility arose from the dead and put an end to the dominion of Pride. Then was the power of Leviathan destroyed for a thousand years, and the Cross was placed on the crowns of the rulers of the world. Light streamed everywhere from the Cross, and the powers of darkness fled with broken forces, now from one nation, now from another, and Christendom was ruled by the law of Christ. Yet pride was still left in the world, for the old Adam continued to produce new children of elation ; and though the spirits of evil were so much weakened in the presence of Christ and of His servants, they were allowed to range the world for the trial of the humble, the victory of the

* *Job* xli. 25.   † *Isaias* xxvii. 1.   ‡ *Ecclesiasticus* x. 17, 18.

faithful, and the punishment of the proud. From the embers of pride blown up by evil wills, heresies arose and dreadful scandals, testing the souls of men, bringing out their hidden qualities, perfecting the humble, revealing the proud.

The dreadful spectacle of the world without humility, that is, of the world without God, must necessarily bring the mind to these two conclusions : First, these monstrous developments of pride completely show the intrinsic malignity as well as the blinding influence of this vice of vices, even as it exists in its first germs and beginnings. He who has within him the fermenting germs ot a life-destroying plant, has only to be left to his own ways for it to grow, and to expand its virulence in the spiritual system, blinding the intellect, corrupting the will, and producing every evil in the soul. St. John says : "Whosoever hateth his brother is a murderer " ;* not that he has actually destroyed his brother, but he fosters the disposition that leads to destruction, and has already destroyed him in his love. And our Lord says that the devil " was a manslayer from the beginning ".† He destroyed the spiritual life of man by pride and falsehood, and gave death to his immortal body. And he who fosters in himself the germs of pride until they corrupt his mind and heart destroys his own soul.

The second conclusion, forced upon us by the actual condition of the world is this : The rejection of the humility of faith and of the Gospel is rapidly bringing the world at large to the old heathen conditions of thought and conduct, and to the old heathen confusion of substituting the powers of the world for the sovereignty of God. This is manifested in many ways. Again, the idolatries of the modern world are in various respects more gross than the idolatries of the ancient world. For the ancient world idealized nature, and, however erroneously, still associated that nature with some ideal of the divine, and ascribed divine attributions to its departed heroes ; but the modern idolatries are given to the gross, unidealized facts and products of nature, and to human inventions, without having associated any divine ideal with their powers ; the ancient world had a sense of religion, however corruptly applied ; and even to the heroes whom they deified they ascribed certain divine attributions. But modern heathenism has dismissed every sense of the divine, and has given its devotion to the bare powers and

* 1 S. *John* iii. 15.　　　　† S. *John* viii. 44.

phenomena of nature ; or to the worship of poor fallen humanity ; to the deification of accumulated wealth ; to the veneration of mechanical inventions ; to the cultivation of material luxury ; and to the superexaltation of pride, independence, and self-reliance. Whatever a man seeks, honours, or exalts more than God, that is the god of his idolatry. There is no need of temples, altars, or statues for material, mental, or social idolatry ; whatever is preferred in mind and heart to God, whatever is chosen as the chief end of man's pursuit in place of God, constitutes the idolatry of these times.

To these we must add the idolatries of the mind, which bring us back to Plato's theory of the end of man in the worship of ideas. This has led to pantheism on the one hand, and to the shallow ignorance of blind agnosticism on the other : the two extreme results of intellectual pride. In the opposite extreme, sensual pride with its idolatries of materialism has led to the revival of the spirit of Democritus and of Epicurus, and even to the worship of human nature, impiously proclaimed to have no end beyond the grave. Nor ought we to omit the worshippers of that science, falsely so called, which excludes God from His works, and is, therefore, devoid of the first principle of science, and is consequently as blind and foolish as when St. Paul rebuked it in the heathens. When the light of God is wrenched from its true position as a gift of God implanted in the mind of man, and the perversity of egotism has claimed that light, that testimony of God to the soul, as a subjective product of the man, there is no theory, however absurd, of which, from his false position, the mind of man, or rather his imagination, will not be capable, even to the deification of his own wide-erring intellect. This fall from the light of truth as it descends from God has led even to the greater folly of setting up material facts for intellectual principles, and thinking them strong enough to encounter and break to pieces the eternal truths which God has imparted to reason or to faith, truths most perfectly adapted to the requirements of the soul.

The destructive influence of failing heresies that have run their time, and in their decay have revealed their utter want of foundation in divine authority, have done much to destroy men's confidence in the Christian religion. Begun in the negation of authority, they have decayed by developing in the direction of negation, which has eaten even into the principles of natural religion, and by its indifference has left free play to the action of godless science, and to the influence of those numerous idolatries that have taken hold of the unreligious world.

Modern States have certainly not claimed divinity for themselves like the old heathen governments; their tendency is to discard religion as a foundation, and to remove its sanctions from beneath their constitutions and laws. Hence their instability, and the ever-growing tendency to substitute temporary expediency for the fixed principles of wisdom, and the unstable voice of the multitude for the maxims of experience and the long foresight of prudence. There is everywhere visible an enormous jealousy of the authority of religion over the souls of men ; and like the heathens of old, the ambition of States is to reign alone, and to have no power above their own in the world. In nothing is this shown more than in those secular systems of education held in the hands of the State, in which all minds shall be trained by compulsion upon the mind of the State, after the fashion of the Spartans, leaving the rights of God and of the family out of consideration, and reducing all minds to one dead level of rationalism.

After this dreary and desolating survey of ancient and modern heathenism, one requires some Christian refreshment. Let us turn then to the ages of faith, and conclude with a parable, not without a moral, that Old Gower poeticized from an ancient chronicle. There was a king both young and wise, the Solomon of his age, who took delight in putting questions that were shrewd and deeply imagined. But a certain knight of his court was quick and skilful in answering them, so that the king was disconcerted at this rivalry of his shrewdness. So he pondered long and carefully in preparing three questions, the answers to which bore a profound signification; he then put them to the knight, and as the sphinx propounded her riddles, so he required them to be answered in a given time on pain of death. The first question was this: What is that which least needs help, but which men help the most? The second was this: What appears to be of the least worth, although it is of the greatest worth? The third was this : What is that which costs the most, although it is worth the least, and goes ever to utter loss?

But the wit of the knight was of a worldly sort, and after many castings about he could not penetrate to the truth hidden in these questions. Fearing for his life, he wasted away in perplexity and grief. Then his daughter, a virgin of innocent heart, and with a mind that looked to God, observed how her father pined away, won his secret from him, and resolved to answer the king's questions. Brought to the king's presence, with eyes cast down, and heart lifted up to God, she said: "Your first question, O king, is this—What is that which least needs help, but which men help the most? What least needs help is the earth. And yet men help it all day, and every day, and at all seasons of the year. They dig and plough it, they sow and plant and enrich the earth; man, and bird, and beast come from the earth; tree and herb, and grass and flowers, spring out of its bosom; yet they all die, and return to enrich the earth already so rich. Justly, then, may it be said, that the earth has the least need of help, although men help it the most.

"The second question of your Highness is this: What appears to be of the least worth, although it is of the greatest worth? I say it is humility. The which from pure love brought down the Eternal Son from the Most High and Holy Trinity unto Mary, chosen to receive Him for her humbleness. Whoever is truly humble wars with no one; he is peaceful in himself, and would have all to enjoy the same peace. Much more might I say of its great worth and little cost, but let this suffice.

"The third question from the king's lips is this: What is that which costs the most, although it is worth the least, and goes ever to utter loss? I tell you that it is pride. For pride could not live in Heaven, but in its fall brought down Lucifer to hell. It cost Heaven to Lucifer, and paradise to Adam. Pride is the cause of all our woes. The whole world cannot staunch the wounds it inflicts, nor wipe out its reproach. Pride is the head of all offence, and the root of all sin, wasting whatever it touches, and putting nothing in the place of what it destroys; pride is the sting of evil, and the malignant element in all wickedness. Let it spring up where it will, it is the most costly and worthless of all things." Then the king was glad, because he had heard the truth from innocent lips, and he laid aside his wrath.

LECTURE XIII.

ON THE FOOLISH VICE OF VANITY.

"Blessed is the man whose trust is in the name of the Lord, and who hath not had regard to vanities and lying follies."—Psalm xxxix. 5.

VANITY, or vainglory, is the offspring of pride, and the eldest daughter of that detestable vice. Pride is her father, self-love is her mother, and cobwebs are her clothing. She is such a light, fond thing, that were it not that her seductions weaken and undermine the best-formed minds and hearts both of men and women, for her own sake she would be unworthy of any serious consideration. A man or woman given up to vanity is filled with light follies unworthy of the dignity of the soul and the noble end for which the soul is created. It may be more secret, as a rule, in men than in women, but is not the less dishonest for that reason. The objects of vanity may also be different in the two sexes, not always, but as the current of vanity runs with our pursuits. If we compare pride in its elation to a dark swelling wave, vanity is the foam upon its surface. If we compare pride to a soul-destroying fire, vanity is the smoke that flies out of it. If we compare that worst of vices to a foul stream laden with death-giving poison, vanity is formed of the bubbles that spring up from the noxious gases that mingle with the black current of pride. The word vanity sounds of things hollow, shallow, and trifling; but that is no trifle which makes the soul light and trivial, and unrobes her of her dignity.

We shall better understand what vanity or vainglory is, after considering the sense of the word *vain*. That is vain which is vacant, or devoid of good, or which is unstable, or unreliable, or unsupporting, or which has no rational object, use, motive, or end. That is a vain thing that fails of its purpose, or that will not do what ought to be done, or will not support what has need of support. Vanity is labour in vain, and labour in vain is labour without fruit. That, again, is relatively vain which is small, trivial, or empty, as compared with things greater and more worthy, and in this sense the Sacred Scriptures call all creatures, as they are objects of desire, vain when compared with God, and all earthly goods vain as compared with heavenly goods.

Every creature has in it a natural vanity, because created from nothing, and unless supported by God, of its own nature it would go back to nothingness. It is vain also, because by the mere force of its own nature no creature can come to its final end. This can only be accomplished through the action of God's providence, and in intelligent creatures by the action of His grace. After Solomon had meditated on all things in the light of that wisdom which God had given him, and had surveyed the world of humanity, and all the toils and solicitudes of men for the uncertain, ever-fluctuating, and unstable things of this world, to the neglect of things eternal and unchangeable, he pronounced this solemn sentence: "Vanity of vanities, and all is vanity".* But before him the Psalmist in his musings on many things, had reached the same conclusion: "Nevertheless all things are vanity, every man living". † And going more profoundly into the subject, St. Paul declares that "the creature was made subject to vanity, not willingly, but by reason of Him who made it subject in hope". That is to say, the creature made vain in its own nature, and become vainer through the fall, is made hopeful of a better end, especially after the resurrection, when all things shall be renewed in Christ. This the Apostle explains: "Because the creature also itself shall be delivered from the servitude of corruption, unto the liberty of the glory of the children of God. For we know that every creature groaneth and travaileth in pain even till now." ‡

Temporal goods are called vain as compared with spiritual goods, because they are unsuited to the nature of the soul, and therefore do not satisfy the mind or fill the soul; because they are uncertain and apt to glide away; and because they cheat the hopes entertained of them, and bring not that happiness of which we are in search. All things are called vain that have much show and little good, that look strong and are weak, that promise to be

* *Ecclesiastes* xii. 8.   † *Psalm* xxxviii. 6.   ‡ *Romans* viii. 20-22.

satisfying, but pall upon the spiritual sense made for eternal things. Hence the wise Solomon again exclaims: "I have seen all things that are done under the sun, and behold all is vanity and affliction of spirit ".*

In this relative sense the Scriptures have applied the words *vain* and *vanity* to temporal good as compared with eternal; to sensual delights as compared with spiritual; to secular science as compared with divine; to beauty of body as compared with beauty of soul; to labours upon earthly motives in grief and vexation as compared with the cheerful work done for God's sake; and to the multiplicity of empty words that fly from the vainglorious as compared with the few and thoughtful sentences of the wise and prudent.

The words *vain* and *vanity* are also attached in the Sacred Scriptures as hollow qualities to every kind of sin, and to every sort of sinner. For sin is vain and unsubstantial, false in its motive, proposing good and doing evil, vain also in finding misery when seeking for content. The sinner is also vain through his sin, losing his foundation in grace, and doing nothing to his final end. Like the passing wind he is unstable, like the loose cloud he is unsolid, like the lamp hastening to extinction he is expiring from life, like some light thing suspended in the air he is tossed about by the breath of temptation. The Book of Wisdom says: "All men are vain in whom is not the knowledge of God". †   And the Psalmist exclaims: "Man is like to vanity; his days pass away like a shadow". ‡   The habitual sinner is vain, that is to say, empty in many ways, vain in his mind and imagination, vain in his acts and conversation, vain above all in his pride and presumption. St. Paul describes the Gentiles as " walking in the vanity of their mind, having their understanding darkened ". §   And the Psalmist rebukes the vanity of all sinners: "O ye sons of men, how long will ye be dull of heart? Why do ye love vanity and seek after lying ?" ‖

After this universal view of vanity as contemplated in the Scriptures, we come to its specific character as it constitutes a special vice. As pride is the inordinate appetite or love of one's own excellence, vanity or vainglory is the appetite or love of making that excellence known, that it may be seen, admired, and praised

---

* *Ecclesiastes* i. 14.   † *Wisdom* xiii. 1.   ‡ *Psalm* cxliii. 4.
§ *Ephesians* iv. 17, 18.   ‖ *Psalm* iv. 3.

by men : whether that excellence has any real foundation, or is only imaginary, and therefore false. As vanity and vainglory are one and the same in different degrees, we shall use these two words indiscriminately.

St. Bonaventure defines vanity with precision as being "the love of one's own praise on account of apparent excellency ". * When the object of vanity is to exalt one's self in the general mind, it is fame. When admiration is sought to be added to praise, it is glory. When we seek this exaltation among friends, it is social reputation. Or it may be sought in the mind of some individual whose good opinion or praise we covet.

The ways of vanity are well known to be manifold, and the methods by which vanity seeks to gain its ends are very numerous ; for it is the most subtle, elastic, and inventive of all human passions. It is not, however, to be assumed that every manifestation of our gifts is vainglorious. Our Divine Lord has said : " Let your light shine before men, that they may see your good works, and glorify your Father who is in Heaven ".† What is not done from ostentation, or to attract notice, praise, or admiration, but purely that God may be honoured, is not vice but virtue. But the humble make no display, they speak not of themselves or their good works except rarely, and with careful measure and prudence. They leave their works to speak, without putting them forward to speak for their author.

Our Lord has said, on the other hand, and with much more emphasis : " When thou dost an almsdeeds, sound not a trumpet before thee, as the hypocrites do in the synagogues and in the streets, that they may be honoured by men. Amen, I say to you, they have received their reward. But when thou dost alms, let not thy left hand know what thy right hand doth. That thy alms may be secret, and thy Father who seeth in secret will repay thee. And when you pray, you shall not be as the hypocrites, that love to stand and pray in the synagogues and corners of the streets, that they may be seen of men. Amen, I say to you, they have received their reward." ‡ Here, and also in the exhibition of fasting, the motive determines the vice : " that they may be seen of men ". And they have already received their reward ; vanity has received its vain reward.

* S. Bonavent., *Centiloquium*, p. i., s. 18.
† *S. Matthew* v. 16.   ‡ *S. Matthew* vi. 2-5.

Vanity may be known, as St. Thomas points out, by one or more of these three conditions. First, when a man vainly glories in what is either wholly or partly false, as when he claims for himself some good, or gift, or ability, that he has not got; or some virtue that he does not possess, or some degree of excellence in these things, or in learning, skill, or accomplishment, or whatever else it may be, beyond what he can justly lay claim to. Again, if one glories in things as one's own that belong to another, or that have been received from another, and especially if one puts forward as one's own what has been received from God. To such St. Paul says: "What hast thou that thou hast not received, and if thou hast received, why dost thou glory, as if thou hadst not received?" *

There is a vainglory, unhappily too common, that boasts of wickedness that was never committed, of errors never entertained, or of seductions never attempted. For vanity, like its parent pride, is voracious of all kinds of reputation and distinction that may awaken surprise, admiration, or envy, and the vain who cannot boast of good will boast of evil. This commonest kind of vanity, made up of false pretensions, is directly opposed to truth and sincerity, as well as to humility; and the Sacred Scriptures call such persons as practise it liars, deceivers, and hypocrites. The Greeks give a very fitting name to this vainglory, and call it *cenodoxia*, which means the acting a part like performers on the stage, though without their justification. They are like the jackdaw in the peacock's feathers of the fable, and are as readily detected by less pretentious birds; although unhappily they can seldom be dealt with in the same way, so that they continue unconscious that they have made themselves ridiculous.

The second mark of vanity is when a man idly glories in things that are not entitled to bring him praise or honour, because they are transient and corruptible, and imply no merit in their owner. Such are personal beauty, showy ornaments, the merits of ancestors, or other things that never came of our own virtues or labours. Again, when the vain seek glory from the vain, whose opinion has no value to confirm anything, who are themselves insincere, who commend but to flatter, and know that what they say is worthless. This is one of the common vices of society.

* 1 *Corinthians* iv. 7.

The third mark of vanity is when a man says things of himself or does acts that are not directed to any good or justifiable end, neither to the honour or service of God, nor to the utility or good of his neighbour, nor yet to his own veritable good, but are said or done solely for his own exaltation or vainglory.*

As vanity is not directly opposed to the love of God or of our neighbour, it is not in itself, as St. Thomas observes, a mortal sin, but venial. Yet in certain cases it is combined with conditions opposed to charity, that bring it under the guilt of mortal sin. The first of these cases is, where the matter on which a man glories is false and contrary to the reverence of God, as when the King of Tyre lifted up his heart and said : "I am God, and I sit in the chair of God in the heart of the sea ".† So also when a man glories in the gifts of God as though he had never received them from above. Again, when a man glories in new and false opinions, knowing them to be contrary to faith. A man also sins mortally if he glories in mortal sins, or seeks praise for them, whether he has or has not committed them ; for this is to glory in the mortal offence of God. Of such persons the Prophet Isaias says : "They have proclaimed abroad their sin like Sodom, and they have not hidden it ; woe to their soul, for evils are rendered to them ". ‡ And the Psalmist says : "The sinner is praised in the desires of his soul ; and the unjust man is blessed ". §

The second condition which makes vanity mortal, is when a man prefers the temporal good in which he glories to God. Of this God Himself speaks through the Prophet Jeremias : "Thus saith the Lord : Let not the wise man glory in his wisdom, and let not the strong man glory in his strength, and let not the rich man glory in his riches ; but let him that glorieth glory in this, that he understandeth and knoweth Me, for I am the Lord that exerciseth mercy, and judgment, and justice on the earth ; for these things please Me, saith the Lord ". ‖

The third condition in which vainglory becomes mortal, is where the opinions of men are preferred to the testimonies of God. This occurs in the vainglories of heresy ; also when men shrink and draw back from avowing the truths of faith from human respect, or neglect their solemn duties to God for fear of human opinion or censure, or for the sake of being thought liberal. This

---

* St. Thomas, *De Malo*, q. 9, a. 1.　　† *Ezechiel* xxviii. 2.
‡ *Isaias* iii. 9.　　§ *Psalm* ix. 24.　　‖ *Jeremias* ix. 23, 24.

was the case with those chief men among the Jews who believed in Jesus, "but because of the Pharisees they did not confess Him, that they might not be cast out of the synagogue. For they loved the glory of men more than the glory of God."* The fourth condition that makes vainglory mortal, is when the man makes it his final end, and refers his works, whether for or against virtue, or anything he does, to the final end of satisfying his inordinate appetite for fame, praise, or glory.

St. Augustine has set forth the evil of this vice and its undermining influence in these impressive terms: "To seek to be loved and feared by men with nothing else in view but the delight that this may give us, is to secure a wretched life of shameful boasting instead of a life of real delight. It comes largely of this that men do not love God, or chastely fear Him. Therefore it is that He resists the proud, but gives His grace to the humble. It is needful in the performance of certain human duties that we should be loved and feared by men; and taking advantage of this, the enemy of our happiness scatters among his snares the exclamations of Well done! well done! And whilst we greedily pick them up, we are caught by them, and letting our delight in the truth drop from us, we take our delight in the deceptive voices of men. But in thus enjoying being praised and feared, not for God's sake, but for our own, we have those with us who are like ourselves, not in the accord of charity, but in fellowship of punishment with him who strove to imitate God in a perverse and crooked way, and who serve that Lucifer in cold and darkness, who declared he would establish his throne in the North."†

Except under the circumstances above stated, vainglory or vanity is but a venial sin, because, however inane, it is not opposed either in its object or motive to charity. Yet it is a habit to be contended against, and shunned, and suppressed by every effort, as weakening to the soul, undermining in its influence, and shameful in its disorder. Even good works done from vanity lose their eternal reward, as our Divine Lord teaches us; and no one can obtain eternal life by sinning, although the sins be venial. But there is a consideration of far more gravity, so grave that we shall express it in the theological words of St. Thomas: "Foras-

---

* S. *John* xii. 42, 43.
† S. August., *Confessiones*, lib. x., c. 36.

much as vainglory makes a man presumptuous and excessively self-confiding, it disposes the soul to grievous sins, and so by degrees to the loss of his spiritual goods ".*

For vainglory is a capital sin from which other vices spring, and was so treated by the Fathers. St. Gregory the Great, who had a most profound intuition into the ways in which the vices spring out of one another, puts pride and self-love by themselves, as the sources of all sin, and then places vainglory as the first of the capital sins. Cassian, who reverses the order of the capital sins, puts vanity or vainglory as the seventh, and pride as the eighth, in which he undoubtedly follows the method of the Ascetic Fathers of Egypt. In explaining the method of St. Gregory, St. Thomas points out that it is not necessary for a capital sin to be mortal in itself, if mortal sins spring from its influence. For, as he further observes, "mortal sins spring from venial sin, when venial sin disposes the soul to mortal sin ". St. Gregory enumerates seven vicious daughters born of vanity. These are " disobedience, boasting, hypocrisy, contention, obstinacy, discord, and the presumption of novelties ".†

The descent of these vices from vainglory or vanity is thus explained by St. Thomas. The end of vainglory is to exhibit our own excellence, and, we may add, to assert our own superiority. A man seeks this in two ways, either in words, and this is *boasting*, or by acts, which if true, but done to excite admiration, have always something new and unexpected in them, which is the *presumption of novelties;* but if these acts are false and deceptive, then it is *hypocrisy*.

There is also an indirect way of exhibiting one's own excellence, by ostentatiously upholding one's equality with others, or one's superiority over them. A person may do this in any of four ways. The first regards his intelligence, and shows itself in *discord*, sticking to his own opinion, and refusing to give way, even after he sees that another is nearer the truth, or is altogether right, whilst he is in the wrong. The second regards the will, and this is *obstinacy*, when a man will not give up his own will and way for the sake of peace and agreement with others. The third regards speech, and this is *contention*, when a man clamorously disputes and contends for no justifiable reason, but only to satisfy his

---

* S. Thomas, *Sum*. ii. 2, q. 1¬3, a. 3, ad 3.
† S. Greg. Mag., *Moralia in Job*, lib. xxx., c. 31.

vanity. The fourth regards facts, and is *disobedience*, when, for any of the above motives, a person refuses to obey his superior.*

Vanity is evidently the root of every one of these vicious habits, and as this same vanity springs from pride and self-love, it is also evident that the one true remedy for all of them is humility. There are disorders in the human frame that cause alarm, because they are visible and painful to the sufferer; but when the physician is called in, he sees that what has caused alarm is only symptomatic of a disorder more deeply seated, of which the patient is unconscious. He therefore soothes and assuages the more sensitive and symptomatic disorder, but directs his chief attention and stronger remedies to the radical disease that is more hidden, well knowing that when that is removed the symptomatic disease will disappear. What cures pride cures vanity, and what cures vanity cures those more ostensible disorders that spring from vanity. The remedy, therefore, will be found in humility. The seven daughters of vanity have all a strong family likeness to pride, with the same bad blood and the same vicious temper.

Vanity also, though of lighter carriage, has this resemblance to pride, that the more hidden it is the more dangerous it is. It is never without some plausible pretext to cover its weakness, and this is not unfrequently the entertainment, instruction, or good of other persons, which seems to ennoble vanity with charity; or it is the removal of misconceptions in doing but fair justice to one's self, and so the pretext is but common justice, although the real object all the while is self-glorification. Some persons, not a few, cover their outward persons with vanity in dress and manners, and make themselves beacons of levity, with as bad a taste socially as mentally and spiritually. They hang out a sign on which this inscription is plainly legible : The vanity of vainglory to be had cheaply within. Others, more grave in outward form, love to parade their knowledge or experience before it is asked for, embarrassing the common right of freedom with the ventilation of their vanity. Others, again, are forward and intrusive, unable to be patient until their singular merits are recognized, and their superiority admitted. Some will tell you, or would have you to think, that they are too proud to be vain, which is a very coarse vanity, out of a pride too gross to understand its offensiveness.

There is a morose and apparently retiring vanity as well as a

* S. Thomas, *Sum.* ii. 2, q. 132, a. 5.

light and salient vanity, and the last is innocent in comparison
with the first.   The thoughtless coquette of vanity is not by any
means so bad as the calculating prude.   A plain exterior will
sometimes cover more vanity than a gay one, as sovereigns dress
plainly for distinction from the brilliant circle around them.   But
whatever the outward shows of vanity, they are but symptoms of
the malady within, and show themselves more in manner than in
material.   For vanity is less in show than in acts, less in acts than
in words, less in words than in thoughts, and less in thoughts than
in those inward movements of self-love, from which, as from their
secret springs, all the shows of vanity proceed.

Vanity is a light, fond motion of the soul, but wonderfully
elastic ; its worst effect is that it makes the soul empty and inane.
For the motive of vanity rests on nothing solid, on nothing that
long abides; neither on God, nor on truth, nor on justice, nor even
on any abiding human affection.   It rests not even on self in any
steady way as pride does, which gives it a sort of evil consistency
that does not belong to vanity.   For in vanity a man seeks himself
in the ever-shifting and uncertain opinions of other persons, and
is always flitting, like the butterfly, from flower to flower, from one
to another, taking its colour, like the chameleon, from what is
nearest at the time.   It is this extroverted and ever-changing
character of vanity, always under the influence of other persons'
opinions, and ever casting about for flattery, that so much weakens
the prudence and judgment of the vain.   It may be taken as a
maxim that where sound judgment and habitual tact is required,
it should never be looked for where vanity is the predominant
weakness.   St. Bernardine of Siena, a man with vast experience
of human nature as well as great spiritual insight, has taken special
note of this fact.   " Much," he says, " is the malice of the
vanities, affecting the mind with such a weakness that when these
vanities pass into the affections, the whole judgment of reason is
thrown into perturbation." *

What St. Bernardine has so justly observed may be noted by
any one who unites a little modesty of mind with observation.
Pride, as we have said, has a certain evil consistency, because its
motive, though false, is within the man.   But vanity has its motive
in other persons, whom it is always endeavouring to conciliate, or
to draw into admiration, and is therefore inclined to a com-

* S. Bernardin. Sienensis, *Serm.* 47 *in Feria* 6ª *post Dom. Passionis.*

promising policy. Then it is always shifting its ground, and is one thing to one person and another to another ; its object is always changing, so that it has no consistent ground, even of the human kind, on which to rest a permanent judgment. Even when judgment concerns other things than vanity, its motives will be constantly intruding, and suggesting how this or that will look in the eyes of those whose esteem or flattery we covet. Thus vanity makes our judgments timid and uncertain, or warps them from their just course, and our conclusions are often hesitating, or contrary to what is wise and just, or not in accordance with the truth. They take not the high ground of what is best before God, but the low one of what is agreeable to men, or what is most for one's own display, and not unfrequently end in some compromising of principle.

Upon the destruction wrought on our good works by vanity, we may take the calm judgment of St. Basil, a most eminent guide of souls. "Most especially," he says, "must we shun vainglory. It will not frighten us from labour, though this would be a less evil, but it deprives us of the crown of labour. This insidious traitress to our salvation is not easily got rid of. She sets her snares in the very orbs of Heaven, bringing down those virtues to the earth that have their ties in Heaven. The good merchant of piety may have well freighted his ship with all sorts of virtue, and vainglory may raise a tempest that will endanger the sinking of his precious goods. He is steering his way to the supernal kingdom ; but if he looks back to the meaner things left behind, and especially to vainglory, the blasts of vanity will scatter the wealth of his soul, and overset the foundation that carries his virtues. When we seek rewards from men for what we have done for Heaven, we destroy the fruit of those labours which ought to be given to God, that He may keep them and reward them. But if we prefer the glory of men to the service of God, and seek the vain reward of human praise, we shall deservedly lose the divine reward. For we have not worked for God, but have hired ourselves out to men, and after boasting of their reward, what right have we to look to God for reward, seeing that we had no intention of acting from His grace? Learn this truth from the Gospel, where Christ says of those who do their works to be seen of men : 'Amen, I say to you, they have received their reward'.

"Let us shun vainglory, then, that agreeable thief of spiritual wealth, that pleasant enemy of our souls, that moth of the virtues, which eats into our good things so sweetly. Vainglory mingles its poison with honey, and hands the fraudful cup to the minds of men, that they may be filled with the vicious draught. For human praise is sweet to the inexperienced. When subject to vanity, they think that nothing can take them from sound judgment into error; yet their thoughts and judgments are so utterly perverted, that whatever the multitude admire they take to be most excellent. If they have little souls, or rash minds, they will be ready to accept anything whatever these wise judges of conduct think the best, however evil it may be, and will be eager to do what may win their praises. Thus vanity not only destroys good but leads to evil. It is just, therefore, that we fix our eyes on right reason with preference, and on the God who rules right reason; and that we take the path on which God moves before us, to lead us right. If some should praise us on the way, we need not take much notice of their praise, except to congratulate their sound judgment, but keep straight on with eyes raised to God, whose praise is always just. If others should dispraise this way, that is no reason for us to turn back, but a reason rather for compassionating their want of judgment and their mental darkness." *

All that we have said brings us to this principle, that true glory depends on the judgment of God, and on the conformity of the human with the divine judgment. But vainglory takes the directly opposite course, and not only values the judgments of men beyond their worth, but neglects to compare them with the judgments of God, as expressed in the conscience. And why this neglect, except in the interests of self-love and pride? Under the influence of these fictitious interests, we not only believe good of ourselves that does not exist, but long for others, and, if possible, for everybody, to believe this falsehood.

The remedy for this disorder is unquestionably in the exercise of that most sincere of virtues, which was against pride and all its offspring, and which bears the name of holy humility. Through the honesty of this virtue we look to the evil within us rather than to the good; we judge the evil and conceal the good, lest vanity corrupt the good into evil. As the evil within us is true, though not according to truth, humility is willing that even

---

* S. Basil, *Constitutiones Monasticæ*, c. x.

that truth be known, where the honour of God and the good of our neighbour do not forbid its being known.

Who can tell how many vanities are united in vainglory? Vanity of vanities, it unites a thousand vanities to the shame of human nature. You have only to watch its interior movements, or even its indicator, the sensitive responsive tongue, as it springs in light wave after wave of emotion from self-love, as it is attracted by one external motive after another, and, with the agile play of subtle contrivances, seeks to win undeserved applause and unmerited admiration. Nay, the scenes of vanity can even be acted in solitude, upon an imaginary stage, before an imaginary audience, where self-love will supply both the vanity and its flatterers. Yet vain are all these little human glories when brought to the light of conscience, the ready dissolver of all such follies. They are vain, because their flatterers are vain, and they are vain because those who accept flattery for truth are vain. The subsistence of vanity is a creature of imagination. For vanity is an artist of fiction, and a servant of self-love; but when truth steps in with its revelations, it causes soreness, sorrow, sadness, or anger. Yet for the sake of these fictions we become the slaves of opinion, and of an opinion that is rarely sincere, and that cannot judge rightly, because the interior is closed against the eyes of opinion. This many-tongued opinion is more capable of imagining than of judging, and of feigning compliments that have no serious meaning attached to them. Yet on this imaginary good the vain think to grow, to become better, and to rise superior to their neighbours. Examine all this, and there is nothing in it but a fantastical folly that makes us first blind, next unhappy, then ridiculous; for to gain the reputation of vanity is to become a jest.

As nothing in human nature is so sensitive as vanity, there is nothing that suffers more. It is easily wounded, often mortified, and frequently disappointed. A word from an innocent child may bring it to confusion; and as vanity is a jealous and an envious vice, it suffers much from the success of others. Hence the vain are censorious, and love to pull down, or to hear others pull down, those who seem to be more in favour. It is said in Holy Scripture that the perverse are with difficulty corrected. This perversity belongs to the dull and the vain, but especially to the vain. For with the dull it is a simple want of intelligence, but the vain man has such an image of his perfection before his eyes, that when you point out his failings he cannot recognise them as belonging to that image. Give a much-needed advice especially intended for him, and if there are fifty persons present, he will applaud its wisdom, and see its application to every one but himself. Give him the same advice in private, and whatever be the wisdom and authority of the adviser, and however kind and gentle the admonition, it wounds him to the quick that any one should think of him that of which he is so utterly unconscious, although everybody sees it but himself. There is no armour so impenetrable to advice as the chain-mail of vanity.

In an ancient book on the Contemplative Life, long ascribed to St. Prosper, we have one of the most complete descriptions of the internal evils of vanity ever written, and with an abridged summary of this description we conclude this lecture ; for if anything will deter from vanity, it must be a knowledge of the evils that it involves.*

Vanity is the inflated affection of a soul that languishes after a variety of inane delights. The vain, eager after honour, know not how to gain honour, but are puffed with a disease of fancied excellence that is hollow, morbid, and restless. The imperious mistress of light souls, vanity has her own bland ways that are unpleasant to solid minds ; and when she has captivated the weak she is tyrannical to her victims. To dissemble her vices she affects the virtues, and often stains her mind with evil thoughts. She has an appetite for those dignities that swell the vainglorious, but are perilous to the weak and bitter to the perfect. Place her in authority, and her vanity will make her imperious to her subjects ; yet will she be weak before the strong, but will captivate the weak, and enjoy their captivity. She will vex the ambitious, but the little-minded she will inflate, and when they become inflated she will humiliate them. The timid will serve her in fear, the vain will flatter her with a show of worship, the feeble and failing will think they stand firm under her protection.

This is that vice of vanity which does not strangle the virtues, as some suppose, but when the vicious embrace it, it gives free play to their vices ; for vanity cannot penetrate a soul that is filled with the solid virtues. What vanity tempts is the empty soul, and the soul inflated with the ruinous pride of ambition, and it brings

* *De Vita Contemplativa, inter opera S. Prosperi*, lib. iii., c. 10.

them to the shame of ravening in the delight of public reputation. Like a ship without ballast, these vain ones are tossed with every wind; like the chaff blown from the solid grain, they are at the mercy of every breath of flattery. Their vanity does not so much make them vicious as show them to be vicious, as they are swept round in the whirl of vain and idle affections.

The vain give up their weak will to every light impulse of their vanity; they boast of things of which they know they are ignorant; they undervalue holy persons as compared with themselves, because they do the vile office of flattery to themselves, and can see no perfection of which they are in want. They love to be talked about, and are not particular whether what is said of them be true or false. They are fond of salutations, are attentive to those who say to them pleasant things, are docile to what delights them, and are pleased with base things. They love to teach what they do not know, and to have great things believed of them, and they will in words express their detestation of what in their hearts they covet. Deluded themselves, they are grateful to those who will help their delusion and will clothe their vice with the name of virtue. Swift to promise, they are slow to fulfil; changeable in good, they are tenacious in evil, and can be grave in words when vile in thoughts. Elated in prosperity, they are frail in adversity, and are soon fretted when reproached; and as they are immoderate in joy, so are they easy-going in human things, and difficult in spiritual things. Such is the morbid softness of vanity, unconscious of its own disease, and intolerant of the physician.

LECTURE XIV.

THE HUMILITY OF FAITH.

"You are all the children of God, by faith in Christ Jesus."—GALATIANS iii. 26.

OUR life begins in utter ignorance of all things, and our mind is first opened by the instinctive faith that we place in those around us. Without this faith we could make no beginning of knowledge. The simple, open, confiding spirit of childhood, and the wonder awakened by the newness of everything, enable us to learn much in a short time. The first labour of learning begins with books, and the reason is that printed words are mere arbitrary signs, twice removed from the things that they represent. But youth advances in knowledge through faith in the teacher as well as childhood. We are now speaking of human faith. There are three moral elements in this teachableness. The first is the consciousness of ignorance, which is an element of natural humility. The second is the opening of the mind with submission to the teacher, which is a second element of humility. The third is the belief given to the teacher, which is a third element of humility.

But the moment the scholar ceases to believe in his teacher, or the disciple in his professor; so soon as he begins to judge and to criticise, he assumes superiority; his faith is gone, and he ceases to learn, for he has closed his mind to the authority of the teacher. If, notwithstanding, there is a real superiority of knowledge and wisdom in the teacher, it is the pride of the pupil that has closed to him the gate of knowledge. But if the pupil remains faithful to his teacher, what he learns on faith will grow into knowledge through subsequent thought, observation, and experience.

This is the human way to knowledge; it begins with faith, and the greater part by far of every one's knowledge has no other ground than faith. Were a man to separate his knowledge into two parts, and distinguish what he knows from his own observation or perception from what he only knows on the testimony of other men, he would be amazed to find how little he knows at first hand, and how much he knows upon the faith of testimony, and on no other ground. Place a son of some wild, untutored tribe by the side of the son of an educated and accomplished family in the civilized world, and compare the contents of their minds. The one has nothing beyond the scanty traditions of his tribe; the other has the whole traditional knowledge of the human race at his service. How does he acquire it? Chiefly on faith. The great map of every one's knowledge rests on faith. What we know not on personal knowledge we take on the testimony of those who had, or who have, personal knowledge. We thus know history, and what passes at a distance from us, and what is in other men's minds; and what others have seen, or investigated, or experienced. It is upon faith in each other that the whole business of life is conducted. Society exists and is held together on the principle of faith, and the cessation of faith in each other would be the dissolution of society. The vulgar man who says that he will believe nothing but what he sees, contradicts his words at every turn by his actions. The man who is habitually sceptical, whether from natural obtuseness or from conceit, is one who ceases to learn, from intolerable dulness or self-sufficiency.

It is important, however, to observe that there is a foundation in the mind itself, into which all communicated knowledge is received, and where it is tested, and that foundation is the light of reason, which God has implanted in the mind. Without that light we should be incapable of knowledge; for as the light of the sun makes all things in the world *visible*, the imparted light of reason makes all things in nature *intelligible*, so that when natural truths are presented to our mind, we see them in that light.

Let us suppose that, like the animals, we knew nothing but what we could see with our own eyes, and feel with our own senses and instincts. Imagine this state of things. But our soul has a light of its own, the light of intelligence, which has in it eternal and unchangeable principles, and laws of justice and responsibility that go straight to the conscience, and tell us of things beyond this visible world, and show us that we belong to the world of spirits, and lead us up to the Supreme Cause of all things. Let us suppose, again, that there was no such thing as faith in the world, no belief of men in each other; the knowledge of every man would be limited to his own observations. We should know nothing of the past, nothing of the distant, nothing of the minds of other men, nothing of their knowledge. What poor shrunken things our minds would be without the help of human faith, and in what a narrow circle our slow minds would move !

But beyond the world of nature and the reach of human reason, there is another sphere of being and of knowledge, which is beyond the report of our senses, beyond the stretch of our natural reason, and which no man living in this world has ever seen. Of that boundless world the boundless heavens are the visible symbol; and from that boundless world comes proofs into this that are accessible to reason and known to reason. Before Columbus undertook to sail to the unknown world, he had much circumstantial evidence to convince him of its existence, and he knew he was nearing the unknown land by the things that drifted from its shores. The testimony of God is everywhere in the light of the mind, whose light partakes of the infinite and unchangeable, and is everywhere the same : in the voice of conscience which proclaims our responsibility to God in all times and places; in the works of God around us that proclaim their Almighty and Intelligent Cause; in the action of His Divine Providence everywhere visible; and in the general voice of mankind. The natural conscience of man leads up to God, and makes him sensible that God everywhere beholds his conduct. Men even punish the violation of the natural law where there is neither human law nor contract, on the principle that every man, even the most savage, has the natural law written in his heart.

Of visible things, and even of rational truths, we only know the human side, and we feel there is a vast knowledge of them that is altogether beyond our reach. There is not an insect or a blade of grass that does not present a great deal more mystery than knowledge, and which does not awaken in us the consciousness of our ignorance. Who can solve these mysteries but Him who made them ? Of ourselves, our nature and destiny, we know little until God teaches us. Everywhere we meet with insurmountable bars to our inquiry, and limits that repel our curiosity. There must be a knowledge of all things, but that knowledge is not in us. Everything around us stretches away towards infinity and eternity; our souls touch upon that infinity, but are far from being infinite; our mind sees eternal principles, though far from being eternal. All around and within us are mysteries beyond our power to understand.

The mind within the man has always and in all times seen, the spirit within the man has always felt, that the soul is immortal, and that an eternal world awaits him. How are we to know that eternal world, or our own destiny, or our duties with respect to our eternal destiny, unless on the faith of testimony from that world? What we know but have not seen with our own eyes in this world, we know by faith on the word of those who have seen. And what we know of the great invisible world, we know on the word of God, whose eye sees all things, and whose mind knows all things. By faith we know from Him what without faith we can never know. As the knowledge and the duties of life rest on faith in man, the knowledge and the duties of religion rest on faith in God, who accompanies His revelations with the demonstration of His power.

But revelation alone is not sufficient to establish a divine faith in man; as there is a medium within us for receiving natural truth in the light of reason, we require a medium within us for receiving supernatural truth, and that medium is the supernatural light of faith. For there is nothing proportioned between the natural man and God that can bring man into a divine communion with God, until God establishes a beginning of proportion, by planting in him a divine light, capable of receiving His supernatural truth. And as to know God truly we must be subject to God and adhere to Him, we need a divine strength to raise up and invigorate the will, before we can either adhere to the divine truth, or love the Giver of it, who has thus established the soul in communion with Him.

These gifts are always ready for all who are ready to receive them. What makes them unready is that pride and self-sufficiency upon which the heathens based their virtues, and from which men in great numbers in these days resist the voice and authority of God. When we look through the heathen world we see what man is without divine faith; when we look through the modern world we see what men become through renouncing that humility of mind and heart to which the gift of faith is given. Outside the Church of God we see nothing but an ever-shifting and restless opinion, from which one truth drops after another, the result of departing from that divine authority upon which faith essentially rests.

Although divine and human faith have sufficient resemblance to justify their having a generic name in common, yet the principles of divine faith are so totally different from the principles of human faith, that they must necessarily be distinguished by specific names from each other. Hence we call the one Christian or supernatural or divine faith, and the other natural or human faith. When men oppose themselves to the principles of divine faith, they very seldom understand them, but most commonly fall into the error of arguing from the principles of human faith. In searching for divine truth they too often take the ground of mere human faith, and apply to it a human measure. It is therefore of the greatest importance to have clear views of the real principles of divine or supernatural faith.

The broad distinctions between divine and human faith may be briefly expressed in these terms : Human faith rests on the testimony of man ; divine faith on the testimony of God. Human faith is received and estimated by the light of the rational soul ; divine faith is received and estimated by a supernatural light given by God to the soul above the light of reason, and without this light there can be no divine faith. In human faith the man gives the assent of his will to a statement on human motives ; in divine faith the assent of the will is given on divine motives. In human faith the assent is given on natural judgment ; in divine faith the will is helped to assent and adhere to the truth by the help of God's grace, divinely communicated to the soul. In human faith one man believes another at a distance through messengers sent with authentic tokens ; in divine faith God sends His messengers duly authenticated to deliver His revelation ; finally, God sends His Son, exercising all the powers of divinity, to deliver His final dispensation to the world ; and He deposited His truth and power in His Church, and invested it with His divine and infallible authority to preserve and to deliver that truth unchanged to men even to the end of time.

22*

When we consider the vast difference between the principles of divine and the principles of human faith, it at once becomes evident that the natural man cannot understand divine faith; he must be prepared for it, and God alone can prepare him. As faith rests on external authority for its teaching and on internal grace for its belief, what has to be externally sought is the authority appointed by God; but what God may teach through that authority, human reason cannot anticipate, because revelation is above reason, and beyond reason, and no one by the light of nature can say what God may reveal or what He may ordain; for it must necessarily be altogether different from the experience of the natural man, yet at the same time suited to the human soul. As the truth revealed is above all created nature, and is divine, the grace of God must dispose the soul for its reception; and this disposition is obtained not by study but by prayer, not by disputation but by humility.

Before explaining more fully what faith is, it will be well to say what it is not. Faith, then, is not a product of human thought, although just thinking upon God and the soul will lead to faith. It is not a work of the imagination or of sentiment. It is not a thinking, but a believing; not an imagining, because the object of faith is independent of the man, and is most certain; not a sentiment, but a truth to which the will assents. It is not opinion, for opinion is uncertain and changeable, whilst faith is fixed and unchangeable. When a man says, "These are my religious opinions," we know he has not faith. When another says, "I respect your religious scruples," we know he does not understand the nature of faith.

Faith, again, is not hope or trust in Christ. This was the error of the early reformers, who confounded the virtue of faith with that of hope. But faith is the foundation of hope and trust. For, as St. Paul says, "He who cometh to God must first believe".* Faith believes in God and in His revelation; hope and trust rest upon the divine promises revealed to faith.

We may consider faith in its object, as it exists in God; in its communication, as it is received by man; in its subject, as it dwells in man; in its action, as it is exercised by man; and in its fruits, as it fills the soul with light and truth, and with the

* *Hebrews* xi. 6.

knowledge of all things available for the sanctification and salvation of the soul.

Let us first draw attention to that very precise and definite term *the faith*, as expressive of the object of faith. This term denotes that there is only one faith, one body of truth revealed by God and imposed by Him on the belief of man; it is always one and the same, one and undivided in all who have the faith, although not communicated to all in the same degree, or with the same expansiveness. "One Lord, one faith, one baptism," * says St. Paul, who unites these three unities with profound significance. For the truth proceeding from the one God must be one, and the way appointed to reach that truth must be one; that way is baptism, the one door of the one Church in which the one God has deposited His truth. God is one, His truth is one, the faith that accepts the one body of truth is one, uniting all believers in one truth; and the divine authority appointed to teach that one truth, and to administer the grace of faith is one. All these unities flow from the unity of God. The truth of faith is therefore one in God, one in the Church, and one in each of the faithful, who in partaking of the one truth become united with it, and so with God. Hence St. Paul describes the fruitful result of the preaching of the Church to be "our meeting in the unity of faith". †

The object of faith is not only one indivisible body of truth, but it is one and the same from the beginning to the end of time. For the substance of the faith is summed up in these words by the Divine Author and Finisher of our faith: "Now this is eternal life: that they may know Thee, the only true God, and Jesus Christ, whom Thou hast sent". ‡

The first revelation of the mystery of redemption was made in Paradise, after the fall, and it became a great tradition, incorporated in the rite of sacrifice. The same revelation was enlarged to the patriarchs, the priests, and religious teachers of their time. It was incorporated in the Law of Moses, and expressed in multitudinous rites and observances revealed from Mount Sinai. To the prophets the whole mystery of Christ was revealed in the fullest details of His divinity and humanity, of His birth, life, preaching, miracles, conduct, sufferings, death, and resurrection, and all this in such minute details, that the prophets have been

* *Ephesians* iv. 5.   † *Ephesians* iv. 13.   ‡ *S. John* xvii. 3.

called the gospel before the gospel. Then came Christ on earth and fulfilled what had been prophesied and believed from the beginning. What God revealed from the beginning was fulfilled in the end, and what He once revealed He never recalled. "The gifts of God are without repentance."* The shadows of truth were absorbed into the very truth present in the world, as the dawning light is absorbed in the full light of day. The revelation from the beginning was not only completed, but enacted by the Son of God in person. He deposited the whole revealed truth from the beginning and His very self, the Truth of truth, with the Apostles and the Church, and promised in solemn testament that both He and the Holy Spirit should be with His Church in her teaching and ministry, even until the end of the world.

For the profoundest reasons the development of the faith was ordained to be progressive until the coming of Christ into the world. And nothing can be imagined more sure or perfect than this unity of the faith in its progressive development. After the fall of man, for a moment all was blank and dreary with dark clouds, as at the moment after the crucifixion, the second great crime of humanity. Then the first dawn of the promise appeared in Paradise, the first rays of the revelation of Christ and of His Redemption. To Noe and the patriarchs that dawning reddened into stronger light. The top of Mount Sinai caught the glow of the yet unrisen sun, and cast it upon the children of Israel. As the Sun of Justice neared the horizon, the stronger beams of light sent before Him fell upon the souls of the prophets, who from their mountain caves saluted Him afar off, and proclaimed the hour of His rising. Then arose the Sun of Truth and Justice, and gradually covered the earth with His splendour. That Light for the revelation of the Gentiles and the glory of God's people was never again to set, or be diminished, except in the hearts of the proud and the incredulous. To this day, as in all days past, the one Church of Christ, having the one Christ with her, shines throughout the world in unbroken descent and unity of authority, with the one undivided plenitude of truth ; most conspicuous to all men, and most distinct from everything of mere human origin or institution ; full of charity, intolerant of error, intolerant of division.

* *Romans xi. 29.*

The very perfection of this unity of truth and society, ever
enlarging, never diminishing in one tittle of divine revelation, is a
stumbling-block to men accustomed to nothing but their own
variable and inconstant thoughts and ever-changing sentiments.
It is equally a perplexity to those born in sects that carry but
fragments of the truth, picked out by their founders from the body
of revealed truths, and ever changing with the change of teachers.
But God is not like men ; His work is perfect. And if a miracle
is asked, no greater miracle can be exhibited than to see one
divine, full, and indivisible truth held unchangeably in the faith
of men of every nation, tongue, and tribe of the earth. Whoever
reflects deeply on what men are, and on what this faith is, must
exclaim : " This is the work of God, and it is wonderful in our
eyes ". * St. Paul has expressed this unity of the faith of all times
in these expressive words : " Jesus Christ yesterday, and to-day ;
and the same for ever ". † Yesterday, that is, as He was believed
before He appeared ; to-day, that is, as He was preached by the
Apostles ; the same for ever, because His truth can never change.
But Jesus Christ is all that He truly is, all that He taught, and
all that He instituted.

The object of faith is God, and the end of faith is God, but in
different ways. For the object of faith is God as He is the
Sovereign Truth who reveals the truth to us. But the end of faith
is God as He is the Supreme Good whom the truth of faith
manifests to us, and as He is our good. The first end of faith
is to make God known to us, and to make known all that He
has done or will do for us, that what we know by faith we may
desire by hope and love with charity. Faith is, therefore, the
beginning of our union with God by making us partakers of His
truth, and that divine truth illuminates His goodness to our
minds. But the final end of faith is God Himself. We were
made for union with God in His beatific vision, in which, as St.
John says, "We shall see Him as He is ". ‡ This is our final
end. But the first beginning of the communication of the
eternal light is in faith, whereby the light of divine truth is placed
in us, and we are placed in that light. Faith is therefore the first
light, the heralding light, the foundation placed in us of what
in its final perfection will be the beatific vision of God. It is the
beginning of the eternal ways in us, the commencement of our

* *Psalm* cxvii. 23.　　† *Hebrews* xiii. 8.　　‡ 1 *S. John* iii. 2.

union with God, and is compared in the Scriptures to a first espousal of the soul with God: "I will espouse thee to Me in faith".* It is the first thing that makes us acceptable to God; for, as St. Paul says, "Without faith it is impossible to please God".† We please Him by the humility with which we acknowledge Him to be the fountain of truth, and subject ourselves to Him as the children of His truth.

Our Divine Lord calls faith the work of God: "This is the work of God, that you believe in Him whom He hath sent".‡ He likewise calls it an attraction of God. When doubts were raised among His hearers about His saying that He had come down from Heaven, He said to them: "Murmur not among yourselves. No man can come to Me, except the Father, who has sent Me, draw him".§ St. Paul also calls faith the gift of God: "By grace you are saved through faith, and that not of yourselves, for it is the gift of God".‖ It is the first great gift to the soul, and the preparation for all the rest. But faith is informal and imperfect without the gift of charity, which quickens it into life, and gives to it form and perfection. Hence St. Paul says: "We in spirit by faith wait for the hope of justice. For in Christ there is neither circumcision nor uncircumcision, but faith that worketh by charity."¶ For what avails it to know God unless we love Him?

It will only serve to our condemnation. Faith without charity is dead, as St. James teaches, who therefore requires the works of charity to prove the life of faith.

St. Paul has described faith in these words: "Now faith is the substance of things to be hoped for, the evidence of things that do not appear".** The word *substance* is here open to two senses, both in themselves true and both beautiful. If we consider faith as it dwells in us, then, as the commentators observe, we must give to the word the Hebrew sense of foundation. As the bones are the foundation of the body, the truths of faith in the soul are the firm foundation in us of the things to be hoped for.†† For the light of those truths, believed though not seen, is a reflection of the things that we hope for. But if we consider these

---

* *Osee* i. 20. † *Hebrews* x. 6. ‡ *S. John* vi. 29.
§ *S. John* vi. 43, 44. ‖ *Ephesians* ii. 8.
¶ *Galatians* v. 5, 6. ** *Hebrews* xi. 1.
†† See *Cornelius à Lapide*, the *Cursus Completus*, and S. Thomas on the text.

truths objectively as they are in God, and of which the image is in a certain way in the lignt of our faith, they are the light reflected from the substance of things in God for which we hope, but which in the time of faith we cannot see until faith is absorbed in the vision of God.

St. Paul has himself explained this word substance a few sentences before, where he says to those who have suffered the loss of their earthly substance for the faith: "Knowing that you have a better and a lasting substance, do not therefore lose your confidence, which hath a great reward. For faith is necessary for you, that, doing the will of God, you may receive the promise."* This would seem to indicate a substance not yet received, but which remains to be received: the substance, or object of faith, as it dwells in God.

Yet there is a certain subsistence of these things in the soul in the faith that gives us the firm conviction of them; and this St. Paul describes as "the evidence of things that do not appear". The Greek word *elenchos* used by St. Paul is much stronger than the word *argument* used in the Vulgate, or the word *evidence* used in our version. It signifies a convincing argument, demonstration, or proof. This proof or conviction is contained in the three elements of faith already described. The first is the light of faith in the mind, which is thus described by St. Paul: "God, who commanded the light to shine out of darkness, hath shone in our hearts, to give the light of the knowledge of the glory of God, in the face of Christ Jesus. But we have this treasure in earthly vessels, that its excellency may be of the power of God, and not of us." † The second is the outward teaching of the Church, delivering to us the form of sound doctrine that accords with the inward light of faith received in baptism. The third element is the inward grace by the help of which the will adheres firmly to the truths of faith. Hence St. Basil defines faith to be "the unhesitating and approving assent given to the truth of the things proposed by the divine gift".‡

These elements of submission to divine authority, and of inward light and grace, helping adherence to the truth revealed, constitute that inward subsistence of truth in the soul, that firm and assured proof captivating the mind, and make those things for

---

* *Hebrews* x. 34-36.   † 2 *Corinthians* iv. 6, 7.
‡ S. Basil, *Serm. de Vera ac Pia Fide.*

which we hope, and which we desire, already to be, after a certain manner, in the mind and the heart. For we already see them, as St. Paul says, "darkly as through a glass," * being even now conscious of their existence. "The substance of things to be hoped for," says St. Bernard, "is no fantasy of things inane. The word substance will not allow you to take liberties with the faith, to dispute at will, or to wander here and there among vain opinions and diverging errors. The word substance implies what is fixed and certain; it fixes you within certain bounds, and keeps you enclosed within certain limits; for faith is not opinion but certainty." †

Whilst, then, the things that we hope for have not their substance in the soul, but in God, they have a subsisting foundation in the soul in their light, grace, and truth. And St. Thomas has expressed this in his definition of interior faith, as being "an act of the mind essentiating the divine truth through the assent of the will moved by grace".‡ The great theologian explains this by a similitude. The things to be hoped for are like a tree still hidden in the virtue of the seed; through faith they already exist in us in a certain way, as the tree exists in a certain way in the seed. Or we may use this comparison. A certain beaming into our eyes of light reflected from mountains in the distant horizon gives us an obscure impression of them; and travellers from that region give us detailed information respecting them. We know, then, that they are no mere clouds or illusions, because they abide always, and are always the same. So in a general light given to our minds we see the objects of faith, which we know in their clear and certain outlines and distinctions from the testimony of God in the teaching of His Church. The more we give our mind and will to them, the more do they grow upon us, become clearer and more vivid, harmonizing most beautifully with each other, and also with the wants and desires of the soul; so that they are constantly infusing greater light and serenity, a joy in the truth, a consolation in believing, a calm peace, and a great hope; and this hope and serenity grow in proportion to the conformity of our life with the faith revealed to our conscience.

After St. Paul has described the heroic faith of the great saints

---

* 1 *Corinthians* xiii. 12.   † S. Bernard, *Tract. de Erroribus Abailardi.*
‡ S. Thomas, *Sum.* ii. 2, q. 2, a. 9.

of the Old Testament, he says of them : "All these died according to faith, not having received the promises, but beholding them afar off, and saluting them, and confessing they are pilgrims and strangers on the earth. For they that seek these things do signify that they seek a country." * But to us who have the grace of Christ and His very presence, these things are not afar off, they are nigh and even at our doors. The sublime effect of Christian faith is to make living and present to us the eternal mysteries of Christ, which are perpetually renewed in the Body of Christ, which is His Church, and all the faithful partake of them, and they become the living things of our hearts and of our love. The soul of the faithful one is actually clothed with Christ, as St. Paul intimates in various places. He says : "As many of you as have been baptized in Christ have put on Christ ". † And to the Romans the Apostle says : "Put ye on the Lord Jesus Christ ". ‡ And elsewhere he speaks of the faithful as having "the sense of Christ"; § but they who have the sense of Christ are not far from Him. The grandeur of those divine things that are in such contact with us, that though we see them not in open day, we feel them close upon us, cannot fail to make us sensible how utterly unworthy we are of the divine condescension and goodness. Like the saints of old we feel ourselves strangers and pilgrims in this low and sensuous world ; but unlike them, who could only salute the eternal mysteries from afar, we feel that nothing but the yet unregenerated body that invests our soul, and the stains upon the soul, keep us back from beholding them in open day ; and we are inclined to exclaim with St. Paul : "Unhappy man that I am, who will deliver me from the body of this death ? " ‖

We will now give two descriptions of the faith, one from a very early writer of the Church, in which we may contemplate its sublimity ; another from the authoritative Catechism of the Council of Trent, in which we may consider its practical value. But let me first invite the reader to reflect on the origin of all truth. The Eternal Word of the Father is the Personal Truth. He is the enlightener of all intelligences, and the revealer of all truth, who revealed the mysteries of God to the angels and then to man. He revealed all truth that was made known to man

* *Hebrews* xi. 13, 14.   † *Galatians* iii. 27.   ‡ *Romans* xiii. 14.
§ *1 Corinthians* ii. 16.   ‖ *Romans* vii. 24.

from the beginning, and then He took the form of man to perfect His revelation.   He is the light of the truth of all things heavenly and earthly, and gives reason to man, and to the humble man the light of supernatural truth.   He "enlighteneth every man that cometh into this world"; and when He described Himself He said : "I am the Light that hath come into the world". *
After a preface of this character, the Book on the Divine Names proceeds as follows :

"God the Word, who is the very truth, is the infallible knowledge of all things.   But divine faith is the abiding firmament of the faithful, founding them in the truth, and the truth in them ; so that the faith of truth becomes one with those who believe, even as iron placed in the fire becomes one with the fire, and operates as the fire operates.   For faith is said to act as well as those who hold the faith ; and who, believing in a certain knowledge that is simple, have no division whatever, and no doubt ; because knowledge unites the things known with those that know them ; whilst ignorance is the cause of division with the ignorant. Nothing therefore can move him who believes in the truth from the household and firmament of the faith.   But, according to the Apostle, he who is in the darkness of ignorance fluctuates in error, and is carried about by every wind of the wickedness of men, like those who are tossed in a tempest ; and they imagine that those who possess this knowledge are out of their senses, as Festus said to St. Paul when he heard him preaching the truth : 'Much learning hath made thee mad'.   But the Christian is one who knoweth Christ, and hath through Him the knowledge of God ; he hath the one knowledge of truth.   This knowledge is outside the world, being by no means concerned with the science of the world or the errors of unbelievers, and knows itself to be sober and free from wide-wandering infidelity.   Wherefore they who have this knowledge die daily for the truth, and are not only daily in peril of death for the truth, but as approved Christians they die to ignorance and live to knowledge." †

From the Catechism of the Council of Trent we select the following paragraphs, as conveying a solid instruction : "As the end proposed to man is his beatitude, and as this end is far above the reach of his natural understanding, he stands in need of receiving

* *S. John* i. 9 ; xii. 46.
† S. Dionysius Areop., *De Divinis Nominibus*, c. vii.

knowledge from God. This knowledge is faith, whose virtue causes us to hold firmly to that which God has delivered, and which the Church sets forth. For as God is the very Truth, the faithful can have no doubt of those things of which He is the Author. From this we understand the great difference there is between the faith we give to God and that which we yield to the writers of profane history. But though faith hath a vast comprehension, it differs in its degree and dignity in different persons. For in the Sacred Scriptures it is said to one: 'O thou of little faith, why dost thou doubt?' and to another: 'Great is thy faith'; and others pray: 'Increase our faith'; and it is also said: 'Faith without works is dead'. Yet these different degrees of faith are of the same kind, and are included in the same definition." *

"Nothing contributes more to confirm our faith and to strengthen our hope than to keep our mind fixed on the truth that nothing is impossible to God. For after understanding the omnipotence of God, we readily and without hesitation assent to whatever He proposes to our belief, however great, however wonderful, however above the order and measure of nature. Nay, more, for the greater the truths proposed by the Divine Oracles, the more readily the mind assents to them. And if any great good is to be expected, the greatness of the gift will not discourage the soul, for she is animated and strengthened with the reflection that there is nothing which God cannot do. With this faith should we strengthen ourselves whenever we have any great work to do for God, or for the service of our neighbour, or when we ask some great favour of God in prayer. Our Lord has taught us the first of these lessons in rebuking the slow faith of His disciples: 'If you have faith as a grain of mustard seed, you shall say to this mountain, Remove from hence to yonder place, and it shall move; and nothing shall be impossible to you'. The other lesson St. James has insisted on: 'Let him ask in faith, nothing wavering; for he that wavereth is like a wave of the sea that is moved and carried about by the wind. Therefore let not that man think that he shall receive anything of the Lord.' The faith also brings with it many advantages. In the first place, it forms the soul to modesty and humility, according to the word of the Prince of the Apostles: 'Be ye humbled under the mighty hand

* *Catechismus Concilii Trident.*, p. i., c. i., n. 2.

of God'.   It admonishes us to fear nothing where no cause exists
for fear, and therefore to fear God alone.   For our Saviour says :
'I will show you whom ye shall fear; fear ye Him who, after
He hath killed, hath power to cast into hell'.   By this faith
we also recognize and honour the benefits of God to us; for
whoever thinks on Almighty God can scarcely be so ungrateful
as not to exclaim: 'He that is mighty hath done great things
to me'." *

   As humility is the receptive foundation of the Christian virtues,
and faith their positive foundation, humility must precede faith ;
for the obstacle to faith is pride, and pride is removed by humility,
which is the first disposition of return to God.   Then faith is by
its very nature a subjection of the mind and will to God as He
is the Sovereign Truth, a subjection to His divine authority as the
illuminator and teacher of the soul, and a subjection to the truth
which He teaches by revealing.   Moreover, as a test and trial of
this subjection to Him, God is pleased to require that this subjection of faith shall be openly made and manifested before all
men, by our open submission to the Church which He has appointed to represent His authority, and to the voice of her teaching, and to her ministry of grace, as exercised in His name and
by His power.   This is not only faith, but the humility of faith,
because it is the subjection of the mind and heart to the authority
of God, and to His truth in the way that He imposes and pre-
scribes.

   Adam first lost his humility and then his faith.   He first
aspired to be as God in knowledge, and then disbelieved the
command of God.   Humility must remove pride and open the
soul that the grace of faith may enter.   The grace of faith subjects the soul that the light of faith may illuminate the soul.   This
order of returning to God is vividly exhibited in the order in
which the catechumen enters the Church.   He is first subject to
a twofold discipline, that of humility and that of instruction.   For
this reason St. Cyril of Jerusalem, in instructing his catechumens
on the nature of faith, warns them that " humility is the key of
knowledge "—an expression also used by St. Augustine.   The
catechumens were kept for a considerable time under a humble
discipline ; they held the position of humble petitioners for the
faith ; they took the last place in the assemblies of the faithful,

   * *Catechismus Concilii Trident.*, p. i., c. ii., n. 13.

and were commanded to withdraw during the celebration of the divine mysteries. When after due probation they were admitted to baptism, they were asked what they sought of the Church of God, and they replied that they petitioned for faith. They are then submitted to exorcisms to expel the proud spirit of evil before receiving the illumination of faith. The whole process plainly shows that the grace of humility is the preparation for the grace of faith; but when faith is received with hope and charity, they perfect the grace of humility.

What prevented such numbers of those who followed our Divine Lord, and, attracted by curiosity, heard His words and saw His mighty power in His miracles, from believing in Him? Our Lord Himself has proclaimed the three causes of their unbelief: their pride, their love of this world's interests, and their human respect. And He proclaimed the two conditions which would alone enable them to follow Him as disciples, and to become members of His kingdom. These were humility and self-abnegation. He says: "Unless you become as little children, you shall not enter into the kingdom of God,"* and, "Blessed are the poor in spirit, for theirs is the kingdom of Heaven". †

After a terrible rebuke to the cities on the Lake of Genesareth, that, after all His miracles worked in the midst of them, they had not humbled themselves and done penance, that they might receive His truth, Christ turns to His Heavenly Father and says: "I confess to Thee, O Father, Lord of Heaven and earth, because Thou hast hidden these things from the wise and prudent, and hast revealed them to little ones." ‡ Those cities were commercial, in which men were absorbed in traffic and gain; and He speaks of the worldly prudent and the wise in their own conceit, from whom the light of truth was hidden even when present before their eyes; and of the simple and humble as the little ones to whom the light was revealed. Both heard the truth from the mouth of God, both saw the miracles of God, but the souls of the humble were open to His light, and the souls of the proud were closed.

When Jesus healed the sick man in Jerusalem who had been five and thirty years on his bed of infirmity, it was the Sabbath day, and for this reason the Jews persecuted Him; and when justifying His healing on the Sabbath day, He said: "My Father

* *S. Matthew* xviii. 3.   † *S. Matthew* v. 3.   ‡ *S. Matthew* xi. 25.

worketh until now, and 1 work," they sought to kill Him because
" He said God was His Father, making Himself equal to God".
Then He said to them, rebuking their unbelief: "I know you,
that you have not the love of God in you. I am come in the
name of My Father, and you receive Me not: if another shall
come in his own name, him you will receive. How can you
believe, who receive glory one from another ; and the glory which
is from God alone, you do not seek ? " *   Christ is speaking to the
doctors of the law, to the men revered in Israel, and He points
to their own hearts for the cause of their unbelief: they sought
not God but themselves, not His glory but their own.

The parable of the sower who sowed his seed is professedly the
parable of faith.   The rocky ground on which the seed withered
up is the soul that is obdurate with pride, where faith cannot
strike root.   The thorny ground is that in which faith is "choked
with the cares and riches and pleasures of life, and yields no
fruit".†   These two obstacles are removed, the first by humility,
the second by self-abnegation.

"Faith demands a certain elevation of the sentiments," as St.
Chrysostom observes, " and a certain energy of soul to surmount
the impressions of the senses, and to triumph over the proud
ignorance of human reason.   There is no true faith but what rises
above the prejudices of custom."‡   What can be so magnificent
to a creature still tied to earth, and earthly sense, and earthly
ways, as to live mentally in a sphere of divine truth invisible to
mortal eyes !   And in that vast sphere of light, whatever its
shadows of obscuration, to tread the secure firmament of truth
with the movements of his mind, and wing his thoughts upwards
from earth to Heaven, from light to light, from truth to truth,
from mystery to mystery, in the wonder of his soul, his heart ever
following his mind with love and veneration !   What so sublime
to him as the meditations of faith, where, whilst the body still
holds to its native earth, the spirit soars to Heaven, and his faith
converses with the Father, the Son, and the Holy Spirit, looks up
with awe unto the glorious Majesty of God, and aspires with
hoping love unto His infinite goodness and clemency !   And the
heart is purified by every ray of descending light, and expanded
with every grace from the eternal love.   Faith looks with lucid

---

* S. *John* v. 42-44.   † S. *Luke* viii. 5-15.
‡ S. J. Chrysost., *Hom.* 22 *in Hebræos*.

eyes upon Jesus Christ, the Author and Finisher of our faith, now glorified in our human nature at the right hand of God. Faith looks upon Him executing His mission of salvation to the world; now listening to His divine words, and opening the heart that they may sink with His light into its depths; now gazing upon the awful spectacle of His passion and crucifixion, inexhaustible in its depths of mystery and grace to faith and love and gratitude. There we behold the living door to the eternal sheepfold, through which all who are saved must pass; and His wounds are as the open gates through which we have access to His spirit and His life. "I am the Alpha and Omega, the first and the last, the beginning and the end. Blessed are they who wash their robes in the blood of the Lamb, that they may have a right to the tree of life, and may enter in by the gates into the city."*

Faith also contemplates the Son of God ever present in His Church, serving in this world of trial, enlightening her with His eternal light, and quickening her life with His spirit; and partaking of His light, the faithful soul partakes also of His crucified, spiritualized, and glorified Body, the sacrament of life, in which the plenitude of the Godhead dwells. United in communion of light and charity with the angels and saints, and with all believing souls, whom the light of Christ embraces, the faithful soul is conscious of being within this vast communion of prayer that extends from the hearts of the poor on earth to the spirits of the seraphim that burn in love and adoration before the eternal throne of God; and is conscious, too, that we, like them, are the children of God, the brethren of Christ, and the heirs of Heaven. O wonderful faith, embracing our spirits with the divine light! Wonderful light, sealing our souls with the seals of eternal truth! Wonderful truth, setting our souls free from the petty confines of this world, and opening the eternal heavens to our contemplation! Wonderful heavens, in which is the Supreme Good for which our souls are made! The soul filled with the light of faith is filled with Christ, and with the Father, and in that soul the Holy Spirit spreads His love; and whilst the wonder of what the soul contemplates in faith grows ever more and more, the wonder grows less and less that men of faith should leave all things for God, and should even cheerfully give their mortal lives

* *Apocalypse* xxii. 13, 14.

to martyrdom, that their faith may be changed more quickly into vision.

As faith rests not on human reason or judgment, but is imposed on man by the authority of God, and is received in humble obedience to that sovereign authority, even before we know by full possession the magnificence of the gift, we must expect to find it taught in the Holy Scriptures from this point of view. Accordingly St. Paul calls the assent of the will to faith "the obedience of faith," * and St. Peter calls the faithful " the sons of obedience".† St. Paul says to the Romans : "We have received grace and apostleship for obedience to the faith in all nations for His name ".‡ And he asks the Galatians : " Who hath bewitched you, that you should not obey the truth, before whose eyes Jesus Christ hath been set forth, crucified among you ?"§ To the Corinthians the Apostle rises into more elevated language to display the power of faith : " The weapons of our warfare are not carnal, but mighty to God, unto the pulling down of fortifications, destroying counsels, and every height that exalteth itself against the knowledge of God, bringing into captivity every understanding unto the obedience of Christ ".‖ The weapons of the Church are the truth, the grace, and the virtue of Christ ; the powers to be overcome are the strongholds of unbelieving science, the counsels of worldly wisdom, and the pride that lifts itself against the knowledge of God. The captivity of the understanding in the obedience of faith is a deliverance from the captivation of error to the captivation of truth. As the Apostle says in another place of the work of Christ : " He led captivity captive, He gave gifts to men ".¶

The whole language of the Sacred Scriptures indicates that faith is a humble submission of the mind as well as of the will to the eternal wisdom and reason of God ; yet not a blind or compelled submission, but a free, enlightened, willing, and contented submission, as all who have the unspeakable gift of faith know by experience. St. Jerome says with great truth : " That it is ridiculous for a man to dispute the faith before he possesses it ". He may dispute on the evidences that lead to faith, but what faith itself is, as it rests on light and grace in the soul, he cannot under-

---

* *Romans* xvi. 26.
† 1 S. *Peter* i. 14.
‡ *Romans* i. 5.
§ *Galatians* iii. 1.
‖ 2 *Corinthians* x. 4, 5.
¶ *Ephesians* iv. 8.

stand before experience. How can he understand the power of that abiding grace that lifts the will to the divine light in the mind, embracing the greatest of all truths without study or effort, yet with a free and grateful adhesion? How can he understand the wonderful harmony that reigns between the truth taught and the light within the mind? How can he understand the marvellous facility with which children, baptized in their infancy, so soon as their minds are opened, drink in the expositions of faith as though their nature assisted them? Yet it is not their nature, but their supernatural light and grace that prepare their mind and will. The two first chapters of the Catechism contain the profoundest questions that have ever engaged the mind of man, and are what human science would call the most abstruse metaphysics; and yet the Catholic child can enter into them with intelligence, can hold them firmly in their order and sequence, and give a clear account of them; whilst the man without faith, however well trained, will labour in vain to make them a part of his intelligence. Why, but because he wants the humility of faith, and his mind is not open to them? Why, but because he is striving to measure the divine reason and truth with his own small measure of reason? Why, but because he never reflects that truths that are so great and so high above the scope of his native mind can only be received by submission to their Author, and must be believed that the soul may possess them, before she can understand them? For, "Unless you believe, you shall not understand ".*

But when faith is established in the soul it illuminates the reason with its divine light; and reason, obedient to the light of faith, devotes its own light to the service of faith as a loyal and devoted servant. For these two lights, which have one and the same origin, though they come to us by different ways, reunite in the soul, and from their union has sprung the most magnificent of sciences, the science of theology. This co-operation of reason with faith has been admirably explained in the authoritative words of the Council of the Vatican, which we here translate :

"The perpetual consent of the Church of God hath held, and doth hold, that there are two orders of knowledge, which are

---

* *Isaias* vii. 9. "You shall not understand " is the common reading of the Fathers from the Septuagint. The Hebrew and Vulgate read : " You shall not be established ". That is, established in the truth.

not only distinct in their principle, but in their object; in their principle, because we know the one by reason, and the other by divine faith; and in their object, because beyond those things that can be reached by natural reason there are the mysteries hidden in God, which are proposed to our belief, and which we could not know unless they were divinely revealed to us. Wherefore the Apostle testifies that God was known to the Gentiles through the things that are made, but in speaking of the grace and truth that is made through Jesus Christ, he says: 'We speak the wisdom of God in a mystery, *a wisdom* that is hidden, which God ordained before the world, unto our glory; which none of the princes of this world knew. . . . But to us God has revealed them, by His Spirit: for the Spirit searcheth all things, yea the deep things of God.'* And the only-begotten Son confessed to the Father, because He had hidden these things from the wise and prudent, and had revealed them to little ones.

"But when reason is illuminated by faith, and seeks diligently, piously, and soberly, it obtains by the gift of God a certain knowledge of the mysteries which is most fruitful, as well from the analogy with things that are naturally known, as from the connection of these mysteries with one another and with the final end of man; yet is never able to comprehend those truths as in their own nature they exist. For in their own nature the divine mysteries so far exceed the created intelligence, that even when delivered by revelation and received by faith, they are still covered with the veil of faith, and remain concealed within a certain darkness, so long as in this mortal life we are absent from the Lord; for we walk by faith and not by sight." †

Thus whilst faith is far above opinion, because the truths of faith are known to us as most certain, fixed, and unchangeable, it is beyond the comprehension of science, from the very nature of the truths revealed, and the limitations of the human intellect. Also, because it is a part of the design of God that faith should be our probation, before we are rewarded with the divine vision. Yet, as we have seen, faith is not without knowledge, and a knowledge increasing with the growth of faith and piety. "We know in part," ‡ says St. Paul; but however much we know, we

* 1 *Corinthians* ii. 7-10.
† *Constitutio Dogmatica Concilii Vaticani de Fide Catholica*, c. iv.
‡ 1 *Corinthians* xiii. 9.

can never comprehend ; for how can the human mind encompass the infinity of God, or take the measure of divine and eternal things ? And what we know is not the cause but the effect of faith, the fruit which the divine revelation produces in the soul. Commenting on the words of Christ, "You shall know the truth," St. Augustine asks : "Did they not know the truth when the Lord spoke it to them ? But if they knew, how did they believe it ? They believed it, not because they knew it, but they believed that they might know it. For what we shall know, neither eye hath seen, nor ear heard, nor hath it entered into the heart of any man to conceive. What is faith but to believe what you do not see ? But to know the truth is to see what you have believed." *

Faith is in its nature catholic or universal, that is to say, it extends to all the truth that God has revealed, and which the Church of Christ teaches from His divine authority. For it is not what a man chooses, but what God imposes, that forms the body of faith, and constitutes its integral object ; and what a man may not know explicitly from want of instruction, he believes implicitly, because he accepts the whole revelation of God without distinction. The divine faith is parallel in this respect with the divine law, which forms a part of the faith. The creed is a law of obedience as well as the decalogue, and both rest on the same divine authority. St. James teaches that "whosoever shall keep the whole law but offend in one point is guilty of all ".† The reason is that he offends against that principle of justice and that authority of God on which the whole law rests, and from which every point of the law proceeds ; so that he who grievously offends in one point offends against the principle of justice and the authority of God, and consequently loses the grace of justice and the friendship of God. So also is it with the law of faith : to reject one point of doctrine revealed by God and proposed by the Church of Christ is to reject the principle on which faith is founded, and is a rebellion against the authority of God ; so that he who disbelieves one point is guilty of all. In other words, as he who sins grievously in one point has lost all justice, he who disbelieves in one point has lost all faith. For this reason the Apostles called those who accepted some points of their teaching and rejected others by the name of heretics, which, translated from Greek into English, signifies *choosers*. For these men set

* S. August., *Tract.* 41 *in Joannem*.   † *S. James* ii. 10.

their own private judgments above the authority of Christ and of His Church, and thrust their natural reason into the revelation of God, from which they choose some things and reject others, reducing faith to human opinion, and destroying the very principle of faith. But who hath known the mind of God? Who can say what is truth with Him? Who can dictate to the Eternal Truth, and say to Him: "This I will allow to be Thy truth, but this I will not allow"?

We hear much outside the Church about the beauty of a simple creed, by which is meant a small low creed that contains much of the reason of man and little of the reason of God, and bears all the marks of human construction on its visage. But these makers of simple creeds forget that the more truth and the higher the truth, the more simplicity; that the greatest of all Beings is the most simple of all; and that the more truth the more liberty; although we must grant that it requires more humility in creatures so far beneath that truth. For the difficulty is not in the truth, but in the disposition of the soul to receive the truth. What gives freedom to the soul? Our Lord tells us: "The truth shall set you free ".* But these choosers think that the less truth the more freedom—more freedom from humility, certainly. For as David says: "In Thy truth Thou hast humbled me ".† For the greater above our nature the truth revealed to us, the less we feel ourselves to be. Again, then, we ask: What gives freedom to the soul? Not less truth, but more truth, provided we enter into it. It is ignorance, not truth, that destroys freedom. Every increase of truth enlarges the soul and increases her freedom. For her liberty is proportioned to the extent and greatness and elevation of the truth in which the soul can live and move and grow. You might as well think of cutting off some of a man's limbs to perfect his body, or of taking out some of his faculties to perfect his soul, as to take away portions of divine revelation to perfect the creed. This is the process of heresy, applying human criticism to divine things, which necessarily ends in negation and protest, for it is the measuring of infinite things with finite intelligence. But that very intelligence tells us that we must expect God to say what we cannot comprehend, and to do what we could not anticipate. The Incarnation and the Cross are the answer to everything.

* *S. John* viii. 32.　　　　　　　† *Psalm* cxviii. 75.

There are not a few persons who would find it equally agreeable to their natural inclinations to choose a simpler code of law out of the Decalogue ; but the cry of conscience and of human law is too strong to allow of this. Yet even to this has the cry of atheism reached in these unbelieving times. So true it is that the destruction of faith leads to the destruction of morality, and all in the name of freedom. But the Eternal Truth has said : " If you continue in My word, you shall be My disciples indeed, and you shall know the truth, and the truth shall make you free ".*

If God has exhibited to us the riches of His truth and the wealth of His grace to make us partakers of His inexhaustible goodness ; if He has offered us such an abundant provision of means for perfecting our souls and bringing us to His kingdom that it rivals and even exceeds the copious provisions of His providence for our earthly life ; who are we, that we should refuse His divine generosity ? Who are we, that we should pick and choose, select and reject, among the divine gifts of the Omnipotent Goodness ? Who or what are we, that we should say : God can do this, but He cannot do that ? Who are we, to prescribe bounds to the power, wisdom, and generosity of God ? What right have we to judge after God, who alone knows what we are, what we want, and what we ought to be ? Or to determine for ourselves what He alone can determine, namely, the conditions on which He will receive us to eternal life. It was after contemplating the state of unbelief in which all men were included, that the mercy of God might reach all through faith, that, struck with the withering poverty of that unbelief by the side of the wealthiness of faith, St. Paul exclaimed : " Oh, the depth of the riches of the wisdom and of the knowledge of God ! How incomprehensible are His judgments, and how unsearchable His ways ! For who hath known the mind of the Lord ? Or who hath been His counsellor ? Or who hath first given to Him, and recompense shall be made him ? For of Him, and by Him, and in Him are all things : to Him be glory for ever." †

God has given His great revelation that He may be glorified in the souls of men ; but the unbelievers refuse Him this glory. What is the revelation of the Holy Trinity but the manifestation of the life of God ? What the revelation of His Eternal Word

* S. *John* viii. 31, 32.   † *Romans* xi. 33-36.

but the manifestation of His infinite truth? But He is also revealed as the Giver of light to all intelligences. What is the revelation of His Holy Spirit but that of His infinite love and sanctity? But He is also revealed as the Giver of grace and sanctity to angels and to men. What is the open and visible Incarnation of the Son of God but the crowning of His creation, and the recovery to its divine end of an intelligent creation lost to God? What is it to believe in Christ but to believe all that He is in his divine and human nature, all that He has taught, all that He has done for us, and all that He has ordained and provided for our salvation and sanctification? Christ is not divided: He was divided on the Cross for our redemption; but He lives for ever, and can be divided no more. Whoever attempts to divide His authority, His truth, His sacraments, or His Church, divides not Christ, but divides himself from Christ.

Humility, then, is the groundwork of faith, and faith the groundwork of the other Christian virtues, which are all exercised in the light of faith. Humility frees the soul from pride and error, faith fills her with light and truth; humility opens the soul that faith may enter; humility brings us to the knowledge of ourselves, and faith to the knowledge of God. But the knowledge of God brings so great an increase to the knowledge of ourselves, when we use that knowledge rightly, that humility may be said to rest on faith as much as faith rests on humility: so that, as St. Chrysostom remarks, humility is the inseparable companion of faith. And indeed it is that element in the virtue of faith that subjects the mind to God and to His truth, and then faith becomes the eye of humility. For it opens to us such a view of God, and of divine and eternal things above and beyond us, and shows us to be so little, so poor and defective by the contrast, that we are led to exclaim with the Psalmist: "In Thy truth Thou hast humbled me ".* And as the light of faith illuminates the creature as well as the Creator, and shows us the horrors of error and vice as well as the splendours of truth and justice, and gives us the power to see and to weigh the value of all things from the divine point of view, faith dispels our errors and rectifies our judgments. Faith, therefore, both exalts and humbles us: it exalts us in the light of God, in the knowledge of what God is to us, and in the knowledge of our noble destiny;

* *Psalm* cxviii. **75.**

it humbles us in the sight of our nothingness apart from the mercy, grace, and providence of God.

But, to quote the great St. Leo : " The force and wisdom of faith is the love of God and of our neighbour ".* For charity is the life of faith, and faith is the light of charity. But each illuminates the other ; for whilst faith gives its luminous truth to charity, charity gives its fire and ardent sense of God to faith ; and so faith works by charity, for charity gives its force to the will to cleave to the truth of God for the love of God. Faith is the end of the Divine Incarnation, and God is the end of faith. Humility is the counterpart of faith in the soul, and charity is its perfection. Wherefore let us cultivate humility, that we may have a larger soul for faith and charity ; and faith, that we may have a greater light from God and deeper knowledge of the eternal mysteries ; and charity, that we may obtain the fruit of faith and humility through the closer union of our soul with God. But faith is cultivated by prayer, and by meditation, and by contemplation, and by living, and thinking, and acting in the light of faith, and in the presence of God.

* S. Leo, *Serm. 7 in Quadragesima.*

LECTURE XV.

ON THE SCHOOLS OF HUMILITY.

"Take fast hold of discipline: leave her not: keep her, for she is thy life."
—PROVERBS iv. 13.

EVERY science is founded upon certain fixed and unchange-able principles of truth, and is guided by rules that spring from those principles. The science of humility rests upon the knowledge of God and of one's self; it fills the whole distance between the creature and the Creator. The Giver of this science is God, whose light descends into our interior, and shows us what we are in His sight, and what we ought to be. But though divine in the origin of its light, it is the most human of sciences, inasmuch as it teaches us the knowledge of ourselves—that most difficult knowledge, which men are most reluctant to enter upon.

The fundamental facts of this science are the spiritual nature of man, considered as he is made for God, and God Himself as He is the Object and the End of man. Its principles arise from the subjective relations of the human soul to the light, the grace, and the bountiful providence of God. Humility not only implies a certain just, truthful, and reverential demeanour towards God, and towards all that belongs to God, but it is intimately concerned with the purification of the soul, for which it is the essential disposition and preparation. But the principle of this purification is the light and the grace of our Divine Redeemer, who purifies the mind from error and delusion with an ever-growing light of faith, and the heart from pride and sin with an ever-increasing grace, proportioned to the increasing humility of the subject soul. Finally, humility is the essential counterpart to that love of God, to that sanctity of soul and wisdom of life, of which the Holy Spirit is the animating principle.

Hence the science of humility is profound, descending as well as ascending beyond the sphere of human comprehension; for the depths of the soul are unfathomable and the heights of God are unattainable in this day of probation. We must therefore learn the great laws of humility from God, who has sent us His Son to teach them, who is Himself their great example, and whose Cross is lifted up as the beacon-flame of His doctrine over the whole troubled sea of human life.

The rules that guide the science of humility spring from all the relations that ought in justice to exist between the soul and God. The first of these relations is the absolute dependence of the creature on her Creator. The second is the relation of the intelligent image of God towards its Divine Original. The third is the relation of justice, which our Divine Redeemer has re-established by His grace between the fallen spirit of man and the sanctifying Spirit of God. The fourth is the relation of human subjection in all things to the divine power, bounty, and supremacy. The fifth is the relation of utter need and want on the part of the soul towards her Divine Illuminator and Provider, who gives to all according to the measure of humility with which they own and confess their wants. The sixth is the relation of humble self-surrender in reverential faith and love to Him who is our Everlasting Good. And the seventh is the relation of gratitude to Him who has given to our native poverty all that we have. There is one unrivalled master in every science, and our Lord Jesus Christ is the Supreme Master of Humility.

But the science of humility is not humility; the science only provides the knowledge and the rules for its exercise. Humility is a virtue, and belongs to practice; it is a divine art or discipline exercised in the deeper regions of the soul; an athletic training of the soul to fundamental sincerity and just bearing towards God and herself; and it implies three things—abstention, endurance, and right action of the spiritual powers, according to the best rules and examples. By this discipline the soul is opened, enlightened, purified, and invigorated to act with freedom in the gifts of God.

Every art and system of discipline has its great schools, which preserve its best traditions, use its best methods, produce its great examples, and send forth its best teachers. The more important and difficult the art or discipline, the greater is the need of maintaining those schools for the general benefit as well as the advantage of their disciples. But the most difficult of all human habits and exercises to understand thoroughly and acquire perfectly is that of humility ; and as the wellbeing of the soul depends on its acquirement, it is the most important. The Church has therefore her great schools of humility in her Monastical and Religious institutions. They may be properly called the schools of the Beatitudes, devoted as they are to the methodical cultivation of the divine counsels that were delivered to mankind by the Son of God. They are founded on the virtues of humility and charity ; their system of training is based upon humility ; and their discipline is perfected in the exercise of that virtue, whose spirit pervades the Beatitudes as it begins with the first of them, and whose true disciples are the choice and privileged portion of the Church of God.

Clearly provided for in the Gospel, anticipated in the schools of the prophets, and traceable in their principle to the apostolic times, these schools of humility took definite shape, form, and expansion so soon as the Church was freed from the pressure of heathen persecution. They were perfected by men of great genius and high sanctity, who reduced the maxims of the perfect life to system and rule, and from these rules of discipline, inspired by the genius of Saints, the great Religious Orders arose in the Church. In the earlier ages of Christianity men and women, of whom the world was not worthy, in their love of God and of justice withdrew from the world, as did the prophets and their disciples, took refuge in solitary places, and there, under the direction of the wisest of their number, obtained great lights on the interior ways of the soul, and a vast experience in the best methods of subjecting the body to the soul and the soul to God. The number of these ardent souls who, in the fervent times of transition from Paganism to Christianity, gave themselves wholly to God was very great ; and their profound experience in the ways of God in souls, their shrewd maxims and heroic examples, preserved with much care, have been a great spiritual light to all subsequent ages. Then St. Basil arose to perfect the form of spiritual life in the East, and St. Benedict in the West, and their rules have been the models of religious discipline to all subsequent ages.

The religious life, matured, like all great things, in solitude and silence after its vigorous and fervid youth had reached a matured constitution, was henceforth called upon to do a great work in the Church of God. Men trained in these schools of humility were placed on the episcopal thrones, and even in the chair of Peter, and became Fathers of the Church and great authorities in the spiritual life. Monasteries spread over the desolated world, and with their spiritual and corporate solidity encountered the barbarous tribes that overthrew the Roman Empire, converted them to Christianity, and replaced the lost civilization of the old world with a new one based wholly on Christian principles; and the old Pagan languages ceased to live that the new ones, imbued with Christian sense and sentiment, might providentially take their place. Thus that spiritual force and discipline that had silently grown to maturity for ages, abiding in the strength of its discipline, reconquered the world to Christ and the Church.

In the thirteenth century, when, through a powerful combination of secular influences, the ministry of the Church had lost much of its spirit and energy, the religious life arose in new forms and restored vigour to the Church. Retaining the spirit and much of the letter of the old monastic discipline, and fed on its traditions, new Orders arose in the Church, who evangelized the people in humility and poverty, or devoted themselves to the revival of sacred learning. These Orders were fertile in saints, as the old ones in their fervour had been, and under their holy guidance many of all classes of the populations took the way of perfect life; and the Third Orders of these great schools of humility became the popular schools of sanctity. In the sixteenth century, when heretical desolation invaded the world in forms that struck at the foundation of all spiritual authority, another combination of the monastical with the clerical life arose to reinvigorate the Church in the various Institutions of Regular Clerics, of which the Society of Jesus was the most conspicuous. They still, however, looked back to those earlier schools of humility, to their spirit, maxims, and examples, and still made humility and obedience the foundation of their discipline, subjecting the whole of life to God.

Hitherto the life of religious women had been wholly secluded from the world, but in the seventeenth century St. Vincent of Paul established the Sisters of Charity, from which time the union of monastical discipline with every kind of active charity in the service of the poor, sick, and ignorant has taken a prodigious expansion among the devoted female sex.

Through all these developments and expansions of the religious life, there is growth, sequence, and adaptation, suited to the requirements of the Church as they arise under new conditions. First, the life given wholly to God was secluded, that its inward spirit might be perfected, and a vast experience might be accumulated of the best methods for the guidance of all the future. Then the rules of religious life were reduced by great and wise saints to what may be called their scientific perfection. Next, at a time of great disorder and confusion, the monasteries, with their corporate strength and discipline, were brought into action to missionarize the world, and restore order and civilization. When secular influences pervaded the Church and wealth brought its many abuses, the life of humility and self-sacrifice arose in a new form, but still in corporate strength, to evangelize the people and to perfect the science of theology in the Dominican and Franciscan Orders. And it is worthy of remark that each of them had special links with the old monastic Order of St. Benedict. When heresy struck at the foundations of faith and authority, and the "new learning" was invented wherewith to put aside the ancient truth—for the criticism of reason was absurdly applied to the authority of divine revelation—St. Ignatius and the other saintly founders of the Regular Clerics united the old religious discipline of humility and obedience with a new order of training, adapted to the apostolic life and the work of Christian education. And here, again, we find a close link between the new and the old, which is thus expressed by Father Alvarez de Paz, one of the most eminent spiritual writers of the Society of Jesus : "St. Benedict, the venerable Patriarch of all holy religious, is in a special way the Holy Father of our Society, for in his most observant monastery of our Lady of Monserrat, our Blessed Father St. Ignatius passed from the service of the world to the service of Christ ".* It is also worthy of remark that that monastery at the time had a special system of Spiritual Exercises, drawn up by a previous abbot, the well-known Cisneros ; although that of St. Ignatius has a special character of its own, and he was the first to popularize the Spiritual Exercises. The purpose of these historical observations is to show

---

* Alvarez de Paz, *Opera*, vol. ii., lib. iv., p. 4, c. 1.

the unity of spirit and tradition which pervades the interior religious life from the earliest to the latest ages.

Finally, after the powers of the world had confiscated or destroyed the old Catholic institutions and provisions for the poor, as well as the monasteries at which they were helped and relieved; after the principles of political economy had supplanted the principle of Christian charity; when money and the distinctions obtainable by money became the ruling passions of the world; when the science of the wealth of nations became the ruling principle of state policy; when systems of mechanical benevolence were substituted for personal charity; when manufactures and commerce with their hard calculating ways opened a yawning gulf between the rich and the poor, and the poor multiplied in numbers and in distress beyond all precedent; then it was that the humble, self-sacrificing life of religion took another shape, and devout women of all ranks gave themselves to God in the severe and heroic life of humility united with active charity.

But all these forms of religious life, however varied in their works, rest on one and the same basis. The three vows are the three forms of self-renunciation that tend to bring the soul to humility and charity. The rules of the great Orders from the third to the seventeenth century have been conveniently brought together in one code; these we have carefully collated, and with them not a few of more recent date, and find them all tending in their chief spiritual provisions to one and the same end of discipline, by the exercise of humility to secure the perfection of every Christian virtue.* Some have a greater and some a less profound apprehension of this spirit; some have a milder and others a stronger discipline; but all have the one aim of subjecting the soul to God with constant reverence and self-sacrifice. But what is striking in all these Orders and Institutes, when we come to examine their spiritual manuals, is the uniform disposition to look back to the maxims and examples bequeathed by the earlier monastic life as most valuable helps in forming the religious life and spirit. Thus the Fathers of the deserts still instruct the religious of both sexes who are combating the evils of the modern world.

If we consider the instruments of religious discipline, poverty gives freedom by removing the world and its concupiscences

---

* Brockie's *Codex Regularum*, enlarging Holstein to 6 vols. folio.

from the soul; purity gives force and elevation to the soul; obedience destroys self-will, which is the root of all sin. Everything receives dignity from its reference to God. Obedience and prayer are direct and immediate exercises of humility, whilst purity of life gives them holiness; for obedience subjects the will to God through the voice of the rule and the superior. Nor is this a capricious authority or obedience, for all is constitutionally regulated; nor can that constitution be changed even in its details without the voice of the governed as well as the voice of authority. Prayer is the subjection of the soul to God in adoration, supplication, and gratitude.

Everywhere within the Church of God humility is exercised, for there can neither be charity nor hope nor faith without this virtue. But there are as many degrees of humility as of sanctity; and as some persons by their natural gifts become skilful artists without the help of schools, so there are not a few souls who, through fidelity to the special help of God, obtain a good degree of humility and sanctity without the training of religious life. For the grace of God is not bound; and sanctity belongs to all states of life that God has ordained, yet always on the same foundation of humility. But when we would learn the higher degrees of its perfection, we naturally go to its great schools or listen to its wisest teachers.

Cassian repeats their instructions when he tells us that the first way to humility is to keep the commandments of God, for this is to subject the will to His eternal law. Then come the divine beatitudes and counsels of Christ, which perfect the subjection of the soul to God. To see this we have only to enumerate them, for they are poverty of spirit, meekness, the mourning over evil and over our distance from God, the hungering and thirsting after justice, mercifulness, cleanness of heart, peacemaking, and the suffering of persecution for justice' sake. Those are nearest to Christ who lead a life of poverty, detachment from the body, and obedience; and the next are they who, though engaged in the secular life, use the world as though they used it not.

Let us hear the great Patriarch of Oriental Monachism demonstrating how all we have lost through pride is recovered by humility. St. Basil says: " If man had but remained in the glory he first received from God, he would have had a true instead of a fictitious elevation; the divine power would have made him apt for this, the divine wisdom would have enlightened him, and he would have delighted in eternal life and all its good. But when he hurried in the quest of something better that could not be, he gave up the desire of divine glory, and lost what he might have had. We can now only recover the ground of our salvation, the healing of our maladies, and the return to our first state by being humble; not by inventing a glory for ourselves, but by seeking the glory of God. We shall thus be corrected in what we have erred, be healed in what we are infirm, and return to the sacred precepts we had left." After proving this at length from the Scriptures, the great founder of the religious life asks: "How are we to get rid of the tumour of pride and come to this health-restoring humility? If we exercise ourselves in those things that express humility, and guard against everything whereby we may encounter loss; for the soul becomes like her pursuits and exercises, and is formed and shaped to what she does." *

In his Rule he replies to the questions: "What is humility? How is it gained? It is to account all others better than yourself, according to the apostolic injunction, and it is gained by reflecting in the first place on the Lord's command: 'Learn of Me, for I am meek and humble of heart'; and in giving faith to the words that 'he who humbleth himself shall be exalted'; and in giving yourself with a steady and determined will to the exercise of humility in whatever you are doing. For what is true of the arts is true of this virtue: thinking will not gain it without practice." † Three more pithy sentences may be added from this Father: "The progress of the soul is the progress of humility. The knowledge of piety is the knowledge of humility and meekness. Humility is the emulation of Christ." ‡

Should some reader be inclined to think that these fundamental truths are too often repeated, though in different forms, he must be requested to reflect on the difference between entertaining the mind and teaching the most difficult of all sciences; and in the following sentences of Father Thanner, the Carthusian, he will find the grave reason for this method. "To reach our object usefully and compendiously we must search after the springs from which this excelling virtue flows; if we come often to them, and by reading and reflecting make them familiar to our

---

* S. Basil, *Hom. de Humilitate.*
† Ibid., *Reg. Brev.*, q. 198.   ‡ Ibid., *Hom. de Renun. Sæculi.*

mind, we shall find humility itself flowing little by little into our soul, and then we shall not neglect to exert ourselves in those acts of humility which the virtue demands."

If there be a stubborn error that is wilfully blind in this sensual world, so ignorant of its own sensuality, it must be in the professing not to know how the humiliation of the body can contribute to the humility of the soul. For this is in direct contradiction to the world's own practice, which, in its corrections, its revenges, and its administration of justice, is constantly afflicting the body to humble and amend the soul. He who has never much reflected on the action of body on soul and soul on body knows little if anything of the discipline of human nature, and less still of the nature of self-discipline. On this subject the shrewd St. Dorotheus has some very pertinent remarks.

. "How," he asks, "is humility of heart obtained through bodily labours? What has corporal labour to do with planting habits and affections in the soul? I will tell you. After the unhappy soul had fallen from her good estate, through transgressing God's commandment, she was given up to various delights, and to all the concupiscences, and was left to her own will and judgment, however erroneous they might be. She then began to love corporal and material things, and became in a manner corporal and carnal. As God said in the Scripture: 'My spirit shall not remain in man for ever, because he is flesh'. For the soul is moved and affected according to what is done and felt in the body. Hence an old man among us used to say that corporal labour leads straight to humility. For the soul is moved and affected one way in health and another in sickness: one way in hunger and another when the body is filled with food. The man who rides a horse feels very differently from the man who plods along on an ass; and he who sits on a throne has a disposition of soul altogether different from him who sits on the ground. He who is clothed in soft, beautiful, and precious garments cannot feel like the man who is begirt with rags and patches. Labour humiliates the body and brings down its pride, and when the body is humiliated the soul is humbled. So the old man justly said that bodily labour brings the soul to humility. . . . And humility frees the man from the greatest evils, and protects him from many and great temptations." *

* S. Dorotheus, *Disciplina* 2ª *ad finem.*

This instruction is gradually leading us on to the practical degrees of humility, and therefore what we have at present to keep in mind is that it is not merely a special but a universal virtue, entering into the composition of all Christian virtue. This is clearly put by St. Thomas in his masterly analysis of the virtues. He observes that though the theological virtues stand higher in dignity, because they command and direct the other virtues from an elevation, yet in this essential respect humility is the most noble, important, and first of the virtues, that the others have each of them but one essential object on which it is exercised, whilst humility has the task of submitting the soul to the whole order of truth, right reason, and justice, and to every good and pious inspiration of grace.* We shall not cease to repeat that the whole labour of virtue is in humility, and that the reward of humility is charity. "If we labour at the first," says St. Augustine, "God will bring us to the last." And now listen once more to St. Laurence Justinian : "When humility shall have filled, brought down, and melted the soul, then shall she begin to be enlarged with charity, irradiated with truth, filled with light, and raised in spirit ".†

This brings us to the question of the right method of building up the soul. We constantly use the word *edification* without much consciousness that it refers to the art of construction. "You are God's building," says St. Paul : "according to the grace of God, which is given to me, as a wise architect, I have laid the foundation, and another buildeth thereupon. But let every man take heed how he buildeth thereupon ; for other foundation no man can lay but that which is laid, which is Christ Jesus."‡ The virtues are the materials of the building, and humility the jointing of every part. How shall we build a temple to the living God on this foundation ? We shall find no better guidance in this work than St. Dorotheus gives us in his admirable discourse on the harmonious building up of the soul.

A man, he says, should take heed to every part of his soul, that the whole edifice may rise together in fit and due proportion. This the venerable Abbot John was wont to say : Give me the man who is constantly adding a little from every virtue, and not

* S. Thomas, *Sum.* ii. 2, q. 161, a. 5.
† S. Laurent. Justin., *Lignum Vitæ, de Humilitate,* c. i.
‡ 1 *Corinthians* iii. 9-11.

the man, of whom there are so many, who is always insisting on one virtue to the neglect of the rest. He gains some mastery perhaps in that one, and feels no conflict from the opposite vice; yet is led away by other passions to which he gives no heed. This is like building a single wall, with no thought beyond making it as high as possible, never dreaming that the first strong wind will bring it to the ground. It is neither bonded nor supported by other walls. No man can put a roof on a single wall; he must wait till the rest are built. This is no sound way of building. Let him who would build and roof his house raise it all up together, and make it as strong and firm as he can. This is the true way of building that St. Paul recommends, that, "doing the truth in charity, we may in all things grow up in Him who is the Head, even Christ: from whom the whole body being compacted and fitly joined together, by what every joint supplieth, according to the operation in the measure of every part, maketh increase of the body unto the edifying of itself in charity." * Mark well that all through the construction there must be truth, jointing of materials, and charity; for humility and charity are universal elements.

We lay the first foundation of faith in the open foundation of humility. Obedience comes to hand. Put in the stone of obedience. Some one is moved to anger with you. Put in the stone of patience. Whatever virtue the order of Providence brings to hand, take a stone from it and place it on the building, raising it all round with steady perseverance. Here a stone of meekness, there a stone of mortified will; here a stone of mercy, there a stone of some other virtue. But look well and carefully to patience and magnanimity, for these are the angels that bind wall to wall and brace the whole building. See also that they neither start nor shrink from each other, for without this you cannot perfect a single virtue. Without some fortitude the soul will endure nothing, nor build what can endure. Hence our Lord says: "In patience you shall possess your soul".+

But the builder must set every stone in a bed of mortar from top to bottom and all through the structure; for unless each stone has its bed, there will be nothing solid and secure. This mortar of the earth on which men tread is humility, tempered with the waters of compunction. Thus the whole building rests on humi-

* *Ephesians* iv. 15, 16.   † *S. Luke* xxi. 19.

lity, and every part of it is couched in humility. For, continues St. Dorotheus, the Fathers say that without humility no virtue is a virtue. And this was the judgment of them all, that it is as impossible to save a soul without humility as to build a ship without nails. Whatever good a soul would do, let her do it with humility, or the labour is lost. The house must also have its beams and its mouldings for increase of strength, for division into compartments, for binding the edifice together, and for ornament. But the roof is charity, which perfects the virtues as the roof completes the house. And round the roof must be a battlement, as prescribed in Deuteronomy : " When thou buildest a new house, thou shalt make a battlement to the roof round about; lest blood be shed in thy house, and thou be guilty, if any one slip and fall down headlong ".* This battlement, again, is humility, crowning and guarding all the virtues and giving them perfection. For the progress of all the saints is through their access to greater humility ; and the closer a man adheres to God the more clearly he will know and the more openly confess that he is a child of sin. But what are these little ones for whom the law provides that they fall not headlong? These are the new-born progeny of our mind, to be kept within the custody of humility lest they fall ; and this guarding of the little ones is per-fect virtue.

The building will now be complete, provided it has had a wise and skilful builder who really understands his work. But it not unfrequently happens that the builder is without knowledge, and undoes with one hand what he does with the other. Like a bungler, he pushes one stone down whilst putting up another, and is so awkward at times, that in setting up one stone he will pull down two. For example, some one hits you with a sharp word ; you take it silently and bear it patiently. Presently you meet a friend ; you tell him how you have been insulted ; you warm upon it, exaggerate the fact, and conclude by saying how patient and silent you were. Don't you see that in putting up one stone you have pulled down two? Another gets some deserved rebuke, and bears it for the credit it will do him. This one cannot dis-tinguish between humility and vainglory ; he pulls down the very stone he is putting up. Another receives rebuke, but without

* *Deuteronomy* xxii. 8. Houses in the East have flat roofs, and the roof is the family resort in the cool of the evening.

knowledge, for he thinks that all that is required is silence, and forgets to submit his heart. But another will even magnify himself in secret, and fancy he is doing great things in bearing rebuke, and that he is very humble withal. Unhappy man! he acts without knowledge, not understanding that he is nothing. Had he reflected in the truth, and reflected justly, his very temptation would have shown him his nothingness.

One has the care of a sick brother, but he does it for some end of his own. This is no wise service. To serve the sick wisely is to do it in loving compassion and with tender kindness. For when we act from mercy we feel nothing to be a difficulty or a trouble. One who acts from this motive believes that the sick man does him more service than he is doing the sick man.

Nor would I have you ignorant of this, that whoever devotes himself to the sick and suffering from right motives will be wonderfully freed from the passions of the soul and the attacks of the devil. Some have been freed from painful and humiliating illusions by assiduously serving those afflicted with sickness; and as the old man Maximus told Evagrius, there is nothing so effectual against passions of this kind as the doing of mercy. Our fathers also, and those before them, were strongly impressed with the conviction that bodily labours, undertaken with right intention, are the certain way to humility. Let every man, in short, so build the virtues into his soul as to consolidate them into habits, and he will be a wise builder.

But whoever would complete his work must beware of thinking that perfect virtue is too high for him to reach. This is to give up confidence in the divine help, and to become drowsy and stupid. If we do what is demanded of us, no grace will be wanting to our prayer; if we exert the will, we shall have the power. It is written: "Thou shalt love thy neighbour as thyself". Stand not on your distance from this virtue, or you will begin to say: "How can I love my neighbour as myself? How can I enter into his feelings and sorrows? They are hidden in his heart; how can I feel them as my own?" If you take to this fashion of thinking, you will imagine the virtue impracticable. Trust in God, and begin as you can. Open to Him your desire, and you will soon feel that His help has come to you.

Imagine you are between two ladders, one of which ascends to Heaven, the other goes down to the infernal abyss. You may say:

"How can I fly to the top of this ladder?" But if God had intended you to do so He would have given you wings. Your first care is not to slip down below; don't injure your neighbour; don't revile him; don't despise him. Respect him; reverence him; and you will begin to do him good. Speak kindly to him; be gentle with him; compassionate his sorrows; and when he has need of you, you will serve him; when he is in want of what you have, you will give it to him; and by degrees you will reach to the top of the ladder that rests in Heaven. From the first little help you will come in the end to wish the same happiness to your neighbours that you wish yourself. You will get as far as this if you choose to try. And if you humbly ask God's help, that help will quickly come. For He says: "Ask and you shall receive: seek, and you shall find: knock and it shall be opened to you". We ask when we pray to God for help; we seek when we look out for occasions of virtue; we knock when we put our hand to the work. He, then, who works with knowledge and skill is the wise architect who builds securely. And our Lord has called him "the wise builder who founds his house upon a rock," that the assaults of his enemies can neither injure nor disturb.*

This ample explanation will enable you to see how humility works through all the virtues, yet not unless this virtue be itself the object of special attention and careful cultivation. Once make a good fire and everything combustible will feed it. Once get a good fouudation of humility, and every virtue that it receives will increase its power. Where a good soil has been well opened out and the heavens are propitious, you may grow any fruit in it; but to humility the heavens are always propitious. For the God of Heaven loves truth, and humility is the truth that makes the man true. The God of Heaven loves justice, and humility is the justice that makes the man just. The God of Heaven loves order, and humility is the moral ordering of the soul. The God of Heaven loves to see a soul that is open to His benefits, and humility opens the soul. The God of Heaven loves to see all things in their due place, and humility gives the soul her right place before Him. The God of Heaven loves to perfect whatever is in a condition to be perfected, and He is able from their condition to perfect the souls of the humble.

* S. Dorotheus, *Disciplina* 14, *De Ædificio, sive Concordia Virtutum Animæ*.

It remains to consider the degrees of humility, and the methods by which they are reached. Those degrees are the successive steps by which a soul advances from her first self-renunciation and conversion to God into greater self-renunciation and subjection to God, until she is able to say with St. Paul: "I live no more, but Christ lives in me".* And with the same Apostle: "Your life is hidden with Christ in God".† Whither shall we go for this instruction but to the great schools of humility which have filled Heaven with saints? But as there are many such schools, each with its own methods, though all have one basis, it will serve no purpose to perplex you with a great diversity of methods, and we shall do best to take the one which takes the largest view, which has exercised the widest influence, and from which the others have derived not a little of their tradition. This will bring us to the celebrated twelve degrees of St. Benedict, which we must put in a more popular way, and with due explanations. The Rule of St. Benedict was drawn up towards the close of the fifth century, but the twelve degrees of humility have an earlier history. St. Benedict drew largely, but with great judgment, from Cassian and St. Basil, who incorporated in their Rules the earlier traditions of the great Eastern saints.

The twelve degrees of humility, which form the 7th chapter of St. Benedict's Rule, are an expansion of the ten signs of the progress of humility contained in the Institutes of Cassian, which he declares he heard delivered in Egypt by the famous Abbot Pynuphius, the history of whose wonderful humility he has recorded.‡ These twelve degrees of St. Benedict have been contrasted by St. Bernard in a special treatise with the twelve degrees of pride; and St. Thomas has scientifically vindicated the sufficiency of St. Benedict's twelve degrees in his Sum of Theology. § The comments written upon them are very numerous.

We must first make three observations of great importance for understanding the twelve degrees. Humility in practice has a negative as well as a positive side. The negative side is self-renunciation, the positive side is the subjection of the soul to God. As Cassian says, after St. Dorotheus, there can be no humility without self-renunciation. We must give up ourselves, and then

---

* *Galatians* ii. 20.   † *Colossians* iii. 3.
‡ Cassian, *De Institutis*, lib. iv., c. 39.
§ S. Thomas, *Sum.* ii. 2, q. 191, a. 6.

give ourselves up with great reverence to God. " Empty yourself, and see that I am God." * Humility must therefore be thought of and acted upon in these two respects. For our second observation what has been already said in this lecture is a preparation. Humility acts not alone, but employs other virtues as instruments for its attainment. This fact will explain why St. Benedict in his twelve degrees introduces other virtues as means for gaining this virtue. As there is nothing isolated in life, there is nothing isolated in virtue, but one works with the other. Hence the remark of St. Basil that all the virtues contribute to humility, though some contribute so much more to its formation and perfection than others, that they may be considered as its special instruments, such as the fear of God and obedience from the heart. The third observation is this, that external conduct, when sincere, emanates from the internal habits of the soul, and gives expression to them ; whilst external reserve and self-control react in their turn in producing internal reserve and solidity of soul. If these observations are kept in view they will greatly facilitate the understanding of the twelve degrees, of which, as St. Thomas observes, some belong to the root of humility, some to its essence, and some to its effects.

FIRST DEGREE.—The first degree of humility is the fear of God. This fear springs from the sense of God and of one's self. It is awakened in the soul by the entrance of divine light, giving us to see what we are in the presence of our Almighty Creator, and showing how unfaithful we have been to His divine law, and how unclean and far removed from Him we are. Then is the soul penetrated and stirred with the fear of God, with the sense of her responsibility, and the dread of His judgments. This fear humbles the soul, awakens the sense of shame in her, and fills her with confusion. She begins to sigh over her miseries, to hate her sins and vanities, and to supplicate the mercy of God.

The more the sense of the goodness of God and of His displeasure grows upon the soul, the more is she humbled down in the sense of her own unworthiness, and is pierced with the thorns of compunction, as though they came from the wounded brow of her Divine Lover and Redeemer to penetrate her heart with the bitterness of self-reproach. The Cross stands before the

* *Psalm* xlv 11.

humbled spirit, and the Divine Victim of her sins, with bleeding arms expanded on its wood, seems to look through His tears into her heart, awakening the movements of repentance with His grace, the tears of contrition, the desires of deeper repentance, and the hope of pardon. This fear generates humility, humility opens the soul, the opened soul receives the grace of repentance, repentance increases humility, humility obtains pardon, and pardon brings the grace of charity and the love of God's commandments. Then servile fear is changed into the chaste fear of God, as of a child for a father who has loved him exceedingly ; and this chaste, loving, and most reverential fear is the fruit of a more advanced humility.

Then the soul becomes grateful, and desires to be faithful, and is watchful of two things—to keep in the presence of God and to keep His commandments in His presence. She knows that in the divine presence she is safe, and that if her heart watches to God He will watch over her. She begins to find light, solace, and protection in that presence, and by degrees begins to suffer when the sense of that presence is lost, as though it were the loss of the sense of life. "God liveth, in whose sight I stand." * And not only knowing but feeling that "in Him we live, and move, and have our being,"† and that He beholds our thoughts and acts at all times and in all places, and is "the God who searcheth our hearts and reins," that soul lives in lowly-hearted reverence before Him, and is ready to say : "Then shall I be without stain, if sins have no dominion over me". ‡

SECOND DEGREE.—The second degree of humility is the renouncing of our own will and desires, that we may be conformable to the divine will. We thus imitate our Divine Lord, who says : "I came not to do My own will, but the will of Him who sent Me ". § After fear has humbled, purified, and subjected us to God in the observance of the commandments, the next step is to perfect our submission to God ; and as the will is sovereign of the man, this is accomplished by the complete subjection of our will to the will of God. But this subjection implies the giving up our own wayward will and fantastical desires that the wisdom of God may rule us ; for self-will is the product of self-love, and the cause of all pride, sinfulness, folly, and vanity. Take away self-

* 4 *Kings* v. 16.   † *Acts* xvii. 28.
‡ *Psalm* xviii. 14.   § S. *John* vi. 38.

will and you take away all evil. Why, then, did God give us this will? He gave us our free-will, but not our self-will; this *self* is the addition we have made to it, and was first inspired by the devil when he said: "Ye shall be as gods".* Our free-will was given us that we might use it magnificently, by uniting it with the truth, the will, the wisdom, and the goodness of God; and might partake of the good that is in the divine will in proportion to the humility and love with which we do His will.

Our own will hath pain, brings confusion, and fails in the end, for it is always crossed by the eternal will of God, which alone will be accomplished in the end. "I am God," says the Almighty; "My counsel shall stand, and all My will shall be done." † Wherefore our Lord has told us for our example: "My meat is to do the will of Him who sent Me";‡ and He gave us a form of prayer for our constant use in which to express the conformity of our will with the divine will: "Thy will be done on earth as it is in Heaven";§ and every faithful Christian, by the title of that prayer which he so often repeats, ought to submit his will with all humility of heart to the all-perfect will of God, and that in all in which the divine will is known to him. But the will of God is so great a good that we ought to seek the knowledge of it in every way that we can, in His truth, in His commandments, in His holy counsels, in prayer, in the inspirations of conscience, in the voice of superiors, in the advice of the wise and prudent, and in the course and order of His providence.

THIRD DEGREE.—The third degree of humility is to obey our superiors for the love of God, imitating our Lord, of whom the Apostle says: "He was made obedient, even unto death". ‖ The interior subjection of the will to God is thus perfected by exterior subjection to the authorities whom God has appointed to manifest His will, that interior subjection may come to expression in exterior obedience. For, as St. Thomas observes, a man comes to humility through two means; first and principally through the gift of grace, in which respect the interior precedes the exterior. But in another respect humility is obtained by labour and effort, which restrains the exterior, and masters whatever resists humility, thus acting from the exterior upon the interior, and so extirpating the interior root of pride. And it is upon this order of acting

---

* *Genesis* iii. 5.   † *Isaias* xlvi. 9, 10.   ‡ *S. John* iv. 34.
§ *S. Matthew* vi. 10.   ‖ *Philippians* ii. 8.

from the exterior upon the interior that St. Benedict arranges the degrees of progress in humility.*

God has ordained authority and obedience in many forms—in the family, in the government of society, in employment, in the Church, and in religion; and this order of things is divinely ordained for many reasons—to preserve us from self-love and pride in judging and deciding in our own case; to place the will under the guidance of those who are wiser and more experienced; to preserve order and subordination; to secure unity in life and in religion; to repair that disobedience by which we have fallen through listening to the external tempter; and, above all, to secure our interior humility and submission to God through the habit of obeying Him in His representatives.

The beautiful chapter of St. Benedict's Rule which treats on obedience opens with the declaration that the first degree of humility is prompt obedience in the fear of God; but in the twelve degrees he places obedience in the third degree. How is this to be reconciled? Very simply. The first degree is the fear of God, and, in the chapter on obedience, obedience is placed under the motive of fear, which brings it under the first degree; but in the twelve degrees it is placed under the motive of the love of God, which advances it from the first to the third degree; for the perfect subjection of humble obedience proceeds from charity. This obedience consummates that interior subjection to God in being prompt to do His will, whether internally, externally, or however manifested.

Humility generates obedience from the heart, and charity makes it prompt and loyal, looking ever to the divine will as its first and ruling motive; but the disobedient one is a proud and ungovernable person, wounded by Lucifer. Speaking of religious obedience St. Basil says: "Rebellion and contradiction argue the presence of many evils—a faith that is diseased, a hope that is dubious, a pride and haughtiness of manners. Whoever detracts from authority has first despised the Author of good counsel; but whoever believes the promises of God, and puts his hope in them, will not be sluggish to obey, even though the command be hard and difficult. For he knows that the sufferings of this time are not to compared with the coming glory that shall be revealed. And he who is convinced that whoever humbles himself

---

* St. Thomas, *Sum.* ii. 2, q. 161, a. 6.

shall be exalted, will show greater swiftness to obey than the superior looks for, because he knows that the present light and momentary trial will bring an eternal weight of glory." *

FOURTH DEGREE.—The fourth degree of humility unites obedience with fortitude and patience. It is the humility that obeys in things hard and difficult to nature, and that silently clings to patience even when the obedient have to suffer insults and injuries, so as to endure and persevere without being discouraged. Such a one will remember what the Scripture says, that "he who perseveres to the end shall be saved ";+ and that other Scripture, "Let thy heart be strengthened, and await the Lord ". ‡ And to show how the faithful soul ought to endure all things for the love of God, the Sacred Scripture speaks in the person of the sufferer : "For Thy sake we are put to death all the day ; we are accounted as sheep for the slaughter ".§ Such was the patient obedience of the Apostles, Martyrs, and all the Confessors of God. Secure of the hope of divine repayment, they followed on, rejoicing and saying : "In all these things we overcome for the sake of Him who loved us ". ‖ And in another place of Holy Scripture we hear them saying : "Thou hast proved us, O Lord, and hast tried us, as silver is tried in the fire ".¶

This patient obedience under every difficulty exalts humility into the grandeur and strength of magnanimity, and gives an heroic greatness to the soul, growing ever more humble, simple, and patient under growing trials. True patience and tranquillity, says Abbot Pramon in the Conferences, is neither obtained nor upheld without profound humility of heart. If it descends from this fountain it will not require to be protected by your chamber nor by solitude ; for what proceeds from humility is supported by that inward generator and protector of its force, and asks for no protection from any external thing. But if we yield to another's provocation, it is certain that the foundations of humility are not firmly laid in us, and a small storm will expose our structure to ruin. Patience would never be worth praise or admiration if its tranquillity had never to encounter adversaries ; but it becomes resplendent and glorious when it abides unmoved amidst a tempest of provocations. Who knows not that patience is the

---

* S. Basil, *Regulæ fusius tractatæ,* q. 28.
+ *S. Matthew* xxiv. 16.   ‡ *Psalm* xxvi. 14.
§ *Romans* viii. 36.   ‖ *Romans* viii. 37.   ¶ *Psalm* lxv. 10.

calm enduring of assaults from passion? No one, then, is entitled to be called patient who cannot endure the inflictions of passion without indignation. Hence Solomon has said that "the patient man is better than the valiant, and he that ruleth his spirit than he who taketh cities ".* And again: " He that is patient is governed with much wisdom; but he that is impatient exalteth his folly ".† When, therefore, a man is so much vanquished by injury as to kindle with the fire of anger, we must not ascribe his sin to the bitterness of that injury, but must take it as the manifestation of his own inward weakness. This was expressed in our Saviour's parable of the two houses, of which one was founded on the rock and the other on sand. On both of them alike the rain fell, and the floods came, and the winds blew, and they beat upon those houses, but the one founded solidly on the rock suffered no injury from all this violence, whilst the one built on the shifting sands fell down, and great was the ruin thereof. ‡ The humility from which this patient and magnanimous obedience is generated is invincible, beeause it rests not on self but on God.

FIFTH DEGREE.—The fifth degree of humility consists in the manifestation of the evil thoughts that come to the heart, and the evil acts committed in secret. The Sacred Scripture exhorts us to this: "Make known thy way to the Lord, and hope in Him ".§ And again: "Confess to the Lord, because He is good, because His mercy abideth for ever ".‖ And the Psalmist says to God: "I have acknowledged my sin to Thee, and my injustice I have not concealed. I said, I will confess against myself my injustice to the Lord; and Thou hast forgiven the wickedness of my sin ".¶ Pride closes up the soul with all her wounds, evils, and temptations, ignoring them, excusing them, or concealing them, even from one's self, and leaving them to fester and ferment together in their death-dealing corruption. Nay, there is a pride so great as to profess to be more shocked at the confession of shameful things, that the heart may be relieved of them, than at the actual committing of them, and the burying of them for ever in the guilty breast. But sincere humility opens the soul, examines what is within, and in her love of justice can keep nothing there

---

* *Proverbs* xvi. 32.   † *Proverbs* xiv. 29.
‡ *S. Matthew* vii. 24-27; Cassian, *Collatio* 18, c. 13.
§ *Psalm* xxxvi. 5.   ‖ *Psalm* cv. 1.   ¶ *Psalm* xxxi. 5.

closed up that is an offence to God, or that contradicts His voice speaking against it in the conscience, but is ever ready to do all that can be done to make atonement, and to punish that self-love which caused the evil. Humility cannot endure that there should be a stain of known sin that is not purged away by confession and repentance.

God knows all, but He would have the sinner to know his guiltiness, to set his iniquity before his face, to humble himself in his delinquency, to confess with shame and sorrow the evil he has done with shameless delight, and to uncover his wounds to the healing blood of Christ, that God may remember them no more. Divine is the remedy of humble confession: divine in its wonderful adaptation to the needs of our weak nature, and divine in its healing power. As in His providence God has provided medicines and surgery for the infirmities and wounds of the mortal body, in His grace He has provided spiritual medicines and surgery for the remedy of the immortal soul. In both cases the man stands in need of a physician, of one who shall examine his case, judge where he is himself incapable of judging, apply the true remedy, and give prudent advice for the future. We first open our soul to God in humility, and then to the physician who bears the remedies of Christ. "Pour out thy heart like water in the sight of the Lord thy God," says the Prophet Jeremias.* "Go show yourselves to the priests," said our Lord to the lepers, "and as they went they were made clean." † "Confess your sins one to another," says St. James, "and pray for one another, that you may be saved." ‡ "If we confess our sins," says St. John, "He is faithful and just to forgive us our sins, and to cleanse us from all iniquity." § Christ has established His tribunals on the earth, to which we freely summon ourselves at the call of conscience; and at which we are our own accusers and witnesses, our own judges, and our own punishers, that, judging ourselves now, we may not be judged hereafter.

There is another mode of manifesting our thoughts and evil inclinations, to which even the children of this world sometimes have recourse, and to which St. Benedict especially refers in this degree; and that is when we find it difficult to manage our own internal troubles without some wise, prudent, and paternal advice.

---

* *Lamentations* ii. 19.　　　† *S. Luke* xvii. 14
‡ *S. James* v. 16.　　　§ *S. John* i. 9.

The very opening of such difficulties is often their solution; for what we bring to open manifestation is much more clearly seen and understood, even by ourselves, when opened out to the calm judgment of another whose virtues we reverence. The very process of humbly opening our mind to a wise, prudent, and sympathizing heart brings light and clearer judgment to ourselves; and we become strengthened and decided by the wise counsel and prudent advice of one who judges without the bias of our own preconceptions and feelings. And when he to whom we open our heart is a man of God, we fail not to obtain some special light and benefit from his wisdom and experience.

SIXTH DEGREE.—The sixth degree of humility is when a man bears all abjection and contempt with an equable and willing mind, and when in all the labours and duties of his state or calling he accounts himself to be an unprofitable workman. This our Lord has commanded: "When you shall have done all these things that are commanded you, say: We are unprofitable servants; we have done that which we ought to do".* And the Psalmist says to God of his own vileness: "I was brought to nothing, and I knew it not; I am become as a beast of burden before Thee, and I am always with Thee".† We have ideal forms in the light of our mind of what is good and perfect, and when we compare our performances with those ideal patterns, we see how far we come short of them in our spirit, life, and works. This light showing us better things than any that we do is given us not only as the measure of good, but also that by seeing how far we fall short of its perfection we may keep ourselves humble. By comparing ourselves with what shines to us of the light of justice we see our vileness, and by comparing our works with their perfect forms in the mind we see their failings. As we owe all things to God, we owe our whole duty to God; but duty is debt; who, then, is entitled to boast that he has done his duty? The servant who does nothing beyond what his lord commands him to do is but an indifferent servant; but when we do what God commands us to do, we have only given Him His own, and we find so many faults and shortcomings in our work, that we have much reason to be humbled and ashamed.

Then, as our Lord tells us: "Without Me you can do nothing";‡ and whatever good we have or do, we must say

---

* *S. Luke* xvii. 10.　　† *Psalm* lxxii. 22, 23.　　‡ *S. John* xv. 5.

with St. Paul: "By the grace of God, I am what I am"; * and
"We are not sufficient to think anything of ourselves, as of our- •
selves, but our sufficiency is from God ". † Plainly, then, can we
ascribe no good to ourselves, but only our defects from grace,
and even our defects from nature in the evils that we do. In
the view of all this truth and of our many ingratitudes, both
truth and justice require that we consider ourselves useless and
unworthy servants, and account ourselves vile and worthy of
contempt. But if this be the true judgment that we form of
ourselves, and not a mere fashion of speaking, how can we in
justice refuse to accept the treatment that accords with this
judgment.

SEVENTH DEGREE.—The seventh degree of humility is to
account one's self lower and viler than all, not merely in words,
but in the innermost belief and affection of our heart, saying
in all humility, with the Psalmist: "It is good that Thou hast
humbled me, that I may learn Thy justification". ‡ The soul
that knows herself has an intuition of the secrets of her nature
and of her heart that are only known to God and herself; and
this knowledge she cannot have of any one but herself. The
further she enters into this knowledge of herself the more fully
she sees that without God she is nothing; and ascribing whatever she sees good in herself to God, she judges herself by what
she sees is not of God, but of herself; and all she sees of this
kind is but failure and deficiency. But she can have no such
perception or experience of any other soul than her own. She
cannot, therefore, judge another as she can herself. She sees
another's exterior, but her own interior. When it comes to the
question of human weakness, vileness, and unworthiness before
God, we must judge the soul by all her lights received and graces
given, and providential helps bestowed from first to last, and from
the whole history of their use or abuse; yet all this is a secret history,
known only between that soul and God; and knowing so much
in our own case and so little in that of any other, upon the known
evidence we can only pronounce that we are the weakest of the
weak, the vilest of the vile, and most ungrateful of the ungrateful.
And when we see another sin openly, we may say in perfect justice with St. Francis: "Had he the graces and advantages that I
have received, he would have been a saint; and had I received

* 1 *Corinthians* xx. 10.　† 2 *Corinthians* iii. 5.　‡ *Psalm* cxviii. 71.

no more than he has received, I should have been a far greater
sinner than he ".

In this profound view of himself St. Paul called himself " the
least of Apostles, not worthy to be called an Apostle ".* In
this profound view of himself David called himself "the reproach of men and the outcast of the people"; † and holy Job
exclaimed : " I am brought to nothing ".‡

Yet this deep sense of one's own nothingness brings no discouragement; on the contrary, whilst producing a great mistrust
of one's self, it fills the soul with confidence in God. For this
light of humility makes it clearly seen that though we can do
nothing of ourselves that is worthy of God, God can and will
do everything in us the moment we surrender ourselves to Him;
for what is required is to renounce one's self as a foundation of
good, and to rest in confidence on God as our foundation. For
He who has given Himself for us will give us all things. Wherefore, whilst we despise ourselves we rejoice in God; and ceasing
to live to ourselves, we live to God. And so, as St. Benedict
says, this descent is a kind of ascent, for whilst we descend into
ourselves by humility we ascend to God by charity. We exalt
not ourselves, but leave God to exalt us, whose prerogative it is
to raise up the poor from the dust; as our most humble and
exalted Lord has said : " Every one who exalteth himself shall
be humbled, and he who humbleth himself shall be exalted ". §

So far is thorough humility from making us weak or little-souled,
that it makes us courageous and great-souled to do great things
for God's service, yet on God's strength and not on our weakness.
This has been well expressed by St. Bernard. " The prerogative of divine grace," he says, " works in the hearts of the elect, so
that humility does not make them pusillanimous, nor magnanimity
arrogant; but humility and magnanimity work together, so that
magnanimity causes no elation, but works with humility, increasing the filial fear of God in the soul, and her gratitude to the
Giver of her gifts. Humility, on the other hand, gives no occasion to pusillanimity, for the less the soul presumes on herself
the more fully she trusts to the divine power, and that even in
the greatest things." ||

* 1 *Corinthians* xv. 9.   † *Psalm* xxi. 7.
‡ *Job* xvi. 8.   § *S. Luke* xviii. 14.
|| S. Bernard, *Serm. infra Octav. Assumpt. B. V. M.*, n. 13.

To sum up this degree in the words of Albert the Great, the true lover of humility should plant its root in his heart, and know his frailty, not only feeling how vile he is, but how vile he might become unless God withheld him by His power from sin and from many temptations. For each one may know this of himself, that by nature he is inclined to the abyss and whirlpool of the vices; according to that of the Prophet Micheas: "Thy humiliation is in the midst of thee ". *

EIGHTH DEGREE.—The eighth degree of humility is to do nothing against the rule or the example of the Fathers. That is, in its full acceptation, that we do nothing either against the preaching of the Gospel, or the doctrine and discipline of the Church, or against the rule belonging to our state of life ; for in all this we have the manifestation of the will of God. As Tertullian told the Pagan authorities of the Roman Empire : "All Christians are religious of the Cross" ; † and St. Paul exhorts us : "That we may be of the same mind, let us also continue in the same rule " ; ‡ and after exhibiting the rule of faith and piety to the Galatians, the Apostle says : " Whosoever shall follow this rule, peace on them, and mercy, and upon the Israel of God ". §

Humility also requires for its perfection that we prefer the common rule, observance, prayer, or duty, as the manifest will of God, to everything of our own private choice or inclination ; for the whole discipline of humility is directed against self-will and self-love, and to the preferring of the sense and will of God to our own, and this is plainly manifested in the common rule of duty and charity. Solomon says that " brother helped of brother is as a strong city " ; and our Lord has blessed the spirit of common duty in a special way, saying : " Where two or three are gathered together in My name, there I am in the midst of them ". ‖   Then it should be remembered that God has condemned those sacrifices in which self-will is found.

The four last degrees proceed from the interior to the exterior, whose careful control protects and fosters the interior spirit of humility and ministers to edification.

NINTH DEGREE.—The ninth degree of humility is to refrain the tongue and moderate its licence. For the Scripture says :

---

* Albertus Magnus, *De Virtutibus*, c. ii.
† Tertullian, *Apologia*, c. xvi.   ‡ *Philippians* iii. 16.
§ *Galatians* vi. 16.   ‖ *S. Matthew* xviii. 20.

" In the multitude of words there shall not want sin; but he that refraineth his lips is most wise ";* and that "a man full of tongue shall not be established on the earth ". † And the Psalmist says again : " I said : I will take heed to my ways, that I sin not with my tongue : I have set a guard to my mouth ". ‡

TENTH DEGREE.—The tenth degree of humility is not to be dissolute or prone to laughter, or to give the reins to levity; mindful of the sentence that "a fool lifteth up his voice in laughter, but a wise man will scarce laugh low to himself". §

ELEVENTH DEGREE.—The eleventh degree of humility is to speak with gentleness and without laughter, humbly and with gravity, in few words, seasoned with the salt of prudence; not clamorously, but in a submissive tone; mindful of those divine counsels : "Speak not anything rashly, and let not thy heart be hasty to utter a word before God. For God is in Heaven, and thou upon earth; therefore let thy words be few." ‖   "The words of the mouth of a wise man are grace; but the lips of a fool shall throw him down headlong;" ¶ and "A man wise in words shall make himself beloved ". **   "The lips of the unwise will be telling foolish things; but the words of the wise shall be weighed in a balance." ††

TWELFTH DEGREE.—The twelfth degree of humility is to be humble not only in heart, but in our whole exterior conduct, and in all times and places, that we may say with David : "Lord, my heart is not exalted, nor my eyes lofty; neither have I walked in great things above myself" ; ‡‡ and that we may fulfil the admonition of the Apostle : "Let your modesty be known to all men ". §§

To the twelve degrees we must add what St. Bonaventure calls the humility of the perfect.   He who has this last degree of humility, however great his virtues may be, however high his gifts, however distinguished his honours, is in nothing lifted up, and takes nothing of them to himself in flattery; he gives all back to God, restores all to Him from whom every good flows.   Such was the humility of our Blessed Lord, "who thought it no robbery to be equal to God, but emptied Himself," always referring all

---

* *Proverbs* x. 19.
‡ *Psalm* xxxviii. 1, 2.
‖ *Ecclesiastes* v. 1.
** *Ecclesiastes* xx. 13.
‡‡ *Psalm* cxxx. 1, 2.

† *Psalm* cxxxix. 12.
§ *Ecclesiastes* xxi. 23.
¶ *Ecclesiastes* x. 12.
†† *Ecclesiastes* xxi. 28.
§§ *Philippians* iv. 5.

things to His Father. Such was the humility of the Blessed
Virgin, who knew she was the chosen Mother of God, but only
called herself His lowly servant. " He hath looked down upon the
lowliness of His handmaid." Such is the humility of the angels
and saints in glory, who, raised to supreme honour and filled with
supreme good, have no movement of pride in them, but are the
more humble the higher they are in God. This is the humility
of the perfect, who, the greater they are the more humble they
become in all things, in their sense, their affections, their words,
their acts, and their habits. *

When a soul has ascended all these degrees of humility, concludes St. Benedict, she will come at once to that charity of God
which casts out fear, and through that charity all that she for-
merly observed, not without the sense of fear, she will now begin
to do without labour, as it were naturally, and with the ease
of custom, no longer from the fear of punishment, but for the
love of Christ, and from good custom and delight in the virtues.
This will the Lord deign to show to His workman, now clean
from vice and sin, through His Holy Spirit. †

* S. Bonaventura, *De Profectu Religioso*, lib. ii., c. 33.
† S. Benedict, *Regula*, c. vii.

LECTURE XVI.

ON HUMILITY AS THE COUNTERPART OF CHARITY.

"God is charity: and he who abideth in charity, abideth in God, and God in him."—1 St. John iv. 16.

IT is to be regretted that the necessity of language compels us to apply one and the same term to things so remote from each other and so contradictory of each other as charity and cupidity; for we have to explain both by the word *love*, and to say that charity is the love of God and cupidity the love of self and of all that feeds the love of self. When we compare these two kinds of love, we shall find nothing in common between them, except that unhappily the love of concupiscence solicits the very same will with its affections as the love of charity. But charity is the cause of all spiritual life, and cupidity the cause of all spiritual corruption and death.

Let us ascend in mind through the grace of God to the Divine Fountain of all charity. God is charity; charity is the life and perfection of His being. What an infinitude of life and love is expressed in these three little words: God is charity! As the shell on the sandy shore cannot contain the ocean that rolls round the world; as the labouring breast of man cannot contain the pure and boundless ether that fills the heavens; as the body of man could not pass into the intense conflagration of the sun without instant destruction; neither can the soul of man embrace, comprehend, or enter into the infinite charity of God. Yet some drops of the ocean are in that shell; some little modified breath of that ether is in the breast of man; and some tempered rays of the warmth of that sun are in our earthly frame. Some created rays from His uncreated charity has God also deigned to impart to the soul of the humble Christian, which are full of divine life and love; and in virtue of that sublime gift, the moment the words are sounded in his ears, he knows and feels to his inmost core that God is charity.

The ardent Apostle of the Gentiles was consumed with charity. Yet with a special reference to this perfecting gift he says: "We know in part, and we prophesy in part. But when that which is perfect is come, that which is in part shall be done away. . . . We see now through a glass in a dark manner; but then face to face. Now I know in part, but then shall I know even as I am known. And now there remain faith, hope, and charity, these three; but the greater of these is charity."* From the part which he saw and felt the Apostle prophesied the whole; and he showed the exceeding goodness of God to us sinful mortals when he declared: "God commandeth His charity towards us".† The innocent St. John drew large draughts of charity from the breast of the Son of God, and was filled to overflowing with divine love; yet he only knew and felt in part, but prophesied the whole when he said that "God is charity".

God is the essential, uncreated charity. There is no charity besides, except the charity imparted from His own eternal charity; for charity can never take its first beginning from the creature. All this is embraced in the words of St. John: "God is charity; and he who abideth in charity abideth in God, and God in him". The supreme beauty of God is the splendour of His supreme goodness, and His supreme truth is the effulgence of that infinite goodness and beauty, and the supreme justice is the order of that goodness; and this infinite goodness, beauty, and justice have infinite sweetness. Of all the attributes of God, charity is the most noble, embracing all, uniting all, in a certain way transcending all, because charity is the life of God, the mode of His action, the perfection of his essence; for God is infinite love, infinitely loving, and infinitely beloved. The reason of His essential love is His essential goodness, beauty, and sweetness, whose nature it is to be infinitely communicated and diffused through His infinite action eternally circling in the Holy Trinity. For the Father is infinite love; and contemplating the character of His substance in His Son, He infinitely loves the Son, and the Son loves the Father equally; and the infinite love of the Father and Son eternally produces the Holy Spirit of love,

* *1 Corinthians* xiii. 9-13.   † *Romans* v. 8.

the divine term of love, the divine person of love, the consummation of the Holy Trinity in love, the active principle of all charity.

As the Holy Spirit is the personal consummation of the charity which God is, through the action of the same Holy Spirit the gift of charity is communicated to us; for all charity is of God, as all truth is of God. Truth comes to us from His Eternal Word, and charity from His Holy Spirit. For as there can be no charity whose principal is not in God, there can be none in any created spirit or soul which is not given by God. Hence charity is the most excellent of all things, and is communicative of its excellence, and by its excellence it unites the created spirit with God.

There is no other reason for the existence of this world than the charity of God and the communication of His charity. The world was made for man, man for the soul, the soul for charity, and charity unites the soul with God. From charity God created the world, and by charity He perfects the end for which the world was made, for that end is the happiness of souls possessed of charity. Hence St. John tells us that "charity is of God, and every one that loveth is born of God and knoweth God".* "Rightly," observes St. Bernard, "is it said that charity is God and the gift of God. Wherefore charity gives charity; the substantial charity gives the accidental charity." † Not that God communicates to us His own uncreated charity, which is His nature, and would be unsuited to our condition of probation; for "our God is a consuming fire," ‡ and He would either consume us by its infinite power, or would absorb and enrapture us into His ecstatic vision; and therefore He said to Moses: "Man shall not see Me and live".§ But from His eternal charity through the action of His Holy Spirit God communicates to us the gift of created charity, as a ray is given from the sun, or, to use St. Augustine's expression, as light produces the light that enlightens us, or as we are warmed by the heat from a fire, though the fire itself would consume us. From this we must understand that charity can come from no power of our nature, from nothing of our own, but it is the divinest grace of God and the noblest habit of virtue in the soul, and is infused by the Holy Spirit; as St. Paul says: "The love of God is spread abroad in our hearts through

---

* 1 S. *John* iv. 7.   † S. Bernard, *Epist.* 11.
‡ *Deuteronomy* iv. 24.   § *Exodus* xxxiii. 20.

the Holy Spirit dwelling within us".* And by this dwelling in charity through charity dwelling in us, we live and move towards God and are united with God; and, as St. Peter says: "We are made partakers of the divine nature," † that is, by a created participation.

On this divine subject St. Augustine has written these golden words: "God is love, and 'they that are faithful in love shall rest in Him'. ‡ When we are withdrawn from the noise of the creature and collected to the inward joy of silence: Behold, God is love. Why do we go running up to the high things of Heaven and down to the low things of earth in search of Him who is with us whenever we choose to be with Him? Let no one say: I know not what to love. Let him love his brother, and he will love that very love; for he will know the love with which he loves better than the brother whom he loves; he will know that love the best because it is in his own interior, and therefore more certain. Embrace the God who is love, and embrace Him with love. That is the love which unites all the good angels and all the servants of God in one bond of sanctity, and that unites us with them, and them with us, and subjects and unites the whole to God. The sounder we are from the absence of the tumour of pride, the fuller we are of love; and of what are we full when full of love but full of God? For I look upon charity, and as far as I can see, I see it with my mind, and believe the Scripture where it says that 'God is charity: and he that abideth in charity, abideth in God'." §

We must first, then, understand that charity is from God, because God is charity, and that charity can only be received from Him, that we may be made like to Him, and may have life from Him, and be united with Him in the bond of His charity. There is a kind of life in the soul without charity, but it is not the life for which the soul was made, not true life, but initiatory and mere infantile life, which is life and pain and sorrow from want of our true life. As St. Irenæus says: "The animal body itself is not the soul, but it partakes of the soul so long as God wills it; and so the soul herself is not life, but she partakes of a life given to her by God". ‖ Secondly, charity is from God because He first

---

* *Romans* v. 5.   † 2 *S. Peter* i. 4.
‡ *Wisdom* iii. 9.   § S. August., *De Trinitate*, lib. viii., c. 7, 8.
‖ S. Irenæus, *Adversus Hæreses*, lib. ii., c. 34.

loved us, and created us to be the subjects and partakers of His charity; so that, as St. Paul says, without charity we are nothing, for we are without the gift and the good for which we are created, and which begins our union with God. When, therefore, that gift was lost to man through pride and sin, God in His infinite condescension put forth that charity anew in a wonderful and surpassing way, which St. John dwells upon in these words: "By this hath the charity of God appeared towards us, because God hath sent His only-begotten Son into the world, that we may live by Him. In this is charity; not as though we had loved God, but because He hath first loved us, and sent His Son to be a propitiation for our sins."* The sublime proof that the Incarnation, ordained for the destruction of pride and the restoration of charity to man, was the work of eternal charity, is shown in its being the work of the Holy Spirit.

Thirdly, charity is from God because He has given us the great law of charity as the fulfilment of all His laws and the perfection of justice. He gives the law of life, and the life by which the law is fulfilled. Fourthly, in the very law of love we have the guarantee that to humble souls—for they alone are capable—the grace of charity will never be wanting; for the God who is charity does not mock His children, but when He commands them to love Him with their whole heart and soul and strength and mind, He gives them the charity by which they may love Him. For as mortal love is from nature, and carnal love from carnal sense, and worldly love is from the world, the love of God must be from God; and this divine gift is always ready to enter the soul whenever humility has expelled the destructive enemy of all charity. Wherefore to sum up this glorious truth in the words of Eternal Charity, He says to the soul through the Prophet Jeremias: "I have loved thee with an everlasting love, therefore have I drawn thee, having compassion on thee". †

But when we speak or think of divine love, we must dismiss from our mind and discard from our feelings every notion and sense of that human love which has not been embraced and purified by being brought within the sphere of charity. To quote the luminous Book on the Divine Names: "When that love which beseemeth God is commended, and not by us only, but by the Holy Scriptures, men who have no insight into that conformity with

* 1 *S. John* iv. 9, 10.   † *Jeremias* xxxi. 3.

God, which the divine name of charity signifies, will fly to that sensual and distracting love with which they are familiar, and which is not true love, but an image, or. rather a lapse from true love; for the multitude cannot form a right notion of the pre-eminence of the one divine love. . . . But the contemplaters of God use the word love in the sense of the divine language, and according to the force it has with those who rightly understand divine things. According to this sense, love is a power that unifies, collects, and excellently tempers together what pre-exists in the good and beautiful, through the good and beautiful, and emanates from the good and beautiful for the sake of the good and beautiful, and contains equals through mutual connection." After this description of the love of the adorable Trinity, the author describes the communication of charity to the creature as " moving in the providence of inferior things, and through a certain conversion uniting what is inferior to what is superior ".

After this exposition of the nature of divine charity, the author enlarges upon its action. " Moreover," he says, "the divine love is ecstatic, not suffering him who loves to be his own, but His whom he loves. This is shown when God descends through His providence from His superiority to inferior existences, and by a divine conversion unites them with His superiority. Thus was St. Paul taken hold of by the divine love, and, partaking of its ecstatic virtue, he was able to say : 'I live, now not I, but Christ liveth in me'. He was a true lover; he went out of himself to God; he lived his own life no longer, but the life of Him whom he so vehemently loved. To this it should be added, that the Divine Author of all things, in the good and beautiful love of all, and from the supreme excellence of His loving goodness, descends through His providence of all, and is imbued as it were with love, and is delighted with it ; and whereas He is above all and exempt from all, He yet descends in power to all, although in exceeding Himself He departs not from Himself; and because of His great and benignant love of all He is called the zealous God, for He awakens the zeal of His creatures to desire to love Him, and puts forth His zeal to make them zealous who desire the good things that He provides for them. Finally, love, and what deserves love, is the truly good and beautiful ; it pre-exists in the good and beautiful, and is made and exists for the good and the beautiful." *

* S. Dionysius Areopagita, *De Divinis Nominibus*, c. iv.

" He who abideth in charity, abideth in God, and God in Him."
He abideth in God because God is charity, and all charity partakes of His charity. Hence St. Paul says to the Christian endowed with charity : "Know you not that you are the temple of
God, and the Spirit of God dwelleth in you?"* For charity is
with God and with us ; the uncreated charity abides with the
created charity, that is, in the living soul, so that in a certain
mysterious way there is a communion with God in the loving
soul, and "we are made partakers of the divine nature". He
therefore who loves abides in God as an object known and loved,
and is endowed with eternal life from God ; and God abides in
him as the Divine Object whom he knows, and whom he loves
with supernatural affection for His own divine sake. For charity
unites God and the soul in a mutual union, transforming the one
who loves into the one beloved, and the one beloved into the one
who loves, according to the degree of love, through the unifying
spirit of the divine gift. †

This brings us to the definition of the virtue of charity, which
St. Thomas defines to be "a certain noble friendship between
God and man, a virtue that is not only one, special, and created,
but is of all virtues the most excellent". ‡ We may enlarge upon
this definition in the words of Albert the Great. That soul has
true and perfect charity to God who moves and advances with all
her powers in the love of God, because of the greatness, goodness,
sanctity, perfection, and blessedness that belong to Him as the
Supreme Good. As God does not infuse His divine gifts into our
soul for His own sake but for ours, and with the sole desire that
we should partake of His beatitude, we also ought to love God
chiefly for His sake, although not ignorant of, or indifferent to,
the good with which He will reward us, because that good is
Himself. Charity is the affectionate recognition of all the good
that God is, and of all the good that He is to us. It is also the
return to Him for His immense and eternal love of us.

Our Lord has given us the genuine proof by which we may
know whether we do love God or not : "He that hath My commandments, and keepeth them, he it is that loveth Me; and he
that loveth Me shall be loved of My Father; and I will love him,

---

* 1 *Corinthians* iii. 16.
† See Cornelius à Lapide on the text of St. John.
‡ S. Thomas, *Sum.* ii. 2, q. 23, a. 1.

and will manifest Myself to Him ".* Go into yourselves, brethren, says St. Gregory; seek within you whether you truly love God; believe nothing of your love but what you can prove by works. Love asks for the tongue, the mind, the life. The love of God is never idle, it works great things; if it refuses to work, it is not love.† There are two other signs of the true love of God. If we rejoice in all the good that is done for the love of God, by whomsoever, wheresoever, and whensoever done; and if we grieve for all that is done displeasing to God, by whomsoever, wheresoever, or whensoever done. For it is the property of charity to love all that God loves, and to be displeased at all that displeases God.

True charity to our neighbour is to love him, whether friend or foe, as we love ourself, in God, unto God, and for God's sake. For the charitable love of our neighbour is embraced in the love of God, proceeds from the love of God, and ends in the love of God. The true test of this charity which our Lord has given us is the love of those who are inimical to us, of which He gives us a great example in His conduct to the traitor Judas. For, knowing that he would betray Him, He still kept him in His company, and gave him His body and blood, and at the moment of betrayal He called him friend, and allowed the treacherous kiss. Nothing makes us more like to God than to forgive those who offend and injure us; and we may certainly obtain more grace and glory from God through persecution than through kindness, if we know how to use it rightly. Thus the persecutors were more profitable to the eternal glory of the martyrs than their friends. But we ought to love our neighbours as ourselves, by desiring them all the good and the absence of all the evil, that we desire ourselves, and by doing for them whatever service we can, especially in their needs. ‡

Charity is the rectitude of the soul, correcting her aberrations, bringing up to straightness what has been bent and deformed in her inclinations, and lifting the affections upwards towards the summit of good. Charity is the beauty and dignity of the soul; this beauty comes to her in the gift of love from the infinite beauty of God, and she receives a reflection of beauty from all the good that she loves in charity. Charity is the living form of the virtues,

* *S. John* xiv. 21. † S. Greg. Mag., *Hom.* 30 *super Evangelium.*
‡ See Albertus Magnus, *De Virtutibus,* c. i.

animating them with life and vigour, and directing them to their final end. St. Paul expresses all the value of charity when he calls it "the bond of perfection".* For it unites the soul with God, and through her union with God unites her also with the angels and saints, and by sympathy with all the good that God has anywhere imparted. For charity is all-embracing of good, as it proceeds from that divine charity which either is all good or is productive of all good, and is therefore inclined to all good. "Being rooted and founded in charity," says St. Paul, "you may be able to comprehend, with all the saints, what is the breadth and length, and height and depth. To know also the charity of God, which surpasseth all knowledge, that you may be filled unto all the fulness of God." † Charity not only unites the parts of the spiritual structure, as St. Antony of Padua observes, but gives to the powers, and to the virtues which they exercise, their proper, pliant, and suitable conditions, and their free and responsive dispositions; for example, the mind to loving faith, the heart to loving obedience, the eyes to modesty, and the body to purity. Glass is a fragile thing, but when fused in the fire it is ductile to new forms and tenacious of the form received. Our sensual nature is as fragile as glass, but is tractable and reformable under the fire of charity. ‡

Charity is the way to man as well as to God. It conciliates all intelligences. And though there may be much excitement in what the world calls pleasure, there is no solid joy of life or peace of heart except in charity. But though charity is one, and all who are in charity are united in one and the same charity, there are many degrees of its communication and growth in individual souls, which is owing to their several conditions. When born in the soul, it is incipient; when nourished in the soul, it advances further within; when rooted and founded in the depth of the soul, it is perfect; when God is desired above all things whatsoever, it is most perfect. As charity and justice are one, St. Augustine measures the advancement of charity by the advancement of justice. "Charity begun," he says, "is justice begun; charity advanced is justice advanced; great charity is great justice, and perfect charity is perfect justice." § St. Bonaventure, the Seraphic

---

* *Colossians* iii. 14.   † *Ephesians* iii. 17-19.
‡ S. Antonius Paduan., *Serm. in feria* 6ᵃ *in Cap. Jejunii.*
§ S. August., *De Natura et Gratia*, c. lxx.

Doctor of charity, has given us the signs by which to know the presence of perfect charity. "It is perfect," he says, "when it has become a great habit, direct in its interior motive, solicitous in its exterior works, firmly consolidated in its root, discreet in its fervour, and consoling in its sweetness." *

What, then, are the relations of humility with charity? This is a most important question. Humility disposes the soul and prepares the way for charity, and greater humility prepares and disposes the soul for greater charity. For the goodness of the divine charity is not restrained, but is always ready to be communicated more generously where the soul is able to receive its abundance, and humility makes her able; and the charity received increases humility, for humility is the counterpart of charity. Both these points we must now explain.

We must first repeat that maxim of eternal truth which is the foundation of the whole economy of grace, and which is therefore repeated in so many forms in the Sacred Scriptures, that "God resists the proud, but gives His grace to the humble"; and we may add, as a necessary consequence, that He gives His greatest graces to the most humble. For pride falsifies the man, but humility makes him truthful: pride is the radical injustice of the soul, but humility strives to be just to God, to self, and to all creatures: pride thinks of self above all things, humility looks to God above all things: pride presumes upon one's own self-sufficiency, humility sees and feels one's utter inefficiency: pride feels no want of the divine help, humility feels the want of God in everything: pride has no desire beyond self-satisfaction, humility can never rest contented without the charity of God: pride is the revolt of the soul from God, and is always aiming at independence; humility is subject to God, and looks on the isolation of independence with horror, as on a desert of solitude. Pride closes the heart against God, humility opens the heart to God. Wherefore humility is the proper disposition and the due preparation for receiving the charity of God, who gives His grace to the humble.

It seems almost irreverent to put the question, but how can the divine generosity dwell with ungodly selfishness? How can God enter with His holiest gift into a soul whose pride resists Him? How can He unite with a soul that prefers herself to Him? How

* S. Bonaventura, *Compend. Theolog. Veritatis*, lib. v., c. 29.

can He spread abroad His love in a heart already filled through all its veins and passages with the love of self? How can He infuse the most precious gift of eternal life into a soul that prefers her own life, and that will only abuse the gift of gifts in the interest of pride? God must recall His gift as soon as given, for there is no society between charity and pride, between the holy and the profane, between Christ and Belial. If God is charity, says St. Basil, the devil must be pride; and as he who abideth in charity abideth in God, he who abideth in pride must abide in the devil. God cannot abide with pride, but only with humility. "For the Lord is high and looketh on the low, and the high He knoweth afar off."* Even when the deadly pride of mortal sin has been vanquished by the grace of humility and penance, and charity is restored, the remains of pride will lurk in certain faculties of the soul and impede the perfection of charity from the want of perfect humility.

Many of the Fathers and Saints have dwelt upon the essential and intimate relations that prevail between these consummate virtues, the relations between which have been repeatedly expressed by St. Augustine in terms like these: If you dig deep within you the foundations of humility, you will come to the summit of charity. By which the Saint intimates, that although humility is founded in divine grace, it is the fruit of great labour, whilst charity is given to the humble without labour. In the celebrated letter to the Virgin Demetriades already quoted, the author says: "Humility and charity are in nowise separate from each other: such is their connection, that whoever is constructed in the one is possessed of the other; for as humility is a part of charity, charity is a part of humility". St. Cæsarius of Arles says: "True humility never was, never is, and never can be without charity. Fire cannot be without heat and brightness, nor charity without humility."† St. Valerian says: "Humility is the intimate associate of charity".‡ St. Peter of Cluny writes to St. Bernard: "Where charity is absent humility is absent, and where humility is absent charity is absent". § Blosius says: "No one grows or advances in charity who does not grow in humility". ‖ Thomas à Kempis writes: "The way to charity is through

---

* *Psalm* cxxxvi. 6.   † S. Cæsarius Arelaten, *Hom.* 35.
‡ S. Valerian, *Hom.* 14 *de Bono Humilitatis.*
§ S. Petrus Cluniacen., lib. iv., Epist. 17.
‖ Blosius, *Speculum Spirituale*, c. viii.

humility, for to indulge in self-elation is to go far from charity ".*
St. Teresa writes: "I can neither understand nor conceive how
humility exists or can exist without love, or love without humility ".† We might quote on indefinitely, but these passages from
such great authorities will suffice to impress this important truth
on the mind.

All sincere love, even in the natural order, has in it a self-
forgettingness, a devotedness, and a submission of inclination to
the person beloved, a kind of natural humility that makes it an
image of the union of humility with charity. To leave lovers out,
though none have, or profess to have, more of this kind of humility than those who sue in courtship, this union of self-renunciation
with affection is realized in friendship, in a happy marriage, and
in a mother's devotedness to her children. The true friend has
no pride with his friend: his heart is open to him, he gives up his
selfishness for him, he is devoted to him, he yields many inclinations to him; and when occasion calls for it, he is ready to make
sacrifices on his account. A happily married pair are not only
devoted to each other and live in each other, but the very foundation of their happiness is in the surrender that each makes to the
other of their selfish inclinations, all which becomes easy through
their mutual affection. Consider the blended humility and love of a
mother towards her children. She is all self-forgetfulness, devotedness, and service. She descends into all their little ways, and
lives in them more than in herself, becoming almost a child with
them whilst retaining her maternal authority; and this humility of
love springs from the united sense of duty and affection.

These examples may help to explain how there can be no true
love of any kind without a proportionate self-renunciation and
humility, for the one element is the essential counterpart of the
other. For humility is the sacrificial element in all sincere love.
For as love is the transfer of our affection from one's self to
another, it includes a surrender of self-love, and this surrender is
humility. But when we give up our love from ourselves to God,
this giving up of our love of self to God is humility, and the love
that we give to God is charity. Hence St. John Chrysostom calls
humility *maximum sacrificium*, the greatest of all sacrifices, because it is the sacrifice of self. Consider the sacrifice of our Lord

* T. à Kempis, *De Disciplina Claustrali*, c. xi.
† S. Teresa, *Way of Perfection*, c. xvi.

Jesus Christ, the model of all sacrifice: perfect humility was its foundation and perfect charity its end. He gave His whole nature to the Father, and the Father gave Him all charity and power for the saving of mankind.

We have drawn more than one illustration of the spiritual from the material world, and we may here introduce another. Electricity is one of the great and secret elements of material nature, which has perhaps a nearer analogy with spiritual power than any other, although the knowledge of its function in the universe is as yet but little understood. This, however, appears to be the fundamental law of its action: that the positive electric force cannot move without the negative; there must be a vacuity or a capacity before this mysterious power can act or move. So it is with charity: God is always ready to impart to souls the fire of divine life, but there must be a negative, a vacuity of self, a capacity to receive its action. Humility and charity are the negative and positive poles of sanctity, and the positive pole of charity will only act where there is the negative pole of humility.

To explain this in another way, we cannot approach one object or place without leaving another; this law arises from our limitation. Here again is the negative and the positive: we cannot approach to God without leaving ourselves; for it is impossible in the nature of things to concentrate our affections on ourselves and yet open and expand them towards God. The leaving ourselves is humility, the approaching to God is charity. In one and the self-same act the will or love of the soul abandons the less for the greater, self for God.

This fundamental law of human sanctity is expressed in the words of the Psalm already repeatedly quoted: "Empty yourself, and see that I am God".* Or, as in the Hebrew text: "Cease and see that I am God". That is to say, cease from yourself, vacate yourself; or, as St. Augustine puts it, pour out yourself that you may be filled with God. There is but one impediment to this, but one adversary of the divine grace, and that is the unjust and extravagant love of one's self. Through this cupidity, not love, for love is not given to self but to another, we form an idol within our heart of which we make a god, and serve as a god, and secretly compare it with God, and without any act of judgment prefer it to God. This false god is a fiction blown

* *Psalm* xlv. 11.

together from many base materials, which in the whole amount to nothing better than a lying pretension to an excellence we do not possess, and to an assertion of merit that in nowise belongs to us. Cease from all this, says the Almighty ; empty yourself of this, and you will see and know that I am God.

As humility is the just thought of what we are, and the right action of our will towards God from the knowledge of what He is to us, we come to see our poverty in the light of His excellence. And then, descending from our conceits and renouncing our fictitious independence, we honestly endeavour to be the subjects of God ; and He gives us His charity and friendship, and we partake in His life, and this infused fire of life passes into our will, and from the will into all the powers, and we live in God. But this new life gives us a new sense, the sense of God, and by this sense we know that without this life from God we are poor, weak, blind, and senseless. And the nearer we bring our hearts to God, the more sensible we become that life is from God and not from us. Thus charity infuses a new grace of deeper humility, which, as we labour to make fruitful, obtains for us yet greater charity. Not that one charity is added to another, for there is but one charity, but that charity penetrates more deeply into the soul, and is more expanded in proportion as the soul is more vacated of self-love, and more subject to the divine gift, and more active in co-operation. Thus the charity that inspires greater humility, and the greater humility that opens the way to still greater charity, augments the virtuous action of the soul in two directions—in greater contempt of self and in greater admiration of God, in more complete abandonment of self and in stronger adhesion to God, in greater hatred of self and in greater love of God.

Who has truly loved God and has never felt those moments of intense peace that arise from forgetfulness of self in God ? Such moments, so filled with life, are a foretaste of the eternal peace. Compare those moments with the hours of trouble : in the one case, self is almost forgotten in God, and time and place seem almost to have receded from us ; in the other, it is our troubled self that is before us, and our wounded self-love is the cause of all our distress. God holds but the second place in our feelings ; time hangs heavily on us, and place seems to reflect our pain. There is no cure for this state of things but the

26*

humility that gives us self-renunciation and the charity that gives us wisdom.

Let us now come to rule. The whole secret of self-management is in two simple principles : the motive of the will and the action of the will ; for the will is the seat of charity. The first thing is to keep the will to the right motive, to the simplest, the purest, the highest, the best. This can be nothing but the love of God, which contains all other good motives as pure light contains all colours. Keep to this motive, foster this motive, be humble for this motive, cherish it by thinking of it with affection. Impulse is not motive ; it is the base intrusion of cupidity. Look to your motive and impulse will drop. Motive is seen in the light of God. When the will deviates to lower motives quietly bring it back. If a selfish motive get mixed with a pure motive, you will know it by its causing trouble and disquiet. Clear it away by concentrating the heart on the true motive, and peace will return. For the best way to clear off the mixture of inferior motive is to transcend it, to rise above it by redoubling the devotion of the will to the will and love of God. And nothing holds the will to its divine motive so effectually as the frequent aspiration of that motive within the soul, which in time becomes the easiest and sweetest of all exercises.

The second principle is the exercise of the will, upon which all virtue depends. It is a great thing to do our best, and with our best judgment on all occasions. This makes the will habitually vigorous and wise. But it requires the keeping up the will above the inferior nature, neither attending to its languors nor listening to its excuses and complaints. Do this, and your inferior nature will learn submission, and you will get into the habit of freedom. A wise man of the world watches over his external conduct ; the wise man of God watches over the inward conduct of his will. Right motive will keep the will right, and when that motive is charity the will does wonders.

Those who first give themselves with ardour to the service of God have generally what St. Benedict calls the fervour of novices. God gives them an ardour and an unction to win them to His love and service. But as they are far as yet from being purified in their affections, this works in them in a mixed way ; for the providence of grace consults their weakness, and draws them partly by the cords of charity and partly by the cords of Adam. They are still much in themselves and in their own sensibilities, and this new wine of charity brings them a new and delightful experience, that not only inebriates the spirit, but flows into the imagination and takes hold of the natural sensibilities. The consequence is that there is much sense of self as well as of God, and enjoyment of self as well as of God. And whoever is experienced in the ways of souls will see that, like the movement of a pendulum, there is a constant vibration of the affections of the will between self and God, which is betrayed not only in much self-ignorance but in a diversity of failures and indiscretions. As a general fact, this first fervour is less a love of God in God than a love of God in self.

But after a certain period this fervour, with its ferment of self-love, comes to an end, and a period is ordained for probation, purification, and self-knowledge. This is a time of labour, a time also for gaining true humility, that the soul may be prepared for a purer gift of charity. To this period we may apply the words of Moses to the Israelites : "The Lord your God trieth you, that it may appear whether you love Him with all your heart, and with all your soul, or not ".* The former sweet, attractive grace is changed to a grace of support divested of sensibility, and the light of justice is left in the soul without the light of consolation. Then that soul finds out her weakness and her self-love, and the failings that spring from them, of all which in her fervour she never dreamed. Yet that weakness was there, and that self-love, even during the inebriation of fervour, though the soul was little conscious of their presence, imagining great things above her strength. But now that soul finds out how much she is still inclined to herself, though but recently she seemed to soar on wings, and how much there is in her to purify and set in order. The desire of God was enkindled in her fervour, and that desire remains when the fervour is gone ; but now God shows her how much it will cost to gain perfect humility and detachment, that she may adhere to God with the whole heart and will. This is the critical time in the spiritual life, requiring great fortitude and perseverance in humble ways.

The one point of difficulty is this : the fear of leaving one's self, the way to which has yet to be learnt. For in that first fervour, so dear to memory, there was, as we have said, a consider-

* *Deuteronomy* xiii. 3.

able mixture of natural sensibility, and the soul still seeks in herself what can only be found in God. The will clings on one side to self, with a sort of dread that to lose one's sense of self is to lose everything, and is unable as yet to distinguish a certain pious sense of self, so to speak, from the sense of God. But it is a long way from self to God, and those who cling to their own house will never make the journey. The venture must be made with faith, and made with sacrifice. This is the reason why the old experienced Fathers of the desert attached so much importance to the giving up one's will with reverence to the wise; it trains the soul to quit her self-love, and so to abandon self for God. Our Lord has told us the solemn truth : " He that shall save his life shall lose it ; and he that shall lose his life for Me shall save it ".* Our true life is not in ourselves but in God. We must lose to gain, we must detach the will from one's self to attach it to God. As long as the heart is divided between self and God, there will be nothing but an unpeaceful swinging of the will backwards and forwards between God and self, so that no great advancement is gained, no solid rest found, no decided peace obtained. But the heart detached from self feels the eternal life, rests in it with peace, and adheres with constancy to God. After all that laborious humility, an infused humility inspires contempt and dread of the fascinating love of self, and gratitude is given to God, and nothing to self.

The pure love of God, indifferent to all changes of mood in one's self, is not only charity but humility. And when a soul reaches this charity of humility, and humility of charity, she will understand these words of St. Francis of Sales : " All that is not God, of God, in God, for God, or according to God, should appear to us as nothing, and even cause in us a sense of horror ".

But there is a more subtle and profound combination of humility with charity in those who are advancing in the perfection of the love of God, a combination that demonstrates their wonderful strength as the soul approaches near to God. For besides the mortification of the passions, there is a more secret and difficult abnegation of self-love and self-will which should be continuous, because it is not the beginning, but the progress and completion of that humility and charity which perfect the soul. This abnegation proceeds from the knowledge and sense of the might, majesty, charity, and will of God. It submits the inmost soul to God, and

* *S. Luke* ix 24.

makes her love her own abjection and contempt, desiring nothing more, and caring for nothing so much as to break down her own will and inclinations, so as if possible to destroy the roots of evil and the opposition to God within her. This has been so well explained from the experience and teaching of the Saints and the devoutly learned by Father Rossignoli that we shall chiefly follow his exposition.

It is certain that we belong to God, and not to ourselves; that He has all rights over us, and that we have no rights against His will. If our will is in our own power, it is so given us that we may freely subject it to the law of the Supreme Wisdom and Goodness, and may surrender it wholly to Him, that He may dispose of us as He sees best for our final good, and to the glory of His grace.

We may ask then : Is it better that God should guide our will to Him by consolations or by afflictions? And the Fathers and Saints reply: It is better that God should draw us to Him through things against our will than through things that allure and soothe the will. For these are the most holy, and such as we should not seek for our own sake, but only for the sake of God. Such are the external trials of poverty, contempt, ignominy, and things of that kind; such are the internal and greater trials of desolation, severe temptations, distress of heart, mental darkness, anxiety of mind, and things of this kind, which make life bitter. For to be conversant and to be exercised in them for the quieting of our will is far better for us than the contrary good, so long as with our will we adhere to God. Let not the proficient, then, prepare for ease and pleasure, but rather for internal afflictions. Let him not look for peace in himself, but for peace in the will of God; and he may look securely for that peace, however much tossed upon the floods of perturbation. The reason for this assertion is, that the chief ground of merit before God is the abnegation of self-esteem and self-love; for the exercise of which adversity is more helpful than prosperity, whether that adversity be external and from the world, or internal and from the soul.

For the repressing of self-esteem the knowledge of our vileness is needful, and although this knowledge comes from God's illuminating the mind, and is so given to the blessed, yet it is best suited to us, who are travelling through this world, when it is born of experience. As God has not the design of destroying but of perfecting our nature, He would have us to know our vileness from experience, and to make good use of this experience. When, for example, we find our will repugnant to the will of God, and it is consequently unquiet, we see clearly what is in us of our own, and what from God. We see what is of our own in the turbid movements against the will of God; but what is of God is that strength by which we refuse to consent to them. That mental darkness also, and that dryness of heart, and that affliction of spirit, are all our own, whilst from God are the gifts that dispel them, as the winds carry away the clouds. Nor does God leave these things in us unjustly, because we have deserved for our crimes to have the whole cup of wrath and bitterness poured upon us, but we only receive a sprinkled drop when we are permitted to be afflicted. If we fly from that drop of bitterness, we unjustly fly the justice of God through an immoderate self-love; for we have been rescued from great evils, and have been reconciled to God through the blood of His Son, and have to be dealt with in a different way than might have been the case if we had never been aliens from God, or had never had a source of corruption in us.

We must therefore bear the branding of vexation and calamity, and feel that the hand of the Lord is upon us, and that we are stricken from Heaven, and crucified, though less by far than we deserve. From this we rise to greater reverence and awe of the majesty of God, and so take His visitations in good part, knowing them to come from His mercy and love. For, in short, spiritual prosperity is apt to blind the soul as well as temporal prosperity, and more, much more. For their inflation creeps in without observation, and injures more secretly, and as the soul is more noble by nature than all bodily things, she is more easily inflated by spiritual prosperity to forget her nothingness; whilst the old self-love and the sense of having been freed from our old iniquities serve the cause of Lucifer in fixing us in our own esteem.

These desolations and miseries break the nerves of self-love and root them from the heart; they compel us to cling to God from the very consciousness of having no other strength or relief; and all the time they endure they are teaching us what depraved propensities and corruptibilities exist in us. This excites one to hatred and contempt of one's self, inspires us with disgust and indignation, and leads us to reproach, persecute, and punish that mean and disgraceful disposition that is ever inclined to oppose the generous designs of God, and even to take possession of His precious gifts, and make them the subject of self-elation. For the delight that flows from sweetness of spirit and gives so much satisfaction is apt to foster self-love more even than its own allurements, because it may then feed on more precious food, and so, like mercenary servants, we are apt to seek the gifts of God more than God Himself. So we are left to bitterness and desolation until we gain the habit of loving God for His own sake and not merely for His gifts, and until the soul is weaned from her attachments to whatever within her is less than God and the sovereign will of God. By this discipline the soul is both purified and fortified, and prepared for the grace of perfect charity.

But this should also be observed, that although we ought to prosecute our sins with undying hatred because of their aversion to God, and because they are sins, yet in so far as they bring us to the knowledge of ourselves, make us vile in our own eyes, and break down that self-esteem and pride which caused them, God draws this good out of their evil, as He draws light out of darkness. On the other hand, when we take a selfish delight in our good acts, and flatter our nature on their account, though they may not alienate us from God, they will not join us to God.

So long then as the vessel of our heart is not well purified from the lees and dregs of self-love, it is not good for us to have much increase of illumination, consolation, or freedom from temptation, lest, like some low vain person raised to sudden affluence, we should become intolerable to our Divine Benefactor. Let the proficient rather strive for a calm indifference to all but God Himself, and leave it to His divine wisdom to give her the gifts He sees best for her condition, whether to change her self-love into humility, or to perfect her charity. For although the soul acts with greater promptitude in the service of God when possessed of inward light and fervour, and for this reason these consoling gifts may be desired and magnified, yet it is more perfect to be able to love God and do His will without the promptness inspired by them. Then the will is stronger and more forcible in its virtue when it acts against inward repugnance and with difficulty, just as it is easy to go down with the stream, but requires much vigour to pull against the stream, and by exerting that vigour the powers are strengthened.

We must therefore clear away from the mind two errors that stand much in the way of conformity to the will and guidance of God. The first is to imagine that merit before God consists in facility of will, even though that canker of all merit, self-love and self-elation, should be hidden in that will; and even though the more difficult way is comparatively or altogether free from them, and therefore produces the real harvest of merit before God. For this reason the most loving God, who desires what is best for us, does not leave His friends in ease and comfort long, but excites, draws, and leads them on to Himself through many difficulties. In Heaven His sons and servants are united with Him so intimately that He beatifies them eternally, and they repose on Him in a torrent of joy; but on earth He exacts of them a service and sub-mission, perfect indeed, and most pleasing to Him, yet full of trial and perturbation.

The other error which the proficient must correct, and which is often fashioned in the imagination, is the desire of seeking a quiet and private life, exempt from cares and troubles, and from inward discomforts as well; desiring this against all the facts of God's providence, and against His obvious will. For He scarcely leaves His greatest friends without troubles in this life, but loves to manifest His power in guiding their vessel through all tempests into the secure port of final rest. Being great and potent, He prepares the souls of His friends for great and arduous works, and through their internal conflicts He strengthens the habits of their souls. For, as St. Paul found, "power is perfected in infirmity";[*] and as the rewards of God are not due to those habits, but to their acts, He gives them much work to do, that their reward may be great and ample. For what God loves in our love is the generosity which forgets the love of self in His service. Such was the love of St. Paul, who desired to spend and be spent in the service of His Divine Master, careless what he suffered, so that the knowledge and love of God might be increased in himself and in the world.[†]

To these instructions we must add two more, which are of great importance. The first is, never to acticipate, but to follow the

---

[*] 2 *Corinthians* xii. 9.

[†] Rossignoli, *De Disciplina Spiritualis Perfectionis*, lib. v., c. 7.

leading of the providence of God. If we anticipate the order of Divine Providence, we put our own will in place of the will of God. This was the severe reproach on the false prophets: "I sent them not, neither have I commanded them, nor have I spoken to them". * The reason is yet stronger why we should never run before, but only follow the light and grace of God, for fidelity to grace is obedience to grace, and no sacrifice is pleasing to God which contains our own will. Our Lord did not tell us to go before Him, but to follow after Him; and the Prophet says: "It is good to wait with silence for the salvation of God". † Nature is excitable, impatient, hasty, and indeliberate; the help of God is calm, patient, and given in due season, according as He sees best for us. To rush in where God has not invited us, or to aim at wonders above ourselves, is to yield to the excitable impulsion of nature; but to follow the divine leading of grace in humility and obedience is to act within the order of the divine gifts.

The second instruction, of very great importance, is this: The hour of prayer is the special hour of grace. But God gives His grace to the humble. The beginning of prayer should therefore be in the profoundest exercise of humility and reverence of which the soul is capable. Nor should time be spared in obtaining this interior position of humble recollection and sense of our nothingness in the presence of the Eternal Majesty, as well as the entire opening and subjection of our spirit to the divine operations of the Spirit of God. Remember that we live and have our being in God; that His light and grace are everywhere present with Him; and that the only obstacles to their communication are the external obstacle of our corruptible body and the internal obstacle of self-love and pride. But we are in God as the bird is in the air and the fish in the water, and humility opens our communication with His gifts. Get your heart as near to God as you can, with profound subjection, that you may feel His life, and not your own nature. Remember also that gratitude is the final expression, and, as it were, the perfect fruit of humility.

We will now conclude this volume with a summary of what it contains, expressed mostly in the language of a very eminent theologian. ‡

---

* *Jeremias* xiv. 14.   † *Lamentations* iii. 26.
‡ Thomassini, *Dogmata, De Deo*, lib. v., c. 10.

26a*

In no other way can our weak and changeable nature be brought to the unchangeable condition of solid good than by virtue and justice. It is by the virtues that rest upon the force of divine grace that we are restored to the form of that Divine Image which touches upon the unchangeable eternity of God, and which gives us a spiritual likeness to God; and when that likeness is perfected in our life, we keep all temporal and changeable things beneath our feet. By the Christian virtues we become spiritual and immaterial, and put off the corruption of matter from our soul to put on the incorruptibility of spirits. The virtues give us stability of mind and will; this stability is derived by gift from the eternal stability, and by the force of this stability we are neither lifted up in prosperity nor cast down in adversity; neither swelled with pride in the one state of our affections, nor sunk into despondency in the other, but either anticipate the alternation of our thoughts and imaginations and the tempest of the passions, or disregard them altogether. For the divine virtues lift us into a calm region above these things.

The fall of man brought us upon a false and treacherous foundation. Pride took us away from God as our foundation, and set us upon no better foundation than ourselves. All the miseries of the human race have come of no other cause than the striving to rest upon this false and fictitious foundation, and the endeavouring to produce the fruits of happiness from this poor and barren soil. What the Christian religion has done is to restore us to our true foundation, and this is effected by the virtue of humility, the special gift of Christ, the virtue of which is to open our eyes to the false foundation on which we have striven in vain to rest our immortal souls, and to transfer us by the act of our will to that divine foundation from which all our strength and good is derived. But as our false foundation is below, and our true foundation is the God above us, we can only adhere to His supreme excellence by subjection. "The Lord is my firmament," says the Psalmist, "and my refuge." * And when we have truly surrendered our trust in ourselves, and have justly subjected our nature to God, He enters our souls with His charity, and we become the loving children of God.

Through the divine force which charity gives the Christian virtues we are brought from much division to a state of unity.

* *Psalm* xvii. 3.

Evil is multiform and the vices are many, presenting as many faces under as many masks as the number of evil affections that we cherish. But the Christian virtues by their very nature tend to one, and to fix us to that one, and that one is the love of God above all things; and through that one they unite us with the divine, unchangeable, and eternal God.

Whosoever has good hold of this one virtue, or rather is held by this virtue of charity, quits the shadows of things, comes to the one true Substance, and leaves the smoke of the vices to vanish. When, therefore, we begin to cultivate this virtue, we begin truly to be, and to take the way to unchangeable being. For the reason of this virtue is unchangeable, its form is everlasting, and it partakes of the Eternal Justice. This virtue is a certain adhesion to God, and so long as it rests on God it is unchangeable. God is the first, the infinite, the perfect virtue; and whosoever receives the light of God and entertains the grace of the virtues hath God for his guest in the home of his soul, and his interior is already gifted with the joyful sense of immortal life. The pleasures of sense are brief, transient, and corruptible, because they are the good of the corruptible body; but virtue is eternal and incorruptible, because it is the good of the incorruptible soul. Among many sublime proofs that God is one and immutable, one is founded on the fact that the nearer a soul approaches to God, the more she finds that she becomes united in herself and the less exposed to change, except in her growth to greater and more unchangeable good. But this is only known by the sincere lovers of God.

THE END.

SELECTION

FROM

BURNS & OATES'

Catalogue

OF

PUBLICATIONS.

LONDON: BURNS AND OATES, Lᴅ.

28 Orchard St., W.

1895.

Latest Publications.

A Retreat : Consisting of Thirty-three Discourses with Meditations, intended for the use of the Clergy, Religious, and others. By the RIGHT REV. JOHN CUTHBERT HEDLEY, O.S.B., Bishop of Newport and Menevia. Second edition. In handsome half-leather binding. Crown 8vo, price 6s.

Journals kept during Times of Retreat. By Father John Morris, S.J. Selected and edited by Father J. H. Pollen, S.J. New volume, Quarterly Series. Cloth 6s.

The Sacred Heart, and other Sermons. By the REV. ALFRED FAWKES. Red buckram, gilt, 2s. 6d.

Bernadette of Lourdes. A Mystery. Translated from the French of E. POUVILLON by HENRY O'SHEA. Blue buckram, gilt, 2/6.

The Inner Life of Father Thomas Burke, O.P. By a Dominican Friar of the English Province. Dark green buckram, gilt, 2s.

The Life of St. Philip Neri. Translated from the Italian of CARDINAL CAPECELATRO. By the REV. THOMAS ALDER POPE, of the Oratory. Second Edition. In two Vols., Price 12s. 6d.

Purgatory. Illustrated by the Lives and Legends of the Saints. From the French of Father F. X. Schouppe, S.J. Cloth, 6s.

"We feel absolutely confident that Father Schouppe's work will soon become one of our most popular works on Purgatory, and that we shall ere long have to notice its second edition."—*Tablet.*

The Jewish Race in Ancient and Roman History. Translated from the 11th corrected edition of A. RENDU, LL.D., by THERESA CROOK. Crown 8vo, cloth, 6s.

Literary and Biographical History; or, Bibliographical Dictionary of the English Catholics. From the Breach with Rome, in 1534, to the present time. By JOSEPH GILLOW. Vol. IV., Cloth, demy 8vo, 15s. Now ready Vols. I., II., and III., in uniform style, 15s. each.

(The fifth and concluding volume will follow shortly.)

History of the Church of England. From the Accession of Henry VIII. to the Death of Queen Elizabeth. By MARY H. Allies. Crown 8vo, cloth, 3s. 6d. Being a Sequel to the History of the Church in England from the Beginning of the Christian Era to the Accession of Henry VIII. By the same Author. Crown 8vo, cloth, 6s.

SELECTION

FROM

BURNS AND OATES' CATALOGUE
OF PUBLICATIONS.

———➤➤➤✦✦✦✦———

ALLIES, T. W. (K.C.S.G.)

A Life's Decision. Crown 8vo, cloth £0 5 0
The Formation of Christendom.
    Vol. I.—Popular Edition. Crown 8vo, cloth. . 0 5 0
    Vols. II. and III. Demy 8vo, . . . each 0 10 0
Church and State as seen in the Formation of Christen-
    dom, 8vo, pp. 472, cloth . (out of print.)
The Throne of the Fisherman, built by the Carpenter's
    Son, the Root, the Bond, and the Crown of Christ-
    endom. Demy 8vo 0 10 6
The Holy See and the Wandering of the Nations.
    Demy 8vo 0 10 6
Peter's Rock in Mohammed's Flood. Demy 8vo : 0 10 6

"It would be quite superfluous at this hour of the day to recommend Mr. Allies' writings to English Catholics. Those of our readers who remember the article on his writings in the *Katholik*, know that he is esteemed in Germany as one of our foremost writers."—*Dublin Review.*

ALLIES, MARY.

Leaves from St. John Chrysostom. With introduction
    by T. W. Allies, K.C.S.G. Crown 8vo, cloth. . 0 6 0
"Miss Allies' 'Leaves' are delightful reading; the English is re-markably pure and graceful; page after page reads as if it were original. No commentator, Catholic or Protestant, has ever sur-passed St. John Chrysostom in the knowledge of Holy Scripture, and his learning was of a kind which is of service now as it was at the time when the inhabitants of a great city hung on his words."—*Tablet.*

History of the Church in England, from the begin-
    ning of the Christian Era to the accession of
    Henry VIII. Crown 8vo, cloth . . . 0 6 0
The Second Part, to the End of Queen Elizabeth's
    Reign. Crown 8vo, cloth 0 3 6

"Miss Allies has in this volume admirably compressed the sub-stance, or such as was necessary to her purpose, of a number of authorities, judiciously selected. . . . As a narrative the volume is capitally written, as a summary it is skilful, and not its least excellence is its value as an index of the best available sources which deal with the period it covers."—*Birmingham Daily Gazette.*

ANNUS SANCTUS:

Hymns of the Church for the Ecclesiastical Year.
    Translated from the Sacred Offices by various
    Authors, with Modern, Original, and other Hymns,
    and an Appendix of Earlier Versions. Selected and
    Arranged by ORBY SHIPLEY, M.A.
    Plain cloth, lettered 0 5 6

ANSWERS TO ATHEISTS: OR NOTES ON

Ingersoll. By the Rev. A. Lambert, (over 100,000 copies
sold in America). Twelfth edition. Paper.   . .£0 0 6
  Cloth 0 1 0

BAKER, VEN. FATHER AUGUSTIN.

Holy Wisdom; or, Directions for the Prayer of Contemplation, &c. Extracted from Treatises written
by the Ven. Father F. Augustin Baker, O.S.B., and
edited by Abbot Sweeney, D.D. Beautifully bound
in half leather 0 6 0

"We earnestly recommend this most beautiful work to all our
readers. We are sure that every community will use it as a constant
manual. If any persons have friends in convents, we cannot conceive
a better present they can make them, or a better claim they can have
on their prayers, than by providing them with a copy."—*Weekly
Register.*

BOWDEN, REV. H. S. (of the Oratory) Edited by.

Dante's Divina Commedia: Its scope and value.
From the German of FRANCIS HETTINGER, D.D.
With an engraving of Dante. 2nd Edition. . . 0 10 6

"All that Venturi attempted to do has been now approached with
far greater power and learning by Dr. Hettinger, who, as the author
of the 'Apologie des Christenthums,' and as a great Catholic theologian, is eminently well qualified for the task he has undertaken."—
The Saturday Review.

Natural Religion. Being Vol. I. of Dr. Hettinger's
Evidences of Christianity. With an Introduction
on Certainty. Second edition. Crown 8vo, cloth   0 7 6

"As an able statement of the Catholic Doctrine of Certitude, and a
defence, from the Romanist point of view, of the truth of Christianity, it was well worth while translating Dr. Franz Hettinger's
'Apologie des Christenthums,' of which the first part is now published."—*Scotsman.*

Revealed Religion. Being the Second Volume of the
above work. With an Introduction on the "Assent
of Faith." Crown 8vo, cloth, ... 0 7 6

BRIDGETT, REV. T. E. (C.SS.R.).

Discipline of Drink 0 3 6

"The historical information with which the book abounds gives
evidence of deep research and patient study, and imparts a permanent interest to the volume, which will elevate it to a position
of authority and importance enjoyed by few of its compeers."—*The
Arrow.*

Our Lady's Dowry; how England Won that Title.
New and Enlarged Edition. 0 5 0

"This book is the ablest vindication of Catholic devotion to Our
Lady, drawn from tradition, that we know of in the English language."—*Tablet.*

Ritual of the New Testament. An essay on the principles and origin of Catholic Ritual in reference to
the New Testament. Third edition   .   .   . 0 5 0

The Life of the Blessed John Fisher. With a repro-
duction of the famous portrait of Blessed JOHN
FISHER by HOLBEIN, and other Illustrations, 2nd Ed.   0 7 6

"The Life of Blessed John Fisher could hardly fail to be interesting and instructive. Sketched by Father Bridgett's practised pen
the portrait of this holy martyr is no less vividly displayed in the
printed pages of the book than in the wonderful picture of Holbein,
which forms the frontispiece."—*Tablet.*

BRIDGETT REV. T. E. (C.SS.R.)—*continued.*

The True Story of the Catholic Hierarchy deposed by
Queen Elizabeth, with fuller Memoirs of its Last
Two Survivors. By the Rev. T. E. BRIDGETT,
C.SS.R., and the late Rev. T. F. KNOX, D.D., of
the London Oratory. Crown 8vo, cloth,   £0   7   6

"We gladly acknowledge the value of this work on a subject which
has been obscured by prejudice and carelessness."—*Saturday Review.*

The Life and Writings of Blessed Thomas More, Lord
Chancellor of England and Martyr under Henry
VIII. With Portrait of the Martyr taken from the
Crayon Sketch made by Holbein in 1527. 2nd Ed.   0   7   6

"Father Bridgett has followed up his valuable Life of Bishop
Fisher with a still more valuable Life of Thomas More. It is, as the
title declares, a study not only of the life, but also of the writings of
Sir Thomas. Father Bridgett has considered him from every point
of view, and the result is, it seems to us, a more complete and
finished portrait of the man, mentally and physically, than has been
hitherto presented."—*Athenæum.*

The Wisdom and Wit of Blessed Thomas More .   .   0   6   0

"It would be hard to find another such collection of true wisdom
and keen, pungent, yet gentle wit and humour, as this volume
contains."—*American Catholic Quarterly.*

BRIDGETT, REV. T. E. (C.SS.R.), Edited by.

Souls Departed. By CARDINAL ALLEN. First published in 1565, now edited in modern spelling by the
Rev. T. E. Bridgett   0   6   0

BROWNLOW, BISHOP

A Memoir of the late Sir James Marshall, C.M.G.,
K.C.S.G., taken chiefly from his own letters.
With Portrait. Crown 8vo, cloth   .   .   0   3   6
Lectures on Slavery and Serfdom in Europe. Cloth   0   3   6
"The general impression left by the perusal of this interesting
book is one of great fairness and thorough grasp of the subject."—
Month

BUCKLER, REV. REGINALD, (O.P.)

The Perfection of Man by Charity. A Spiritual Treatise.
Second edition. Crown 8vo. cloth   .   .   .   0   5   0

"The object of Father Buckler's useful and interesting book
is to lay down the principles of the spiritual life for the benefit
of Religious and Seculars. The book is written in an easy and
effective style, and the apt citations with which he enriches his
pages would of themselves make the treatise valuable."—*Dublin Review.*

CARMINA MARIANA.

An English Anthology in Verse in honour of the
Blessed Virgin Mary. Edited by ORBY SHIPLEY,
M.A. Second and cheaper Edition. Crown 8vo,
472 pp., bound in blue and red cloth   .   .   0   7   6

"Contains everything at all worthy of the theme that has been
written in English verse to the praise of the Blessed Virgin Mary
from Chaucer's time to the present year, including the best trans-
lations from Latin, French and other languages."—*Irish Monthly.*

CATHOLIC BELIEF: OR. A SHORT AND
Simple Exposition of Catholic Doctrine. By the
Very Rev. Joseph Faà di Bruno, D.D. Twelfth
edition . . . . Price 6d.; post free, £0 o 8½
  Cloth, lettered, ... o o 10

CHALLONER, BISHOP.
Meditations for every day in the year. Revised and
edited by the Right Rev. John Virtue, D.D., Bishop
of Portsmouth. 7th edition. 8vo . . . o 3 o
And in other bindings.

COLERIDGE, REV. H. J. (S.J.) *(See Quarterly Series.)*

DALE, REV. J. D. HILARIUS.
Ceremonial according to the Roman Rite. Translated
from the Italian of JOSEPH BALDESCHI, Master of
Ceremonies of the Basilica of St. Peter at Rome;
with the Pontifical Offices of a Bishop in his own
diocese, compiled from the "Cæremoniale Epis-
coporum"; to which are added various other Functions and copious explanatory Notes; the whole
harmonized with the latest Decrees of the Sacred Congregation of Rites. New and revised edition. Cloth,   o 6 6

The Sacristan's Manual; or, Handbook of Church
Furniture, Ornament, &c. Harmonized with the
most approved commentaries on the Roman Ceremonial and latest Decrees of the Sacred Congregation of Rites. Cloth . . . . . . o 2 6

DEVAS, C. S.
Studies of Family Life: a contribution to Social
Science. Crown 8vo . . . . . . o 5 o
"We recommend these pages and the remarkable evidence brought
together in them to the careful attention of all who are interested in
the well-being of our common humanity."—*Guardian.*
"Both thoughtful and stimulating."—*Saturday Review.*

DRANE, AUGUSTA THEODOSIA, Edited by.
The Autobiography of Archbishop Ullathorne. Demy
8vo, cloth. Second edition . . . . o 7 6

"As a plucky Yorkshireman, as a sailor, as a missionary, as a
great traveller, as a ravenous reader, and as a great prelate, Dr.
Ullathorne was able to write down most fascinating accounts of his
experiences. The book is full of shrewd glimpses from a Roman point
of view of the man himself, of the position of Roman Catholics in this
country, of the condition of the country, of the Colonies, and of the
Anglican Church in various parts of the world, in the earlier half of
this century."—*Guardian.*

The Letters of Archbishop Ullathorne. (Sequel
to the *Autobiography.*) 2nd Edit. Demy 8vo, cloth   o 9 o
"Compiled with admirable judgment for the purpose of displaying
in a thousand various ways the real man who was Archbishop
Ullathorne."—*Tablet.*

EYRE MOST REV. CHARLES, (Abp. of Glasgow).

The History of St. Cuthbert : or, An Account of his Life, Decease, and Miracles. Third edition. Illustrated with maps, charts, &c., and handsomely bound in cloth. Royal 8vo £0 14 0

"A handsome, well appointed volume, in every way worthy of its illustrious subject. . . . The chief impression of the whole is the picture of a great and good man drawn by a sympathetic hand."—*Spectator.*

FABER, REV. FREDERICK WILLIAM, (D.D.)

All for Jesus	0	5	0
Bethlehem	0	7	0
Blessed Sacrament	0	7	6
Creator and Creature	0	6	0
Ethel's Book of the Angels.	0	5	0
Foot of the Cross	0	6	0
Growth in Holiness	0	6	0
Hymns	0	6	0
Notes on Doctrinal and Spiritual Subjects, 2 vols. .	0	10	0
Poems . . . . . . , .	0	5	0
Precious Blood	0	5	0
Sir Lancelot	0	5	0
Spiritual Conferences	0	6	0

Life and Letters of Frederick William Faber, D.D., Priest of the Oratory of St. Philip Neri. By John Edward Bowden of the same Congregation . . 0 6 0

FAWKES, REV. ALFRED.

The Sacred Heart, and other Sermons. Red buckram, gilt 0 2 6

"Nor do we wonder at the fascination which Father Fawkes's sermons must have for a man of letters, if they at all approached in power and charm those which are brought together in the little first volume he has put to press. Every page of these sermons shows him to be an original and cultivated Catholic thinker. The substance of his discourses never wanders astray from the unchanging doctrines of the Church, and yet there is found throughout them all a freshness of view as welcome as it is uncommon. This preacher has something to say—something worth saying that he wants to say."—*Weekly Register.*

FOLEY, REV. HENRY, (S.J.)

Records of the English Province of the Society of Jesus.

Vol. I., Series I. . . . . net	1	6	0
Vol. II., Series II., III., IV. . . net	1	6	0
Vol. III., Series V., VI., VII., VIII. . net	1	10	0
Vol. IV. Series IX., X., XI. . . . net	1	6	0
Vol. V., Series XII. with nine Photographs of Martyrs . . . . net	1	10	0
Vol. VI., Diary and Pilgrim-Book of the English College, Rome . . . . . . net	1	6	0
Vol. VII. Part the First : General Statistics of the Province; with Biographical Notices and 20 Photographs . . . . . . net	1	6	0
Vol. VII. Part the Second : Collectanea, Completed ; With Appendices. Catalogues of Assumed and Real Names: Annual Letters ; Biographies and Miscellanea. . . . . net	1	6	0

"As a biographical dictionary of English Jesuits, it deserves a place in every well-selected library, and, as a collection of marvellous occurrences, persecutions, martyrdoms, and evidences of the results of faith, amongst the books of all who belong to the Catholic Church."—*Genealogist.*

FORMBY, REV. HENRY.
Monotheism: in the main derived from the Hebrew nation and the Law of Moses. The Primitive Religion of the City of Rome. An historical Investigation. Demy 8vo £0 5 0

FRANCIS DE SALES, ST.: THE WORKS OF.
Translated into the English Language by the Very Rev. Canon Mackey, O.S.B., under the direction of the Right Rev. Bishop Hedley, O.S.B. . .
Vol. I. Letters to Persons in the World. 3rd Ed. . 0 6 0
"The letters must be read in order to comprehend the charm and sweetness of their style."—*Tablet.*
Vol. II.—The Treatise on the Love of God. Father Carr's translation of 1630 has been taken as a basis, but it has been modernized and thoroughly revised and corrected. 2nd Edition 0 6 0
"To those who are seeking perfection by the path of contemplation this volume will be an armoury of help."—*Saturday Review.*
Vol. III. The Catholic Controversy. . . 0 6 0
"No one who has not read it can conceive how clear, how convincing, and how well adapted to our present needs are these controversial leaves.'"—*Tablet.*
Vol. IV. Letters to Persons in Religion, with introduction by Bishop Hedley on "St. Francis de Sales and the Religious State." 2nd Edition . . 0 6 0
" The sincere piety and goodness, the grave wisdom, the knowledge of human nature, the tenderness for its weakness, and the desire for its perfection that pervade the letters, make them pregnant of instruction for all serious persons. The translation and editing have been admirably done."—*Scotsman.*

GALLWEY, REV. PETER, (S.J.)
Precious Pearl of Hope in the Mercy of God, The. Translated from the Italian. With Preface by the Rev. Father Gallwey. Cloth 0 4 6
Lectures on Ritualism and on the Anglican Orders. 2 vols. (Or may be had separately.) 0 8 0
Salvage from the Wreck. A few Memories of the Dead, preserved in Funeral Discourses. With Portraits. Crown 8vo 0 7 6

GIBSON, REV. H.
Catechism Made Easy. Being an Explanation of the Christian Doctrine. 9th Edition. 2 vols., cloth. . 0 7 6
"This work must be of priceless worth to any who are engaged in any form of catechetical instruction. It is the best book of the kind that we have seen in English."—*Irish Monthly.*

GILLOW, JOSEPH.
Literary and Biographical History, or, Bibliographical Dictionary of the English Catholics. From the Breach with Rome, in 1534, to the Present Time.
Vols. I., II. III. and IV. cloth, demy 8vo . . each 0 15 0
5th, and concluding vol. in preparation.
"The patient research of Mr. Gillow, his conscientious record of minute particulars, and especially his exhaustive bibliographical information in connection with each name, are beyond praise."—*British Quarterly Review.*
The Haydock Papers. Illustrated. Demy 8vo . 0 7 6
" We commend this collection to the attention of every one that is interested in the records of the sufferings and struggles of our ancestors to hand down the faith to their children."—*Tablet*
St. Thomas' Priory; or, the Story of St. Austin's, Stafford. With Three Illustrations. Tastefully bound in half leather 0 5 0

GLANCEY, REV. M. F.

Characteristics from the Writings of Archbishop Ullathorne, together with a Bibliographical Account of
the Archbishop's Works. Crown 8vo, cloth . . £0 6 0

" The Archbishop's thoughts are expressed in choice, rich language,
which, pleasant as it is to read, must have been additionally so to
hear. We have perused this book with interest, and have no hesitation in recommending our readers to possess themselves of it."—
Birmingham Weekly Mercury.

GRADWELL, MONSIGNOR.

Succat, The Story of Sixty Years of the Life of St.
Patrick. Crown 8vo, cloth 0 5 0

" A work at once bright, picturesque, and truthful."—*Tablet.*
" We most heartily commend this book to all lovers of St.
Patrick."—*Irish Ecclesiastical Record.*

GROWTH IN THE KNOWLEDGE OF OUR LORD.

Meditations for every Day in the Year, exclusive of
those for Festivals, Days of Retreat, &c. Adapted
from the original of Abbé de Brandt, by Sister Mary
Fidelis. A new and Improved Edition, in 3 Vols.
Sold only in sets. Price per set, ... 1 2 6

" The praise, though high, bestowed on these excellent meditations
by the Bishop of Salford is well deserved. The language, like good
spectacles, spreads treasures before our vision without attracting
attention to itself."—*Dublin Review.*

HEDLEY, BISHOP.

Our Divine Saviour, and other Discourses. Crown
8vo 0 6 0

" A distinct and noteworthy feature of these sermons is, we certainly think, their freshness—freshness of thought, treatment, and
style ; nowhere do we meet pulpit commonplace or hackneyed phrase
—everywhere, on the contrary, it is the heart of the preacher pouring
out to his flock his own deep convictions, enforcing them from the
'Treasures, old and new,' of a cultivated mind."—*Dublin Review.*

A Retreat : consisting of Thirty-three Discourses with
Meditations, intended for the use of the Clergy,
Religious, and others. Crown 8vo, half leather . 0 6 0

" This ' Retreat,' which will remain as a treasure with Catholics
of English speech, shows forth once more, and very attractively, his
(Dr. Hedley's) qualifications as a preacher and a guide of souls. It
gives amplest evidence of his piety and his literary gift, his keen insight into the motives and the weaknesses of the human heart, and
withal such a winning humility as leaves the erring one unwounded,
though he is enlightened and rebuked."—*Weekly Register.*

INNER LIFE OF FATHER THOMAS BURKE, O.P.

By a Dominican Friar of the English Province. Dark
green buckram, gilt. 0 2 0

" In this little work the writer has endeavoured to depict that side
of Father Burke's character which, if it is least known, gives the
truer as well as the higher idea of the well-known preacher of fifteen
years ago.
" It is a singularly pleasing picture of a most attractive character,
in which humour, humility, and piety each found an appropriate
place."—*Scotsman.*

KING, FRANCIS.

The Church of my Baptism, and why I returned to
it. Crown 8vo, cloth 0 2 6

" Altogether a book of an excellent spirit, written with freshness and distinction."—*Weekly Register.*

LEE, REV. F. G., D.D. (of All Saints, Lambeth.)
Edward the Sixth : Supreme Head.   Second edition.
Crown 8vo   .   .   .   .   ,   .   £0   6   0
"In vivid interest and in literary power, no less than in solid historical value, Dr. Lee's present work comes fully up to the standard of its predecessors ; and to say that is to bestow high praise. The book evinces Dr. Lee's customary diligence of research in amassing facts, and his rare artistic power in welding them into a harmonious and effective whole."—*John Bull.*

LIGUORI, ST. ALPHONSUS.
New and Improved Translation of the Complete Works of St. Alphonsus, edited by the late Bishop Coffin :--
Vol. I. The Christian Virtues, and the Means for Obtaining them.   Cloth   0   3   0
Or separately :—
1. The Love of our Lord Jesus Christ   .   .   0   1   0
2. Treatise on Prayer. *(In the ordinary editions a great part of this work is omitted)*   .   .   .   0   1   0
3. A Christian's rule of Life   0   1   0
Vol. II. The Mysteries of the Faith—The Incarnation ; containing Meditations and Devotions on the Birth and Infancy of Jesus Christ, &c., suited for Advent and Christmas.   0   2   6
Vol. III. The Mysteries of the Faith—The Blessed Sacrament   0   2   6
Vol. IV. Eternal Truths—Preparation for Death   .   0   2   6
Vol. V. The Redemption—Meditations on the Passion.   0   2   6
Vol. VI. Glories of Mary.   New edition .   .   .   0   3   6
Reflections on Spiritual Subjects   .   .   .   0   2   6

LIVIUS, REV. T. (M.A., C.SS.R.)
St. Peter, Bishop of Rome ; or, the Roman Episcopate of the Prince of the Apostles, proved from the Fathers, History and Chronology, and illustrated by arguments from other sources.   Dedicated to his Eminence Cardinal Newman.   Demy 8vo, cloth   .   0 12   0
"A book which deserves careful attention. In respect of literary qualities, such as effective arrangement, and correct and lucid diction, this essay, by an English Catholic scholar, is not unworthy of Cardinal Newman, to whom it is dedicated."—*The Sun.*
Explanation of the Psalms and Canticles in the Divine Office. By ST. ALPHONSUS LIGUORI.   Translated from the Italian by THOMAS LIVIUS, C.SS.R. With a Preface by his Eminence Cardinal MANNING. Crown 8vo, cloth   0   7   6
" To nuns and others who know little or no Latin, the book will be of immense importance."—*Dublin Review.*
"Father Livius has in our opinion even improved on the original, so far as the arrangement of the book goes. New priests will find it especially useful."—*Month.*
Mary in the Epistles ; or, The Implicit Teaching of the Apostles concerning the Blessed Virgin, set forth in devout comments on their writings. Illustrated from Fathers and other Authors, and prefaced by introductory Chapters.   Crown 8vo, cloth   0   5   0
The Blessed Virgin in the Fathers of the First Six Centuries.   With a Preface by CARD. VAUGHAN. Cloth 0 12   0

" Father Livius could hardly have laid at the feet of Our Blessed Patroness a more fitting tribute than to have placed side by side with the work of his fellow-Redemptorist on the ' Dowry of Mary,' this volume, in which we hear the combined voices of the Fathers of the first six centuries united in speaking the praise of the Mother of God."—*Dublin Review*.

MANNING, CARDINAL. Popular Edition of the Works of

	£	s	d
Four Great Evils of the Day. 6th edition	£0	2	6
Fourfold Sovereignty of God. 4th edition	0	2	6
Glories of the Sacred Heart. 6th edition	0	4	0
Grounds of Faith. 10th edition	0	1	6
Independence of the Holy See. 2nd edition	0	2	6
Internal Mission of the Holy Ghost. 5th edition	0	5	0
Miscellanies. 3 vols. . . . the set	0	18	0
Pastime Papers. 2nd edition	0	2	6
Religio Viatoris. 4th edition	0	1	6
Sermons on Ecclesiastical Subjects. Vol. I. . (Vols. II. and III. out of Print.)	0	6	0
Sin and its Consequences. 8th edition	0	4	0
Temporal Mission of the Holy Ghost. 3rd edition	0	5	0
True Story of the Vatican Council. 2nd edition	0	2	6
The Eternal Priesthood. 11th edition	0	2	6
The Office of the Church in the Higher Catholic Education. A Pastoral Letter	0	0	6
Workings of the Holy Spirit in the Church of England. Reprint of a letter addressed to Dr. Pusey in 1864	0	1	6
Lost Sheep Found. A Sermon	0	0	6
Rights and Dignity of Labour	0	0	1

The Westminster Series
In handy pocket size. All bound in cloth.

	£	s	d
The Blessed Sacrament, the Centre of Immutable Truth	0	1	0
Confidence in God.	0	1	0
Holy Gospel of Our Lord Jesus Christ according to St. John.	0	1	0
Love of Jesus to Penitents.	0	1	0
Office of the Holy Ghost under the Gospel	0	1	0
Holy Ghost the Sanctifier	0	2	0

MANNING, CARDINAL, Edited by.
Life of the Curé of Ars. Popular edition . . . 0 2 6.

MEDAILLE, REV. P.
Meditations on the Gospels or Every Day in the Year. Translated into English from the new Edition, enlarged by the Besançon Missionaries, under the direction of the Rev. W. H. Eyre, S.J. Cloth   0 6 0 (This work has already been translated into Latin, Italian, Spanish, German, and Dutch.)

" We have carefully examined these Meditations, and are fain to confess that we admire them very much. They are short, succinct, pithy, always to the point, and wonderfully suggestive."—*Tablet*.

MEYNELL, ALICE.
Lourdes : Yesterday, to-day, and to-morrow. Translated from the French of Daniel Barbé by Alice Meynell. With twelve full pages water colour drawings by Hoffbauer, reproduced in colours. Royal 8vo, blue buckram, gilt 0 6 0

MORRIS, REV. JOHN (S.J., F.S.A.)

Letter Books of Sir Amias Poulet, keeper of Mary
Queen of Scots. Demy 8vo .   .   .   . net   £0   3   6

Two Missionaries under Elizabeth   .   .   .   0   14   0

The Catholics under Elizabeth   0   14   0

The Life of Father John Gerard, S.J.   Third edition,
rewritten and enlarged   0   14   0

The Life and Martyrdom of St. Thomas Becket. Second
and enlarged edition.   In one volume, large post 8vo,
cloth, pp. xxxvi., 632, ...   0   12   6

or bound in two parts, cloth .   .   .   0   13   0

" Father Morris is one of the few living writers who have succeeded
in greatly modifying certain views of English history, which had long
been accepted as the only tenable ones. . . To have wrung an
admission of this kind from a reluctant public, never too much inclined to surrender its traditional assumptions, is an achievement not
to be underrated in importance."—*Rev. Dr. Augustus Jessopp, in
the Academy.*

MORRIS, REV. W. B. (of the Oratory.)

The Life of St. Patrick, Apostle of Ireland.   Fourth
edition.   Crown 8vo, cloth   0   5   0

" Promises to become the standard biography of Ireland's Apostle.
For clear statement of facts, and calm judicious discussion of con-
troverted points, it surpasses any work we know of in the literature
of the subject."—*American Catholic Quarterly.*

Ireland and St. Patrick.   A study of the Saint's
character and of the results of his apostolate.
Second edition.   Crown 8vo, cloth.   .   .   0   5   0

" We read with pleasure this volume of essays, which, though
the Saint's name is taken by no means in vain, really contains a
sort of discussion of current events and current English views of
Irish character."—*Saturday Review.*

NEWMAN, CARDINAL.

Church of the Fathers   0   4   0

Prices of other works by Cardinal Newman on
application.

PAGANI, VERY REV. JOHN BAPTIST,

The Science of the Saints in Practice.   By John Bap-
tist Pagani, Second General of the Institute of
Charity.   Complete in three volumes.   Vol. 1,
January to April (out of print).   Vol. 2, May to
August.   Vol. 3, September to December .   each   0   5   0

" ' The Science of the Saints ' is a practical treatise on the principal
Christian virtues, abundantly illustrated with interesting examples
from Holy Scripture as well as from the Lives of the Saints.   Written
chiefly for devout souls, such as are trying to live an interior and supernatural life by following in the footsteps of our Lord and His saints,
this work is eminently adapted for the use of ecclesiastics and of religious communities."—*Irish Ecclesiastical Record.*

PAYNE, JOHN ORLEBAR, (M.A.)

Records of the English Catholics of 1715.   Demy 8vo.
Half-bound, gilt top   0   15   0

" A book of the kind Mr. Payne has given us would have astonished Bishop Milner or Dr. Lingard.   They would have treasured it,
for both of them knew the value of minute fragments of historical
information.   The Editor has derived nearly the whole of the information which he has given, from unprinted sources, and we must
congratulate him on having found a few incidents here and there
which may bring the old times back before us in a most touching
manner."—*Tablet.*

PAYNE, JOHN ORLEBAR, (M.A.)

English Catholic Non-Jurors of 1715. Being a Summary of the Register of their Estates, with Genealogical and other Notes, and an Appendix of Unpublished Documents in the Public Record Office. In one volume. Demy 8vo . . £1 1 0

" Most carefully and creditably brought out . . . From first to last, full of social interest and biographical details, for which we may search in vain elsewhere."—*Antiquarian Magazine.*

Old English Catholic Missions. Demy 8vo, half-bound. 0 7 6

" A book to hunt about in for curious odds and ends."—*Saturday Review.*

"These registers tell us in their too brief records, teeming with interest for all their scantiness, many a tale of patient heroism."—*Tablet.*

St. Paul's Cathedral in the time of Edward VI. Being a detailed Account of its Treasures from a Document in the Public Record Office. Tastefully printed on imitation handmade paper, and bound in cloth 0 2 6

PERRY, REV. JOHN,

Practical Sermons for all the Sundays of the year. First and Second Series. Sixth Edition. In two volumes. Cloth 0 7 0

POPE, REV. T. A. (of the Oratory.)

Life of Philip Neri. Translated from the Italian of Cardinal Capecelatro. Second and revised edition. 2 vols, cloth 0 12 6

" Altogether this is a most fascinating work, full of spiritual lore and historic erudition, and with all the intense interest of a remarkable biography. Take it up where you will, it is hard to lay it down. We think it one of the most completely satisfactory lives of a Saint that has been written in modern times."—*Tablet.*

POUVILLON, E.

Bernadette of Lourdes. Translated from the French. By Henry O'Shea. Blue buckram, gilt, . 0 2 6

" A very charming little miracle-play. It is in the form of prose-narrative, interspersed with dialogue and lyrical snatches; simple, devout, and strewn with tender fancy."—*Weekly Register.*

"A creditable version of a clever and original work."—*Birmingham Daily Gazette.*

QUARTERLY SERIES. Edited by the Rev. John Gerard, S.J. 91 volumes published to date.

Selection.

The Life and Letters of St. Francis Xavier. By the Rev. H. J. Coleridge, S.J. 2 vols. . . . 0 10 6

The History of the Sacred Passion. By Father Luis de la Palma, of the Society of Jesus. Translated from the Spanish. 0 5 0

The Life of Dona Louisa de Carvajal. By Lady Georgiana Fullerton. Small edition . . . 0 3 6

The Life and Letters of St. Teresa. 3 vols. By Rev. H. J. Coleridge, S.J. . . . . each 0 7 6

The Life of Mary Ward. By Mary Catherine Elizabeth Chalmers, of the Institute of the Blessed Virgin. Edited by the Rev. H. J. Coleridge, S.J. 2 vols. 0 15 0

The Return of the King. Discourses on the Latter Days. By the Rev. H. J. Coleridge, S.J. . . 0 7 6

QUARTERLY SERIES—*(selection) continued.*

Pious Affections towards God and the Saints. Meditations for every Day in the Year, and for the Principal Festivals. From the Latin of the Ven. Nicolas Lancicius, S.J.	£0	7	6
The Life and Teaching of Jesus Christ in Meditations for Every Day in the Year. By Fr. Nicolas Avancino, S.J. Two vols.	o	10	6
The Baptism of the King : Considerations on the Sacred Passion. By the Rev. H. J. Coleridge, S.J.	o	7	6
The Mother of the King. Mary during the Life of Our Lord.	o	7	6
The Hours of the Passion. Taken from the *Life of Christ* by Ludolph the Saxon	o	7	6
The Mother of the Church. Mary during the first Apostolic Age	o	6	o
The Life of St. Bridget of Sweden. By the late F. J. M. A. Partridge	o	6	o
The Teachings and Counsels of St. Francis Xavier. From his Letters	o	5	o
The Life of St. Alonso Rodriguez. By Francis Goldie, of the Society of Jesus	o	7	6
Letters of St. Augustine. Selected and arranged by Mary H. Allies	o	6	6
A Martyr from the Quarter-Deck—Alexis Clerc, S.J. By Lady Herbert	o	5	o
Acts of the English Martyrs, hitherto unpublished. By the Rev. John H. Pollen, S.J.	o	7	6
Life of St. Francis di Geronimo, S.J. By A. M. Clarke.	o	7	6
Aquinas Ethicus ; or the Moral Teaching of St. Thomas By the Rev. Joseph Rickaby, S.J. 2 vols.	o	12	o
The Spirit of St. Ignatius. From the French of the Rev. Fr. Xavier de Franciosi, S.J.	o	6	o
Jesus, the All-Beautiful. A devotional Treatise on the character and actions of Our Lord. Edited by Rev. J. G. MacLeod, S.J.	o	6	6
The Manna of the Soul. By Fr. Paul Segneri. New edition. In two volumes.	o	12	o
Saturday dedicated to Mary. From the Italian of Fr. Cabrini, S.J.	o	6	o
Life of Father Augustus Law, S.J. By Ellis Schreiber.	o	6	o
Life of Ven. Joseph Benedict Cottolengo. From the Italian of Don. P. Gastaldi.	o	4	6
Story of St. Stanislaus Kostka. Edited by Rev. F. Goldie, S.J. 3rd Edition.	o	4	6
Two Ancient Treatises on Purgatory. A Remembrance for the Living to Pray for the Dead, by Father James Mumford, S.J. ; and Purgatory Surveyed, by Father Richard Thimelby, S.J. With an Introduction by Rev. J. Morris, S.J.	o	5	o
The Lights in Prayer of the Venerable Fathers Louis de la Puente and Claude de la Colombière, and the Rev. Father Paul Segneri. Edited by the Rev. J. Morris, S.J.	o	5	o
Life of St. Francis Borgia. By A. M. Clarke.	o	6	6

QUARTERLY SERIES—*(selection) continued.*

Life of Blessed Antony Baldinucci. By Rev. F. Goldie, S.J.	£o	6	o
Distinguished Irishmen of the Sixteenth Century. By Rev. E. Hogan, S. J.	o	6	o
Journals kept during Times of Retreat. By the late Fr. John Morris, S.J. Edited by Rev. J. Pollen, S.J.	o	6	o

VOLUMES ON THE LIFE OF OUR LORD.

The Holy Infancy.

The Preparation of the Incarnation	o	7	6
The Nine Months. The Life of our Lord in the Womb.	o	7	6
The Thirty Years. Our Lord's Infancy and Early Life.	o	7	6

The Public Life of Our Lord.

The Ministry of St. John Baptist	o	6	6
The Preaching of the Beatitudes	o	6	6
The Sermon on the Mount. Continued. 2 Parts, each	o	6	6
The Training of the Apostles. Parts I., II., III., IV. each	o	6	6
The Preaching of the Cross. Part I.	o	6	6
The Preaching of the Cross. Parts II., III. each	o	6	o
Passiontide. Parts I. II. and III., each	o	6	6
Chapters on the Parables of Our Lord	o	7	6

Introductory Volumes.

The Life of our Life. Harmony of the Life of Our Lord, with Introductory Chapters and Indices. Second edition. Two vols.	o	15	o
The Passage of our Lord to the Father. Conclusion of The Life of our Life.	o	7	6
The Works and Words of our Saviour, gathered from the Four Gospels	o	7	6
The Story of the Gospels. Harmonised for Meditation	o	7	6

ROSE, STEWART.

St. Ignatius Loyola and The Early Jesuits, with more than 100 Illustrations by H. W. and H. C. Brewer and L. Wain. The whole produced under the immediate superintendence of the Rev. W. H. Eyre, S.J. Super Royal 8vo. Handsomely bound in cloth, extra gilt. . . . . net.   o 15 o

"This magnificent volume is one of which Catholics have justly reason to be proud. Its historical as well as its literary value is very great, and the illustrations from the pencils of Mr. Louis Wain and Messrs. H. W. and H. C. Brewer are models of what the illustrations of such a book should be. We hope that this book will be found in every Catholic drawing-room, as a proof that 'we Catholics' are in no way behind those around us in the beauty of the illustrated books that issue from our hands, or in the interest which is added to the subject by a skilful pen and finished style."—*Month.*

RYDER, REV. H. I. D. (of the Oratory.)

Catholic Controversy: A Reply to Dr. Littledale's "Plain Reasons," Seventh edition . . .   o 2 6

"Father Ryder of the Birmingham Oratory, has now furnished in a small volume a masterly reply to this assailant from without. The lighter charms of a brilliant and graceful style are added to the solid merits of this handbook of contemporary controversy."—*Iris Monthly.*

SCHOUPPE, REV. F. X. (S.J.)
Purgatory. Illustrated by the lives and legends of
the Saints. Cloth £0 6 0
"We feel absolutely confident that Father Schouppe's work will
soon become one of our most popular works on Purgatory, and that
we shall ere long have to notice its second edition."—*Tablet.*

STANTON, REV. R. (of the Oratory.)
A Menology of England and Wales; or, Brief Mem-
orials of the British and English Saints, arranged according to the Calendar. Together with the Martyrs
of the 16th and 17th centuries. Compiled by order of
the Cardinal Archbishop and the Bishops of the Province of Westminster. With Supplement, containing
Notes and other additions, together with enlarged
Appendices, and a new Index. Demy 8vo, cloth . 0 16 0
The Supplement, separately 0 2 0

SWEENEY, RT. REV. ABBOT, (O.S.B.)
Sermons for all Sundays and Festivals of the Year.
Fourth Edition. Crown 8vo, handsomely bound in
half leather 0 10 6

THOMPSON, EDWARD HEALY, (M.A.)
The Life of Jean-Jacques Olier, Founder of the
Seminary of St. Sulpice. New and Enlarged Edition.
Post 8vo, cloth, pp. xxxvi. 628 . . . 0 15 0
"It provides us with just what we most need, a model to look up to
and imitate; one whose circumstances and surroundings were suffi-
ciently like our own to admit of an easy and direct application to our
own personal duties and daily occupations."—*Dublin Review.*
The Life and Glories of St. Joseph, Husband of
Mary, Foster-Father of Jesus, and Patron of the
Universal Church. Grounded on the Dissertations of
Canon Antonio Vitalis, Father José Moreno, and other
writers. Second Edition. Crown 8vo, cloth 0 6 0
Letters and Writings of Marie Lataste, with Critical and Expository Notes. By two Fathers of the
Society of Jesus. Translated from the French.
3 vols, ... each 0 5 0

ULLATHORNE ARCHBISHOP.
Autobiography of, (*see* Drane, A. T.) . . . 0 7 6
Letters of, do. ,, . . . 0 9 0
Endowments of Man, &c. Popular edition. . . 0 7 0
Groundwork of the Christian Virtues; do. . . 0 7 0
Christian Patience, . . do. do. . . 0 7 0
Memoir of Bishop Willson 0 2 6

WATERWORTH, REV. J.
The Canons and Decrees of the Sacred and Œcumenical
Council of Trent, celebrated under the Sovereign
Pontiffs, Paul III., Julius III., and Pius IV., translated by the Rev. J. WATERWORTH. To which are
prefixed Essays on the External and Internal History
of the Council. A new edition. Demy 8vo, cloth. 0 10 6

WISEMAN, CARDINAL.
Fabiola. A Tale of the Catacombs. . . 3s. 6d. and 0 4 0
Also a new and splendid edition printed on large
quarto paper, embellished with thirty-one full-page
illustrations, and a coloured portrait of St. Agnes.
Handsomely bound 1 1 0